Space as
Storyteller

Space as Storyteller

Spatial Jumps in Architecture, Critical Theory, and Literature

✦

Laura Chiesa

NORTHWESTERN UNIVERSITY PRESS
EVANSTON, ILLINOIS

Northwestern University Press
www.nupress.northwestern.edu

Printed in the United States of America

10 9 8 7 6 5 4 3 2 1

Library of Congress Cataloging-in-Publication Data

Names: Chiesa, Laura, author.
Title: Space as storyteller : spatial jumps in architecture, critical theory, and literature / Laura Chiesa.
Description: Evanston, Illinois : Northwestern University Press, 2016. | Includes bibliographical references and index.
Identifiers: LCCN 2016014075 | ISBN 9780810133457 (pbk. : alk. paper) | ISBN 9780810133464 (cloth : alk. paper) | ISBN 9780810133471 (e-book)
Subjects: LCSH: Literature, Modern—20th century—History and criticism. | Space and time in literature. | Architecture, Modern—20th century—History and criticism. | Architecture and literature. | Cities and towns in literature. | Benjamin, Walter, 1892–1940—Criticism and interpretation. | Marinetti, F. T., 1876–1944—Criticism and interpretation. | Calvino, Italo—Criticism and interpretation. | Perec, Georges, 1936–1982—Criticism and interpretation. | Tschumi, Bernard, 1944—Criticism and interpretation. | Koolhaas, Rem—Criticism and interpretation.
Classification: LCC PN56.S667 C466 2016 | DDC 809.9384—dc23
LC record available at https://lccn.loc.gov/2016014075

For if the sentence is the wall before the language of the original, literalness is the arcade.

—Walter Benjamin, "The Task of the Translator" (260)

[Gerard Dupuy:] By its size, *Life A User's Manual* is a book with which one can settle in. You can take your time. "You'll be reading it all winter," remarks G. P. on the phone with somebody who just bought his book. Sure, you can settle in with it, but the book is not very favorable to it.

[Georges Perec:] At the beginning, people were reluctant to read it, because of the volume and of the stories that are not related to each other. It's like a train that's starting up: the locomotive has to work hard to pull. But, as soon as it gets moving . . .

—Georges Perec, *Entretiens et Conférences* (vol. 1, 233)

CONTENTS

ILLUSTRATIONS

ACKNOWLEDGMENTS

This book couldn't even have been imagined without my leaving Europe on the cusp of a new century and landing in the United States to pursue a PhD in comparative literature at UCLA. Indeed, I went there intending to stay only one year (having received a Fulbright Research Fellowship), but I recognized in UCLA's program in comparative literature an unparalleled direction, one that fostered comparatist and interdisciplinary quests, and so, with enthusiasm, I applied to be admitted. I am therefore grateful to the Fulbright Commission, to the Department of Comparative Literature at UCLA for having supported my intellectual curiosity and my desire to bridge interdisciplinary fields (to start to jump), and also to the city of Los Angeles, even for (really, mostly for) having set me adrift—disorienting me.

Among individuals, I wish to thank first of all Lucia Re, my doctoral thesis director, who introduced me to Futurism and encouraged me all through the writing process—during our countless conversations—to pursue my project; Re's research taught me the force of Italian studies in the comparativist field and has certainly animated this book. Samuel Weber's research crossing the fields of critical theory, theatricality, and old and new media has inspired my project; continuous interaction with Sam and with the incredible network of scholars he fosters—in Los Angeles, in Paris (both during and after my participation in the Paris Program), and in Chicago (while I was a predoctoral visiting fellow at Northwestern University)—played a determinant role in the organization of this book. I extend my gratitude therefore to him and also to the Program in Comparative Literature at Northwestern University. Many thanks go also to Françoise Lionnet, Ali Behdad, and Efrain Kristal, who supported my trajectory toward the PhD. At the preliminary stages of this project, Sylvia Lavin kindly opened to me the doors of the Department of Architecture, introducing me to architectural critical studies. Though my stay in Los Angeles was very brief (only three years), UCLA has fostered an incredible network of friendships, and among my peers I would like to thank at least Alisa Hartz, Lori Lantz, Deborah Levitt, Paola Giaconia, Erika Tasini, and James Tobias, stellar friends and companions during and even after my graduate studies.

The Department of Italian at Yale provided some relief while I was looking for a tenure-track position; I thank Giuseppe Mazzotta and Millicent Marcus for their care.

The completion of this book and my path toward a more stable academic situation were delayed by all that happened in 2008, but (in contrast to the innumerable terrible stories that originated in that year, at a global scale) I am pleased that I nonetheless found my way to the University at Buffalo's Department of Romance Languages and Literatures. The many intellectual exchanges I had the opportunity to be part of at the University at Buffalo (UB) during the revision of the manuscript sparked unexpected new lights upon the project. In the Department of Romance Languages and Literatures at UB, I wish to thank Jean-Jacques Thomas, who has fostered and supported my research since my arrival at the University at Buffalo, and certainly David Castillo, who has accompanied me in the last stages of the rewriting of the manuscript, deserves my highest gratitude; Margarita Vargas's friendship and care has breezed into my research at any and all moments, and she too deserves my gratitude. A semester of leave from teaching helped me to devote myself almost entirely to the completion of the project. I am grateful to my friend John Long for his professional competence in publishing and his invaluable advice. Gregory Epp, an exceptional editor, has accompanied me in editing the manuscript; his clarity of mind earns my gratitude. I am also grateful to Simona Riva (CASC–Università di Parma), Cristiano Toraldo di Francia, Bernard Tschumi, and Rem Koolhaas/OMA for having granted me permission to publish their work. I thank the Julian Park Fund of the College of Arts and Sciences at UB for supporting the publication of this book. I have benefited greatly from the assistance of the librarians at Yale University and then at the University at Buffalo.

Finally, working with Henry Carrigan and Nathan MacBrien at Northwestern University Press has been a very positive experience; the peer reviewers' attention in reading my manuscript, in supporting its publication, and in suggesting critical interventions have been vital to the writing of the final revision.

To come to the closer, affectionate circle of my life, I wish to thank my parents, Maria Rosa and Nini, who brought me in tears to the Milano airport the first time I left for the United States; I am grateful to them and to my sweet brother, Valentino, and his son, Andrea, for having been close to my life, despite the distance. Without Jacoba the completion of this book would have been much harder, perhaps without room or space for storytelling. I am deeply grateful to her, for her patience and for the inventive twists and turns that she brings to reality, that she brings to life and into the lives of others. A final thank-you goes to Lola, who, at only thirteen, was able in a blow to send me by email the detailed definition of the term *colportage* as found in the French dictionary; this is certainly not the only reason to thank her: to her go my best wishes for a formidable future.

NOTES ON THE TEXT

All translations are my own unless otherwise indicated.

A portion of chapter 3 appeared in "Italy and France: Imagined Geographies," ed. Laura Wittman, special issue, *Romanic Review* 97, nos. 3/4 (2006): 401–21. Reprinted by permission.

A very short portion of chapter 1, in a much different form, appeared in "Khoraographies for Jacques Derrida," ed. Dragan Kujundzic, special issue, *Tympanum* 4 (2000). Reprinted by permission.

INTRODUCTION

This book focuses on new and extreme notions of polysemic space that developed—from the beginning of the twentieth century to the beginning of the twenty-first century—at the transdisciplinary intersection of architectural experimentation, literary and critical theory, and the practice of writing, leaving indelible marks. The five chapters of the book focus on selected works by Walter Benjamin, the later Italian Futurists, Italo Calvino, and Georges Perec, and on experimental architects from the 1960s (Superstudio, in particular) to more recent times, especially Bernard Tschumi and Rem Koolhaas/OMA (Office for Metropolitan Architecture). My point of departure is the notion of "space as storyteller" that I derive from a selective reading of Benjamin's seminal *Arcades Project*. Space becomes a storyteller in constructing time to come; the different authors and works considered are embedded in such a space, to which they respond with multilayered proposals that eventually challenge their own time. In order to do so, they more or less implicitly invite readers, observers, spectators, passersby, and participants to reconfigure established assumptions, playing out transdisciplinary interpretative gestures and soliciting any stable disciplinary ground. The performative gesturing activated at specific moments—but along a wide span of time—simultaneously implies and demands the possibility of repetition and of the unexpected.

Space as Storyteller, despite its generic title and mixed contents, directs attention to specific moments when space speaks, entrains, performs, or is questioned in order to imagine the new or, conversely, to display its junk-like side.

To begin with a few introductory remarks at the level of generality, in scholarship in the humanities for a few decades now, the "spatial turn" has mobilized the critical debate to renew the articulation of the discourses of not only human geography and urban studies but also the broader field of cultural studies. One key aspect of the spatial turn is that it fosters researches that explore a sense of locality combined with a sense of hybridity and mobility, implying the necessity of experimental fieldwork and a quest for the meshing of the theoretical with the ordinary and the outside, in their manifold margins and temporalities. This book asserts the necessity of this turn—it is in sync with such a turn—but it also considers what in ordinary language, and also in the field of comparative literature, has been associated with the turn: the twist. I mention the twist here not as any specific figural form or shape but because a twist implies both a sudden change and a sense of intertwining.

This book indeed looks at sudden changes, springing moments of adventures of/in space; it also implies, because of the scattered relationship among its different parts, spatial jumps.

Hence: Space as storyteller? Anyone could whisper the question "What will happen here?" But how can something so abstract as space possibly be a storyteller? The two words clash, don't they? Indeed they do. However, exactly because one term tends toward abstraction (and universality) and the other one tends to relate to something very singular, it is possible to trace a trajectory, yet this trajectory can both allow for a multiplicity of stories to narrate and (indissolubly) allow for a set of mobile, spatial stages where backdrop and foreground, plot, narrativity, and both human and nonhuman characters or actors are interspersed and meshed. Benjamin starts off his essay "The Storyteller" by affirming that "the art of storytelling is coming to an end." Benjamin maintains that "it is as if a capability that seemed inalienable to us, the securest among our possessions, has been taken from us: the ability to share experiences."[1] Benjamin wrote "The Storyteller" in the same period that he was drafting a project he never finished, the *Arcades Project*, which among its many directions of inquiry seeks to give an account of experience in the cityscape, even as the very notion of experience changes and is questioned (or, if you like, contested) in its pure and proper sense. At a certain moment, Benjamin writes that space speaks to the flâneur, saying: "What do you think may have gone on here?" (M1a,3). It is as if space has acquired a fleeting ability to impart experience, becoming a storyteller.

Space as Storyteller does not limit its field of inquiry with a subtitle like, just as examples, *Theater and Literature at the Time of Mussolini*, *Place and Locality in French Contemporary Philosophy*, *Benjamin and Architecture*, *Heidegger and Space*, *Lefebvre's Space and Its After-Life*, *Autonomia and Counterculture Architectures*, or *Junkspace and Its Others*. This is possible because of the specific and interdisciplinary intersections that this project selects and establishes. Instead, the subtitle—*Spatial Jumps in Architecture, Critical Theory, and Literature*—stresses jumps among disciplines, because the scope of the book is to highlight how in several different instances the relationality of literature, theater and theatricality, and space and architecture recurs and meshes and how each instance or occurrence gives form to different ways of interspersing these motifs and disciplines, inventing new way of imagining, understanding, performing, or constructing in the cityscape.

Readers who look only for a foundational organizing intention or a method to apply may lose their way in such a book, but readers who begin with an understanding of the nature of the book will be prepared to embark on the journey, the trajectory, that this book proposes. The scope of the book is to highlight fleeting yet pivotal scenes that are singularly staged by a multiple—but limited—set of authors, architects, and artists, who are not all experimenting and doing, saying, imagining the same thing. Instead, their experimentations may either collide or, on the contrary, share traits, but they never come together in one unified concept. Stated concretely, it is not that I have operated in a kind of critical hands-off way from the material I consider—or, if you will, that I have simply piled the material up—instead, I have given attention and respect to several of the lines that may connect singular occurrences and have brought into convergence different parts that communicate or conflict with each other without any intention to form an entire, unified whole. Stated in another way, the materials, motifs, and modes in the chapters relate, yet there is no general theory of space, nor is there a "concept of space" that will permit an approach to them that will straighten them toward a universal, unifying paradigm. Notions such as "space as storyteller," "architecturability," and "colportage of space"—as we will see shortly and throughout the book—do nevertheless coalesce or merge to make of this comparatist project a determined concurrence or animation of communicable or puzzle-like motifs.

To situate this comparatist project, instead of undertaking an academic exercise that would try to revisit the term "space" in modernity, it will be more effective to give recent scholarship its due and to make clear the project's indebtedness to it. The published work of several scholars has guided the reading of the material considered here and may share at least the articulations, if not the jumps, that construct this comparatist project. Giuliana Bruno's *Atlas of Emotion*, with a density oxymoronically lightened by the modality in which the author weaves together interconnected lines of thought experiments among disciplines, mapping a totally new voyage, as she mentions in her preface, has "tried to learn how to 'space' differently,"[2] but in turn, implicitly, also allows for imagining alternative routes. Anthony Vidler, from many alternate angles—questioning indeed the very idea of representation and perspectival space—has opened up a new way of studying architecture and modern space. With *Warped Space*, Vidler takes on the challenge offered by "the forced intersection of different media in a way that breaks the boundaries of genre and the separate arts in response to the need to depict space in new and unparalleled ways," studying in a single stroke "the psychological culture of modernism from the late nineteenth century to the present."[3] Samuel Weber's writing on theatricality that is by no means limited to theater has rehearsed and articulated the term "theatricality" as a distinct medium apt to think anew situatedness, allegory, moving stages, old and new media, and space. Referring to the pieces, meaning chapters, collected in *Theatricality as Medium*, Weber writes:

> At the center of their concerns stands the tension between the effort to reduce the *theatrical medium* to a *means* of meaningful representation by enclosing its space within an ostensibly self-contained narrative, and the resistance of this medium to such reduction. Theatricality resists the reduction to a meaningful narrative by virtue of its ability to signify. This ability associates it with what is called "language." As

> the most ubiquitous of signifying media—a pleonasm insofar as *all* media are such through signifying—language demonstrates the priority of the signifying function over that of representation. In so doing, far from reducing the materiality and corporeality of theater, it marks their irreducibility.[4]

This is readable, argues Weber, when staging is not subordinate generically to its narrative function. Opening up new paths in scholarship, these authors have never been shy about (or hostile toward) bringing together avant-garde experimentations and more contemporary ones, and their way of proceeding has accompanied in part the making of this present project.

It is by following in part(s) their new and yet already rigorous researches, which certainly also engage in a transdisciplinary take on space, that *Space as Storyteller* defines and demarcates, or delimits, a comparatist project that bears a singular, yet open, trajectory, one that brings to the fore significant transdisciplinary intersections without tending toward a flattening of the texts in order to find a unifying concept. *Space as Storyteller* brings closer together and compares a set of writers, performers, and architects for whom the tensions between the theoretical and the experimental, the narrative and the performative, the abstract and the material, and the mappable and the yet-to-be-mapped are always at issue.

The additional but connected complication that a reader may encounter is that this book is not, let's say, a book that considers a series of literary texts concerned with architecture or a book that critically engages only a series of architectural experimentations and architectural projects. Instead, as a comparatist project, it considers the relationality among several disciplines, specific works, and trajectories that break through the containing disciplinary boundaries. Although architecture is a focalizing agent and space a storyteller, this doesn't imply that *Space as Storyteller* is a book about architecture. It is, rather, a comparatist project that includes architects. Indeed, even though chapters 4 and 5 are devoted to architectural studios, my approach to the materials highlights not only constructed architectural projects but also the literary and critical strategies that are at the core of these architects' ways of thinking through modernity and the mediascape in order to open up the discipline to the outside and to its others. The challenge is to maintain attention within a set of chapters in which the critical and experimental focus is, because of the jumps, continually displaced; moreover, this set of chapters imports in its texture the experimentality that the materials considered may transmit; though the selection of the material spans a century, there is no intention to be comprehensive or treat the century exhaustively.

Certainly this project activates critical interpretations, yet it is attentive to the specific manifestations in which these materials have been produced, imagined, delivered, left to their contemporaneity and their future. The materials studied demand that they not be read with a single standard format throughout the book; somehow they demand to be rescued according to the way they have been imagined or thought, and that is why each chapter avoids equating their reading and interpretation in one paradigmatic modality of interpretation with the intent to form a unified whole.

While each chapter follows a clear line in the way the texts have been selected, each chapter also searches for an alternate mode of interpretation in approaching them. The *Arcades Project* is an endless scattered cumulus of annotations and quotations and also demands a respect for its rhythm; scattered Futurist experimentations can be rediscovered in their endless reiteration among originality and reproduction—this book asserts—if one keeps up to speed by quickly detailing splinters of multiple, ephemeral, small projects. To bring together in the middle of this book the strange couple Italo Calvino and Georges Perec makes it more readable, because it offers an interdisciplinary perspective from which to map out the comparatist project in its previous and later instantiations; here in this book, Bernard Tschumi's riddle of conceptual/literary investigations and praxis at work in architectural projects makes more sense and finds its critical space when seen in a temporal, timeline-oriented trajectory; the apparently enormous experimental production of not simply Rem Koolhaas alone but also OMA—an ever-bigger team, multilocalized and extremely mobile—invites consideration of many projects. Now, I do not read these OMA projects, as is clearly explained later in this introduction and in chapter 5, as separate *big* objects but mostly as parts, what I call "architecture-characters" of the novel *S,M,L,XL*, which then give the space over to other "architecture-characters" that, resisting their cartoonish quality and retail value, pop up in a strange publication, an almanac, *Content*, colporting architectures in contemporary space.

Benjamin's *Arcades Project* is not the text from which to interpret this comparatist project. Nevertheless, it is important to highlight the way Benjamin regards modernity as proceeding: with jolting, irregular, staccato movement and temporality. Such a logic is pertinent to the configuration of this project, and it *maintains* the relation of the project's parts.

What does "maintains" imply?

Interestingly enough, my project has been motivated, or triggered, in part by an occasional text by Jacques Derrida. Writing about specific architectural experimentations of the architect Tschumi in the text "Point de folie: Maintenant l'architecture," Derrida expands on the ideas of "maintaining" and the "now." There, in a quite rhapsodic way, while considering the singularity of Tschumi's experimentation, Derrida interprets the Parc de la Villette and its *folies* (small-scale constructions) as an architecture that "*maintains the dis-jointed per se* . . . [to] give dissociation its due but to implement it *per se* in the space of reassembly."[5] Derrida notices that the *folies*, as points articulated in the space of the park, maintain and divide. Without implying any generalization—if I may be permitted a quasi catachresis (and if it will not be received as an abuse or a misuse)—the relation among the parts of this book also tends toward such a relationality; the experimental side of this book project implies ties among disciplines and a play of a certain nonsynchronicity, a disjunction among the way the different aspects or disciplines connect for each occurrence.

This project studies multiple areas: theater and stage design, literature, critical theory, and architecture. These areas acquire different relevance in each chapter; each chapter relates to the others as a pulse of modernity, as a city and a room, as freeze-frames, as strange, sliced sections that Tschumi or OMA might have imagined. None of them explains the other, yet they communicate, and each chapter, presenting an interspersion of fields, displays different constellations—spaces of comparison—that relate in contrasting and concurring modes. Each chapter considers different gestures of interspersion among disciplinary fields, but what is maintained for each chapter is an attention to architecture when it relates to other media (printed matter, theater, and film, to mention just a few)—what I call "architecturability"—at moments when the potential to imagine the field and its outside is mobilized. To make use of narrative terms, space becomes a storyteller, thereby implying a multiplicity of potential and actual stories and tellers and certainly also many participants, fictional or real, who will never form a unified whole or a simply passive audience or readers who listen and agree to one new or well-established story. Perhaps this notion of "space as storyteller," because of the constrained stretch between abstraction and singularity, even leads us beyond or, better, elsewhere in comparison to a sometimes more reassuring and comforting term like "everyday life," often considered to be in contrast with modernist or in tune with postmodernist narrative takes (or otherwise the notion that allows a bridging of the cusp between modernism and postmodernism). To express these ideas in another way, in terms borrowed from the theatrical and staging dimension of the project, the chapters relate one to the other as if spotlights illuminate moments and zones of interspersion more or less distant in time; there is no pretension to illuminating an entire stage or a whole theater, hence readers are invited to share and to participate in these spaces and eventually to bring some additional spots of light (or of darkness) so as to show additional constellations, to reinvent them.

"Interspersion" and "interpenetration" are words that recur throughout Benjamin's *Arcades Project*. To the Nietzschean dictum "We are no longer contemporary to architecture: its time is gone," Benjamin responds with his unfinished project, which is a constellation of his notes disseminated among quotes from disparate sources and different languages; Nietzsche's take on architecture is diverted into a complex and stratified materiality of a recent past: that of Paris of the nineteenth century. The noncontemporaneity to architecture is allegorically affirmed and negated at the same time. It is affirmed because Benjamin refers to architectures that have just passed, but it is negated because the architectures of Paris of the nineteenth century participate allegorically to define the way Benjamin proceeds. The temporality of these architectures is similar to the one that pulsates in the *Arcades Project*; it is a temporality affected by abrupt changes, whose immanence is captured in its passing. But Benjamin's writing distends this convulsive temporality, expanding it within the multiple written perspectives that render the *Arcades Project* an open-ended text into which the reader is invited to enter. The *Arcades Project* has a structure that has the unique characteristic of allowing the reader to select an access to it from several entrances and to move in it along different paths. Each section (*Konvolut*) has a specific title that corresponds to a proper name ("Baudelaire," "Fourier," "Marx") or to particular materials and aspects of the society of Paris of the nineteenth century ("Fashion," "Iron Construction," "The Stock Exchange," "Mirrors") or to spaces of Paris ("The Street of Paris," "The Interior, The Trace"). The sections are also related; each one contains passages that echo the "materials" discussed in others. Rolf Tiedemann, the German editor of the text, argues that the *Konvolute* can be considered as provisional divisions into chapters, yet the reading of the unfinished project presents the different sections in an allegorical relationship, communicating one with the other, while still insisting on their difference, or apartness. The arcades become at the same time material architectural constructions that shelter without enclosing and also the perfect allegorical image that lets many elements of an epoch pass by and circulate, without imposing any essential meaning or access but instead fostering the movement of thought.

I divide chapter 1—which is devoted to this movement of thought—into two interrelated parts: "Legibility: A Methodology of Composition" and "Spaces of Knowability." In the first part, I select three of the many "script-images" of which the *Arcades Project* is constellated and which articulate Benjamin's distinctive way of thinking-through-writing the spatiotemporal experience of modernity; his method is defined by scattered and perspectival images embedded in the tempo of modernity: the blow (*Umschlag*). Exactly because architecture is considered only tangentially, and not as a self-contained object of study, Benjamin's attention to it becomes potential: as a sense of abrupt and ruinous decay but also as the potential for architectures still to come, still to be invented; in any case, the reading of these architectures requires that we consider them in their specificity but yet among many media. More than one commentator on Benjamin has highlighted the importance of the debates that started at the end of the nineteenth century on space and architecture; one of the breaking points in the consideration of architecture among the scholars of that time was that architecture was not to be considered as a self-contained object (a mass) but instead for its space-impulse, what August Schmarsow called *Raumgefühl* (sense of space). Benjamin translates this art history term in his *Arcades Project*: in this cityscape that is always fleeting and always changing, space becomes a storyteller. The second part of chapter 1 follows Benjamin's immersion in certain literary texts (in particular Baudelaire, Proust, and Aragon) as he interprets and intersperses them with aspects of architecture and cityscape. I argue that the arcades are considered for their "architecturability," to use a neologism that opens up within their actuality and their potentiality. It is at this point that the notion of "colportage of space" opens a path to conclude the selective reading of the *Arcades Project*. Benjamin makes use of an old term, "colportage," but stretches its meaning beyond its previous uses: it is not simply a question of transporting small goods, of spreading information and news, or of defining the "colportage literature"—little popular books (with mixed contents) sold by peddlers between the sixteenth and the nineteenth centuries. Benjamin indicates that "the colportage phenomenon of space" (which one would argue is certainly not a "pure" phenomenon as defined in philosophy by phenomenology) is the flâneur's elemental experience; according to Benjamin, the "colportage of space" imparts the ability to perceive different occurrences or events happening in the same place, but he also indicates that interpenetration (one of the terms with which, above, I began to approach this chapter) is a principle of colportage (as it is for cinema and new architecture). In the Benjaminian interpretation of the "colportage of space," space transforms and transports, and the city becomes a theatrical display.[6] It is a space that speaks, becomes a storyteller, echoing the overlapping of mirrors and psyche, of inside and outside, at the threshold of bodily experiences and dreams, performing its plays in streets that are a "vascular network of imagination." In the constructed but moving cityscape, everything—temporality as much as spatiality—asks to be rethought, and the *Arcades Project*'s way of inscription opens up beyond the locale of Paris of the nineteenth century. Such storytelling derives its rhythm from the always-changing theatrical display into which the city transforms, and it is experienced, to phrase it in a contemporary fashion, affectively.

One of the pivotal moves scholars make when considering the look Benjamin casts on the cityscape is to expand beyond the *Arcades Project*—because of Benjamin's direct interests—toward the Surrealist avant-garde, and toward Le Corbusier in architecture. Just to come back momentarily to the *Arcades Project*, Benjamin notes therein: "To encompass both Breton and Le Corbusier—that would mean drawing the spirit of contemporary France like a bow, with which knowledge shoots the moment in the heart" (459). Many studies have been devoted more or less directly to these connections, and that is not the objective of this book. From chapter 1 to chapter 2 the book does a twisted jump to a series of Futurist experimentations. Certainly, the most striking take on F. T. Marinetti and Futurism as a whole is the one flashed out by Benjamin in his "The Work of Art in the Age of Its Technological Reproducibility"; in his essay discussing the misuses of technology in relation to national state building and imperialism, and the consequent disastrous and epochal changes they brought forth as destruction, the German critic finds in Marinetti's manifesto the exemplification of the experience of annihilation as aesthetic pleasure: "'Fiat ars—pereat mundus,' says fascism, expecting from war, as Marinetti admits, the artistic gratification of a sense perception altered by technology" (122).

The Benjaminian sentence, which with a single short quote from Marinetti closes his masterpiece, has focalized in one essential direction—like a permanent magnet—all subsequent scholarship: in a stroke, Benjamin has been able to perform an act of thought that, it is not very hazardous to say, no scholarship will ever be able to reproduce. After such a critical stroke, the scholarship that has followed—whether in studying Futurism or comparing Benjamin's thought with Futurism—has been circumscribed to producing critical moves that swing closer to or further from its lodestone but always remain constrained by the permanent magnetic field. Benjamin has established a compass, which directly or indirectly, aloud or silently, directs the scholarship. At the same time this antinomy, Marinetti/Benjamin (and also Futurism/Surrealism, just to mention another related one), has gone through a reconfiguration because of the archival materials that since the 1970s have brought into the open the multifarious experiments that Futurists performed, which have only recently been more widely translated from Italian into other languages. These archives have surfaced not by themselves but through the assiduous work of many: beginning slowly and then with much more intensity, over the last twenty years international scholarship and, in large part, Anglophone scholarship have achieved a spectrum of research that reaches nearly *n*-dimensionality in its intent and scope. It is perhaps worth mentioning that in the field of theater in particular and in what is now called performance studies, Futurism has been embraced as a cardinal point, starting with RoseLee Goldberg, passing on to Giovanni Lista and Günter Berghaus, and arriving at Chris Salter. This being so, it should not be too shocking for me to pass on from the way I read Benjamin's take on the cityscape to a consideration of how a series of Futurists experimented at the crossroads of theater and performance with attention to the cityscape. And to come back to the Futurist archives, my selection from them is only a splinter of the whole.

Futurism, from its inception, had an incredible impact in Europe and beyond, for its effects of rupture. As Luca Somigli writes, Futurism was crucial for artists who "attempt to articulate new strategies of legitimation of their activity."[7] Futurism, in this respect, since its "origin" in the first of Marinetti's manifestos, was the result of a process that forced Marinetti "to confront and discard a series of options regarding the place of the intellectual in modernity. . . . [It] will present the traces of what have been discarded—left behind in the whirlpool of the original moment—and at the same time will open up space for the emergence of a new project whose features remain, at least initially, undefined" (95). Marinetti, the impresario of an impressive renewal, fostered new spaces for literary and artistic activities; he did so by encouraging the disentanglement of previous ways of writing, acting, painting, constructing, and by permitting the new mass media to circulate among these arts, while reconfiguring them in new ways. This is interesting to consider, not just at the time of the Futurist's heroic moments, but also at a later time when Futurist experimentations, entangled in complex international political scenarios as well as altered by international cross-pollination of the historical avant-gardes, still exhibited reluctance toward a *retour à l'ordre*—moving still within the Futurist tropes but absorbing Surrealist and Constructivist moods. In chapter 2, I look at many Futurist experimentations often considered as belonging to the Second Futurism (from the mid-1910s to the mid-1930s). Benjamin in the *Arcades Project* writes in reference to Le Corbusier: "Today, the watchword is not entanglement but transparency" (419). The Futurist experimentations considered in chapter 2 are entanglements—abstract and imaginary—in which the technological imagination, to quote the title of a recent collection of essays on Futurism,[8] presents not an architecture proper of master builders but instead ways of articulating at an intermedial level extreme relations between space and architecture, between the fleeting and the stable, between the tactile and the optical, between the close and the distant. All, along the trajectory selected for chapter 2, take place on the stage, and more and more beyond the Futurist *macchinolatria*, allegorically.

I read closely several instances in the "Futurist Reconstruction of the Universe" and some of the many experimentations disseminated in journals, exhibitions, and theatrical performances. I look at instances that articulate the moment of passage from the Futurist art of rupture to *artecrazia*, when many experimentations were worked out, activating new spaces of modernity. Claudia Salaris has given a well-informed historical perspective on Futurism during the fascist era, a time for which *artecrazia* is the term that best defines the priority of the experimental dimension. Salaris, in her *Artecrazia: L'avanguardia futurista negli anni del fascismo*, writes about the activities of Marinetti and other Futurists: "During the 'ventennio' occurs a substantial revision of futurism that moves from the global contestation to a more limited objective, the union-like defense of the avant-garde, and the conquest of a space."[9] I closely analyze manifestos and experimentations that inventively connect theater, architecture, and other mixed-media experimentations. The Synthetic Futurist Theater disrupts the rules of classical theatrical plotting, and it encourages the auditors to participate on the stage, onto which are brought simultaneous but split and superimposed scenes from the cityscape. The scenographical constructive and architectural inventions are integral parts of the Synthetic Futurist Theater. Futurists experiment in mobile places that are invented among oblique, abstract, ephemeral, invisible constructions within a dynamic of interruption, jumps, and distortions, which will never come to form a static whole. At the limits of invention and abstraction, the constructed spaces become either actors or magical multiplicities of disproportionate planes. These are extreme spaces: on the one hand, there is an insistent experimental search for experiencing and performing yet again the sense of space, the space of sensation within a technological frame; on the other hand, these are abstract possible reinventions, a laboratory for possible future cityscapes, which indeed take place and take shape allegorically on the stage. Abstraction is transmitted and also translated through allegory, or, if you wish, allegory is transmitted and also translated through abstraction. The art historian Roberto Longhi in the 1910s pointed out the Baroque take of Futurism. Indeed, we could define Futurism as an abstract Baroque for the twentieth century: Futurism presents, in a distorted mirror, possible new inventions. No wonder, therefore, that one of the late unfinished works by Marinetti is a theatrical piece that has architectures as its main characters: "mass-mediauric" architectures, invisible and imaginary. *Reconstruct Italy with Futurist Sant'Elia Architecture* is a recollection of many of the proposals that Futurism launched on its mobile stages, with manifestos, theater, and architectures. It performs the war between the old and the new that takes place in an imaginary version of Venice, a privileged Baroque city, a place of exchange and traveling, one of the most visited and studied cities for its marvelous architecture.[10] Throughout this allegorical theatrical piece, the characters, who act out proposals for alternative constructed cityscapes for Venice, are vividly defined but are abstractly divided among groups: "speed people," "space people," and "passéists." Imagined architectural scenarios with their forms and spatial connections are once again a possible allegory of a time to come; they are an interrogation about the multiplicity of new tasks that future architectures will have to work on, as well as possible spectacular outcomes.

The quest for storytelling and the novel in a constructed and media-saturated cityscape is crucially re-elaborated by Italo Calvino and Georges Perec. Chapter 3, looking at cross-pollination of their activity as writers of fictions and as essayists, shows the radicalism of their spatial literary takes. I read Calvino's *Invisible Cities* and Perec's *Life A User's Manual* by forcing their relational elliptic focuses: these two texts share common literary and critical spaces, which I define (recalling Giuliana Bruno's *Atlas of Emotion*) as a "geographical tenderness," while at the same time they contain extreme but not exclusive tensions. While in *Invisible Cities* everything is exteriorized and the text offers a multiplicity of well-defined perspectival images of cities, in *Life A User's Manual* everything converges with centripetal force on a fictional Parisian building's inside, an inside that is always chopped, if not contested, by a massive amount of interviewing and potential stories. The cultural potentials of the localities of Venice (the place of departure of Marco Polo's adventures, the Baroque city par excellence, the enchanting stage for many literary texts as much as for tourist clichés) and Paris (one of the loci of the modern novel, if not of recent modernity) are allegorically put to flight; the insistent tangential reference to these two enchanting literary mobile stages is questioned fictitiously, drifting upon their respective grounds. From the mid-1960s to the mid-1970s, Calvino and Perec actively participated in the literary laboratory of the Oulipo, experimenting with diversified literary patterns and forms. *Atlas de littérature potentielle* is a collection of many samples that sprang from the "inner" circle of the Oulipians; nevertheless, the title ushers in the necessity to allow alternative literary patterns to surface within and beyond already-known literary atlases. Fredric Jameson, in *The Geopolitical Aesthetic*, suggests that the apartment building of *Life A User's Manual* has a formal centrality in relation to the apartments.[11] The building in Rue Simon-Crubellier is just a scaffolding, which holds no centrality; indeed, it stands constructively, interrogating the notion of centrality. In *Life A User's Manual* storytelling is constructed within a web of stories that present themselves at the edge of their emergence while suddenly disappearing. The scaffolding articulation of this novel has a double emptying-out function in relation to the form of the novel. On the one hand, the profusion of characters, most often potential because not well defined, echoes spatial patterns of the novel at the times of its splendor in the nineteenth century, which Alex Woloch has so intensively studied. Woloch writes: "For the character-system offers not simply many *interacting* individuals but many *intersecting* character-spaces, each of which encompasses an *embedded* interaction between the discretely implied person and the dynamically elaborated narrative form. While characters themselves might or might not gain a relationship, character-spaces inevitably do. To put this differently, all character-spaces inevitably point us toward the character-system, since the emplacement of a character within the narrative form is largely comprised *by* his or her relative position vis-à-vis other characters."[12] On the other hand, the novel, whose subtitle is *Romans* (in the plural), gestures toward morphed samplings of many literary texts and literary genres, already written or yet to come. In a similar experimental gesture, Calvino's *Invisible Cities* depicts a multiplicity of cities, diagramming and abstractly mapping their relationships from a distance while at the same time drawing architectural forms close up with unsurpassed and forceful precision. *Invisible Cities* may be said to experiment with form as force in its spatial and architectural dimensions as well as allegorically in relation to potential ways of writing fictions. In this respect, *Invisible Cities* seems to be an abstract subtext of what Franco Moretti has recently written in his *Graphs, Maps, Trees*: "As in an experiment, the force 'from with-out' of large national processes alters the initial narrative structure beyond recognition, and reveals the direct, almost tangible relationship between social conflict and literary form. Reveals form as a diagram of forces; or perhaps, even, as *nothing but force*."[13] While Calvino's and Perec's experimentations are definitively literary, they are highly and densely informed through the filters of many mass media, pointing indeed toward a media-saturated cityscape. In this regard Calvino mimics the estrangement at work in avant-garde and neo-avant-garde contemporary experimentations; Perec, who was in a long-lasting conversation with interlocutors such as Paul Virilio and Henri Lefebvre, seems to playfully activate a *détournement* of the *détournements* of the Situationist poetic. Calvino's and Perec's experimental storytelling, positioning on the edges of their time as well as of the literary and critical tradition, certainly points toward the quest for reimaging and reexperiencing life in the constructed cityscape.

These texts search for a dimensionality of literature that is not flat or, if you will, not mappable; instead, they search for the conditions of countless literary worlds, indicating the potential of imaginative space "made of sets of differences, implications, rules and exclusions."[14]

In chapters 4 and 5, I turn my attention to architecture proper, balancing the specificity of architectural experimentations with a simple, general fact: architecture is always something relational, mundane, and shared. But the attention focuses more on specific experimentations than on this fact; in other words, if a less obvious space is made for these experimentations, architecture is more than just a backdrop. The first part of chapter 4 is devoted to the intermediality of the counterdesign practices of the Italian architecture group Superstudio, which in the 1960s and early 1970s marked the international architectural experimental and critical debate in the way they mined any utopian flight. In reading Superstudio's *12 Ideal Cities* (1971) and other related counterprojects, I consider the strategies at play in their nightmarish, escapist takes on architecture, showing how from the one side they seem to mimic a dead end of space as storyteller while on the other side they aim to reimagine the practice of architecture within an increasingly urban population and also a highly saturated mediascape, even if that is yet to come, or yet to deploy itself in its actuality.

The inventive and experimental atmosphere of the many international neo-avant-gardes, and in particular the atmosphere produced by Superstudio and Archizoom (another Italian architectural radical group), resonated in the first steps of the two architects I consider next: Bernard Tschumi and Rem Koolhaas. Rather than Superstudio's intermedial criticality or the neutral, non-figurative quality of Archizoom's *No-Stop City*, Tschumi prefers to interrogate space via many different media and disciplinary fields that he experimentally imports, as is amply documented in his collection of essays, *Questions of Space*. With these essays and many performance-based interventions, Tschumi reinvents a new space of comparison for architecture, one that deviates from and offers resistance to any modern or contemporary canonical master narrative of architecture and its theorization. Tschumi intersperses the stable ground of architecture with performance practices from Futurism to Vito Acconci, with literary texts from Borges to Calvino, and with *détournement* of advertisement to show the temporary and eventful aspects of architecture. With the *Manhattan Transcripts* Tschumi shows a way to turn cinematic practices to work for/in architecture and to articulate space, movement, and event in an unprecedented relationality; the relations established among these terms allows for imagining an architecture that is detached from the conventional mode of representation, an architecture that acquires its potential from the broken and fleeting experiences in the cityscapes and from cinematic nonlinear narrativity. The project for the Parc de la Villette in Paris, France, is mobilized by many of Tschumi's previous reflections and practices, which coalesce in a design-gesture that seems to be triggered by a kind of programmatic fission. Tschumi invents an urban park for the new millennium. A zone at the outskirts of Paris, a *terrain vague* in a troubled neighborhood, obtains a second chance and is rehabilitated as a park that offers an openness of uses for participants and passersby. The park maintains and disjoints a complex system of cultural and entertainment facilities and open-air spaces. The intermingling of programs interspersed in the park does not require the user to grasp it: it can be lived and perceived in a state of distraction. To this may be added that no picture can encompass it: eventually a montage of images may begin to approximate it, but a passerby, a walker, a runner, or a user will get only some fleeting points of view. The accesses to this park and to the activities are several in number, the desires or reasons to go there may be many, and what can potentially take place there and give space for storytelling is essentially unknown. Chapter 4 focuses also on more recent projects by Tschumi, highlighting the well-calculated interdisciplinary projectuality that Tschumi Studio activates: thinking of architecture as one desirable medium, envisioning and imagining the cityscape for its everyday life and eventual aspects. For Tschumi, architecture is a form of knowledge, and chapter 4 strives to show the ways in which architecture can be radically inventive while thinking out the conditions that produce new relationships among architecture and its others (its potential participants as well as the other media and all the spaces in between them). While Tschumi's incursions into other fields appear only to (apparently) disappear again, with a flash-like modality similar to fireworks, they conceptually punctuate a new way of thinking, practicing, and writing about architecture, exemplary for the way theoretical, theatrical, literary, and visual experimentations and concepts are imported—to use one of Tschumi's idioms—into the field of architecture and of the urban. This chapter, like the one that follows, aims at approaching just such a modality, so as to learn from it and also to import it into the field of literary studies. In the end, chapters 4 and 5 also generate other ways of reading the materials studied in the previous chapters. Because what this book contends for, or searches for, is not to apply a theory to several different practices but instead to see how the imparting of insights from different fields of research may bring new and unexpected understanding of the space of modernity. This said, while chapters 4 and 5 are in some respects parallel, the intent of this study is not principally to define what ties or unties them but, ultimately, to get glimpses of how the two offices, Tschumi and Koolhaas/OMA, "space differently," to quote Bruno, their specific ways of inventing new architecturabilities among different media. To put it another way, even if chapter 5 highlights moments that punctuate how Koolhaas/OMA unfold their interdisciplinary way of thinking about architecture and the urban differently from Tschumi, this is not the most important concern of the chapter.

Chapter 5 plunges into a reading of the massive book *S,M,L,XL* (1995)—a novel of architecture by Koolhaas/OMA and Bruce Mau—to encounter astonishing architecture-characters that acquire life as they are imagined and put on stage. My reading of *S,M,L,XL*, a book that alternates without any clear-cut distinction among essentially critical project-texts, built projects, and unbuilt ones, aims at highlighting some moments that articulate the adventure of architecture or some of the many ways in which architecture is adventured. The changing and captivating flow of architectural/urbanistic stories (always presented in different formats and through different media) that one learns of from this publication makes one want to know more about OMA's operating projectuality. No wonder that one of the recent publications on OMA sprang from the impulse to dedicate two years to participant observation in the OMA office in Rotterdam. Albena Yaneva has documented the specificity of OMA's design practice with ethnographic glances, gathering "small accounts of different design trajectories, reminiscent of short stories";[15] these stories, Yaneva writes, "'just' offer the world lived in the office, and depict it, deploy it, whenever the story allows. They recount how models, as virtual beings, gain concrete reality little by little; they tell of how story-telling reveals traces of their metamorphoses, some of their *trajectories*" (16). My take on OMA derives neither from a close encounter with the architectural firm nor from archival researches; I work with the materials publicly available, either published or built. The chapter takes time to unpack the many genres, modalities, and tones that the book assumes, recycles, or reinvents. OMA's works have been studied in relation to eminent precedents: Surrealism and Russian Constructivism, Le Corbusier, Mies van der Rohe, and Oswald Mathias Ungers, just to mention a few; here I approach the singularity of OMA's practice, and at times I look at weak ties through which it can be put in relation to the previous parts of the book, even if several motifs are tilted—if not turned inside out—by OMA. For example, the complex project for Euralille—which inscribes at its core a transport network that alters the very meaning of address—is Futurist in its intent (at least in Koolhaas's words), but in *S,M,L,XL* we find only the most minimal quotation of the historical avant-garde, Futurism—and those few are taken, apparently with a quite ironic intent, from the 1930s publication *The Futurist Cookbook*. Otherwise, the adjective "Futuristic" may well define the developer and architect John Portman as a producer of a "city of clones." While projects like Euralille aim at activating a renewed sense of urbanism and the metropolis, text-projects like "The Generic City," assess the state of the city, with tones that challenge the surreal Calvinian *Invisible Cities* as much as Superstudio's *12 Ideal Cities*: in "The Generic City," streets become the residual, the public has been evacuated, and the city is sedated. Koolhaas texts always read like performances, or like a one-man show, as much as each of the OMA projects imagines unexpected and nonstandard architectures; the engineer Cecil Balmond, who has a long-standing collaboration with OMA, imagines informal structures for the Kunsthal in Rotterdam for which, as he writes, space entertains. Space, never a critical term for Koolhaas, becomes one when in "Junkspace" he records a proliferation of constructed spaces that massively contrast with any avant-garde scenarios. Futurism, in its "Futurist Manifesto of Aerial Architecture," was seeing junk from a distant, bird's-eye view; now Koolhaas sees the entirety of constructed spaces as immersed in and permeated by junkspace. If *S,M,L,XL* is a big novel of architecture assembled in part on the basis of the projects' scales, a later Koolhaas publication, *Content* (2004), is assembled in part from projects whose motto is "Go East"; as an almanac of recent OMA adventures, *Content* seems to operate a colportage of architecture in junkspace; as David Joselit posits, "In this kaleidoscopic, multigenre graphic novel/journal/luxury retail catalogue/retrospective, *content* is laid out like junkspace—the term Koolhaas invented to define an architecture of pure optimization—of time, money, and real estate."[16] But splinters of exceptional projects are also presented, immersed in this junk-like edited publication; among these are the Seattle Public Library, which aims at the design of a public space that hosts old and new media alike in an unprecedented way, and the CCTV/TVCC complex, headquarters of the Chinese national television network, built in downtown Beijing. The CCTV project, a huge palindrome and "a true enigmatic signifier,"[17] is a loop that "poses a truly three-dimensional experience";[18] it is also an allegory of data flow: it integrates the different activities of the process of television broadcasting, exposes and makes public the backstages and the production of the media flows, gives different vistas on the city and offers different views as seen from the outside, and interrogates the public at the time of data flows and fosters spaces for public and temporary events.

Looking at Tschumi's and Koolhaas's posturban projects, yet searching for the public, wherein architectures and infrastructures are in a continuous process of contamination, I show how Tschumi, with his architecture of movement, lightens the projects of the hypermodern spaces and how Koolhaas—in a cityscape altered from congestion to data flows—creates an almost allegorical mise-en-scène of interlocking spaces.

This book explores a multiplicity of authors whose abilities to read constructed spaces of modernity result in active and polysemic transformations. Architecture is the focalizing agent of change considered from several perspectives: tangential and passing by Benjamin, abstract and experimental by the Futurists, invisible and multiple by Calvino and Perec. The effective, constructive gestures by Koolhaas/OMA and Tschumi are also read in relation to the fleeting and temporary ones analyzed in the previous chapters. In each instance, space is the storyteller of the different transdisciplinary interpretations that these authors set in play on the stages of modernity.

Chapter 1

✦

In the Primeval Fields of Modernity

Introduction

In an essay on Walter Benjamin's Parisian *passages* and Siegfried Kracauer's hotel lobby, Anthony Vidler emphasized the way emblematic architectural spaces haunt these texts. Vidler points to the artifice implied in these writings: "In a real sense these are purely textual spaces, designed, so to speak, by their authors; they possess an architectonic of their own, all the more special for its ambiguous status between textual and social domains; they are, so to speak, buildings that themselves serve as analytical instruments."[1] Vidler underlines the spatial and constructive side of Benjamin's writing and the spatialization implied in his practice of inscribing motion and temporality within the arguments themselves.

In the *Arcades Project*, the spatiotemporal open framework of Paris in the nineteenth century allows Benjamin to work within the complex relationship between past and future, at the moment that initiates the provisional relationship that appears at the encounter between the "what has been" and the "now." This relation is configured in a dialectical image that emerges when the "what has been" and the "now" crystallize into a constellation ("Paris") of a certain period ("the nineteenth century"). Benjamin writes: "It's not that what is past cast its light on what is present, or what is present its light on what is past; rather, image is that wherein what has been comes together in a flash with the now to form a constellation" (N2a,3).[2] Benjamin's method of interpretation is guided by the moment of twilight of the relationship between past and future: it is a moment and a space-time from which can emerge the new and the unexpected as well as the ruinous aspect of what was new, the "has been." Indeed, Benjamin discerns a specific relationship, or directionality, between the present and the past:

> We can speak of two directions in this work: one which goes from the past into the present and shows the arcades, and all the rest, as precursors, and one which goes from the present into the past so as

> to have the revolutionary potential of these "precursors" explode in the present. And this direction comprehends as well the spellbound elegiac consideration of the recent past, in the form of its revolutionary explosion. (O°,56)

In this chapter I approach a number of passages from Benjamin's *Arcades Project* that are related to what he defines, if disruptively, as a "method." Benjamin conveys his method through figural language and images that, while communicating with each other, are self-enclosed in a monadic style. These images require a continuous suspension and interruption of straightforward logic.

Through fleeting images characterized by a sense of transience and interruption, Benjamin defies language so that his writing loses any self-evidence. He suspends the conciliatory mode of understanding that allows the direct association of a description with an image. Thus my reading focuses on the singular way in which language inhabits images but always exceeds and overflows the confines of a single image or concept. I am particularly interested in the logic of a method composed of diffracted perspectives. Benjamin's use of nonlinear, dialectical figures allows for multiple configurations of perspective. Benjamin proceeds not by providing a method that may then be applied but by elaborating a manifold study of a specific epoch, in which each point of view relates to another and at the same time differentiates itself from another. The *Arcades Project*, because of its in-progress format, can be accessed by selecting from among Benjamin's numerous perspectives. The ones I have selected show how Benjamin captures the emergence of two terms that are in tension: construction and space. "Construction" (and scaffolding) will give us access to the way Benjamin envisions the "origin" of a new way of understanding and experiencing architecture and the cityscape. "Space" results, not as a simple extrasubjective extension but instead as a site of experiment that requires the reader and the inhabitant to participate. I will show how Benjamin situates his writing within these perspectives, how he brings the reader into this perspectival method, and how his figural language disseminates images that appear and disappear in a space and time suspended between writing and materiality. This chapter, traversing the *Arcades Project* and a few other related texts of Benjamin's, will show how architecture, rather than constituting a self-contained object, emerges instead primarily for its potential, for its "architecturability," as a medium and in relation to other media, where repetition and the unexpected converge in unprecedented ways; it will show too that space, as inscribed in the intriguing term "colportage phenomenon," is not a static entity but instead a storyteller in the moving cityscape.

Part 1. Legibility: A Methodology of Composition

Setting the Sails—Experience, Sea Voyages, and a Method of Drafting

> *December 30, 1929.* No sooner do you arrive in the city than you feel rewarded. The resolve not to write about it is futile. You reconstruct the preceding day just like children who reconstruct [*aufbauen*] the table full of presents on Christmas Day. This, too, is a way of expressing your gratitude. Still, I'm holding to my plan [*Veranstaltungen*] that someday soon I will do more than just this. For the moment, at least, the plan prevents me—as does the space for reflection that I need in order to work—from abandoning my willpower and surrendering myself to the city.[3]

This quote is from the beginning of a piece, *Paris Diary* (1930), in which Benjamin reports on his meetings with various Parisian intellectuals during his stay in Paris (between December 1929 and February 1930). Stepping into the city demands that he write about it in a way that is like reconstructing the day just passed; Benjamin writes that he does not have time or, better, does not have "the space of reflection" for his plan to write on the city. The end of the piece concludes with a moving cityscape in which Benjamin walks:

> Spring has come with the cold, and when you come striding down the Champs-Elysées as if down a snowy mountain slope, with racing pulse and flushed cheeks, you suddenly call a halt in front of a small lawn behind the Théâtre Marigny—a lawn in which spring is in the air. Behind the Théâtre Marigny, an impressive building is in the process of construction; a tall green fence surrounds the site, and behind it the scaffolding [*Gerüste*] rises. . . . And as I walked along, my thoughts became all jumbled up as a kaleidoscope—a new constellation at every step [*Und wie ich im Gehen meine Gedanken so kaleidoskopisch durcheinanderfallen fühlte—mit jedem Schritt eine neue Konstellation*]. Old elements disappeared, and unknown ones came stumbling up—figures of all shapes and sizes. If one remained, it was called a "sentence." And among thousands of possible ones, I found this one, for which I had been waiting for many years—the sentence that wholly defined the miracle that the Madeleine—not the Proustian madeleine, but the real one—had been from the first moment I saw it: in winter the Madeleine is a great furnace that warms the rue Royale with its shadow.

The end of this piece draws the attention toward an actual theater, the Théâtre Marigny, but behind it appears a building in the process of construction and a scaffolding being erected. New constellations spring from each step as he walks among those constructed spaces. Benjamin's remark that "old elements disappeared, and unknown ones came stumbling up—figures of all shapes and sizes" seems to point toward images, yet what remain are not images, figures, shapes, but instead a "sentence" from among "thousands of possible" sentences. The sentence refers to a monument and its relation with the atmosphere of the cityscape, which could be defined as the "aura" of a specific place in the cityscape. At the end of the piece, just before giving us the "sentence," the text, like a photograph or a film, superimposes two different kinds of locations, a theater and a building in the process of being constructed, blurring theatrical and architectural spaces in a way that, I will show, occurs in many passages of the *Arcades Project*.

While this text shows Benjamin's endless stylistic power to translate or convey images through sentences, it does not embrace the avant-gardist tone that he works out in the citational style of the *Arcades Project* or in the style of *One-Way Street*. Michael Jennings argues that *One-Way Street* marks the attempt to establish, not simply a new avant-gardist form, "a new, montaged, and non-narrative form," but a form that in turn "places unusual demands on the reader."[4] For Jennings, such a text is Benjamin's attempt to achieve a fusion of many avant-garde expressions (Dada, Constructivism, and Surrealism), as part of a collective venture of the G-Gruppe, the Berlin-based artists' collective Benjamin associated with in the 1920s. Compared with *One-Way Street*, *Paris Diary*'s style tends toward an auratic rather than avant-garde experience of the cityscape: the vision of the city and the walking are embedded in a specific locality, while in *One-Way Street* places lose their sense of unique locality. Whereas in *Paris Diary* the spatial dimension is embedded in ordinary (even if enchanted) walking, in *One-Way Street*, as Jennings has noticed, space resides in disorientation; according to Jennings, "the most brilliant evocation of this form of spatial displacement occurs toward the end of the volume, in 'Stand-Up Beer Hall.'" Jennings writes, "The bourgeoisie experience the disorienting power of commodities in a mediated manner . . . For the sailor, however, whose work 'in the rump of the ship maintains contact with the commodity,' the world actually travelled and lived in ceases to have any local character" (27).

Certainly the numerous notes and citations constellated in the *Arcades Project* bring the disorientation of *One-Way Street* to the cityscape of nineteenth-century Paris, whose assemblage Benjamin invites the reader to navigate. The passages of the *Arcades Project* move the reader between orientation and disorientation, and while insisting on a specific time and a specific place, their interrelationships destabilize any simple totality and produce a flash-like multitude of perspectives on an epoch. There are some passages that pose the "I" of the writer, who, while proceeding in his writing, gives moving images in which he indeed seems to move and transport the reader. I have selected some of them in order to show how the tension between space (never a simple extension) and architecture (never an isolated object) is embedded in *Arcades Project*. Oddly enough, one of the first passages from

Konvolut N introduces not a cityscape but instead a sea voyage (*Schifffahrt*), which alludes to Benjamin's own way of proceeding: "Comparison of other people's attempts to the undertaking of a sea voyage in which the ships are drawn off course by the magnetic north pole. Discover *this* North Pole. What for others are deviations [*Abweichungen*] are, for me, the data which determine my course.—On the differentials of time (which, for others, disturb the main lines of the inquiry), I base my reckoning" (N1,2).

A sea voyage implies a relation to space and to experience that inflects the way of proceeding and draws it off course (*abgelenkt*); movement can no longer be completely calculated. Whatever calculations figure in the sea voyage must also cope with the magnetic field, which actively inflects the normal course of the vessel. The spatial deviation of the trajectory and the "differentials of time" are crucial to Benjamin's thought. In the comparison with navigation, the writer is a sailor, and the "differentials of time" are decisive in Benjamin's method.

The passage cited above is a "script-image" (*Schriftbild*), which Samuel Weber defines as both "an image that calls for reading" and "a *scenario*":[5] this script-image exhibits a way of proceeding that is not simply in motion but also diachronic, deviating, and destabilized in its direction. If Benjamin compares his way of thinking with navigation, this implies that there is an experientially crucial aspect, connected also with time and movement, in his way of proceeding. Here as in the rest of this *Konvolut*, Benjamin's notion of experience involves disorientation and danger. The differentials of time are indispensable to the method Benjamin adopts in composing the *Arcades Project*; in the image of the sea voyage, his method (a quasi-calculated navigation) is thus never completely totalized into a single perspective. While this quote introduces the experience, if not the feeling, of navigating, the comparison with navigation returns in other passages of *Konvolut* N in a strange metonymy. Indeed, the way of proceeding by navigating and sailing corresponds to the method of a dialectician who, Benjamin writes, has the "wind of world history" in his sails (concepts). During the navigation, phenomena are rescued. "The rescue that is carried out . . . can operate solely for the sake of what in the next moment is already irretrievably lost" (N9,7). The metaphors of the "rescue" and of navigating are conjoined in a group of passages from *Konvolut* N to comprise a metaphor for Benjamin's way of proceeding. Phenomena are rescued from the "wind of the absolute": "They are saved through the exhibition of the fissure within them" (*Sie werden durch die Aufweisung des Sprungs in ihnen gerettet*) (N9,4). "Thinking means . . . setting the sails" (N9,6). The emphasis is on knowing "*how* sails are set"; otherwise there would be no movement (no history) and only concepts. Why? Because sails are words, and "the way they are set makes them into concepts" (N9,6), just as having sails is different from sailing and knowing how to set the sails. Benjamin claims that it is necessary to articulate words and concepts in a differential mode and "to dissipate [*zerstreuen*] the semblance of eternal sameness, and even of repetition, in history" (N9,5). It is not enough, emphasizes Benjamin, to have the sails; "what is decisive is knowing the art of setting them" (N9,8).

Knowing how to set the sails is thus the dynamic basis for Benjamin's method: it is a dialectical method that situates the historian in the epoch "he himself must live in" (N9a,8), while the past is the prehistory of his own epoch. Such a method is "distinguished by the fact that, in leading to new objects, it develops new methods, just as form in art is distinguished by the fact that it develops new forms in delineating new contents" (N10,1). In the same way as there is a tension between words and concepts, between having the sails and knowing how to set them, for Benjamin it is also important to explain the determinant intensity of the method of composition (*Abfassung*), drafting, writing, or reporting. Benjamin articulates or, better yet, disarticulates the very idea of method, situating the inquiry between intensive and extensive dimensions. Everything that one is thinking should be "incorporated into the project" (N1,3); this is what gives intensity to the method of composition. A *telos* is required, such that everything converges virtually at a specific moment, but paradoxically this can be attained only when "the intervals of reflections" (N1,3) are preserved and the distance between the parts (*Teilen*) of the work is maintained. On the one hand, because of the intensity, everything is virtually present from the start in the project; on the other hand, as Benjamin writes, this method of composition "aims to characterize and to preserve the intervals of reflection, the distances lying between the most essential parts of this work, which are turned most intensively to the outside" (N1,3). In the split of knowledge described in this passage, an epoch in history becomes a set of fields through a movement that Benjamin describes as a paradox of civilization and madness: "cultivated fields [*Gebieten*] where, until now, only madness has reigned" (N1,4). There is a moment in which these fields, which Benjamin calls a "primeval forest" but also employs as the materials of the method, "must have been cleared of the undergrowth of delusion and myth" (N1,4). And Benjamin's aim is that this "be accomplished here for the terrain of the nineteenth century" (N1,4). Benjamin's method of composition maintains intervals that are cuts or breaks, in which the figural dimension of the method should persist. Benjamin wants to avoid establishing oppositions, as is clear in another passage:

> It is very easy to establish oppositions, according to determinate points of view, within the various "fields" [*Gebieten*] of any epoch, such that on one side lies the "productive," "forward-looking," "lively," "positive" part of an epoch, and on the other side the abortive, retrograde, obsolescent. (N1a,3)

In order to avoid dichotomies, for Benjamin displacing the angle of vision is decisive. "It is therefore of decisive importance that a new partition [*neuem eine Teilung*] be applied to this initially excluded, negative component [*Teile*] so that, by a displacement [*Verschiebung*] of the angle of vision [*Gesichtswinkels*] (but not of the criteria!) a positive element emerges anew in it too—something different from the previous signified. And so on" (N1a,3). It is a question, for Benjamin, of moving beyond negative and positive *parts*, and locating where "the firm, seemingly brutal grasp" belongs in the process of rescue.

Legibility, Interpenetrations, and the Interspersing of the What-Has-Been and the Now

> In the fields with which we are concerned, knowledge comes [*es gibt*] only in lightning flashes. The text is the long roll of thunder that follows. (N1,1)

The very first passage that Benjamin annotates in *Konvolut* N is a remarkably suggestive one; it points to what may be his most elusive and least linear definition of knowledge. If this passage draws its strength from an image, the image is less an illustration than a way of defining a particular *mode of knowledge*, one that operates with a recurrent but scattered rhythm. This image, moreover, gets its own strength from the relation between lightning and thunder, implying movement and transformation at its very core. Indeed, relationality, movement, and transformation are central to Benjamin's fleeting and often explosive images.

There are several further elements that I want to point out. First, "we are concerned" with *Gebieten*, or fields, a term indicating spatiality, an expanse, zone, or region, but in these fields knowledge arrives only intermittently. Knowledge may be situated in these fields, but its object is not determined; instead, one learns only the rhythm by which knowledge proceeds.[6]

The sentence's imagery transports the reader into stormy fields of knowledge, exposed to forces without any defined contour or spatial reference. And in fact, for most of the passages of the *Konvolut*, the reader is brought into an expansive and incompletely defined field, scattered in different places, and is never fully able to situate him- or herself in advance. But, in this first passage of *Konvolut* N, the reader is asked to be situated in this scenario, for the moment suspending all reference to the object of knowledge. Knowledge is given only in lightning flashes; it is thus a kind of knowledge that can be obtained only at intervals, when the intermittent lightning offers images that are at their strongest in the moment of their disappearance.

In the first passage from *Konvolut* K, knowledge arrives repeatedly and at the same time abruptly; it arrives as it passes; it is ephemeral, appearing only for an instant. But knowledge is attended by thunder, the text, "coming after." There is a temporal relationship between the knowledge and the text, necessarily, but this relation is not simply a function of linear time. It also is function of a time as a moment of surprise and repetition that can be dangerous. The audibility of the text takes on its strength only at a temporal distance from the visibility of knowledge. As an image, this implies a disjointed relationship between visibility and audibility, between image and text; if these two poles are neither completely disconnected nor in opposition, there is still an interval between them, a division at the very core of their relation. The dynamic of lightning flashes and thunder is interrupted and scattered; since their temporal relation cannot be simply linear or progressive, the spatialization of the two cannot be thought of only in terms of a movement between two points. Benjamin places us in fields (*Gebieten*) but not yet in the force field (*Kraftfeld*) with which he will pose, as we will shortly see, his understanding of history, marked by divisibility and virtuality.[7]

It is Adorno who, commenting on Benjamin's writings, illuminates our understanding of how history is disarticulated in the *Arcades Project*. History in the *Arcades Project* is captured by what Adorno defines as Benjamin's intellectual energy, a "kind of mental fission," an "insistence" able to "dissolve the insoluble."[8] Or, as Adorno writes: "Everything that fell under the scrutiny of his words was transformed, as though it had become radioactive." Benjamin, who in the *Arcades Project* is also concerned with a particular access to history, thinks through image and history with a kind of a mental force, dissolving the interpretation of history as continuous and linear. For Benjamin the knowledge of history is not a self-contained and well-defined object but instead is constituted as the rescue of an object. And history—or more specifically the object of history—is not self-present but instead decomposes, disintegrates, decays (*zerfällt*) "into images, not into stories" (N11,4). This disintegration of history into images is the way the "method" operates: history is not a classical historiography, if historiography is supposed to show things "as they really were." Instead, Benjamin highlights a historiographical method that resembles the splitting of an atom, which liberates the enormous energies of history by detaching and disentangling the bounds of the "'once upon a time' of classical historiography" (N3,4). This allows Benjamin to construct a history in which "every dialectically presented historical circumstance polarizes itself and becomes a force field in which the confrontation between its fore-history and after-history is played out. It becomes such a field insofar as the present instant interpenetrates [*hineinwirkt*] it" (N7a,1). Benjamin grafts a force field onto the study of a specific epoch to avoid substantializing a historical moment and to instead divide and disrupt the continuum; the emergence of a differential understanding of space ("as a space of propagations and effects")[9] intervenes, interpenetrating with time and historicity.

How, then, is knowledge of history constituted as an object's rescue? As Benjamin establishes a relationship between knowledge and text in the first passage of *Konvolut* N, so in another passage he opens up this question in relation to the historian, the way he takes part in events, and the relationship between legibility and citation of history. The process of splitting of events is one in which the "historian takes part" (*er teil nimmt*) (N11,3). Taking part, or partaking, is also a way of emphasizing that this knowledge is in parts. This way of proceeding therefore splits not only the object but also the subject of the analysis. "The events surrounding the historian, and in which he himself takes part, will underlie his presentation [*Darstellung*] in the form of a text written in invisible ink" (N11,3). This passage suggests that the part-taking in the present is implied in the presentation (*Darstellung*) of the past, as a text written in "invisible ink" that structures that presentation of the past. But in this same passage, things become even more complicated; in fact, what the historian will present are "citations," and "it is only these citations that occur in a manner legible to all" (N11,3). Benjamin thus breaks the bounds of straightforward logic (as Adorno posits in his short introductory essay to Benjamin's texts); to cite, and to cite history, is not simply to record but to tear, pull, or rip (*rissen*) a historical object from its context and continuity (*Zusammenhänge*). In this sense, to cite is to cite out of a context and to set in motion, to estrange a historical object from its context, to reanimate something that is of the order of an object's rescue. For the Benjaminian historian, "To write history means to *cite* history" (N11,3). But this again does not bring us to continuity; instead, this "concept of citation," as Benjamin indicates, implies exactly that "the historical object is torn . . . from its context" (N11,3).

Now to get back to Benjamin's images, or script-images, their relation to history is again not linear or transparent. If history is given in stories not as continuum but as images, these images, as Benjamin remarks in another passage, are not essences; on the contrary, they are historical indexes, whose "legibility" (*Lesbarkeit*) emerges only at a critical point.[10] Acceding to "legibility" is a movement, a motion (*Bewegung*), within the images themselves. The legibility is given at a moment defined as the critical point "wherein what has been comes together [*zusammentritt*] in a flash with the now to form a constellation" (N3,1). Such legibility therefore is one that comes together, that coalesces at a certain moment. A split, a distance, and a certain spatiality in this process are underscored so that this process is not "purely temporal" but also "figural" (*bildlich*), something that inscribes a lapse or a spacing within this immediate moment. The first image of *Konvolut* N exposes the relationship between the lightning flashes and the thunder, between knowledge and text, and now knowledge transforms into knowability (*Erkennbarkeit*): "The image that is read—which is to say, the image in the now of its knowability—bears to the highest degree the imprint of the perilous critical moment on which all reading is founded" (N3,1). The relationship between the what-has-been and the now is considered dialectical by Benjamin precisely because it is not simply temporal but figural (*bildlich*); immediate and punctual, it nonetheless bears within itself spacing, an *écart*, and also, as the German term *bildlich* implies, a constructive aspect. The image that is read has the mark of "*gefährlichen Moments*" (N3,1), the critical moment, and therefore the legibility implies experience and perilous trajectories. The figural interrupts continuous time or progression; it is *sprunghaft*, erratic, spasmodic; it jumps and leaps. In fact, as Benjamin writes: "Image is dialectics at a standstill. For while the relation of the present to the past is a purely temporal, continuous one, the relation of what-has-been to the now is dialectical: is not progression, but image, suddenly emergent—*sprunghaft*" (N2a,3). In exploding, cracking the continuity of history, Benjamin's method provokes the "interspersing [*durchsetzt*] it with ruins—that is, with the present" (N9a,6). There is an interspersing and disentangling of past and present that is necessary to this process.

We have seen that Benjamin emphasizes that the image is read at a critical, perilous moment (*gefährlichen Moments*), as in a "constellation of dangers." The risk and the critical moment are also at work when Benjamin considers "construction" and "constructing," to which I will devote the next section.

Constructing on the Mobile Scaffolding

There is a third image, a vista of modernity, drawn from the architectural critic Sigfried Giedion, that Benjamin uses to convey the way to "garner fresh perspectives," as he writes, into his net:

> "In the windswept stairways of the Eiffel Tower, or better still, in the steel supports of the Pont Transbordeur, one meets with the fundamental aesthetic experience of present-day architecture: through the thin net of iron that hangs suspended in the air, things stream—ships, ocean, houses, masts, landscape, harbor. They lose their distinctive shape, swirl into one another as we climb downward, merge simultaneously." Sigfried Giedion, *Bauen in Frankreich* (Leipzig and Berlin), p. 7. In the same way, the historian today has only to erect a slender but sturdy scaffolding—a philosophical structure—in order to draw the most vital aspects [*aktuellsten Aspekte*] of the past into his net. (N1a,1)

This reflection on Giedion's moving image draws the attention to architecture and specifically to the questions of construction and the image of the scaffolding; these themes are exposed in some passages of *Konvolut* N, from Benjamin's "Paris, the Capital of the Nineteenth Century" ("Exposé" of 1935), and from the correspondence between Benjamin and Adorno regarding this text. In the Benjaminian method, the term "construction" functions as both an architectural/technological term and a linguistic/conceptual term, such that it opens up possibilities in his conception of architecture and in his mode of writing and thinking. While Benjamin focuses on a specific historical moment, he also opens the past moment to possible unexpected effects in the future. Benjamin draws the themes of "construction," its gerund form "constructing," and "building" from Giedion's *Building in France, Building in Iron, Building in Ferroconcrete*, and these terms are at work in many of the *Arcades Project*'s *Konvolute* in order to articulate different concrete and abstract elements of this epoch. The term "construction" is never a fixed term but functions almost allegorically. In ordinary language, the relation between "function" and "allegory" can be carried on only as a disjunctive, if not oxymoronic, one. The disjunctive tension between the two terms characterizes many parts of the *Arcades Project* exactly because the term "construction," while playing a crucial role in the *Konvolute*, does so in the allegorical mode of signification. "Allegory," writes Samuel Weber, "is the traditional means of investing a manifestation with a signification that it cannot possibly have in terms of a purely immanent, self-contained structure."[11] Just as Giedion apprehends the aesthetic experience of his time from the Pont Transbordeur, Benjamin posits a kind of scaffolding (*tragfähiges Gerüst*) that is also a philosophical structure.[12]

The scaffolding structure supports an opening toward a scenario of writing and interpretation. Benjamin's elaboration of Giedion's text provides an example of how Benjamin simultaneously incorporates and problematizes several of Giedion's arguments. In this scaffolding image, Giedion's argument is inscribed between methods and materials, raising the question of Benjamin's notion of construction.

In order to understand this notion of construction, it is crucial to read some exchanges between Adorno and Benjamin regarding the term. After reading Benjamin's "Exposé,"[13] Adorno writes to him: "You have left the concept of construction [*Begriff der Konstruktion*] completely unclarified; as both alienation and mastery of material, it is already eminently dialectical in character and should therefore, in my view, be expounded explicitly as such (with a clear differentiation from the current concept of construction; perhaps the term engineer, which is very characteristic of the nineteenth century, would provide a suitable starting point!)."[14] But for Benjamin the question is not so much one of engineering versus beaux arts;[15] rather, it is exactly the tension between function and ornament, and between useful and useless/no-more-in-use, that Benjamin considers in order to question a specific origin (*Ursprung*) of modernity. What interests Benjamin in the Paris arcades is a process in which the encounter between architecture and technology (and production) is as determinative as it is "fragile." He writes: "Glass before its time, premature iron. In the arcades, both the most brittle and the strongest materials suffered breakage; in a certain sense, they were deflowered" (F1,2). In fact, Benjamin is interested in the arcades as the *origin* of modern architecture both because of the way they use materials in their constructions and the way they rearticulate the relationship between public and private dwelling.

Benjamin began the *Arcades Project* in 1927, and Giedion's groundbreaking new way of studying architecture, *Building in France, Building in Iron,*

Building in Ferroconcrete, was published in 1928.[16] In the beginning of his book Giedion writes:

> **CONSTRUCTION.** Is CONSTRUCTION something external? We are being driven into an indivisible life process. We see life more and more as a moving yet indivisible whole. The boundaries of individual fields blur [*Die Grenzen einzelner Gebiete verwischen sich*]. Where does science end, where does art begin, what is applied technology, what belongs to pure knowledge? Fields permeate and fertilize each other as they overlap [*Die Gebiete durchdringen sich, befruchten sich, indem sie sich durchdringen*]. It is hardly of interest to us today where the conceptual boundary between art and science is drawn. (87)

It is clear from these opening words of Giedion's book that the term "construction" plays a complex role in what he calls an "indivisible life process"—a process that cannot be considered within containing and definitive boundaries. His book aimed "to extract from the vast complexity of the past those elements that will be the point of departure for the future" (85). After reading this text, Benjamin sent a letter to Giedion, writing, "The few passages that I read electrified me."[17] What was it that interested Benjamin so much in Giedion's work? Giedion considers the arcade to be the prototype of architecture in glass and iron, a calculated structure that would be used to construct exhibition buildings, stations, stores, and other structures that might be called "mediauric," in Samuel Weber's sense. Weber coins this neologism in his reading of Benjamin's reading of Baudelaire's poetry in light of the question of mass reproduction.

For Weber, the specificity of Benjamin's interpretation of Baudelaire's "A une passante" underlines how the poem articulates an experience of the "aura" that is more an experience of desire than of a uniquely apprehended reality—and how this experience originates according to the law of dispersion and collection of the masses.

> The mass qua crowd appears as what it is in withdrawing before what seems to be an individual, feminine figure, that of the *passante*. But the ostensible individuality of this passerby is anything but individual: she comes to be only in passing by. And in so doing, she reveals herself to be the allegorical emblem of the mass, its coming-to-be in and as the other, in and as the singularity of an ephemeral apparition. The mass movement—the mass in/as movement—produces itself as this apparition, which provides an alternative to the formed and mobilized masses of the political movements of the Thirties.[18]

This poem is an alternative to the collective spectacle of the emerging mass-industrialized society. "*Un éclair . . . puis la nuit!*" stands for an alternation of the aura that "is no longer" writes Weber, "that of the original moment but of its posthumous aftershock" (104–5). Weber writes in relation to this moment of coming-to-pass, of fleeting flash:

> Mystery happens dramatically when language overshoots its semantic-thematic function and takes place as an event. To the extent to which it eludes or exceeds signification, such an event can only be fugitive, fleeting, like a falling star or a flash. What this meteoritic event leaves behind can be called—if a neologism can be allowed—the *mediauric*: auratic flashes and shadows that are not just produced and reproduced by the media but which *are* themselves the media, since they come to pass in places that are literally inter-mediary, in the interstices of the process of reproduction. (106)

Weber's argument on Baudelaire's poetry "in the age of mass reproduction and on the threshold of the arrival of masses" shows that in it emerges an aura that "is no longer unique, no longer the *other* of reproduction and repetition, but their most intimate *effect*" (104). A similar *effect* can be ascribed to the urban fabric. Indeed, Giedion's analysis lets itself be carried forward so as to interpret architectures themselves as media. In his analysis of the introduction of glass and iron into architecture as the shift from "craftsmanship to industrial building production" occurs, Giedion writes:

> It started with the introduction of iron in roof framing. The wooden beams of theaters and warehouses burned like tinder. One tried to replace them with iron. Soon one saw that iron construction required little space, allowed much light to stream in, and, when used in combination with glass, was especially suited for the roofing of courtyards. Glass and iron galleries appeared the true point of departure for railroad stations, market halls, exhibition buildings. . . . Glass houses, with their—compared to walls—virtually invisible exterior shell, provide the impetus for the introduction of cast-iron supports and skeleton constructions. (103)

Here Giedion underlines how determinant glass and iron turned out to be in construction, though they were first introduced only for temporary use. The architectural historian Sokratis Georgiadis traces the genealogy of cast-iron forms from nineteenth-century architectural history to Giedion's time to clarify the sources for Giedion's book. Georgiadis refers us to nineteenth-century architectural critic Gottfried Semper, who wrote that cast-iron structures, which he considered "invisible structures," were appropriate only for "plain iron roof trusses of the railroad engineer in terminals and other such things as symbols of their provisional nature."[19] It seems that Benjamin points to these invisible structures because their cast-iron supports and skeleton constructions participate in the ambivalence inherent in modernity, an ambivalence in which they could become the terminus of predetermined uses but are also the mobile places and spaces of a potential that announces new and provisional possibilities. Benjamin's conception of the term "construction" goes beyond real constructions, but without negating them. In architectural construction, the iterability of new materials like cast iron opens up possible futures; in the same way, the iterability of the philosophical meaning of the new constructions inflects Benjamin's method. It is thus all the more striking that Adorno denounces the indeterminacy of the concept of construction in Benjamin's writings, for it is precisely the concept's indeterminacy that Benjamin is putting to work in his method.

Benjamin explicitly relates the "new architectural materials" of glass and iron to sites like railroad tracks that evoke not stability but movement. Thus iron, which is used to stabilize architectural constructions, is also used to negate this stability, or at least to make constructions that allow for movement. In the *Exposé* Benjamin writes:

> For the first time in the history of architecture, an artificial building material appears: iron. It undergoes an evolution whose tempo will accelerate in the course of the century. This development enters a decisive new phase when it becomes clear that the locomotive—on which experiments have been conducted since the end of the 1820s—is compatible only with iron tracks. (4)

Adorno critiques some of Benjamin's claims about iron's role in the history of architecture. In a letter to Benjamin, he writes:

> With regard to page 3, I would ask whether it is really the case that cast iron was the first artificial building material (what about bricks!); in general, I am not always comfortable with the notion of "first" as used in the text. . . . Page 4: the phrase "the new and the old are intermingled" (*durchdringt*) is highly suspect to me, given my earlier critique of the dialectical image as regression.[20]

What Adorno's reading misses is the effect of Benjamin's perspective. Through his perspective, Benjamin can articulate a relationship between the new and the old that takes into account their dialectic, their intermingling—not their equivalence. Adorno, regarding the relation between the old and the new, writes that Benjamin should consider Adorno's analysis of the "interior," as developed in his book on Kierkegaard, in which Adorno claims to demonstrate the false existential temporality at stake in the Danish philosopher's description of the interior. A crucial passage of Adorno's book is quoted at length in the *Arcades Project*, and here I extract some parts of it:

> The contents of the interior are mere decoration, alienated from the purpose they represent, deprived of their own use value, engendered solely by the isolated dwelling-space. . . . The ordering of things in the dwelling-space is called "arrangement." Historically illusory [*geschichtlich scheinhafte*] objects are arranged in it as the semblance of unchangeable nature. In the interior, the archaic images unfold: the image of the flower as that of organic life; the image of the orient as specifically the homeland of yearning; the image of the sea as that of eternity itself. For the semblance to which the historical hour condemns things is eternal. (I3,a)

Benjamin quotes a long part of this book without adding any comment, and in the reply to Adorno he does not really address Adorno's specific comments. Instead, his answer points toward a fundamental question related to his project that appears as a work in progress. Envisioning the project as an archer's bow, he says he still lacks some elements of "training" for the project, which would allow him to "bend and string" the "calculated plan of the whole."[21]

> What are other elements of "training"? The constructive ones. If Wiesengrund expresses reservations about the way in which the chapters have been divided up, he has certainly hit the nail on the head. For as yet the arrangement still lacks the constructive moments. . . . The only thing that can really be said about this at present is that it will have to rearticulate the opposition in which my book stands in relation to all previous and traditional historical research in a new, succinct and very simple fashion. How this will be done remains to be decided.[22]

Benjamin is still in search of an arrangement that will articulate the difference between his method and all previous historical research, and still in need of the "constructive elements" for such an arrangement. Therefore, how the project will be constructed is deferred into the future. I would like to advance the argument, anticipating what I will address more directly in a little while, that the *Arcades Project*, as a labyrinthine construction site, offers an unprecedented way to consider architecture and the urban for their architecturability, rather then simply their actuality.

It is worth noticing that while Benjamin does not respond here directly to Adorno's analysis of Kierkegaard, he does write a quite concise note in a previous letter about Adorno's in-progress manuscript on Kierkegaard. In that letter, Benjamin opens up an expanse within the interior itself, or interpenetrates interior and exterior: "Not since reading Breton's latest verse (in the 'Union libre') have I felt myself so drawn into my own domain as I have through your exploration of that road map [*Wegekarte*] of land of inwardness [*Innerlichkeit*] from whose bourn your hero never returned."[23] Even in these very short exchanges with Adorno, Benjamin acknowledges the crucial role that arrangement plays, even with the chaotic material of interior life. Imposing a road map upon an inwardness implies that within and beyond the "phantasmagorias of the interior,"[24] an active and complex process is at work, a process that Benjamin tries to push beyond Giedion: "Attempt to develop Giedion's thesis. 'In the nineteenth century,' he writes, 'construction plays the role of the subconscious.' Wouldn't it be better to say 'the role of bodily processes'—around which 'artistic' architectures gather, like dreams around the framework [*Gerüst*] of physiological processes?" (K1a,7). Beyond announcing an intermingling between the inside and the outside, Benjamin sketches a close look at the relationship between the two terms—one in which the body takes part. Here we see that Benjamin is starting to consider architecture to be as implicated as corporeality in preparing for the mutated psyche of modernity. For the body and the psyche to be embedded into the constructed space of modernity implies an interpenetration that intrinsically relates to the outside. In his book, Giedion comments on the vista from the Marseille harbor in this way: "A mobile ferry suspended by cables from the footbridge high above the water connects traffic on the two sides of the harbor. This structure is not to be taken as a 'machine.' It cannot be excluded from the urban image, whose fantastic crowning it denotes. But its interplay with the city is neither 'spatial' nor 'plastic.' It engenders *floating* relations and interpenetrations [*Es entstehen schwebende Bezeichnungen und Durchdringungen*]. The boundaries of architecture are blurred" (90).

Such structures from 1905 suggest the connection between "construction" and "interpenetration," resulting in an urban fabric that is no longer entirely stable or fixed but that shifts between movement and fixity. Movement disrupts the relationship between space and stability; it disrupts the ontopological[25] understanding of architecture as something that delimits as well as contains. Architecture becomes unstable in time and space in an epoch when place is called into question and attains a differential split and acceleration.[26] This split is to be understood as taking place at the interconnections at which Benjamin was aiming by demanding that architecture at large be considered as an eminent and complex phenomenon, as "architecture" just begun anew in that epoch. Benjamin telescopes expanse and interior without annihilating or equating them. He seeks a dynamism of change in the multifarious, polyrhythmic cityscape that requires a reconsideration of space and time. The body, too, is implicated in this dynamism and technology; a passage in *Konvolut* N shows that the "tempo" of technology significantly affects bodily perception:

> The momentum of primal history in the past is no longer masked, as it used to be, by the tradition of church and family—this at once the consequence and condition of technology. The old prehistoric dread already envelops the world of our parents because we ourselves are no longer bound to this world by tradition. The perceptual worlds [*Merkwelten*] break up more rapidly [*zersetzen sich schneller*]; what

> they contain of the mythic comes more quickly and more brutally to the fore; and a wholly different perceptual world [*Merkwelt*] must be speedily set up to oppose it. This is how the accelerated tempo of technology [*das beschleunigte Tempo der Technik*] appears in light of the primal history of the present. Awakening. (N2a,2)

Benjamin's *Merkwelten*, more accurately translated by the neologism "note-worlds,"[27] imply something more articulated than perception, a process of individuation that bends with the experience of living in the cityscape with technics. *Merkwelten* evokes notes and marks that are embedded in different aspects of the epoch; in this way the term focuses on the way the "many glittering points" of an epoch create a constellation. Because phenomena for Benjamin are historical indexes, it is less a question of perception than of rescuing the marks.

The notions of construction and scaffolding that emerge in the time period Benjamin studies work together to articulate his method, and his method emerges from the very cityscape and fabric he considers. Because such a space is not a stable one, neither is the method a stabilizing, self-enclosed one. As Giedion stresses, the invisible architectural structures need to be considered within an "indivisible life process." Such an indivisible life process, Benjamin emphasizes, is determined by an accelerated tempo of technology in which the "note-worlds" break up rapidly; therefore, this tempo affects intrinsically not only architectures but also the body and the psyche, and nothing remains stable. The notions of construction and scaffolding are not thought of and understood as stable and fixed terms but are instead deployed to foster the possibility yet to come that is inherent to the space of modernity. Such a space, therefore, as I will expand upon in the next section, is more a space of knowability than a space to know: a space that exceeds a contained knowledge.

Part 2. Spaces of Knowability

Pas-sages: *Wise-Paths or Not-Wise? The Hollow Mold of Modernity and Architecturability*

Benjamin reiterates the method established in the very theoretical *Konvolut* N throughout the *Arcades Project*. Even though each individual *Konvolut* appears to be self-contained, in each one Benjamin's method is to relate the parts without making a contained whole. This method resembles the modality of language that Samuel Weber has discerned in Benjamin's writing. "Language," writes Weber, "names a modality rather than a substance or substantive. It describes the possibility of a particular *way* of being: that of being communicated."[28] Weber focuses on the German term *Mitteilbarkeit*, which he translates not as communicability but, in a more literal rendering, as impart-ability. Therefore, argues Weber, "the being of language has more to do with parts, and indeed with partitioning, than with wholes" (117). This modality of language can be read in the *Arcades Project*; the parts relate through a process of partitioning with respect to disparate objects ("material objects" as well as literature) and their specific relation to space and time. Benjamin's notions of "dialectic at a standstill" and the "now of knowability" and his insistence on the monadic structure of knowledge serve to relate the individual elements of the *Arcades Project*. Benjamin's way of imparting his method between spaces and words resonates with and in his writing on architecture and on specific features of the arcades. Benjamin emphasizes the shift in techniques of construction, paying allegorical attention—allegorical because always exceeding the simple signification of "construction"—to the "origin" of modern architecture. In so doing, he respects the specificity of the architectural dimension but in the same gesture carries "architecture proper" beyond its containing domain. The importance of architecture in Benjamin's text helps us understand the potential mass-mediauric effect of architecture at a time when cinema was becoming the preferred medium for reading the urban fabric. Anthony Vidler's "Metropolitan Montage"[29] discusses the necessity and the impossibility of simply considering the *Arcades Project* as a movie or a screenplay of Paris. Vidler writes: "The only way to render architecture critical again was to wrest it out of its uncritically observed context, its distracted state, and offer it to a now attentive public—that is, to make a film of the building." While obviously no "film" of this kind was ever made, Vidler suggests that an attempt to answer the hypothetical question "What would Benjamin's film of Paris have looked like?" would clarify what we might call Benjamin's "filmic imaginary" (115). Vidler emphasizes that such a movie would have presented the prehistory of modernity as realized by "modernity's own special form of mechanical reproduction" and that Benjamin would have constructed new "kinds of optical relation between the camera and the city, film and architecture" rather than a realistic, expressionist, or idealist movie of that time. This thought experiment underscores the way Benjamin gives a critical role to architecture: architecture is a medium, a mass medium, but for exactly the same reason a space to experiment and take part in. Benjamin's drive toward presenting an impossible film of the past brings us into the ghostly arcades, to make critical the spatial, and temporal, experiential dimension and mediality they convey.

Passagen (in German), or *passages* (in French), form the core of Benjamin's research. The "passage" is a very important architectural metonymic and material structure because it lets Benjamin elaborate a way of thinking that copes with specific material and experiential epochs and yet still remains open to a kind of virtuality. The arcades are architectural structures and public spaces, but as "passages" they also have the temporal significance of something that is passing or transient. A passage may lead from a beginning to an end, but Benjamin focuses less on the point of departure or arrival than on the idea of a passing experience that takes place within it.

Moreover, by fostering movement in space and time, the arcades are places that contest the idea of place as a stable entity and negate the idea of self-contained construction. These particular architectural constructions, which Benjamin inscribes in a dialectical process,[30] can be understood only after they are no longer in use, once their complex contemporary function has decayed, the moment after their apogee. Benjamin is interested in them not as monuments of the past but for the inherent dynamism between their novelty and their decay. Benjamin is careful to distance his conception of decay both from an idea of decline and from mythology, as is evident in his treatment of the writer Louis Aragon. While Aragon's work is of enormous interest and provides an opening for Benjamin's research on the history of the arcades, Aragon maintains an attitude that, for Benjamin, insists too much on "dream" and mythology. Aragon is plunged into a "mythology" that needs to be dissolved in the space of history (*Auflösung der "Mythologie" in den Geschichtsraum*) (N1,9). For Benjamin, Aragon's writings on the arcades remain in mythology because he keeps an impressionistic tone that evades a confrontation with history.[31] For Benjamin, a confrontation with history implies "an awakening of a not-yet-conscious knowledge of what has been" (N1,9). Benjamin indicates a specific moment of awakening that corresponds "with the 'now of knowability' in which things put on their true—surrealist—face" (N3a,3). This moment of awakening is a moment of rupture; the first image in Proust's *A la recherche du temps perdu* is for Benjamin the emblematic scene: "Proust begins with an evocation of the space of someone waking up" (N3a,3).[32]

Benjamin is in search of this modality of knowledge in his writing on the arcades. The arcades, or, even more so, the entrance to the arcades, are thresholds (*Schwellen*); they give access to a temporality, a moment in which change takes place. Many meanings stream out of the word "passage"; in French, *passage* can be heard as *pas sage*, meaning not wise. Or again, still playing with French words and sounds, we can nearly hear a *paysage* or landscape of modernity, a landscape that is not so wise; the passage thus becomes a place of change that inscribes in itself a kind of madness.

Benjamin directs his myth-dissolving impulse toward the arcades so as to develop an understanding of architecture and of the genesis of temporary, ephemeral structures that bear within themselves the possibility of both change and repetition. The complex space to which Benjamin lends his attention is the architecture that precedes the architecture contemporary to him, for which "interpenetration become[s] sober reality." "The intoxicated interpenetration [*Durchdringung*] of street and residence such as comes about in the Paris of the nineteenth century—and especially in the experience of the flâneur—has prophetic value. For the new architecture lets this interpenetration become sober reality" (M3a,5).

By tying together a singular understanding of space and time with material and literary "objects," the material constructions and the significations of the "arcades" are multiplied by Benjamin so as to allow for a certain *potentiality* or *possibility*, thus also implying repetition and iteration. Samuel Weber has pointed out the importance of the suffix "-ability" (*-barkeit*) to Benjamin's terminology:

> If a leap or a crack is the way Benjamin describes the way "thinking" gains access to the "domain of writing," one rather unusual stylistic trait that recurs throughout his writings may help readers "push forward" into the labyrinthine realm of his thought. It is the tendency to formulate certain key concepts in nouns that employ the suffix *-ability* or *-ibility* (in German *-barkeit*). . . . Nouns formed in this way refer to a *possibility* or a *potentiality*, to a *capacity* rather than an actually existing *reality*. Communic*ability*, for instance, does not refer to an accomplished act as does *communication*; the same holds true for *knowability*, which is by no means equivalent to *knowledge*.[33]

I would like to follow Weber's logic and coin the word "architecturability" as a way to access Benjamin's mode of knowledge (knowability) as it pertains to the passages. By architecturability I mean a way of understanding the origin of modern architecture in which repetition and potentiality are at work at the same time (instead of simple reality or, if you prefer, a fixed, specific structure). Architecturability, then, rather than the architectonic, characterizes Benjamin's conception of construction in relation to both the built environment and the construction of his own writing and thinking. Understanding architecture and construction more for their potentiality than for their reality implies that they do not establish a principle of coherence or unity but instead proliferate in a manner that can never be unified.

Several *Konvolute* in the *Arcades Project* are primarily concerned with architecture (A, E, F, G, K, and P, among others), interspersing quotes from multifarious fields of research, genres, and authors, with Benjamin's remarks. In these passages the span of Benjamin's thought extends from Grandville's drawings to the Crystal Palace and the Universal Exhibitions to Haussmann and up to Le Corbusier's "indivisible space."[34] The passages in *Konvolut* F are concerned with architecture in a tangential way.[35] Benjamin was interested in capturing the specificity of the arcades at the moment when new materials in architecture began to be used in new ways.

> Around the middle of the past century, it was not yet known how to build with glass and iron. Hence, the light that fell from above, through the panes between the iron supports, was dirty and sad. (F1,2)

> The first structures made of iron served transitory purposes: covered markets, railroad stations, exhibitions. Iron is thus immediately allied with functional moments in the life of the economy. What was once

> functional and transitory, however, begins today, at an altered tempo, to seem formal and stable. (F2,9)

While the arcades in their vertical dimension were the last example of Baroque architecture, they were nevertheless expanding on a field of horizontal amplitude.[36] A new unstable synthesis between form and construction materials was taking shape, and the brittleness of the material made them barely able to give shelter. The arcades are defined by Benjamin as *Schwellen* (thresholds). For Benjamin the word *Schwelle* is important because of the different meanings that it contains (or, better, encrypts). On the one hand, the word has a tectonic context and meaning, a "structural support"; on the other hand, it refers to a moment and a place of change, a constructive meaning telescoped into an organic one. "The threshold must be carefully distinguished from the boundary. A *Schwelle*—threshold—is a zone. Transformation, passage, wave action are in the word *Schwelle*, swell, and etymology ought not to overlook these senses" (O2a,1). Benjamin wants to maintain the tension of meanings that are present in this spatial term: construction and transformation. Transformation, for the arcades, is sudden:

> No decline of the arcades, but sudden transformation. At one blow, they become the hollow mold from which the image of "modernity" was cast. Here, the century mirrored with satisfaction its most recent past. (S1a,6)

Benjamin does not want to delimit the arcades' interpretation as a mythology, nor does he want to consider them in terms of decline, which would indicate a linear dimension of historicity. Instead, he demarcates them within an *Umschlag*, a sudden transformation, a blow, *un coup*. This expression, so intense and dense, demands that the reader consider at the same time the *Umschlag* as an envelope and an upturn, a sudden change, a crack, a knock-over, a warp, and a transfer in a spatial-time dimension. The relation posed in the sudden transformation indicates an abrupt temporality, while the *Umschlag* implies also a sense of overturning, a quick covering-up. The transformation in modern architecture takes place in a violent blow, leaving the arcade, the emblematic construction, as a hollow mold. The arcades' transformation into hollow molds implies, on the one hand, that they are no longer a delimited sheltering structure but, on the other hand, that their structurality shelters possibilities yet unknown. They are, in my coined word, pointing toward architecturability.

In this hollow mold, the image of modernity was cast, formed, and informed. Modernity was cast into the arcades with an accelerated tempo, like the one that also affects the "note-worlds," *Merkwelten*, as we have seen in the previous section. "Note-worlds" and casting both relate to mark, impression, imprinting. As I will address in the next section, the "note-worlds" are allegorically imprinted also in Baudelaire's poetry, and Baudelaire's poetry is interpreted in the *Arcades Project* through the question of mold and imprint.

Baudelaire's Allegory, Schwellen *of Interpretation, and the "Colportage Phenomenon of Space"*

Like the image of modernity cast by Benjamin's arcades, Baudelaire's poetry has made its mark, which Benjamin delineates in *Konvolut* J: "What I propose is to show how Baudelaire lies embedded in the nineteenth century. The imprint [*Abdruck*] he has left behind must stand out clear and intact, like that of the stone which, having lain in the ground for decades, is one day rolled from its place" (J51a,5).

Underlining how the "Tableaux parisiens" start with a "transfiguration of the city" (J72,1), Benjamin notes that Baudelaire does not seem to have thought about the arcades as the "classical *corso* of flânerie." Yet in the last poem of the "Tableaux parisiens," "Le crépuscule du matin," Benjamin can find "the canon of the arcade" in the construction of the lyric: "The central portion of this poem is composed of nine couplets which, while chiming one with another, remain well sealed off from the preceding as well as from the following pairs of lines. The reader moves through this poem as through a gallery lined with showcases" (J88a,2). In this way, Benjamin retraces a certain movement of the reader that resembles that of the flânerie inside the arcades. In another passage, he questions the relation between images and words, between the optical and the linguistic, in Baudelaire's writing:

> Explore the question whether a connection exists between the works of the allegorical imagination and the *correspondances*. In any case, these are two wholly distinct sources for Baudelaire's production. That the first of them has a very considerable share in the specific qualities of his poetry cannot be doubted. The nexus of meanings might be akin to that of the fibers of spun yarn. If we can distinguish between spinning and weaving activity in poets, then the allegorical imagination must be classed with the former.—On the other hand, it is not impossible that the correspondences play at least some role here, insofar as a word, in its way, calls forth an image; thus, the image could determine the meaning of the word, or else the word that of the image. (J24,3)

Spinning involves making thread or yarn out of cotton or wool, while weaving takes that thread or yarn and makes fabric out of it. While they both work toward the same end, there is a temporal relation between them (you cannot weave unless something has already been spun). Spinning, as the more primary act, creates something that is still in a state of potentiality (yarn, thread). On the one hand, Benjamin poses that, if we could compare the poets' activities with spinning and weaving, spinning would be classed with the allegorical imagination and the optical—it creates out of the raw material of existence the somewhat less raw materials (images) that are then worked (woven) into poems. But then, on the other hand, he introduces a different model for the relation between word and image, one in which the temporality is not as clearly linear as the one between spinning and weaving. The movement of Baudelaire's lyric is not a movement forward, but it is similar to the flight of images in Baroque lyrics that "'swell up from within'" (J54,3). This flight of images, which proceeds from the shock that occurs as the allegory breaks up, is connected, for Benjamin, to an endless and spasmodic relation between movement and rest: one of the most explicit allegorical elaborations is the image of "petrified unrest" found in Baudelaire's poem "La Destruction," in which the bloody apparatus of destruction is defined by Benjamin as "the court of allegory." The poet is forced to contemplate "the scattered apparatus by dint of which allegory has so disfigured and so unsettled the world of things" (J68,2). But this contemplation, as a petrification, is destabilized by a convulsed movement and therefore is not immobile. While the "court of allegory" insists on spatiality, it is also agitated by a movement that breaks off in an abrupt temporality. The poem ends suddenly and unexpectedly.

More than once Benjamin cites what Marcel Proust wrote on the poetic stanzas in Baudelaire: they are often constructed as a "strange sectioning of time" (J44,5).[37] The nexus of meanings in Baudelaire's allegory is syntactically articulated, as a process of signification that moves among discontinuities where, Benjamin says, the "sign is pointedly set off against its meaning" (J83a,3). This discontinuity between the temporality and the nexus of meaning, implied by the sudden breaking-up, also works a certain violence. Baudelaire's allegorical intention implies a violence (*Gewalttätigkeit*) "that was necessary to demolish the harmonious façade of the world that surrounded him" (J55a,3). It is a violence that, like the allegory, simultaneously shatters and preserves (J56,1), as Benjamin points out in the following passage:

> Baudelaire's destructive impulse is nowhere concerned with the abolition of what falls to it. This is reflected in his allegory and is the condition of its regressive tendency. On the other hand, allegory has to do, precisely in its destructive furor, with dispelling the illusion that proceeds from all "given order," whether of art or of life: the illusion of totality or of organic wholeness which transfigures that order and makes it seems endurable. And this is the progressive tendency of allegory. (J57,3)

The necessity of destroying the façade does not negate the necessity of construction and calculation in Baudelaire's allegory. In fact, Benjamin retraces "hidden constructions,"[38] or stanzas, which are built in such a way that "it would seem almost impossible to construct them" (J68a,8).

If Benjamin insists so much on the specificity of the cast-iron and skeleton construction in the more methodological *Konvolut* N, in his interpretation of Baudelaire's poetry he unfolds the "skeletal element," a term that, along with "estrangement," plays a crucial role: "The unique importance of Baudelaire resides in his being the first and the most unflinching to have taken the measure of self-estranged human being [*selbst entfremdeten Menschen*], in the double sense of acknowledging this being and fortifying it with armor against the reified world" (J51a,6).

This interpretation, which functions both to acknowledge the self-estrangement and fortify it, emphasizes that a corporeal *Gerüst*, or armor, was allegorically necessary in order to endure and respond to the estrangement of the human condition. The term *Gerüst*, translated as "armor," also means "armature," "scaffolding," and "skeleton" and thus indicates a provisional structure that is never stable. In this allegorical mode, the body is embedded in a relation to the inorganic, to the nonliving, and to technics.

This dividing relationship between the living and the nonliving is at the heart of Benjamin's conception of allegory (and mourning) in his *Origin of the German Mourning Play*. But in Baudelaire's allegory, this relation is pushed farther still, and mortality and decay are seen in the "contexts of life" (329); in fact, Benjamin writes: "Baroque allegory sees the corpse only from the outside; Baudelaire evokes it from within" (J56,2). Baudelaire's allegory bears traces of, and thus a relation to, the Baroque allegory.

This relation is also to be found in the theatricality that Samuel Weber has traced in his reading of *The Origin of the German Mourning Play*.[39] Weber's reading dwells on the role of theater in the tension between the Reformation and the Counter-Reformation, and the role of theatricality and allegory in Benjamin's historical and critical interpretation. In this tension, Weber finds the struggle of modernity and the aporia of singularity. Before the Reformation, the Church guaranteed a stable relationship between immanence and transcendence, while afterward a "'storm against the works' is directed not merely against 'good works' and their redemptive capacity but against *all* 'works as such'" (169); at the same time, Weber emphasizes, this change "opens the way for a very traditional institution to assume a radical new role. That institution was the theater" (172). The Baroque theater is important as a place and space that tries to give responses to the isolated self and its relation to the community.

Theater, on the one hand, offers a locality where the individual is determined by the "here and now," a place that relates to the immanence of an audience. Because temporality cannot follow an eschatological narrative, theater offers a spatialized temporality that tries to arrest a catastrophic terminus. In this way, secularization is brought into theater, in a process that Benjamin refers to as "the conversion of originarily temporal data into a spatial inauthenticity and simultaneity" (quoted in Weber, 172). Weber adds that on the stage (in the *Schauplatz*) "such an inauthentic simultaneity is thus the sole chance available to an individual otherwise condemned to perish by virtue of its unredeemable authenticity" (173). On the other hand, because it is allegorical, and because of the repetition implied with theater, this theater negates a simple immanence. It is this articulation of arguments that leads Weber to insist also on the changing locality of the stage: it is not yet a fixed National Theater. If Weber considers theatricality an effect of modernity and vice versa, it is because the theater insistently testifies to the aporias of singularity as well as the "storming of the works." Thus this theatricality also exceeds the question of genre. Weber views the theatrical *medium* as a modern paradigm of works that are not self-contained.

The shift from theater to theatricality is still determinant in the *Arcades Project*. As architectonic and cityscape elements, the arcades offer access to change, a demarcating *Raum* (space, place, and room) of the Benjaminian "threshold" (*Schwelle*) of interpretation. The constructed space in its brittleness also takes on a new theatrical importance with respect to theater "proper." The theatrical dimension remains: Baudelaire assumes a posture that Benjamin more than once compares to the posture of the mime "who has taken off his makeup" (J52,2).[40] This trembling prosodic construction negates and violates "intimacy." The allegorical and textual space is also broken in the confrontation with living experience; if there is no habit that can contain this experience in allegory, everything is always already obsolete. Benjamin emphasizes that "to become obsolete means: to grow strange." The "self-estrangement" I have previously underlined can here be linked to a "becoming obsolete" or a growing strange; it is a discontinuous process in which "modernity has, for its armature, the allegorical mode of vision" (J59a,4). The self-estrangement of and in modernity, in its allegorical dimension, also has a theatrical dimension; not only is Baudelaire a mime, but he, like the flâneur, also has no native ground (*Heimat*) in his own city, or perhaps, if he is ever "at home," it is in a theater. The city, for Baudelaire and for the flâneur, is a "theatrical display, an arena [*Schauplatz*]" (J66a,6). This locality thus maintains some connotations of the theatrical and "open" display; this locality is in the city, and therefore defines the writing of and on the city by surprise and transience, change and repetition. In Baudelaire's cityscape, immanence is contested and at the same time rescued in the theatrical dimension of the city that Benjamin underlines. The city is marked by the transience of modernity and its accelerated tempo, and *Les fleurs du mal* are exemplary of a temporality that constitutes a close echo between antiquity and modernity. Benjamin nevertheless argues that there is the risk of an overly direct correspondence between antiquity and modernity in Baudelaire's work, in which a secularization of space eludes any confrontation with time. Benjamin interprets Baudelaire's poems allegorically, yet he also underlines the fact that the "constructive [*konstruktive*] conception of history," the correspondence between modernity and antiquity, "is a rigid armature [*Armatur*], it excludes every dialectical conception" (J59a,5). In the

1938 essay "The Paris of the Second Empire in Baudelaire," Benjamin finds in Baudelaire's poetry the traces of "shock-like changes" and a specific "way of living life to extremes."

> In all his endeavors, Baudelaire was subject to abrupt, shock-like changes; his vision of another way of living life to extremes was thus all the more alluring. This way becomes apparent in the incantations which emanate from many of his perfect verses; in some of them, it even gives its name.
>
> Vois sur ces canaux
> Dormir ces vaisseaux
> Dont l'humeur est vagabonde;
> C'est pour assouvir
> Ton moindre désir
> Qu'ils viennent du bout du monde.
>
> [See, on the canals, / Those sleeping ships—/ They have a vagabond spirit. / It is to satisfy / Your least desire / That they come from the ends of the earth.]
>
> This famous stanza has a rocking rhythm; its movement seizes the ships which lie moored in the canals. To be rocked between extremes: this is the privilege of ships, and this is what Baudelaire longed for.[41]

How should one read the "extremes" to which Benjamin was pointing in Baudelaire? Two expressions in the *Arcades Project* bring us closer to Benjamin's constellation of thought: "threshold" (*Schwelle*) and the "colportage phenomenon of space" (*Kolportagephänomen des Raumes*) that constitutes the flâneur's basic experience. Benjamin in the same essay from 1938, comparing Victor Hugo's all-embracing acceptance of progress and attitude toward the crowd with Baudelaire's hesitation and resistance, points to a *Schwelle* in Baudelaire's poetry. Benjamin writes:

> The masses of the big city could not disconcert him [Hugo]. He recognized the urban crowds and wanted to be flesh of their flesh. Secularism, Progress, and Democracy were inscribed on the banner which he waved over their heads. This banner transfigured mass existence. It was the canopy over the threshold [*Schwelle*] which separates the individual [*Einzelnen*] from the crowd. Baudelaire guarded this threshold, and that differentiated him from Victor Hugo. (39)

According to Benjamin, Baudelaire maintained a critical stance toward the crowd and so rescued the threshold that separates the individual from the crowd. But this does not imply that the individual is self-contained. The other term that has a definitive importance is the "colportage phenomenon of space [*Raum*]"[42] that Benjamin defines for two aspects that are crucial in relation to my argument. "Colportage," the French dictionary informs us, is the action of transporting goods as well as books, of transmitting information to several people, of reporting and spreading news. But in *Arcades Project* who/what does the action is not a person but space—space narrates and scatters the news. Colportage is defined as the "flâneur's basic experience," in which "everything potentially taking place in this one single room is perceived simultaneously" (M1a,3); in another instance Benjamin connects it in a fragment to interpenetration: "Interpenetration [*Durchdringung*] as a principle in film, in new architecture, in colportage" (O°,10). This expression—"colportage phenomenon of space"—determines my reading of Benjamin's *Schwelle* of thought in the modern city, where an accelerated tempo occurs and is experienced as a shock and as desire. The experience of the flâneur is liminal because it is determined by estrangement and can no longer be contained within regular habits. Habits are the armature of experience as *Erfahrung*, but they are disarticulated, displaced, put out of joint by "individual experiences" as *Erlebnisse* (J62a,2). The ongoing movement between *Erfahrung* and *Erlebnis* in Benjamin's articulation is similar to the movement between the singular and the collective. Benjamin insists on this relationship in *Konvolute* C, K, M, and R, and he interprets it with an overturning and dialectical reversal.

> The nineteenth century a spacetime [*Zeitraum*] (a dreamtime [*Zeittraum*]) in which the individual consciousness more and more secures itself in reflecting, while the collective consciousness sinks into ever deeper sleep. But just as the sleeper—in this respect like the madman—sets out on the macrocosmic journey through his own body, and the noises and feelings of his insides, such as blood pressure, intestinal churn, heartbeat, and muscle sensation (which for the waking and salubrious individual converge in a steady surge of health) generate, in the extravagantly heightened inner awareness of the sleeper, illusion or dream imagery which translates and accounts for them, so likewise for the dreaming collective, which, through the arcades, communes with its own insides. We must follow in its wake so as to expound the nineteenth century—in fashion and advertising, in buildings and politics—as the outcome of its dream visions. (K1,4)

It is very important that Benjamin emphasizes bodily experiences that negate a "clear-cut antithesis of sleeping and waking" and therefore determine the unending variety of "concrete states of consciousness conditioned by every conceivable level of wakefulness within all possible centers" (K1,5); Benjamin puts the emphasis on the transfer of such a variety of levels of consciousness, inscribed in a singular epoch, from the individual to the collective. While considering this transposition, Benjamin also says that all that is external to the individual (fashion, architecture, etc.) becomes internal for the collective. He constructs a relation between an inside and an outside in which the two remain disjointed even as they are bound tightly together. Benjamin underscores how the ambiguous space-time that unsettles and excites the opposition between the individual and the collective results in the experience of singularity. The colportage phenomenon of space affects the experience of the flâneur as a singularity. The colportage phenomenon of space insists on the overlapping of different spaces. This overlapping of spaces takes place in Paris such that the city steps apart into dialectical poles; it becomes a landscape and a cozy den. Paris is determined by the threshold (*Schwelle*) of boundaries (*Grenzen*) and "only apparently is homogeneous" (C3,3); Benjamin poetically comes to say that "even its name takes on a different sound from one district to the next" (C3,3). Paris is an overlapping of boundaries that weave the city—now beyond the arcades—with its railroad crossings, parks, and riverbanks, constructed among thresholds; at each threshold "a new precinct begins like a step into the void—as though one had unexpectedly cleared a low step on a flight of stairs" (C3,3). This phenomenon, a step into the void, is an originary (*ursprünglicher*) phenomenon, and the mode of experiencing it is close to the experience of dreams. "Nowhere, unless perhaps in dreams, can the phenomenon of the boundary be experienced in a more originary way than in cities" (*Nirgends, es sei denn in Träumen, ist noch ursprünglicher das Phänomenen der Grenze zu erfahren als in Städten*) (C3,3). The streets are a "vascular network of imagination," where Benjamin telescopes particular experiences of an epoch by intermingling possible bodily experience with his methodological interpretation. The walking of the flâneur is precipitous, and the space comes close to him with "an irresistible magnetism of the next street corner," as a desire that is never fulfilled. The steps of the flâneur "awaken a surprising resonance" (516) in the space of Paris, "*la ville qui remue*": the city "that moves" or, even better, the city "that never stops moving" (P1,1). This does not imply that Benjamin considers the experience in space and the cityscape as empathy. Indeed, here we find again the active tension between space and construction.

In the revision of the first published version of the essay "The Work of Art in the Age of Its Technological Reproducibility,"[43] while defining his understanding of the relation between collective reception and distraction in the new medium of cinema, Benjamin considers that the "laws" of architectural reception are "highly instructive" (120); this is because "architecture has always offered the prototype of an artwork that is received in a state of distraction and through the collective" (*dessen Rezeption in der Zerstreuung und durch das Kollektivum erfolgt*) (119–20).[44] Architecture is apprehended in a twofold manner—tactile and optical—and the tactile reception "comes about not so much by way of attention as by way of habit" (120). Benjamin remarks that "even the distracted person can form habits," therefore architecture's specificity resides in the fact that it can be apprehended in a state of distraction. John Macarthur, writing on movement and tactility in architecture in Benjamin, refers to the following passage from Benjamin's essay on Heinrich Wölfflin:

> Architecture is not primarily "seen," but rather is imagined as an objective entity and is sensed by those who approach or even enter it as a surrounding space [*Umraum*] *sui generis*—that is, without the distancing effect of the edge of the image space [*Bildraum*]. Thus, what is crucial in the consideration of architecture is not seeing but the apprehension [*durchspüren*] of structures.[45]

Macarthur comments that "Benjamin here insists that the perception of architecture is spatial before it is visible. Or rather, we sense space visually in a way that differs from our appreciation of pictorial space with its 'distancing effect of the edge of the image space.' "[46] Therefore, the image space cannot in itself define the apprehension of architecture, which in "The Work of Art in the Age of Its Technological Reproducibility" is considered a medium or, if you will, an art that is experienced or apprehended in a distracted way.

If architecture is considered as a medium, even within its specificity, this has very interesting connections to the question of technics, or what Mark Hansen has called "technesis." Hansen points to a specific moment of Benjamin's essay *Surrealism* (1929), adopting Benjamin's term "innervation" in order to define Benjamin's ("mature") theory of technology:

> Benjamin initially takes up this issue in his surrealism essay of 1929, where he develops the notion of a "collective innervation" of mankind's body through technology. Here Benjamin again invokes the new *physis* that was being organized for mankind by technology and emphasizes the sensuous nature of our collective contact with it: "Only when in technology body and image-space [*Bildraum*] so interpenetrate [*so tief durchdringen*] that all revolutionary tension becomes bodily collective innervation, and all bodily innervations of the collective become revolutionary discharge, will reality have surpassed itself to the extent demanded by the *Communist Manifesto*." The operative vehicles of such innervation are precisely those reproductive technologies that Benjamin would come to focus on in the 1930s: photography, radio, gramophone, and especially film.[47]

As we have seen throughout this chapter, the term "interpenetration" (which is indeed a modernist and avant-garde term) frequently recurs in Benjamin's texts, as well as in those of Giedion, who uses the same term to highlight the complexity of the architectural cityscape. In the scattered logic of Benjamin's method, architecture not only takes the part of a complex palimpsest of the cityscape but also plays a crucial role among the different media. Architecture is considered as a medium, and not only is interpenetration at play in the cityscape, but so is collective innervation among the experience of space and constructions.

Hansen defines Benjamin's leap in "On Some Motifs" as one "into a posthermeneutic analytical model that not only refuses to contain the physiological dimension of shock within the dialectical space of the image [*Bildraum*]—to reduce it to the *content* of a dialectical image—but also positively insists on grappling with the conversion of the imagistic into the affective" (260). Hansen's insight gives force to my argument on architecture as one of the mass media in Benjamin's *Arcades Project*.

Thus Benjamin insists on paying attention to the constructed city, while also looking for the most brittle and unexpected experiences, sounds, and voices, all appearing, disappearing, and superimposing as allegory is wont to allow. This overlapping is such that truth is no longer an essence but "becomes living," and it has the rhythm "by which statement and counterstatement displace each other in order to think each other" (M1a,1). This rhythm is possible because of the potentiality of the colportage phenomenon of space, the hinge of my reading of Benjamin. To repeat: with the colportage phenomenon of space, "everything potentially taking place in this one single room is perceived simultaneously" (M1a,3). In an ongoing movement, the expanse and the distant parts of the city clash with what is close and communicates allegorically. The colportage phenomenon of space brings that which is outside and distant to the inside, performing unexpected theatrical scenes, which nevertheless are now within the city.

This theatricality is enhanced by the other modern material that Benjamin reframes in the *Arcades Project*: glass (and mirrors).[48] The specificity of the materiality of glass is respected and at the same time is made into a spectacle, something that composes the space, a multifarious interconnection of the points of contact of the cityscape. The mirror "brings the open expanse, the streets, into the café—this, too, belongs to the interweaving of spaces [*Raumes*], to the spectacle by which the flâneur is ineluctably drawn [*verfallen ist*]" (R1,1). In *Konvolute* M and R, Benjamin annotates the most striking passages concerning this material, interweaving the mirrors with psychic experiences, vision, and voices, and so rejoining the question of space as a character, which is thematized as a *storyteller*. In passage R2a,3, in a close-up description, Benjamin passes from a brittle mosaic threshold extending to a glass door to an adjacent glass door "promising to bring you to a theater," but it is an ambiguous entrance:

> Brittle, too, are the mosaic thresholds [*Mosaikschwellen*] that lead you, in the style of the old restaurants of the Palais-Royal, to a "Parisian dinner" for five francs; they mount boldly to a glass door,

> but you can hardly believe that behind this door is really a restaurant. The glass door adjacent promises a Petit Casino and allows a glimpse of a ticket booth and the prices of seats; but were you to open it—would it open into anything? Instead of entering the space of a theater, wouldn't one be stepping down to the street? Where doors and walls are made of mirrors, there is no telling out from in, with all the equivocal illumination. Paris is the city of mirrors. The asphalt of its roadways smooth as glass, and at the entrance to all bistros glass partitions. A profusion of window panes and mirrors in cafés, so as to make the inside brighter and to give all the tiny nooks and crannies, into which Parisian taverns separate, a pleasing amplitude. (R1,3)

This passage takes an anonymous yet singular snapshot of the cityscape, an ongoing play between streets and theater, transparency and reflection, glass and mirrors, time and space; glass is now not only that specific material but also the asphalt, such that this glass-like effect expands. The play of the colportage phenomenon of space is exemplified in the arcades whose entrances are *Schwellen* and whose spaces are apprehended in their ambiguity. The specific characteristic of space lies in fact in the ambiguity of the space of the arcades. In the arcades, the abundance of mirrors "amplifies the spaces and makes orientation more difficult" (542). Orientation and bodily orientation are deranged by the montage of glass and cast iron in the arcades, whose effects exceed their simple functional aspect. Even if mirrors have an infinite, unending aspect, space still remains ambiguous; it is always different, it negates universality, while insisting on double-edged and dialectical poles.[49] The space of the arcades, with their mirrors, is a space that blinks: "It blinks [*blinzelt*]: it is always this one—and never nothing—out of which another immediately arises" (R2a,3). These mirrors, comparable to the "eyes that don't see" in Baudelaire's "A une passante," "blink" again and again. Samuel Weber has pointed out the importance of the "experience" of the aura also as an "experience" of *desire*, in which Baudelaire "succumbs most entirely to the fascination of the 'eyes that do not see,'" eyes that Weber relates to the blinking eye of the camera. This blinking is an unconscious intermittent action of the eye that differs from winking. Weber writes: "The recording apparatus, whether visual or auditory, 'takes up' everything but never looks back, never returns the glance. It *blinks* but never *winks*. Instead what it does is to arrest and separate and reproduce the 'here-and-now' again and again in a proliferating series of images which go here and there, a mass of pictures that cannot keep still even if they are instantaneous 'snapshots.'"[50]

The space of the arcades, where the image of modernity was cast, is always different and changes into the "bosom of nothingness." The gazes in the space of the arcades appear as they disappear; it is a whispering that "fills the arcades," a colportage of voices: "To the whispering of these gazes, the space [*Raum*] lends its echo. 'Now, what' it blinks [*blinzelt*], 'can possibly have come over me?' We stop short in some surprise. 'What, indeed, can possibly have come over you?' Thus we gently bounce the question back to it. Flânerie" (R2a,3).

Benjamin creates a chiasmus between the blinking of gazes that abruptly becomes a voice, transposing this intermittent blinking to the whispering of gazes. The fugitive eye, which blinks and is quickly gone, is similar to the whispering of voices that are unexpected and quickly gone.

Space blinks, and then whispers, in an anonymous voice, in the tight spaces of the arcades. This whispering of space returns in *Konvolut* M, where Benjamin works out a relationship between bodily experience and the materiality of the city, thus opening up room for space as storyteller. Indeed, space now blinks (*blinzelt*) at the flâneur, says, "What do you think may have gone on here?" (M1a,3).

Thematizing the space of modernity as storyteller implies that one cannot know in advance what will happen; instead one must traverse the cityscape and the *Arcades Project*, singularly embedded in experience and equally in criticality; space, as a site of experience, is open to the unexpected, in a cityscape where architectures acquire importance precisely because of their specific mass-mediauric consistencies and effects, because of their architecturability.

Chapter 2

✦

Abstract Theatricality as Impossible Synthesis

Part 1. Staging the Ephemeral and the Bursts of the Cityscape

From the Benjaminian "Constructors" to the Second Waves of Futurism

During the years in which Benjamin wrote the *Arcades Project*, he wrote a brief text entitled "Experience and Poverty" (1933).[1] Both "poverty" and "experience" are to be considered together; according to Benjamin, the poverty of experience was one of the determining features of the human condition during the 1930s. The capacity to experience, and then to communicate that experience, to narrate it, had been diminished in an unprecedented way for the generation of the First World War, Benjamin tells us, because experience itself had been arrested, as had daily life by war, economic life by inflation, physical life by hunger, and finally moral life by the forces of government. As the result of an intense intertwining of destructive events and technological changes—what Benjamin calls a force field of destruction—he says that "a completely new poverty has descended on mankind" (732). Benjamin specifies that such poverty affects the individual as well as humankind, and leads to a new barbarism. But Benjamin intends to introduce this concept through a new, positive perspective. "For what does poverty of experience do for the barbarian? It forces him to start from scratch; . . . to begin with a little and build up further, looking neither left nor right. Among the great creative spirits, there have always been the inexorable ones, who begin by clearing a tabula rasa" (732).

These barbarians are, principally, constructors: Descartes, Einstein, the Cubists, Paul Klee, and Adolf Loos. These "constructors" are grouped together by Benjamin because their projects "obey the laws of their interior [*Innern*], . . . rather than their inwardness [*Innerlichkeit*]" (733). Benjamin considers the architect and writer Paul Scheerbart[2] a primary example both of acceptance of the contemporary world and of such a turn-of-the-century change. Scheerbart, writes Benjamin, directs attention toward the functioning of telescopes, airplanes, and other sophisticated technological constructions in order to understand how they can "transform human beings as they have been up to now into completely new, lovable, and interesting creatures" (733). Equally important is the fact that Scheerbart writes about an arbitrary language, a constructed language not unlike that of the Russians, who preferred to give children "dehumanized" names, with the aim of a "mobilization in the service of changing reality instead of describing it" (733). Benjamin also associates the writer of *Glasarchitektur*, and his fantastic imagination, with what would soon afterward become the modern architecture of Le Corbusier and the Bauhaus. Houses that have no "aura" are constructed with a new combination of materials: glass and steel are materials that are considered incompatible with the concept of a "plush apartment"; they are materials on which no traces are left. They are emblematic, for Benjamin, of houses where people who are no longer capable of having experience can reside, "long[ing] for a world in which they can make such pure and decided use of their poverty—their outer poverty, and ultimately also their inner poverty—that it will lead to something respectable" (734). Here, in contrast to what Benjamin investigates in the *Arcades Project*, there is no more space for *l'intérieur*—interiors are eventually the laws that govern constructors' acts, and the intoxication of the interpenetration through which Baudelaire was exposed among the inside and the outside has given way to glass, "a hard, smooth material to which nothing can be fixed" (734). While Benjamin maintains the idea of construction, he now associates it with a new barbarism.

In the *Arcades Project*, *Konvolut* S, "Painting, Jugendstil, Novelty," while analyzing Jugendstil's reactionary relation to technology—which is to assume technological forms as "natural"—Benjamin sees in this specific aspect a similarity to what Futurism later accomplished: "The reactionary attempt to sever technologically constituted forms from their functional contexts and turn them into natural constants—that is, to stylize them—appears, in a mode similar to Jugendstil, somewhat later in Futurism" (S8a,7).

This excerpt from the *Arcades Project* will be one of the hinges with which I will read a selection of experimentations by Futurist artists that dwell on motifs of construction, architecture, space, and theatricality. In these experimentations, there is certainly a stylization of functional constants, but mostly what is at work is the search for ephemeral and abstract constructions within new spatial configurations. The concrete attention to the making of specific necessary technologies is not at the core of these experimentations; it is only a technological potential—left to be actualized in the future.

In his *Architectures of Time*, in an argument that has partially opened paths for my own, Sanford Kwinter foregrounds an investigation into the ways in which new conditions of possibility might have occurred at the beginning of the twentieth century. Between the end of the nineteenth century and the beginning of the twentieth, Kwinter individuates the emergence of modernity understood as "a reverse stream that is present *virtually* (but relatively rarely actualized) throughout history, emerging here or there as a kind of counterhistory or counterpractice."[3] According to Kwinter, the first figures, in the aesthetic realm, to participate in this modernity were the Futurists, and in particular he considers the architect Antonio Sant'Elia and the

Futurist artist Umberto Boccioni. Both Sant'Elia and Boccioni participated in the first wave of Italian Futurism, and both died early while serving in the army in the First World War. Kwinter sees their writings and their drawings as participating in a modernity in which time and space would no longer "distribute their contents in quite the same ordered way. . . . They would no longer remain separate from one another, but had merged to create a new field, one that would characterize the rest of our century, yet for which a properly solid map never emerged and will certainly never exist" (36).[4] Time is no longer finalized eschatologically, transcendentally, or historically but is instead much more fragmented, intricate, proliferating, and immanent to phenomena, and space loses certain oppositional metaphysical determinations such as body/nonbody, inside/outside, and part/whole "as it weds with time to become more intensive, dynamic, or continuous" (36).

In the chapter "The New Plasticity," the architectural drawings of Sant'Elia are read through the lens of quantum field theory, which, contrary to Euclidean space, can be thought of as "a space of propagation, of effects. It contains no material points, but rather functions, vectors, and speed" (60). In this respect, the field is concerned with dynamism as its plastic structure takes part in, and is influenced by, physical events. The architecture of Sant'Elia strives to be consistent with the new technological mutations, in relation to a "constellation of needs and desires," without, however, losing its artistic and expressive role. In particular, analyzing Sant'Elia drawings, Kwinter writes:

> In this *mise-en-abyme* system, where every element seems in part only fortuitously there, in part *already* there, relaying forces received from other similar elements, the earth as first principle or ground seems no longer to exist at all; rather, there is a homeostatic system of circulating currents, which, thanks to the visionary use of reinforced concrete, seems virtually untouched by gravity or any other *absolute* (grounded or original) cause. (80)

Sant'Elia's urban architectural drawings, according to Kwinter, imply that the observer is a mobile part of the system and that a space loses its consistency and univocity in order to make room for the flux of continual and intricate space with multiple surfaces of connection. In Sant'Elia's *La città nuova*, an architectural space "does this by willfully embracing the city block into which it has been literally submerged, continuing the city's existing lines of flow (streets, tram routes, passages) through its own, pausing only to effect additional convergences by means of ramps, catwalks, steps" (86). For Kwinter, in Sant'Elia's architectural drawings, the function of the architectural object supersedes its formal and functional self-containment and is embedded in its interaction with the other functions of the city: it is difficult to say about Sant'Elia's drawings, writes Kwinter, whether his train station for Milan rests within the city or the city runs through the train station. Discussing some of Sant'Elia's drawings, Kwinter continues, "The 'station' comes to be seen as an allegorical representation of the city itself, and necessarily, in terms of the transformation of 'place' into a swirling manifold of circuitry, switching points and deterritorialized, nongrounded flows" (86).

Beyond these "founding" Futurist moments, or authors—which in Kwinter's analysis stop at 1915—many others worked through new ways of rethinking and experimenting with space and construction. Kwinter does not consider a longer trajectory of Futurism that traces a specific internal history of Futurism. For the artists on whom I focus—in particular, Giacomo Balla, Fortunato Depero, Filippo Tommaso Marinetti, and Enrico Prampolini—the dynamic and plastic space they privilege is the theater.[5] Such a mobile place is at play in the space of modernity, announcing totally new spatial scenarios, and over time these experimentations become more and more abstract from reality, as an impossible abstract theatricality.

In *The Sphere and the Labyrinth*, written much earlier than Kwinter's book, the architectural historian Manfredo Tafuri refers to Futurism as a key moment in what he calls "the stage as the 'virtual city.'" Within the experiments of Futurist theater, Tafuri recognizes all the premises of avant-garde theater, yet he speaks of it as "the metropolitan universe seen as a pure anarchic market, a flow of events without place or sense that in the theatre comes to be revealed and exalted."[6] Tafuri pauses to demonstrate the ways in which conflictual tensions of modernity are brought into play by the avant-gardes and draws particular attention to the new inclusive and interactive relationship between "authors" and "audience." Nevertheless, Tafuri does not look closely at the inventive aspects introduced by the Futurist theatricality.

My objective is to highlight the possible, unactualized concepts that relate to architecture and space at play in these experimentations—where space as storyteller and architecturability converge in abstract and allegorical ways. While these experimentations often make use of "construction," "architecture," and "space," they do so in abstract or theatrical contexts, not in concrete constructions. In addition, they always require the audience's participation in these spaces. If Futurism aimed to introduce the dynamic life of the metropolis into the theater, these artists, over time and through a series of different presentations as well as with different media, brought greater attention to architecture, although to an architecture not imagined according to a rigid notion of the object. Their interest in architecture is oblique, and it is not the only field being investigated: architecture, construction, and materials are inscribed within different media—painting, theater, cinema. Thus these artists deform spaces by making them complex, working through the use of a mobile "location": the theatrical *stage*.

Balla, Depero, and Prampolini are often associated with what is referred to as the second wave of Futurism (*secondo futurismo*). Before arriving at a careful reading of this material, it is worth considering the particular association of *secondo* and *futurismo*. On the one hand, the idea of a "second" implies that it follows a first, thus adding to the original, almost as a supplement. On the other hand, within the word "Futurism" exists the essential idea of the future: that which is still to come, not yet known, unscripted by a preanticipated, prestabilized plan. This idea of the future, of an investigation always in progress, is one of the conditions of Futurist experimentations. It seems that this double registry of "second" and "Futurism," together, can shed light on some of the productions of Balla, Depero, Marinetti, and Prampolini, in which a certain singularity invents itself in each encounter between Italian and European perspectives, in each inscription into a particular medium, and is finally brought into question and reinvented through the formulation of new proposals.

In relation to the second wave of Futurism, one of the most attentive critics, Enrico Crispolti, has defined the relationship between Balla, Depero, and Prampolini as "the knot 1914–1915."[7] Balla and Depero's manifesto "Futurist Reconstruction of the Universe," writes Crispolti, "places itself effectively at a key moment of the Futurist evolution, and announces a qualitative leap," a leap in relation to pictocentric and Boccioni-centric experience.[8]

I intend this chapter to chart a singular trajectory among multiple Futurist experimentations from 1914 up to the 1930s; the chapter will follow this second wave from the first impulse and formation, through transformations, turbulent fluctuations, and changes along time up to the moment when, moving ashore, it deposits the debris of the Futurist theatrical space. As the wave reaches the shore, it forms a specific crest, an unfinished theatrical text by Marinetti. This piece uncannily theatricalizes a space-time activated on the mobile stages, which resonates not only within the internal history of Futurism's turbulent waves (now gone) but perhaps, in part, also with our time. Finally, this unfinished text demands to be read extensively because it tackles many critical questions, questions that it elaborates while apparently storming away any temptation toward high-theory impulse; instead it lets the questions flow over long fetches toward the coastline, allegorically, in both theatrical and intermedial narrative moods.

Ultimately, the trajectory defined in this chapter has been motivated partly by the fact that there is a strong division as to appreciation in the scholarship that considers Futurism, in this case between studies done in theater and performance studies and those done in critical theory: the former are generally more enchanted and curious, the latter more resistant to or dismissive of the Futurist experimentations.

Plastic Complexes and "Theatrical Instantaneous *Acts": Balla, Depero, and the Synthetic Theater*

In 1914 Fortunato Depero created a mural manifesto entitled "Plastic Complexity—Free Futurist Game—The Artificial Living Being." This manifesto is divided into three parts. It is concise and synthetic; rather than making a specific announcement regarding one art form in particular, it proposes a renewal based and built on complex plasticity. The first part states eleven points, which Depero defines synthetically as a marvelous plastic complex into which are woven poetry, painting, sculpture, and music. The plasticity that Depero describes is portrayed as dynamic and as an ungraspable emotion; because it is therefore not immobile, heavy, or opaque, according to Depero, it must be abstract. This type of complex is constructed from elements that are both light and transparent: Depero speaks of an emotion that springs from the merging together of the plasticity, the colorfulness and the lightness of the complex—"everything appears and disappears, very lightweight, impalpable."[9] In addition to being colored, dynamic, and "continually moved," it must also be "suspended in space." Why suspended? Because, writes Depero, a plastic complex such as this "develops around an unstable center"; Depero means to draw attention neither toward the idea of a fixed location nor toward a static space but rather toward a complex whose location stems from motion. Without this movement, such a construction would be static, colorless, and heavy, and most likely noisy as well. Depero indicates a few "necessary means," the requisite construction tools required for building an iridescent and lightweight complex such as this one: "colored metallic threads in cotton, wool, silk, transparent papers of any kind, colorful glasses, light very malleable substances, superfine textiles, feathers, waddings, . . . electrical and musical devices."

However, a question remains: what is this complex? The theories of complexity recently developed in humanities research have opened the floodgates to the investigation of such a term, though perhaps it would be anachronistic to refer to these. A return to the etymology of the word shows it is derived from Latin: *complexus* is the past participle of *complectĕre* (to encompass), which means, as the *Oxford English Dictionary* (*OED*) suggests,"to encompass, embrace; but partly taken in the analytical sense of Latin *com-* together + *plectĕre* , *plex-* to plait, twine."[10] Therefore, it indicates something not unitary whose elements are plaited together. We can wonder: what is Depero proposing? The manifesto, which until this moment he had sketched through a manipulation of opposites, now advances across a series of adjectives that are related in their abstraction rather than in opposition. It is architecture that allows the manifesto to proceed: "It will be realized miraculously the complex of the invisible—impalpable—improbable—imperceptible—the instinctive ARCHITECTURE—fleeting—light's spiral blows that enlace invisible to the phonic emanations of the squeeeeaaaaks—wheeerrrrrriiiings—all the nooOOOIIIsszzzTT." This section of the manifesto, beginning in a succession of adjectives referring to what is immaterial, suddenly ties the complex to architecture, written in capital letters, only to let it run away, as a suspended and intuited material, between lights and phonic emanations.

Into the spatiality (and the temporality as well) of the plastic complex, Depero introduces sound, not unlike what Marinetti had already indicated in "Technical Manifesto of Futurist Literature" (1912). Marinetti proposes in his manifesto to "substitute, for human psychology now exhausted, **the lyrical obsession with matter,**"[11] in which he does not humanize materiality but instead intends to develop a prose and a poetics that emphasize the technological and material aspects of modernity.

> Nothing, for a Futurist poet, is more interesting than the action of a mechanical piano's keyboard. Film offers us the dance of an object that disintegrates and recomposes itself without human intervention. It offers us the backward sweep of a diver whose feet fly out the sea and bounce violently back on the springboard. . . . All these represent the movements of matter which are beyond the laws of human intelligence, and hence of an essence which is more significant.
>
> Three elements which literature has hitherto overlooked must now become prominent in it:
>
> 1. **Noise** (a manifestation of the dynamism of objects);
> 2. **Weight** (the capacity for flight in objects);
> 3. **Smell** (the capacity of objects to disperse themselves). (122–23)[12]

In his manifesto, Depero employs a language that gives form and space to an interdisciplinarity of thought and one for which interaction, rather than hierarchy, exists between verbal language and other languages.

The following year, Depero and Balla wrote "Futurist Reconstruction of the Universe." Even more than Depero's previous effort, this manifesto insists on the invisible and "the interpenetration of planes and states of minds";[13] it concerns itself with giving "skeleton and flesh to the invisible, the impalpable, the imponderable, the imperceptible" (209), where the plastic complex is volatile, a fast, noisy apparition. The abstract style, preface, and primary point of this manifesto aim to counter the "an anxious re-evocation of an Object lost (happiness, love, a landscape)" (210) with the construction of a new reality. Consequently, the manifesto indicates a series of means through which the plastic complex can be constructed, and some modalities of the assemblage are mentioned: rotating (oblique, vertical, horizontal), with varying speeds, in opposite directions, according to varied forms and varying decompositions and sounds, with different rhythms and speeds. The abstract transposition of reality is analogical: for example, the shape of a cloud is suggestive of a transformable building, the takeoff of an airplane can give the rhythm to a "**Plastic-Motornoise-ist Concert in Space** and the **Launching of Aerial Concerts** above the city" (211).

With this manifesto, a different coherence of construction—autonomous and not chained to any predetermined reality—is indicated through various means of abstraction. The last section describes Futurist toys, the "innocence and playfulness" of whose construction, Günter Berghaus notes, "ensured that they would create wonder and amazement, fascination and joy, rather than fear and loathing."[14] A principle of construction passes without rest throughout the manifesto, defined as always in motion, remaining elusive and fleeting. If architecture is a recurrent motif, it returns as a potentiality, the product of an event rather than as a stable form in and of itself. From this manifesto comes forth a scene in motion; it strikes like lightning, in a temporary manner, seizing the moment and a potential outcome, rather than an outcome that has been predetermined. By means of abstraction, the manifesto places on stage (and perhaps also in the streets) a new relational complex. This abstraction is similar to the one described by John Rajchman as "an attempt to show—in thought as in art, in sensation as in concept—the odd, the multiple, unpredictable potential in the midst of things of other new things, other new mixtures."[15]

Balla and Depero's manifesto was written in 1915, the year in which Bruno Corrà, Marinetti, and Emilio Settimelli wrote the manifesto "The Futurist Synthetic Theater (*A-technical-Dynamic-Simultaneous-Autonomous*)."[16] This theater is introduced with terms of affirmation and rebellion and various strategies simulating bellicose violence in order to distance it from "passéist"[17] theater. This theater is "synthetic" because it lasts only a few minutes; its acts can "last but a moment" (205).[18] Synthetic theater is sometimes called antitheatrical due to its brevity and its lack of any intent to provide an illusion of life. Yet, paradoxically, its antitheatricality is due to its desire for closeness with life and with all of life's manifestations, which offer "*innumerable possibilities for the stage*" (206). The signers of the manifesto propose experiments that bring into theater the reality that "throbs around us, assaulting us with *bursts of fragments of interconnected events* [*fatti*], *interlocking together*, *confused*, *jumbled up*, *chaotic*" (206). The logic of synthetic theater pertains to a tension between imminence and immanence,[19] in which events emerge by means of time and movement. "For example: it's stupid to act out a contest between two persons *always* in an orderly, clear, and logical way, since in daily life we nearly always experience mere *flashes of argument* which have been rendered *ephemeral* by our activities as modern men, passing in a tram, a café, a railroad station, so that experiences remain filmed in our minds like fragmentary dynamic symphonies of gestures, words, lights, and sounds" (206; translation modified).

Thus, synthetic theater is simultaneous and dynamic, with interpenetrations "**of different times and environments**" (207). Such theater, while it borrows aspects of contemporary life, is autonomous, as far as concerns reality, even photographic reality: photographic technology is not considered by Futurists a primary area for realistic undertakings, even though Futurists experimented in many ways with the photographic medium. Rather, beginning with pieces of reality, which it then combines, synthetic theater has the capacity to lead the audience "through a **labyrinth of sensations imprinted with the most exacerbated originality and combined in unpredictable ways**" (208). The flow of time in this kind of theater is that of modernity itself—it is a disconnected time, in which events with varying rhythms and tones can take place simultaneously. In his *Theatricality as Medium*, Samuel Weber traces criticism of theater from Plato's Allegory of the Cave through Guy Debord, noting that this criticism opposes theater that "'turns reality on its head' by causing 'a world that is no longer directly perceptible to be seen,' by transforming 'mere images . . . into real beings.'"[20] Weber is not referring to Futurist theater; however, it is not difficult to compare the criticism of conventional theatrical logic with the "theatrical" proposals of the synthetic theater. Synthetic theater is spectacle that, through images and splinters of reality, refuses to concern itself with "usurp[ing] the role of 'reality' and threaten[ing] 'life'" (11). Synthetic theater is radical in its proposal: it aims to eliminate many of the techniques and forms of theater of the past, including even farce, vaudeville, and the *coup de théâtre* if these were written within a narrative *plot* in which the characters and events functioned according to a linear, explicative logic. As the critic Giovanni Lista writes, "Following this poetics of the fragment, the Futurist synthesis ought to be done as 'theatrical knots,' that is to say dramatic syntagms devoid of any narrative connection. . . . The 'theatrical,' as a specific value of the stage, constitutes the content of a 'futurist synthesis.'"[21] This theater is atechnical in not being based on the traditional theatrical techniques dictated by the presence of theatrical *plot*; in addition, it is autonomous, meaning that it brings a labyrinth of sensations to the stage with abstractions, throwing "nets of sensations between the stage and the audience" (208), to the extreme of body-madness.[22] A strange postscript concludes the manifesto, as a kind of supplement, calling for a building able to host such ephemeral, mobile, lightning-like performances. Anticipating the near future, it announces: "In Milan we soon shall have the great metal building, driven [*animato*] by many electromechanical inventions, that alone will enable us to realize our freest conceptions on the stage" (209). This building is only announced; it is not constructed, nor is it even designed, as Sant'Elia's train station is. Nevertheless, it is evident that the Futurists would obtain some of the results proposed in the manifesto through sophisticated technological innovations, drawn from the interactions with the modern city.

The manifesto traces lines for innovative ways of playing with theater, and we can find many examples of experimentations, of "theatrical knots" that challenge the traditional theatricality, importing in their making various cinematic devices, from montage to editing, interpenetration of splinters of action, abstract scenes and stages devoid of actors, always attentive to turning ordinary everyday life upside-down so as to cause to appear, in passing, the contemporary dissonance embedded in the cityscape.

Prampolini and the Abstraction of the Emotive Theatrical Space

Enrico Prampolini began his artistic activities during the same years in which Balla and Depero worked together, paralleling Futurist experimentations without belonging to the Futurist movement.[23] Like Balla and Depero, he produced manifestos that referred to architecture and theater. Prampolini's manifestos, however, placed significantly more emphasis on space and atmosphere than on plastic complexes.

In "The Atmosphere-Structure—Bases for a Futurist Architecture"[24] (1914) Prampolini explicitly connects, in an analogous, abstract manner, the concepts of habitation and the city with the atmospheric elements of space (motion, light, and air). Air and light (or other natural forms of energy) and force (artificial energy) determine the scenario within which Prampolini sees the potential for a Futurist architecture.

> Futurist architecture will need to be molded by these energetic entities, which when *amalgamated*, create a single *abstract entity* that I call spherical diathesis, abstract consequence of energies, which establishes the *value-relationship* between the *natural influence of the atmosphere and man's material necessities*. (23)

Here architecture is shaped, molded (*plasmata*) as an abstract entity that ties together natural and artificial energies in the atmosphere. Prampolini is not referring to an invisible architecture; instead, by making a connection between fields of energy and the constructed, he employs abstraction to define a new configuration in which architecture is an integral, active part of the "atmosphere." With an abstract and ethereal tone, the manifesto points toward the need to harmonize natural and artificial factors in the constructed urban fabric. In "A New Art? Absolute Construction of Movement-Noise" (1915),[25] Prampolini develops further his ideas regarding the impossibility of any art's remaining isolated; he advocates that an abstract and absolute construction is necessary in order to communicate a new sensibility with the immaterial values relative to the "crackling and spiral dynamic life of today, of movement-noise" (24). An incredible torsion plays between materiality and abstraction, through which some of the aspects of the modern cityscape are developed. At the beginning of his manifesto, Prampolini insists on inserting noise and motion, two elements noted for being difficult to control, into atmospheric space; he also notices the similarity of his "absolute-constructions of movement-noise" to the plastic complexes. He writes: "It's about the abandonment of the traditional picture in painting, the statue in sculpture, the apartment block in architecture, the orchestral concert, and finally the book; to arrive directly, without intermediary means and excluding any cerebral elaboration, at the *forms of pure sensibility*" (24).

It seems from this excerpt that Prampolini bypasses any intermediality and any technological estranging effect so as to gather directly a new synthesis between sensations (smell, plasticity, and color) and absolute expressions of motion-sound, which are connected in such a way that their development finds form in material expression. Prampolini in this way has suspended any material and technical mediality, along with the shocks of modernity that transform—as Benjamin has clearly indicated—the way of experiencing. Therefore he is able to continue:

> To concretize with more efficiency, to excite with greater vehemence this emotionality, these life sensations of the infinitely small and of the universe that surrounds us: these are the foundations of these *absolute-constructions-of-movement-noise* that reunite in themselves not only the material values of all the arts, but all the sensations which up until now had been singularly fixed by each art. (24)

While Prampolini advocates for "actually setting in motion plastic scaffoldings" that will give a "*construction of sensations*," he maintains his proposal at the most abstract and remote level from construction. His aim is to construct forms whose movement comes from a continual transformation, wherein each element is transformed in its formal and chromatic aspect, as well as in its movement and noise—"transforming these plastic units, changing aspect, detaching themselves from one part to interpenetrate with another, propagating a noise in relation to the movement and to the plastic evolution that a given element requires" (25). Through abstraction, dynamism is imprinted and fixed into shapes, into constructions, the forms of motion. However, no tension is embedded in such constructions; they interpenetrate smoothly in the space of the manifesto. Twice in the manifesto Prampolini suggests such proposals as the vowels of a new alphabet or embryos like a "protoplasm" that has already at its center a possible equivalent. The manifesto concludes with a possible and fleeting actualization of such "embryonic research," in which Prampolini opens a scenario of the contemporary metropolis: it is a complex urban fabric, in which multiple architectural and mechanical elements connect together through material elements that are capable of motion. In the manifesto's last part, in order to render Futurist architecture tangible, he imagines "dynamic architectures that move, metallic arms that detach from doorposts, floors that will unhook themselves from the walls, transporting us smoothly through a pneumatic stairwell from one floor to another" (25).

This manifesto is accompanied by some architectural drawings that furnish examples of possible architectural experiments, yet Prampolini left behind architecture and continued to orient his interests toward set design.

In 1915, almost simultaneously with the preceding manifestos on architecture, Prampolini published "Futurist Stage Design" (a literal translation would be "Futurist Stage and Choreography Design").[26] For Prampolini, who aimed at innovations in scenography, "it is no longer a matter of reforming only the structural concept of the stage design, but of creating an abstract entity that can be identifiable with the action taking place on stage in the theatrical work" (213). In order to reform scenography, it was necessary to rethink the relationship between author and scenographer. Even if, to be reformed, the set design must abandon a relationship with reality, abstraction does not imply an abandonment of the "emotive picture"; instead, the setting must awaken "all the impressions [*sensazioni*] necessary to the drama's development, so that it creates an atmosphere which renders the internal ambience of the work" (213). For Prampolini, a set should be neither realistic, nor painted, nor a reproduction of past clichés—those "dusty, moldering corners of classical architecture" (214)—but rather an architecture made of light with special effects.

> The stage will no longer have a colored backdrop, *but a colorless electromechanical architectural structure, enlivened by chromatic waves from a source of light*, produced by electric reflectors with colored filters arranged and coordinated in accordance with the mood demanded by every dramatic action. (214)

Innovation in the scenography occurs through interpenetrations of light, color, and chromatic fugues he defines as "unreal clashes," which intersect with the dynamic architecture of the set (the metallic arms with the mobile plastic planes return in this manifesto).

Prampolini writes that abstraction should not be separated from emotional intensity, from particular special effects, nor from a direct relationship with sensation and the effect it provokes in the audience. He is explicit in positing his differences in painting from Kandinsky's "Pure Painting" (1915). Colors and shapes exist in relation to the interior laws of the construction of a work of art, writes Prampolini; otherwise they become "purely cerebral results, instead of psychic—this presupposed the total lethargy of the senses, while these should participate, so that the emotion, saturate with elements, transmits to the sensations the immaterial or formal values of the material's interior."[27] Prampolini maintains the idea of purity: he is for a "pure" process of painting, even if he thinks of theater as the medium in which the relationship between the arts is most active. Prampolini considers pure painting a synthesis of "*psycho-physical product=plastic-chromatic construction*." He refers to construction to differentiate it from composition: construction, in this sense, offers the possibility for an abstract art derived "through its own sensitiveness and not from outside itself," which "requires construction (or internal value) and not composition (or external value)." Therefore, we could add, Prampolini is a "constructor" in the Benjaminian sense, one who believes that the senses participate even in a translated way with the inner laws of the work.

Prampolini is occupied more with construction than with composition, as far as set design is concerned. Just as he inverts the importance between static and dynamic, he inverts the value attributed to light: in "Futurist Stage Design," the stage is *illuminating* rather than *illuminated*. The stage is never a regulated Cartesian space but is instead a place of action and construction and also a place of surprise, where "electrochemical colors, using fluorescent salts which have the chemical property of being sensitive to electrical currents and emitting luminous colors of every tonality" (215) will activate a dynamic stage of architectural structures. This is a primary example of a Futurist theatrical stage, based on a Futurism that, before it had assumed its own name, might have been called "Elettricismo." Prampolini's proposals concerning abstract theater downplay the role of the actor and the marionette, both of which lose their central position.[28] Prampolini proposes that the actors be replaced by special effects, strange hybrids of the inorganic and incorporeal which he refers to as *gas-actors*.[29] Prampolini thus gives form on the theatrical stage to an idea he had for architecture. In other words, the stage, as a place that is only apparently contained, can permit experimentation in possible scenarios that give architecture space in a dynamic and active manner.

Although Prampolini had not been accepted by the Futurist circle, his highly sophisticated international avant-garde journal—*Noi*—was able to establish a connection with a well-known French avant-garde journal, *SIC*. Prampolini asked *SIC*'s editor, the French poet Pierre Albert-Birot, to perform his *Matoum et Téviban*. In 1919 Prampolini was able to perform the piece; as Berghaus notes, although the theme and the storyline of the piece were too dull for the Futurists' tastes, Prampolini's stage design did finally get their attention. Berghaus writes: "The creation of a mobile scenic architecture with its active and dynamic integration of the stage set into the plot of the play was indeed innovative. The use of colored lights to indicate the protagonist's states of mind was a novel and startling device."[30]

Part 2. Toward Futurist Allegories of Architecture

From Machine-Age Art and the Actor-Space to the Magnetic and Magic Theaters

From the beginning of the 1920s on, Prampolini's multifarious activities related to set design brought him in contact with many strands of the emerging international avant-garde (Dada, De Stijl, Esprit Nouveau, and Bauhaus, among others). Among those activities, one that caused contention between the left and right factions of Futurism at the time was the rewriting of the 1922 "Manifesto of Futurist Mechanical Art" by Ivo Pannaggi and Vinicio Paladini, which is still targeted by critics even today. The manifesto by the two Futurist artists advocates a revolutionary new machine style:

> Today the MACHINE distinguishes our era. **Pulleys and flywheels, bolts and smokestacks, all the polished steel and odor of grease. . . . Gears** wipe away the misty and the indecisive from our eyes, everything

> is more **incisive, decisive, aristocratic, sharp**. We feel mechanically, and we sense that we ourselves are also made of steel, we too are machines, we too have been mechanized by our surroundings. The beauty of transport wagons and the *typographic pleasure* of solid thick advertising signs, trucks shuddering and trembling of a TRUCK, the fantastic architecture of a construction crane, lucid and cold steels.[31]

Maria Elena Versari has traced the microhistory of the multiple rewritings of this manifesto, locating it in a macrohistory related to politics and to the emergence of Constructivism in art and architecture. At the May 1922 International Congress of Progressive Artists, in Düsseldorf, a schism arose between Russian Constructivists who remained in Russia and those who relocated to Western Europe.[32] Versari writes that a "trans-national network of collaboration, which had been promoted by Prampolini himself" (164), was dismissed at the Congress, and it was in this context that Prampolini brought to the manifesto a crucially different take on the theme of the machine. The first part of the new version of the manifesto, "Mechanical Art—Futurist Manifesto," published in *Noi* and signed by Prampolini along with Pannaggi and Paladini, contains an internal genealogy of Futurism that explains how "Modernolatry" had finally attained the new sensibility of the machine. It then argues for a distinction "between the exteriority and the spirit of the Machine." If the artist's work stops at the "exteriority of the Machine," explains the version from 1923, this leads to "purely geometric paintings, shouting and exterior (comparable to certain engineering projects) . . . plastic constructions executed with real mechanical elements (screws, gearings, gears, steels, etc.) that don't enter the creation as expressive material, but that only are ends in themselves)."[33] The tension between the mechanical and human is transposed to "the infinite analogies that the Machine suggests"—the Machine is the new divinity that illuminates and initiates the Religion of the New.[34]

Among Prampolini's most significant international encounters was certainly the one with Frederick Kiesler, the Austrian artist/architect who organized the *International Exhibition of New Theater Techniques* in 1924 in Vienna. The exhibition, a turning point in set design innovation, was attended by George Grosz, Fernand Leger, László Moholy-Nagy, and Oskar Schlemmer, among many others; Kiesler himself presented his groundbreaking project "Space Stage," a towering construction of complex scaffolding that "consisted of several performance spaces staggered on top of one another, which could be performed on simultaneously."[35] The different proposals presented made clear the international cross-pollination of constructive experimentations as they were taking place in set design. The exhibit also featured Prampolini's presentation of his manifesto "Futurist Scenic Atmosphere" (1924).[36] In this manifesto, Prampolini begins by referring to his earlier manifesto on scenography, which agreed with Marinetti and Settimelli's manifesto of Synthetic

Theater in insisting on the necessary negation of the classic stage setting "as description of the apparent reality, as a realistic *verismo*'s fictionality of the visual world"; this is contrasted with the "*scenic dynamism*, the essence of theatrical action" (226). Then he writes: "The fundamental principles that animate *Futurist scenic atmosphere* are the very essence of spiritualism, of aesthetics and of Futurist art, that is: *dynamism*, *simultaneity*, and *unity* of action between man and his environment" (226). The occurrence in a single phrase of "metaphysical" words like "essence," "spiritualism," and "unity" confirms that theater, a place in motion though contained, was for Prampolini the site where modernity merged with abstraction, where the relationship between humans (which he calls the "dynamic element") and environment (the static element) is not out of joint and there is no dualism. It is in theater that Prampolini hopes to achieve such a harmony between human life and modernity, between the dynamic and the static, between the human and the other, the environment. Theater is no longer the place for dissonance and conflict. Everything is held in balance by a scenic atmosphere.

But how? The earlier technique of the theater, according to Prampolini, consisted in an unresolved dichotomy between mankind (as dynamic element) and environment (as static element). In place of this, Prampolini proposes a new synthesis, an interpenetration of the two: a living synthesis. In what Prampolini refers to as the "magic triangle" of synthesis, plasticity, and dynamics, a scenic Futuristic atmosphere develops out of a trajectory that he sees as integrating and synthesizing. The point of departure is the empirical scenography, as a pictorial and realist description; then comes a *scenosynthesis*, elaborated through chromatic surfaces; this is followed by a *scenoplastics*, in which the scenic environment becomes three-dimensional and the architecture intervenes as "a living plastic reality"—in this case, the stage is abolished. Subsequent to such integrations, Prampolini introduces the *scenodynamics*, a four-dimensional environment where there is a "predominance of spatial architectural elements, intervention of rhythmic movement as a dynamic element essential to the unity and the simultaneous development between environment and theatrical action" (228). This is the polydimensional scenic space that breaks the rules of the traditional stage and the proscenium arch: "By breaking the horizontal surface through the intervention of new vertical, oblique, and polydimensional elements, by forcing the cubic resistance of the scenic arc by means of the spherical expansion of rhythmic plastic planes in space, we arrive at the *creation of Futurist polydimensional scenospace*"(229).

Prampolini's abstract architectural scenarios are possible, but they are only experimented with, or imagined, on the stage. He proposes a scenodynamic architecture in which the fixed plane, and the *ground*, jump, substituting a rhythmic turbulence of planes in/of movement and in/of circulation. Theater and stage become a laboratory for continuous experimentation. In relation to his earlier manifesto on scenography, Prampolini has elaborated his manner of presentation, maintaining and even intensifying certain proposals by again presenting the self-illuminating set design and clarifying different ways of performing it.

> *Electrodynamic polydimensional architecture of luminous plastic elements in movement in the center of the theatrical concavity.* This new *theatrical construction*, owing to its location, enlarges the perspective *visual angle* above the horizontal line by displacing it at the vertex and vice versa in simultaneous interpenetration toward a centrifugal irradiation of infinite visual and emotional angles of scenic action. (229)

In the preceding text Prampolini spoke of *gas-actors*; here he is even clearer in this respect. He writes of the actor "as the *useless element* in the theatrical action," for his scenographic formulation is the absolute, and "the actor always represents the *relative viewpoint*" (230). In fact, it is the unknown variable of the actor that must be eliminated (230). Prampolini, whose starting point is experimenting with theater as a medium, as a place of exchange between what is constructed and what is living, consequently arrives at the negation of the actor, having followed a discourse previously elaborated by Edward Gordon Craig, Adolphe Appia, and other directors and set designers—and having brought to the extreme his imposed and not experimental idea of unity. The actor is defined as the unknown, and therefore cannot be entirely constructed, programmed, or anticipated. For this reason he refers to the *actor-space*, to the *personification of space* as "a dynamic and interacting element between the scenic environment and the public spectator" (230). He negates even the experimentality of the theater, the "episodic extemporization on the life of a singular person" (230). If the aspects of Futurist theater that I have considered are indeed an allegory of modernity, what I defined in chapter 1 as the *colportage de l'espace* seems to be negated: events, actors, and participants are negated or unknown, yet to be determined. At this moment of his research into scenography, Prampolini, who started with an exploration of the possible and of the inventive, now blocks the unexpected and the incalculable. In fact, by the end of the manifesto the theater has become "a center of spiritual abstraction for the new religion for the time to come," and space becomes, respectively, the "*metaphysical aureole of the environment*." If, for Baudelaire, the poet has lost his halo, here Prampolini picks it up and places it on the constructed and illuminating theatrical space. It remains extremely unclear whether, within this reconstructed space, spectators actively participate while differentiating themselves from it or whether they simply become hypnotized by it.

A prime example of such a set design is Prampolini's Magnetic Theater, presented at the Exposition Internationale des Arts Décoratifs et Industriels

Modernes in 1925, for which he won the Diplôme d'honneur and the Grand Prix Mondial. At this international exhibition, the architect Robert Mallet-Stevens presented many projects, such as the provocative garden with trees in cement that infuriated the artist Fortunato Depero (also present) because he had submitted the same idea a year earlier and been rejected. In the architectural section, Le Corbusier presented his pavilion *l'Esprit Nouveau* and the *Plan Voisin*, the Russian Konstantin Melnikov designed the Soviet pavilion, while Kiesler in the part dedicated to set design presented his *City in Space*—a walk-through model that consisted of "panels and beams suspended in space without supports" that he called "a system of tension in open space."[37] Kiesler's project is a strong instance of utopian abstraction at the crossing of architecture and set design.

The model of Prampolini's Magnetic Theater no longer exists, although drawings and photographs survive that illustrate the manner in which it functioned mechanically, as well as the way the lights were displayed. The drawings, in elevation and in plan, clarify some of the mechanical motions that are at play in the model. From the frontal view, it is evident that it consisted of a constructed set, articulated along different horizontal and vertical movable planes. The center of the set was cut horizontally by a circular surface, to which were connected, at its sides, different movable structures: for example, in the upper area of the central circular surface on the left, a vertical construction could move in a circular motion; it seemed to be able to rotate, as Lista writes, "with a slow rhythm pivoting on the side fixed to the three horizontal planes."[38]

From the various photographs, it is possible to discern the play of lights and of constructions designed by Prampolini in the Magnetic Theater. Two photos shows that the model could be illuminated in different ways, in order to create different contrasts of light and shadow. It is in this sense that Prampolini's mechanical theater is also a magnetic one, a *stage* of magnetic fields, and is constructed through the use of special effects.

One of the important theatrical productions by Prampolini in these years was the *Théâtre de la Pantomime Futuriste*, performed in Paris in 1927.[39] This production was a way to present a multiplicity of stage experimentations in which dance, music, and mime converged; this repertoire is interesting because it shows how several different avant-garde artistic media—as a sign of the times—were merged as samples, as constructed and performed Futurist theatrical moments, rather than presented as total works of art. Lista makes clear that the production was not a homogeneous project and that "the program proposed a stylistic pluralism deliberately chosen by Prampolini" (394). The brochure for the *Theater of Futurist Pantomime* states: "It is about abandoning the mimetic decorativism, which is the surface, to enter into the domain of architecture, which is the depth."[40] The "depth" of architecture was indeed only mirrored in the most ephemeral way. The project was a mix and a confluence of Expressionism, Theater of Color, Constructivism, and Futurism, which—as Lista emphasizes, based on the few documents that remain—was an attempt to obtain "a maximum of stage vitality by using the most exterior signs of the theatrical action: rhythm, intensification of gestures, plastic masses, lightings' dynamism, mobile elements" (394). The project attempted to bring together interpenetrations of dance, gestures, music, and scenography, and, as a magazine of that time wrote, "to transport mechanized, modern life into the fragile world of dance and gesture."[41] Therefore, volatile and fragile aspects of gestures and dances were given space in the *Théâtre de la Pantomime Futuriste*, certainly more space than any violent and powerful mechanized aspects of modernity. They were, as Berghaus call them, *folies du futurisme*, which in French suggests a sort of vaudeville presentation with lively dances and noisy music.

Among the repertoire of the performed pieces, *Three Moments* and *Cocktail* mixed performers and animated objects. *Three Moments*' first act is set in the forest: a satyr seduces a nymph and brings her to a modern city; in the second act the two lovers are replaced by a ventilator and a gramophone—on hearing the two lovers, an elevator "in his excitement moves frantically up and down, emanating green and red light beams from his watchful 'eyes' " (451).[42] The nymph and the satyr reappear wearing modern dress, but soon the world outdoors calls them and they are "enveloped in a flood of light and a deluge of noise. Overwhelmed by the forces they have summoned, they are sucked into the hustle and bustle of the metropolis, leaving behind their clothes, which perform a dance" (451). The music was by Luigi Russolo's *rumorarmonio*[43] and filmed décor was introduced. These metonymic exchanges (objects for persons, lights and noises for the big cities) are also at work in the two-level stage of *Cocktail* (written by Marinetti): enormous, human-sized bottles start moving when a customer orders, preparing cocktails and dancing among colorful lights coming from a huge soda siphon. Therefore the *Théâtre de la Pantomime* was not performed with an absolute absence of actors; instead, puppets and dancers activated the space of the stage, pointing toward the complex novelty of life in the city. The only piece that was never staged was Prampolini's *Saint Speed*, but from the indications that he gives in the short text, we can suppose that there would have been no actors, only modern architectural and cinematic cityscapes:

> Very modern city: metropolis. Neon signs. Cinematographic life at night, electric, dazzling. Apartment blocks. Wide streets. Sky. The only human intervention: a song which stops and smothers the speed. But the song slowly comes to an end and the speed of modern life picks up again in a crescendo which is extraordinary, magical, unlimited, resounding. (460)

Prampolini develops performances that are connected to the space-time environment of the Magnetic Theater. While *Théâtre de la Pantomime*'s repertoire is not performed on the spaces of the Magnetic Theater, it becomes nevertheless fluid and open to cross-pollination of different theatrical avant-garde practices.

In the same years in which Prampolini worked on the Magnetic Theater, Depero wrote about it in his own 1927 *Bolted Book*,[44] a unique example of assemblage, a monograph that combines writing and typographic presentation of multifarious proposals. Depero includes the manifesto for his own "Magic Theater" with typographic characters of different dimensions; the proposals of Prampolini and Depero are in tune, and both search for expanded theatrical and scenographical dimensions. Depero, in proposing a completely amplified construction of the stage "in all the electrical and mechanical directions," says that most scenographers are illiterate as far as the grammar of set design is concerned. He proposes to bring to life inside the theater a new grammatology of theater—if this neologism is permitted—one that assumes gestures in the constructed cityscape, that "most agitated world of lights, winds, reflections; upside-down realities, absurd and multiplied in mirrors and plate-glass windows; scenes turning spirals in a stairwell, spectacles in the turmoil of storms, or dancing and vertiginous as if perceived at high-speed."[45] Depero is in search of a new grammar of constructed spaces, and here he abandons his recurrent fantastic transposition of the natural realm into the artificial one, aiming instead at facilitating anyone to jump into the contemporary cityscape. Regarding the study of set design, Depero makes the observation that, barring the rare exceptions, the contrast between

Drama Dance song and music	and the stage setting

is **enormous.**

Violent and synthetic dramas,
modern dance, very original and ultra-dynamic,
songs, choruses, and powerful orchestras and
pyrotechnics, etc. etc.
SET DESIGN, bad and grey,
bland imitations, fifteenth-centuryish. (101)

Scenography must be mobile, so that it can "express rapidly, awaken interest, amuse, and inexhaustibly variate-create." Depero's concept of set design finds inspiration in the cinema for its capacity to bring "contrasts-findings-panoramas-facts," for the possibility of presenting brief sequences: "a hand that steals," "a forest that flees," "one runs, navigates, flies, travels, lives incessantly remaining seated in an armchair." Depero considers cinema as an art of the future, though he emphasizes what is lacking in the seventh art at the moment: the palette of the cinema is limited to black and white; while cinema does not present living people, nor constructions nor anything of importance, it will become the powerful means of artistic creation because "it is fast, it moves and transforms." He returns then to the theatrical set, proposing a magnified vertical floor that multiplies the floors with superimposed planes:

> To create the perspective of characters with automatic
> figures, giving spatial sensations, magic distances and depths,
> accompanied by analogous vocal deformations.
> The voice is also on the same level.
>
> To distanciate,
> To disproportion
> people—voices—dimensions—time.
> . . .
> Deformation of the running time and magic of the distances.

In contrast to Prampolini, the last section concludes not with the omission of the actors but rather with the introduction of automatons, which "are used for dividing, multiplying a character in its various dimensions. . . . One's own shadow, the different aspects of oneself, repeated, shrunken and enlarged one can render efficiently and simultaneously only with the help of robots." This manifesto shows the work of Depero as mature set designer. The moving scenario that Depero imagines includes actors as well as the actors' shadows; a lively staging of modernity is therefore embedded in living, ghostly, and mechanical presences.

When Depero was able to realize his designs, he incorporated earlier Futurist elements, including elements of typography, into his constructions. Perhaps the clearest example is the *Book's Pavilion*, which he produced in 1927 for the publishers Treves-Besteretti-Taminelli for the book exposition in Monza. This cube-shaped pavilion, built out of cement, is structurally simple; the complexity of its design lies in the constructions with letters that advertise the publishing house. This project illustrates a transformation in the application of abstraction: rather than serving as a means to break the bond with language and within the stage, it has become an instrument for advancing the trade of letters, as well as for product promotion and publicity.[46] The *Book's Pavilion* and Prampolini's *Futurist Pavilion* for the International Exhibition in Turin 1927 share design aspects with Depero's *Futurist Campari Pavilion*, which Kwinter considered to be derived from Sant'Elia drawings in which "information dissemination processes (ads, signs, graffiti) constitute nothing less than a *material* intervention in the urban continuum."[47]

Kwinter, interweaving his reading of Sant'Elia's manifesto and drawings, writes: "By adding another totally heterogeneous material to those enumerated in the manifesto (glass, iron, textile), the introduction of language—and presumably later, of images—into the urban/architectural domain would, besides having far-reaching consequences for the Russian and Dutch avant-garde of the 1920s and the later Italian work of architects such as Depero, Dazi and others, create the conditions for the truly polymorphous, procedural—action- or information-based—architectures that began to emerge in the late 1950s and 1960s" (90).

The architectural poetics of these temporary constructions was overtaken by other fringe movements of Italian architecture, such as Rational and Functional Modern Architecture, while Prampolini's temporary spatial constructions, in particular, captured the attention of the Mussolini regime, which included him in many crucial exhibitions such as the *Mostra della Rivoluzione Fascista* (1932), *Mostra Nazionale del Dopolavoro* (1938), *Mostra Autarchica del minerale italiano* (1938), and *Mostra Triennale delle Terre d'Oltremare* (1940).

A Theatrical Synthesis in Chains: Reconstruct Italy with Futurist Sant'Elia Architecture

During the 1930s, Marinetti wrote a series of theatrical works that are regarded by Lista as more conventional than his previous Futurist theatrical experimentations.[48] Lista locates within these texts a formal effort that is paralleled by an ideological "void," uniting in a regressive movement toward dramaturgical forms that merely imitate the avant-garde set in a Mannerist way. Lista also notes another characteristic shared by these theatrical texts: a style of writing that is invested with subtexts referring to the internal history of Futurism, which include public and private moments from Marinetti's life.

Giovanni Calendoli, the first to edit a collection of Marinetti's theatrical works, provides a contrasting reading that traces several of Marinetti's themes as they develop over time and are made manifest in these works. Calendoli does not even touch on these works' Mannerist qualities; instead, he makes evident the Futurist themes he sees developing in Marinetti's theatrical work, such as the stage directions with an abundance of colors and wild images, the recurrent use of a technique of interpenetration, and the staging of a rejection of psychology "understood in the traditional sense as an instrument for the construction of the characters and refusal of the assumed succession as support for the progress of the action."[49]

The last of Marinetti's theatrical works, never performed and considered unfinished, is *Reconstruct Italy with Futurist Sant'Elia Architecture*, described as a "*divertimento* performable in many syntheses."[50] The *OED* indicates that *divertimento* derives from the Latin *dīvertĕre* (to turn in different directions, turn out of the way), blended with the Latin *dēvertěre* (to turn away or aside); *divertire* in Italian means "to amuse," and divertimento is a musical genre that generally features light, informal pieces. The musical term was allegedly first used by Carlo Grossi, an Italian composer in Venice in 1681, and since then the genre has undergone a number of variations: even Igor Stravinsky wrote some divertimenti for ballets. Though there are ballets in *Reconstruct*, there is no music; it is all about what Goethe called "frozen music": architecture. This text is interwoven with proposals by the Futurists taken from their works and manifestos, and it also imaginatively reworks the debates that animated the architectural field from the end of the 1920s to the early 1930s. The major participants in this debate were Futurist architects and another group, the Rationalists, who considered their ideas more advanced and in tune with their times, with what is commonly called "modern architecture." What is important to note is that both groups aimed at obtaining the patronage of the fascist regime.[51]

In 1933 Marinetti and other Futurists proposed the First Competition of Aerial Architecture, as one of the first examples of an open-call-for-ideas competition. Never realized, it is now known as the "Futurist Manifesto of Aerial Architecture." The manifesto is strikingly eccentric in destabilizing the most advanced trends in architecture of that time. From the airplanes, the cities seem a "stack of junk," with scattered bricks and rubble, without color or rhythm. Instead, the manifesto proposes the "Uni-City with continuous lines"; it will run throughout the entire nation along with Aero-ways and Aero-canals. The manifesto borders on the psychedelic in its description of how the city "will show to the sky its parallelism with aero-ways turquoise gold orange, bright aero-canals, bright and wide provider residences with mobile surfaces."[52] While it avoids verticals and horizontals, the manifesto proposes all other possible regular and irregular, sinuous and folding forms to produce visual and lighting effects, so as to avoid any standardization of the forms. The surfaces of both interiors and exteriors will be on different levels and, accompanied by what remains of Futurist violence, will ecologically mold the configuration of the landscapes. Today this manifesto lets itself be interpreted in part as something resembling contemporary avant-garde architecture's experiments with forms and geometry: movement is interior to the forms, not only exterior to architecture. The Italian writer Massimo Bontempelli, who was passionate about Rational Architecture (and in particular Giuseppe Terragni), participated for a time in the architectural debate.[53] Bontempelli considered this manifesto not an architectural but a theatrical text. In *Quadrante* Bontempelli proposes

> a clean break between Futurist ideal and the architecture that is so near to our heart, whether rational or functional. . . . Our architecture derives from, and tenaciously recalls, the principle that every aesthetic expression grows directly out of the practical necessities that generate

> it. . . . Futurism, on the other hand, departs from the opposite point of view: its first thought is a decorative thought, really theatrical or scenographic, actually. The city is above all a city to be admired in flight. . . . We pull for the side of engineering, Futurism pulls for literature. It prescribes a form for the inhabitants: spheres, cones, pyramids, prisms. . . . Allegorism is imposed over functionality.[54]

Bontempelli regards this late Futurist manifesto as not even allegorical and dismisses it as allegorism. In *Reconstruct* these debates—volatile Futurist memories—are staged perhaps as a counterattack, or with the intention of outbidding Bontempelli's criticism and all that he advocated.

While one can find in the piece echoes of previous Futurist experimentations, the text lacks any explicit reference to the historical moment; instead, what is performed is the tension among different ways of thinking of past, present, and future. Venice is the city where this piece takes place, and it becomes the playful emblem and stage of hyper-Baroque constructed spaces, an allegory of architectural potentiality.

The theatrical work is composed of nine syntheses, and although it seems to contain a plot, it is continually interrupted by *coups de théâtre* and pervaded by dialogues and monologues that tend to show extreme internal logics that are performed for the sake of enjoyment. The architectures, or potential future metropolitan complexes, become the principal characters, as well as the sites of the primary conflict of dispute and tension. Architecture, and how to conceive of it, is in play throughout this concatenation of syntheses, in which the characters are divided into three primary groups: the *Velocisti* (speed people), the *Spazialisti* (space people), and the *Mollenti* (flabby people). On one level is the juxtaposition of the past and future; the longest syntheses are those that are most colorful and dynamic, while the briefest are those in which various *Mollenti* make an appearance. Strong contrasts exist between *Spazialisti* and the *Velocisti*, but both are opposed to the *Mollenti*. Two tendencies become apparent among the *Spazialisti*: one aims to change the architecture of the city through forms that are solid even if only temporary; the other aims toward a lighter, colorful, and unpredictable architecture.

The *Spazialisti* must complete six new cities in three years. The plan is to construct one hundred new aeromarine cities in ferroconcrete along the sea so that the Italian coast will increase by two hundred kilometers. The first synthesis, *The Living Space*, opens to a colored architectonic scenario that is set in motion mechanically. The scene opens to a view of a "Sant'Elia city, most colorful buildings with graduated hanging gardens and sheaves of elevators. Balls of solar rays run on the edges of joyful immense geometries. The sun runs, golden ball along the brass balustrade. In the glass panels, the luminous segments of the curved marine horizon with plumes of smoke from the ships and sails moving mechanically in every direction" (479).

Vasto, a *Spazialista* who is determined to defend the eternal-but-new spatial aesthetics, enters the stage and speaks: "Finally we possess the living space that constructs and determines itself. In our hands is now developing the new spatial aesthetic of the torpedoes, still and eternal, on the seas' ephemeral disorder and the decorativism of their foamy furies" (481). Vasto supports ferroconcrete, which is fixed and permanent, while Ballamar, a *Spazialista* who would like to ally himself with the *Velocisti*, is against the straight line and the eternal; he desires instead the unexpected and bizarre. Vasto accuses him of plunging into the void; Ballamar agrees that he prefers it to fullness. Once they have achieved some steps that Ballamar considers possible/feasible—"infinite constructability [*costruttibilità*], a perfect nutritive chemistry of the State, manual labor reduced to two hours, humongous choice of new, flexible, strong and portable materials" (484)—his ideas will be possible. Somehow, he lightly takes as solvable many of the major social issues of that time: a nation-state that supports continuous invention, reduced labor time, and infinite availability of different materials, ready to be used.

Ballamar celebrates "the fury of the colors in freedom exploding and jarring. The future [*avvenire*] of architecture is in the color, not the form. Form imprisons and limits. Color breaks, expands, immensifies" (484).[55] Thus, if form is important, plasticity neither blocks nor closes. Ballamar supports "*disproportionalism*," "the modification of the perspectives, of the panoramas, and the glimpses. By means of oblique planes of terraces on which we will get used to walking, we will have to create new arches of marine horizons with slopes of thirty and forty degrees" (485).[56]

Ballamar supports an architecture of shapes that construct themselves through movement. This architecture destroys the façade, as the architect Volt wrote in his manifesto in 1919, where he refers to the façade as the "hypocritical plaster mask that hides the mysterious and suggestive life of the houses and the scaffoldings. Our houses will either have no facades, or they will have twenty-seven, which is the same. They will allow glimpses of all the complications of their skeletons and all the undulations of their *musculature*."[57] To Vasto, who would destroy the scaffolding in order to wind up with a solid, fixed façade, Ballamar responds that scaffoldings are wings: "We will create theaters of projected shadows, buildings whose mobile profile decorated with artificial clouds of aluminum, crystal or cloth will impress on the surrounding plains a drama of magnifying shadows. We will reshape the sea with new kinds of waves! . . . Expansive and polymateric architectures will join with the clouds, the rain, the snow" (486).[58] This hyperbolic refashioning of the environment and of the cityscape is certainly to be read allegorically, within the Futurist theatrical trope.

Ballamar is for inequality, not unlike Volt, who wrote: "We shall rebel against the tyranny of the cube. We shall construct conical, spherical, icosahedric, pyramidal, polyhedral, halo, funnel, spiral houses, houses without any preestablished form. . . . The rooms of the dynamic house will attract, push back, run back, turn in, interpenetrate, jut out of the walls with excrescences and crystallizations of glass windows, pushed by an indomitable thirst for movement, for air, of light" (89). Splinters of memories from the Futurists' previous experimentations are here enmeshed among impossible superimpositions with theatrical and cinematic strategies; they are therefore imagined as staged within a multiplicity of media.

Ballamar, after having explained how to construct and reshape the environment, continues along the same lines, now discussing how to create architectures that assemble together natural and electrical illumination and light displays. He proposes architectures that are self-illuminating—certainly reminiscent of Prampolini's proposals; this reconstruction includes a series of magical technological innovations, such as the "lightning seducer" (a gigantic porcupine of lightning rods), the "stars seducer," and the "sun buster." He then continues, uncannily announcing many conceptual and visual features that will later, in the 1960s, be proposed by the experimental architectural group Archigram with *Instant Cities*: "We shall create the celestial cities suspended by free-floating balloons and helicopters! I haven't finished! . . . We will continue tomorrow!" (487). Alata, the *Spazialista* wife of Vasto, addresses Ballamar: "You confound the possible with the impossible!"

But the lively discussion continues, and a decision must be made as to whether to construct the new cities with or without proportions. Ballamar supports an architecture in which attention is paid to both small and large details; he supports "unequalism," which connects "dis-pro-por-tion-ate-ly [*spro-por-zio-na-ta-men-te*]" "the enormous things to the dwarfish, the microscopic links up to the gigantic, the grey to the very colorful, the dazzling to the dark!" (487): Depero's "Magic Theater" returns. Being in favor of "disproportionalism and unequalism," Ballamar declares his opposition to the hegemony of stone, "the big cadaver," and iron, preferring instead aluminum "and its infinite alloys" (488). Alata listens to the conversation but, being a *Spazialista*, is worried that the *Velocisti* will destroy the "conquered and constructed space" that the *Spazialisti* have already achieved: "The *Velocismo* will strangle the *Spazialismo*. We have destroyed the old world to create a perfect and lasting one" (490). However, alliance becomes necessary. To those whose duty it is to construct, the *Spazialisti*, assistance is required from the *Velocisti* in order to rearticulate what must be constructed within space-time. In this first synthesis, a distance separates the *Spazialisti* from the *Velocisti*, which cannot be maintained as it is but needs to be re-elaborated. It's as though space and speed belong together, according to changing spatiotemporal rhythms; however, this does not point to an inevitable absolute where speed is concerned. At the end of the synthesis, while Ballamar proposes to blast the old city, Furr, the leader of the *Velocisti*, suggests postponing the attack; to voices who are astonished by the fact that a *Velocista* prefers to delay, he replies, "We know how to drink centuries, but also how to sip hours" (492). Furr is a *Velocista* who is aware of frenetic modern rhythms and is able to synthesize them whenever required. Here Marinetti seems to suggest that speed is not an absolute, in contrast to what he wrote in his 1911 manifesto "Electrical War": "We are creating a new aesthetics of speed. We have almost abolished the concept of space and notably diminished the concept of time."[59] In *Reconstruct*, he seems to suggest that speed is the experience of difference of forces that, for the moment, Furr appears able to synthesize.

The second synthesis contrasts with the first in its brevity and by containing only one character, a *Mollente*. As he constructs a hut out of magazines, he expresses his opinion about several of them, saying, "I hate all magazines." He then comments on them individually: *Tepid Water* is a daily periodical that aspires to be weekly, but its publisher is conspicuously absent; *The Saint Pond* is his favorite, as it is anti-*Velocisti*, though without energy; he recommends to the audience *The Healing Immobility* over *Slow Down*, which he claims has an extortionist style. Marinetti obtains a sharp shift by presenting a solitary *Mollente* as he contemplates the respective tones of various magazines symbolizing change, events, happenings; this shift is intensified by the action of constructing a home out of periodicals—apparently useless as a construction material.

A new synthesis turns attention toward a postwar landscape, where the new Sant'Elia city as well as part of the old Venice has been destroyed (it will be reconstructed by Furr, and destroyed again by Lord Antiquity's troops). The *Spazialisti* must be taken to court to receive judgment for having destroyed Saint Venice, but Furr defends them and makes a proposal to Mollazon, who moderates the trial, offering to "immediately" reconstruct Venice in its entirety.

Furr says: "Above your Saint Venice I propose to have my sprinter-glass *velocisti* blowers blow out of the top of their tubes a super-strong crepuscular sky sphere of Murano glass; so that the colored gondolas of the good old days with the long floating trains of silks, velvets, moirés, blue brocades are enriched by green reflections. I speak of the traditional gondolas, properly worm-eaten by us . . . with the by-then patented mechanical worm-wood-eater" (497).

Ariella, atmospherist poet, fails to believe Furr; through crying and hiccups he asks, "What will these braggarts do to reconstruct the Foundations, the Campos, the Campiellos, and the Rio Terrà, and on its wharfs the furtive shadows of the women in zandalo and the venerable historic mold on the stones, and the suggestive patina of time?"

Furr responds: "You do not know then about the marvelous machine we invented called Past-ery? In ten minutes it can remake two centuries of green mold. . . . We will try to avoid the introduction of new pieces. Everything will be made utilizing the old pieces conjoined by soldering of electric mold" (498).

Mollazon asks: "Will it be real or artificial mold?" Furr responds, "I ask permission to avoid this discussion about the true and the artificial. It would require a hundred years of real mold." No clear division exists between what is natural and what is artificial; rather, what is original and what is artificial will be connected "with electrical molds."

Pattumol, the head of the *Antiquari* (Antiquarians), is seduced and accepts Furr's offer to reconstruct the old Venice. Vif-Glin presents a dance and sings the hymn of the *Antiquari* to put them to sleep while the *Velocisti* work. It is clear from the structure of this synthesis that during the time Vif-Glin sings and dances, the set design would have been changed completely. While entertaining the *Mollenti* to sleep, Vif-Glin also incites the *Spazialisti* and *Velocisti* to speed up: "If you don't mind please accelerate—otherwise I fall asleep or I get distracted. The past's dust is morphine" (501). Pattumol and Mollazon awaken and see the reconstructed Venice. Embedded in this totally renewed architecture, possibly without distraction, they must decide whether or not the project has been well executed and whether, as a result, the *Spazialisti* will be discharged. Mollazon does not accept before consulting several persons: Pattumol is ecstatic on seeing again the old patina, "delightful slipway of death"; Ariella thinks that "the textile fabric of the noises and the silences" are not well done, to which Furr replies: "How come? [Where can you find] this lagoon of silent liquid obtained by means of 300 dribbling parliamentarians that I have signed up?" (504). Lord Antiquity, the dean of the ambassadors of the nations who ally with Venice, asks: "Above all, we are inclined towards the most absolute disinterest when it comes to events that happen in the interior of the country. . . . But I turn to you, representatives of the great nations of the world. . . . Can what happens in Venice be considered external or internal?" (504). Lord Antiquity wonders whether the reconstruction of Venice should be administered internationally or nationally. Since it is an international affair, the imperialism endorsed by the *Spazialisti* cannot be accepted; either they are convicted or Lord Antiquity's troops will destroy Venice again. Mollazon accepts, satisfied that the "damned religion of Speed" will be extinguished at last; Pattumol is for the war so that the prices will skyrocket, and the *Spazialisti* and the *Velocisti* are condemned to exposure to the sun among ruins.

In the fifth synthesis, *The Death of the Last Train*, Mollazon confesses his deepest idiosyncrasies as a *passéist*, and declares the end of urbanism, artificial light, and speed; as he raises from the ruins of the train station three living statues—Vasto, Alata, and Furr—he declares: "Space and Time in chains, living statues rightly martyred" (507). In this synthesis, a mechanic speaks sadly about the ruins of modernity. While trying to reanimate a train, he recounts the tricks played by the tentacles of dead stations in small villages that wanted to hook and capture the train and to throw it to old "timephages." These villages or perhaps the inhabitants (it is not clear from the text), motivated by nostalgia and memories, "wanted to avenge themselves for my train, which, I must confess, brutally cleaned them of their worldliness and universality. They have a formidable explosive, memory! On the other hand, it's a question of different rhythms that hate each other" (511). Reflecting on his experience, the mechanic sets forth a particular logic, according to which any novelty quickly becomes passé. "Believe me, the more fast cars multiplying on the earth, the more the ruins swelled with threatening nostalgic forces. The ruins smoke grey weather, while all around the new things resonates the electricity of the future, like a halo and like a glass mask" (511). This is a logic that does not differ greatly from that of modernity, for which everything grows old quickly, similar to some motifs of Baudelairean allegory; however, perhaps it also suggests what has happened "to the mechanic" in love with machines.

The seventh synthesis opens with the three chained characters in front of an emblem of the Baroque, a clock, which here moves backward; two postmen look at the ruins and talk about what was there before, and they remember the fate of the last electrician, who was struck by the lightning of the past. The two meet Vif-Glin, who claims to have hidden several objects belonging to her different lovers that contain memories of her past "speed loves." Among these items is a radio-phone, which would provide a large amount of money if they sold it to a historian. The postman tells her that historians no longer exist because "history is dead" (585). Future time has been blocked; ruins and useless objects abound now that the past is the only temporal opening by which time can be comprehended. Attentiveness in defining "the before" and "the after"[60] is not facilitated now. We are no longer in a labyrinth of sensations—instead we are in a labyrinth of ruins. Vif-Glin claims she will be able to sell all of these hidden objects to the nostalgics, but the postman responds, "Every nostalgic by now knows how to fabricate false memories for himself. What do you take us for?" Vif-Glin replies, "For antiquarians," to which the postman protests: "Come on! We're letter-carriers." Vif-Glin continues: "Letter-carriers, like merchants of antiquity, are intermediaries. The intermediary of love praised by Socrates! I don't care for love-letters, sad surrogates that they are!" (522).

An immobile deadly rhythm has overtaken life in the city, where the postmen gossip about whether the letters arrive to living or to dead people, until the scene is interrupted by a person snoring in the audience, whom they promptly wake up.

Before the action can continue, the eighth synthesis presents the solitary thoughts of the wealthiest *Mollente*:

> Bent under an intricate and heavy tangle of telephonic apparatuses, pocket-radios, metallic wires, electric light bulbs turned on, electric light bulbs turned off, neon tubes, etc. he muttered.
>
> I fear that the Mollenti were mistaken in their struggle against money. It would have been better to moderate, not kill the finance of the world. . . . But my old prudence doesn't abandon me. For a year I've been hoarding telephonic apparatuses and light bulbs. . . .

> I hid about eight-hundred-thousand apparatuses of every kind in an unknown and deserted valley a hundred miles from the Deceased City. You will ask me: for what purpose? I'll tell you my secret: life and death are two fashions, which alternate. Today, death triumphs. But soon we'll get bored and we'll return to life. Then I'll be the exclusive provider of every dynamism. In a few days I will be able and know how to reanimate a continent! (527–28)

The thoughts of this *Mollente* will have no final outcome at the end of the theatrical piece; what should be highlighted is the logic that governs his thoughts: he too affirms that time has different rhythms, as in Furr's statement at the beginning of the piece, hence everything in these last reflections is capsized.

The ninth and final synthesis aims to turn the audience into active participants: it begins with a lively discussion among the audience members regarding whether or not snoring in the audience is disrespectful, anarchic, or permissible. Leaving the trapdoor, Vif-Glin frees Vasto, Alata, and Furr, who subsequently join the discussion on theater. Vif-Glin exclaims, "We can continue the performance that will be all reserved for empty chairs! These most ancient and good slaves that have ferried so many rivers with vain chatter and so many imbeciles, carrying them in their arms for three hours" (531). One of the postmen asks, "The spectators then are always right and not the author?" Vif-Glin answers: "Only as much as they become authors themselves, and put on a show" (531). One can only wonder what might have been the stage and set design for this piece that, all along its unfolding, brings the readers to follow the performances of these abstract characters and to imagine mutant, impossible architectures. Yet certainly the participatory boost of the end of the piece aims to encourage the audience to invent in their turn.

The destruction of Venice recalls the manifesto "Against Passéist Venice" by Marinetti, Boccioni, Carrà, and Russolo (1910), but now, twenty years after, many things have changed, and Marinetti theatrically performs a different relationship between destruction/reconstruction. In the manifesto we read: "Let us burn the gondolas, rocking chairs for cretins, and raise to the heavens the imposing geometry of metal bridges and factories plumed with smoke, to abolish the cascading curves of the old architecture."[61] *Reconstruct* is no longer a text distributed during the time of the "Futurist political action theater"[62]—the *serate*—that often later turned violent,[63] nor is it a "futurist fiction of power."[64] In the speech given by Marinetti at the Teatro della Fenice after the presentation of the manifesto, he calls upon the Venetians to become "constructors of the time to come" (*costruttori dell'avvenire*), in the sense that they should not be manipulated by the future but ought to be capable of composing with what is still to come, as opposed to decaying in their "filthy waters so as to enrich the Consortium of Grand Hotels" (70). In the same speech he accepts being referred to as a barbarian: "Shrug your shoulders and scream at me that I'm a barbarian, incapable of savoring the divine poetry that flows among your enchanting isles!" (69). The "constructors of the time to come" and the barbarians—if they can be recognized in *Reconstruct*—are represented with an allegorical tone, acting in an abstract and complex setting. Italo Calvino, while talking about his *Invisible Cities*, refers to the city as "complex symbol."[65] To approach this piece for its "complexity" would be somehow to overinterpret it. Many of the real events, facts, and fearful political decisions appear as flashes in *Reconstruct* only to make us laugh: financial crisis, war, the Fascist expansionist campaign, force fields of influences among different nation-states; the costumes and the constructions of this divertimento cannot mask for us what was happening and going to happen shortly after.

It is quite clear why Bontempelli accuses the "Futurist Manifesto of Aerial Architecture" of "allegorism," and one can imagine he would have said something similar about these imaginary architectures that become theatrical protagonists. *Reconstruct* introduces new architectural spaces, defined by colors, nonstandard geometries, oblique planes, and plays of reflections on the surfaces of new materials. We do not know anything about the use and the function of these "possible/impossible" architectures. It is as if Marinetti put to one side the functional and constructive aspects of architecture and instead let the design imagination run without constraints outside the boundaries of a prescriptive modern universalism. The forms and complexes imagined in this piece can be defined by the notion of "virtual" as Kwinter considers it: "The virtual does not have to be realized, but only actualized (activated and integrated); its adventure involves a developmental passage from one state to another. The virtual is gathered, selected" (8).

Reconstruct's "virtual stage" reinforces what Futurists have claimed since their first experimentations: architecture should be a space to construct but also to experience; therefore, it also becomes a spectacle in which the audience is invited to participate. Bontempelli poses a clear-cut difference between spectacle and use in architecture: the first is associated with Futurism, the second with "modern architecture." Such tension appears again today in contemporary debates on architecture, in which the two poles are inflected by concerns about architecture's relation to the capital that makes it possible.

For example, as Anthony Vidler explains in his introduction to the collection *Architecture between Spectacle and Use*,[66] the "curvilinear forms, computer-generated and titanium-covered" of Frank Gehry's Guggenheim Museum in Bilbao have come under attack by the critic Hal Foster as "arbitrary, perverse, and oppressive." For Foster, under the rule of the market economy, architecture "serves marketing more than either architecture or society" (viii). Foster is recalling Guy Debord's definition of spectacle as "capital accumulated to the point where it becomes an image." For architecture, according to Foster's argument, this implies several questions (as Vidler underlines) relating to freedom in design, architecture's responsibility to the public, and the formal language of architecture; at its extreme, the criticism implies that "the very process of design" adopted by such architects as Gehry, with its "value-free iteration of computer-generated forms," is "driven by neoliberal capital expansion" (viii).

While acknowledging Foster's critique as "severe but serious," Vidler still returns the debate between spectacle and use to its earlier modernist manifestation, one that is contemporary to the one in *Reconstruct*. To criticize Bilbao for "expressionist excess" (because it "betray[s] avant-garde modernist anti-monumentality") recalls an argument that was common in the early modernist avant-garde, a conflict between

> a universalist, standardized, abstract language of pure geometrical forms appropriate to the gamut of tasks demanded by the technologies and social mores of industrial mass society, and a personalized, psychologically generated language that at once expressed the alienation of the individual in such a society and its triumphant overcoming. . . . While these debates were momentarily subsumed with the attempt of the Congress of International Modern Architecture (CIMA) after 1929 to bring together all modernist factions under a singular umbrella as a way of institutionalizing the social and the material concerns of modernist planning, the aesthetic divide was never quite resolved, haunting the attempts of postwar modernists to refine a corporate style against the critiques of countermodernists like Frederick Kiesler and Bernard Rudofsky in their quasi-surrealist, quasi-anti-architectural revolt against universalism. (viii–ix)

Marinetti brings to the stage an excess of expression, a quasi-Futurist revolt against universalism in architectural forms. Although this piece was never staged, we find some similarities with contemporary constructed architectures, in which oblique, not orthogonal, algorithmically generated surfaces reshape and redesign, in part, coastal harbors. But this concerns a more architectural context, not Futurist abstract theatricality.

Chapter 3

✦

Cities and Puzzles

Multiple and Contrasting Emotions

Of Tenderness and Tension

The texts of Italo Calvino and Georges Perec are sometimes associated in contemporary literary criticism, but this association is often made in such a way that a simple cross-reference to one author is used to shed light on the poetics of the other, on which the critic then develops a position. In fact, this association is sometimes presented in a way that transforms the shared places of the two writers into something like a common place—or, rather, these places become commonplace, trite, or taken for granted, concealing any spaces and moments of tension. In underlining the relationship between these writers, we run the risk of ignoring the singularities of each. In this chapter, I intend to bring together, starting with *Invisible Cities* and *Life A User's Manual*, some of the places, geographies, and spaces that Italo Calvino and Georges Perec have in common, juxtaposing spaces the two writers exchange and share while taking care not to cancel out their singularities.

If the question of estrangement is emblematic and inescapable in the literary criticism on Calvino,[1] for Perec, on the other hand, the question is that of the *infra-ordinaire* and of the *contrainte du reel*.[2] I will try, beginning with these two poles (estrangement and *infra-ordinaire*), to demonstrate the connections and the disjunctions in how the two authors articulate and dislocate space and imaginary geography. The texts I will discuss insist on geographies not merely imaginary but also interdisciplinary, geographies that are at work in the specific elaborations of the two authors, shared and contended for in a multiplicity of interconnected spaces that are never made whole.

There are many common spaces and places of predilection shared by Calvino and Perec. They can be united by their critical distance from the *nouveau roman*, by their interest in and ironic stance toward travel literature (J. J. Grandville, Jules Verne, up to Michel Butor), and finally, certainly, by their membership in the Oulipo (*Ou*vroir de *Li*ttérature *Po*tentielle).[3] An example in the realm of geography is the title of the Oulipo's second collection, *Atlas de littérature potentielle* (1981),[4] which was suggested by Calvino. Pieces of work in progress by Calvino and Perec and many members of the Oulipo appear in this collection. The words "atlas" and "potential" are placed together and in relation to literature, which means that we are dealing with a collection of literature and with geographical maps not yet drawn, with atlases and literatures to come, yet to be discovered by the emotions.

Giuliana Bruno, in *Atlas of Emotion*,[5] develops an interdisciplinary research project at the heart of which she places *La Carte du Pays du Tendre* (1654), a map designed by Madeleine de Scudéry to accompany her novel *Clélie*. Bruno proposes this text as inaugural of a new genre of narrative in which geography is not a cold scientific discipline but rather is in a relationship with psychology and emotion; the voyage and the open space of the map open paths to narrative, in a movement both real and emotional, in the relationship between image and text. The map incarnates a narrative voyage for which, writes Bruno, "it visualizes, in the form of the landscape, an itinerary of emotions which is, in turn, the topos of the novel" (2). On the subject of *tendre* or tenderness, the author reminds us that this word in romance languages recalls, if not a romantic attachment, at least an affectionate tie between people. Still today in common speech one says *il y a du tendre* when speaking of a budding romance. In nearly opposite ways, the texts I analyze are pervaded by this emotive connotation of the map, and furthermore, as we will see, *il y a du tendre*, there is tenderness between these texts. Or to express it another way, the texts of Calvino and Perec that I consider deal with spaces and geographies brought near to each other eccentrically. On one hand is Calvino, with the glare of cities both potential and surreal, and on the other hand Perec, who plays at blowing up maps and their universes of sense, yet both touch on themes that, thanks to the elaboration and construction of the narrative space, lose their analytical coldness.

Nevertheless, if there is tenderness, geo-graphical tenderness, between the texts, there is also tension, the tension between singularity and the complexity of the modern metropolis, a tension not unlike that which Walter Benjamin describes in his unfinished *Arcades Project*. It will become clear that certain tensions described by Benjamin—such as those between the collector and the *flâneur*, between the inside and the outside, between the public and the private—set off sparks in a determining way when we compare *Invisible Cities* and *Life A User's Manual*. In comparing them, I will show the strong echo of tension inherent in modernity, as described by Benjamin, in which the city becomes an ambiguous space between a room and a landscape. Regarding the experience of the *flâneur*, Benjamin writes: "Landscape—that, in fact, is what Paris becomes for the *flâneur*. Or, more precisely: the city splits for him into its dialectical poles. It opens up to him as a landscape, even as it closes around him as a room."[6] Benjamin develops a mode of thought in which the vast open space of the landscape or the metropolis and the closed space of a room are confused, or, rather, alter and alternate with each other; such an interchange takes place between the texts of Calvino and Perec. For Calvino, space is a well-defined cartography that is placed in check by the singularity of each city; in Perec, space is a puzzle of rooms across which we see mimicked the attempt to contain, delimit, and close off the other and the elsewhere. My reading therefore concentrates on grasping the strong bond between the two authors, paying close attention to the tension that brings to extremes the outside in Calvino and the inside in Perec, while also keeping close to the rhythm and dialectic of modernity as indicated by Benjamin. I will exhibit common spaces and places of the two authors, so as to place in evidence the tenderness and the tension inherent in the singularity of their texts, texts that are at once mirrors and mirages of their times.

Italo Calvino and *Invisible Cities*: Dialogical and Descriptive Illuminations

> Calvino had been unusually thrilled to recount his recent experiences in Spain: he had spoken at the Menéndez Pelayo International University about fantastic literature and had then gone to watch the *encierro* of a bullfighter. . . . Calvino relived without reserve the deception of the Andalusian crowd, all the apparent thrills and ill-concealed interior torments. He did not interrogate the causes, recondite or near, of that theatrical hesitation of a people otherwise sensible and even attracted by the flashy proofs of modern power. . . . He spoke as if he were about to refer to an event, or about to illustrate a toponymic map on which not all the strategic points, the troughs, the plains, or the deserts were indicated. (J. L. Borges, "L'ultima volta che ho visto Calvino," *L'Unità*, September 20, 1985)

> My work as a writer has from the beginning aimed at tracing the lightning flashes of the mental circuits that capture and link points distant from each other in space and time. In my love of adventure stories and fairytales, I have always searched for the equivalent of some inner energy, some motion of the mind. I have always aimed at the image and the motion that arises naturally from the image, while still being aware that one cannot speak of literary result until this stream of imagination has been turned into words. (I. Calvino, *Six Memos for the Next Millennium*, 48)

Themes of travel and the map are two of the main foci of Calvino's poetics. For example, in drafting *Invisible Cities*, Calvino was interested in the map as plot, the tracing of a route, *in fieri*, and also as the opening of a landscape and a way of giving the coordinates of a new landscape that has just begun to make itself known. In "Com'era nuovo il Nuovo Mondo" (How new the new world was),[7] Calvino, referring to the discovery of America, writes, "How new the world was, discovering the New World was a difficult undertaking, as we all learned" (417), and he adds that it was even more difficult to see that new world and to understand that it was new. The map, or the chart, implies also the act of mapping, as design and outline of the already known. In "Il viandante nella mappa" (The wayfarer in the map),[8] Calvino writes that "the initial need to fix places on a map is linked to the voyage: it is the memorandum of the succession of stages, the tracing of a route" (426) and adds that a map always presupposes an idea of an itinerary and of a narrative. Calvino is fascinated by the map both as the possibility of an outline and selection and as a metaphor of the invitation to enter into the new.[9] In this essay, which moves quickly from one century to another, Calvino contrasts Opinicus de Canistris, a fourteenth-century priest who projected "his own interior world on the map of earth and of the seas," with the "society of the 'precious' in the seventeenth century that sought to represent psychology according to the code of geographic maps: the 'map of the tenderness' devised by Madeleine de Scudéry in which a lake is Indifference, a rock is Ambition, and so on" (433).

At the end of this brief essay, Calvino points out that the extensive topography of psychology as in Madeleine De Scudéry, which "indicates relationships of distance and perspective between passions projected on a uniform extension," is then replaced in Freud with "a more vertical tension, a psychology of depth, and of overlapping strata" (433). There is thus a tension in Calvino's text between an extensive psychological space and a more intensive one, formed by superimposed layers.[10]

These occasional essays, written by Calvino in the 1980s and later collected under the evocative title *Collection of Sand*, are preceded by many other essays that insist on a reading of literature in graphical and spatial terms. From the well-known question of the labyrinth, which begins to pervade Calvino's writing from as early as the 1960s, to certain titles such as "Definitions of Territories: Comedy," "Definitions of Territories: Eroticism," and "Definitions of Territories: Fantasy," the theme of territory leads us astray, causes us to make a detour, in the sense that, in each case, Calvino tends not to propose borders and barriers but rather to provoke them critically and deconstruct them.

Invisible Cities, published in 1972, insists on space and geography as hidden and apocryphal territories. In an essay on the Canadian critic Northrop Frye, "La letteratura come proiezione del desiderio" (Literature as projection of desire),[11] Calvino postulates a relationship between society's repressed desires as transferred in literature and texts he calls "hidden" or "apocryphal."

Desire, Calvino claims, paraphrasing Frye, turns out to be the social equivalent of emotion at the literal level, or rather, an impulse toward expression that can only take place through poetry. Calvino schematizes and updates

Frye's intention: "The reference to the element of desire, which in literature finds forms that enable it to project itself beyond the obstacles met on its way, seems to me extremely topical, based as it is on the unlivable situation of the present and the drive toward the project of a desirable society" (52). In this essay, Frye's position results in an overly "teleological" tone; Calvino focuses on his maniacal and insistent desire to supply schemas and sieves through which nothing can escape and for which we would need "a play of mirrors through which each work refracts the entire encyclopedia of human civilization" (58). To express this methodical insistence more adequately, Calvino contrasts it with the critical choices of Tzvetan Todorov (in "La quête du récit"), which, on the contrary, "closes the work in on itself, without leaving any windows to look out of and, indeed, by his very method rules out the existence of an 'out-of-doors' to be looked at" (58). Precisely in regard to this relationship between the inside and the outside of a text, Calvino affirms his choice of a critical analysis and a literature that, "by exploring the 'indoors' of the text and going deeper and deeper in its centripetal movement, succeeds in opening up some unexpected glimpses of that 'out-of-doors'" (58). Calvino returns to Frye's obsession with the encyclopedic and the archetypal but reiterates his idea of literature as a relationship among a multiplicity of works, in which the books are divided according to periods and interpretative traditions of the "canonical" and "apocryphal." Calvino's ideal library is hidden or yet to come, and his idea of literature is the search for the book hidden far away: "It is the pull toward the new apocryphal text still to be rediscovered or invented" (61).

Invisible Cities[12] is a geography of tensions between inside and outside, between the new and the past, between the fantastic and the real, between the invisible and the unlivable, but perhaps they all speak of the "hidden" and "apocryphal" city. There is a synoptic and holistic perspective on *Invisible Cities* in the form of the table of contents, the logic of which the critic Claudio Milanini skillfully displays. Following some handwritten notes by Calvino and the text's own table of contents, Milanini proposes a diagram of the network of the fifty-five invisible cities. Milanini's lucid interpretation is worth quoting in full:

> Elucidations more or less fitting were successively provided by the critics. Some made use of metrical metaphors, like Pier Vincenzo Menegaldo, who spoke of "seven stanzas of sestinas framed by two double sestinas." Others resorted to tables and diagrams. Proceeding with this latter course in our own turn, we propose a graphic that seems to have the benefit of both fidelity and immediate evidence: a skewed and downwardly sloped chessboard with square cells, each of which correspond to one of the fifty-five paragraphs. The halved squares, or rectangles on the borders, indicate the eighteen extracts—of a prevalently dialogic nature—that serve as introduction

> and conclusion in every chapter . . . If we go over this scheme as we would in a normal reading (line after line, from left to right), we would arrive at a sequence which is the same as that suggested by the continuing progression of the pages. However, if we go over it rather from top to bottom, and then from left to right (skipping the frames), we will discover the paragraphs ordered into neat columns that compose the eleven rubrics.[13]

These cities are related to each other through a diagrammatic scheme; in their multiplicity, they are woven together into a well-built and clearly mapped tapestry. Yet this is merely one method of reading the text. It is certainly not the only one. If we move forward in the exploration of these cities, we find them to be readable, certainly, but in a manner quite different from the legibility and "imageability" proposed in 1960 by the city planner Kevin Lynch, and we immediately begin to distance ourselves from a stabilizing and totalizing concept of mapping.[14]

Before embarking on the adventures of the individual cities, I would like to bring together the different dialogues between Marco Polo and Kublai Khan, to see how the new and the foreign are negotiated between the two and how the importance of the map changes throughout the course of the book.[15] The italics, the places where we find the dialogues between Marco and Kublai, theatrical and placed into an abstract set, begin by emphasizing that the most important thing for Kublai is not believing everything this ambassador tells him but rather listening to the tale. The passages in italics tell of a relationship between the two, in which Marco, who has yet to learn the emperor's language, at first communicates through pantomime, using leaps in the air, "*exclamations, . . . ramified and leafy discourses, metaphors and tropes*" (38). Then, with the passing of time, Kublai and Marco are able to communicate with each other; at times, they understand each other best in moments of silence.[16] When the emperor begins to understand that "*Marco Polo's cities resembled one another, as if the passage from one to another involved not a journey but a change of elements*" (43), he too begins to want to describe the cities and to ask Marco if he recognizes them. In this way the emperor begins his descriptions of the dreamt cities, and the dialogue with Marco becomes almost a psychoanalytic task, which gives us concise profiles of the desires and fears on each of their minds. As time passes, the relationships between past, present, and future and between the real and the imaginary become an interrupted exchange, to which each brings pieces of the mosaic (73). Their dialogue becomes increasingly more abstract until it takes place in a confrontation on a chess board, on which a variety of differentiated things (canals, princely palaces, market squares, island gardens) are given shape and formalized (85–87). At times, Kublai accuses Marco of feigning, and despite the abstractness of the scene their exchange finds itself in motion with improvised theatrical moments, as when Kublai "*had Marco with his back to the wall, attacking him, putting a knee on his chest, seizing him by the beard: 'This is what I wanted to hear from you: confess what you are smuggling: moods, states of grace, elegies!'*" (98). It is only in the last two dialogues/meetings that they speak of the Khan's atlas. The exchange between Marco and Kublai, which at any rate remains in parts, is also interrupted, according to the general outline of the text, by the descriptions of the various cities. Kublai wishes to come to know his empire by studying his atlases at Marco's side; Marco, on the other hand, wishes to escape from the premapped with stories of one who has visited and experienced, even if briefly, every single city. The result of their interaction is a complex intersection of spaces mapped, told, and/or experienced. Between Kublai and Marco, as with the construction and articulation of the invisible cities, two impulses alternate: on the one hand the need to schematize with a map, on the other hand the desire to know different spaces, which present themselves as an outside yet to be lived or read by one who is still searching; they activate a colportage of space and of stories.

Many of the descriptions of the cities begin by transmitting a sense of movement, often by using a gerund or a verb of actual movement. Take the very first city, Diomira, which begins with a gerund and movement of detachment: "Leaving there and proceeding for three days toward the east, you reach Diomira" (7). Then comes Isidora: "When a man rides a long time through wild regions he feels the desire for a city. Finally he comes to Isidora" (8). This sense of movement and a tendency toward the not yet known introduce the reader to each city; once inside a city, though, the reader is forced to stop in his or her tracks, and it is in this way that, reading, we see the city as an image burnt onto closed eyelids, at a kind of standstill. Yet this steadiness of the image simultaneously contrasts with the sense of change and iridescence to which each city exposes the reader. We see, read of, and move about Sophronia, part amusement park, part ephemeral city:

> The city of Sophronia is made up of two half-cities. In one there is the great roller coaster with its steep humps, the carousel with its chain spokes, the Ferris wheel of spinning cages, the death-ride with crouching motorcyclists, the big top with the clump of trapezes hanging in the middle. The other half-city is of stone and marble and cement, with the bank, the factories, the palaces, the slaughterhouse, the school, and all the rest. One of the half-cities is permanent, the other is temporary, and when the period of its sojourn is over, they uproot it, dismantle it, and take it off, transplanting it to the vacant lots of another half-city.
>
> And so every year the day comes when the workmen remove the marble pediments, lower the stone walls, the cement pylons, take down the Ministry, the monument, the docks, the petroleum refinery, the hospital, load them on trailers, to follow from stand to stand their

> annual itinerary. Here remains the half-Sophronia of the shooting-galleries and the carousels, the shout suspended from the cart of the headlong roller coaster, and it begins to count the months, the days it must wait before the caravan returns and a complete life can begin again. (63)

Fedora stands in contrast to this provisional half-Sophronia, free and oblivious to its relationship with time. Fedora is a metropolis of stone, and in its center is a building that jealously conserves in each room a sphere containing unrealized possible models of Fedora, which have been conceived over the course of time.

> These are the forms the city could have taken if, for one reason or another, it had not become what we see today. In every age someone, looking at Fedora as it was, imagined a way of making it the ideal city, but while he constructed his miniature model, Fedora was already no longer the same as before, and what had been until yesterday a possible future became only a toy in a glass globe. (32)

At the end of the description of Fedora, Marco addresses the Khan, telling him: "On the map of your empire, O Great Khan, there must be room both for the big, stone Fedora and the little Fedoras in glass globes. Not because they are all equally real, but because all are only assumptions. The one contains what is accepted as necessary when it is not yet so; the others, what is imagined as possible and, a moment later, is possible no longer" (32–33). The little Fedoras contrast the archontic position of the big Fedora, and the logic that springs from them points toward the possible and the variable, which cannot be contained by or in the one big Fedora.

These descriptions push themselves toward the limits of impossibility; they move us into the "territory of the fantastic," if not into that of contradiction or contraposition of the ordinary and the known. Like Marco Polo, who emphasizes in his *Travels of Marco Polo* things that in his time were unknown, Calvino's Marco gives us details that are hardly adapted to the description of a city. Take, for example, Dorothea, which Marco says can be spoken of in two ways. The first is a strange spatial assembly of the separate parts and the relationships that exist among the people who live there; the second is the way in which a foreign camel driver remembers his initial arrival in the city (9). Or perhaps Armilla, which has none of the elements needed to compose a city except for the forest of water pipes.

> At any hour, raising your eyes among the pipes, you are likely to glimpse a young woman, or many young women, slender, not tall of stature, luxuriating in the bathtubs or arching their backs under the showers suspended in the void, washing or drying or perfuming

> themselves, or combing their long hair at a mirror. In the sun, the threads of water fanning from the showers glisten, the jets of the taps, the spurts, the splashes, the sponges' suds. (49)

Armilla is made by the subtraction of all the elements except that of cool spurts of water, while in Zaira each architectural element signifies a moment of the city's past. Marco says: "In vain, great-hearted Kublai, shall I attempt to describe Zaira, city of high bastions. I could tell you how many steps make up the streets rising like stairways. . . . The city does not consist of this, but of relationships between the measurements of its space and the events of its past" (10).

Consider, for example, the stories the old people tell one another while sitting on a dock, in which each part of the city remains in relationship with the different stories that have taken place; natural, relational, and constructed aspects of the city interpenetrate:

> . . . the rips in the fish net and the three old men seated on the dock mending nets and telling each other for the hundredth time the story of the gunboat of the usurper, who some say was the queen's illegitimate son, abandoned in his swaddling clothes there on the dock.
>
> As this wave from the memories flows in, the city soaks it up like a sponge and expands. (10)

We understand the relationships that make up many of these cities, yet we are obliged each time to reopen spaces of sense in order to orient ourselves; everything seems to point toward the external, the outward appearance, but in reality each city immediately transforms itself into a secret, into something as complex as it is hidden. In *reality*, we know very little about each city. We are given merely flashes of each city; afterward it may be up to us to find, imagine, or invent other connections. In the descriptions of the various elements that make up the cities, a fantastic prefiguration is at work, never lacking in irony, for which opposite pairs, such as innovation/repetition, east/west,[17] melancholy/euphoria, or movement/stasis, frequently spring and leap, as do architectural and typological determinations, such as primary and secondary, work and ornament, tending to obey a sort of interior logic unique to each city rather than an abstract treatise of architecture. The methods of estrangement and deformation of the Russian Formalists enter into the very heart of elaboration of the form and content of the text.

In fact, Calvino also plays with the idea of construction as proposed by the Russian Formalists, which he uses allegorically to describe the simultaneous fabrication of the text and the vision of each city, with a knowing and virtuoso use of language, rhythm, and phonetic construction. The prose is articulated on the basis of a dynamic and polysemous principle of construction like that espoused by the Russian Formalists. The Russian Formalist

Yuri Tynianov writes in "The Concept of 'Construction' ": "This dynamism reveals itself firstly in the concept of the constructive principle. Not all factors of a word are equivalent. Dynamic form is not generated by means of combination or merger (the often-used concept of 'correspondence'), but by means of interaction, and, consequently, the pushing forward of one group of factors at the expense of another."[18] In *Invisible Cities*, the concept of construction is incessantly reiterated and experimented with; construction pervades the entire text, thereby exceeding the idea of city and metropolis and also precluding a comprehensive methodology that could encapsulate and subsume it; it is a quest for architecturability.

In this way, *Invisible Cities* incites the reader to await further cities as much as to discover already-known cities. Each city has its own internal logic and dynamically distances itself from the other cities, to which it nevertheless binds itself, through the effects of reiteration and subtraction of elements.[19] The architectural space is described each time with details that become determining, and also, in a defamiliarizing way, the description learns from and plays a bit with the will to teach the clear methodology for looking at architecture that the architectural historian and critic Bruno Zevi presented in 1948 in his *Architecture as Space: How to Look at Architecture*.[20] The visionary ability of Calvino's writing transports us to a reading that becomes a three-dimensional image[21] in which we almost seem to hold in our hands not typeset pages but the travel journal of an architect and in which we feel ourselves in front of if not inside a maquette, like a scene from *Alice in Wonderland*. The fact that Calvino does not take the exterior for granted is closely related, if in an estranging way, to his search for form, for the describable, for the portrayable. In the invisible cities we find articulated a multiform space and cities of *n* dimensions, which echo the graphical dimensions of the artist Saul Steinberg, whom Calvino greatly admires. With his drawings, writes Calvino, Steinberg allows one "to move in a space of limitless *n* dimensions of the drawn and the drawable, to establish communication between the most contradictory stylistic universes, to make elements belonging to divergent figurative cultures or conventions of perception coexist within the horizon of the same page."[22] The reflection on form and style is fundamental for Calvino, and he finds it also in the New York graphic artist; in Steinberg's drawings, the reflection on forms, connected to hypotheses of visual formalization, is at the same time "criticism of the permanent world's fair in which we are involved, playing the triple role of exhibitors, exhibits, and audience" (296). Thus, for Calvino, exposing and being exposed stand in relation to one another and interact in his writings with the theme of travel and adventure. Calvino, through multidimensional language, through language that explains and exposes itself, truly smuggles states of mind from architecture to imaginary geography and back again: this in turn encourages the readers to expand or reinvent the interdisciplinary maps.

Architectures as Mass Media and Supercities in an Interdisciplinary Geography

> With the Industrial Revolution, philosophy, literature, and art have experienced a trauma from which they have not yet recovered. . . . We may say that if up until this point [the moment exemplified by Émile Zola in Calvino's text] the antithetical term to the unpoetic-inhumanity of advanced industry was sought in a previous humanistic conception, or better yet, in an image of the naturalistic-humanitarian world in which one tried to incorporate industrial reality as well, then from this point on one moves toward the adoption—Cubism, Futurism—of a new antithetical term, that is to say, the image of an industrial future that has rediscovered beauty and moral significance, not those of the past, but different ones; an image which has found—which has expressed—a style. (Italo Calvino, "La sfida al labirinto," *Saggi*, vol. 1, 111–12)

So far, I have considered some of the continually abstract and estranged relationships between geography and space, between architecture and the city; a further step must be taken in order to fully understand and "localize," in this multifarious abstraction, the *interdisciplinary geography* that communicates with Calvino's time and pervades this text.

Invisible Cities is in an unstable relationship with a previous project of Calvino's, of which it is a reworking. The critics most attentive to the Calvinian oeuvre have underlined the affinities and differences between *Invisible Cities* and the unfinished cinema project of *Il Milione* (chronicling the adventures of Marco Polo in the Orient) that Calvino worked on in the 1960s.[23] The critic Marina Zancan underlines the continuity between the two texts for their relationship with the elsewhere and with travel, and she notes that *Invisible Cities* is also a response to a conversation through time with *Cities of the World* by Elio Vittorini.[24] Bruno Falcetto, on the other hand, points out that the emotive tone of *Invisible Cities* is considerably more melancholic and that the experience of a youthful Marco is replaced by an experience of shadows and ashes.[25] Yet if one considers Calvino's perpetual search for prefiguration, and a possible "inheritance," albeit a dislocated one, from Vittorini as an avant-garde interdisciplinary figure,[26] could one not read *Invisible Cities* as a response to a totalizing criticism like that of the critical school of Venice in the 1970s and after?[27] In the fourth dialogue Kublai spends an entire day asking Marco to tell him again and again about his embassies in the various cities.

> *But this time Kublai seemed unwilling to give in to weariness. "Tell me another city," he insisted.*
>
> *". . . You leave there and ride for three days between the northeast and east-by-northeast winds . . ." Marco resumed saying, enumerating*

names and customs and wares of a great number of lands. His repertory could be called inexhaustible, but now he was the one who had to give in. Dawn had broken when he said: "Sire, now I have told you about all the cities I know."

"There is still one of which you never speak."

Marco Polo bowed his head.

"Venice," the Khan said.

Marco smiled. "What else do you believe I have been talking to you about?" (86)

Marco explains to the Khan that Venice is always implicated in the descriptions of the other cities.

And Polo said: "Every time I describe a city I am saying something about Venice."

"When I ask you about other cities, I want to hear about them. And about Venice, when I ask you about Venice."

"To distinguish the other cities' qualities, I must speak of a first city that remains implicit. For me it is Venice." (86)

In my interpretive hypothesis, which moves between fiction and theory, between fiction and "reality," Venice and the school of Venice remain implicated, involved, perhaps even as resistance. "Venice" remains implicated in the "other cities." By "Venice," I mean the almost abstract Venice, one that challenges projects like rational and totalizing theories.

This interpretation brings us back to the question of modernity and to the singular way in which Calvino listens to the "methodological" tone and style of Walter Benjamin.[28] It is well known that during the time Calvino wrote *Invisible Cities* Walter Benjamin's texts were already being circulated and discussed in Italy and France. Calvino participates in this dialogue in a more or less silent way, but always, I think, with awareness.[29]

The relationship between Kublai Khan and Marco makes reference to a relationship between movement and stasis, and Marco's stories repeatedly bring the reader back to the implied question, perhaps to the *doute absolu* and the *écart absolu*,[30] whether or not Marco has really traveled in and experienced these cities. Has Marco really traveled? Or are his tales merely the fruit of a storyteller's imagination? The succession of the cities, which is also a succession of images of the city, perhaps of a single city (Venice) presented from different perspectives, strongly recalls the experience of modernity as read by Benjamin in his *Arcades Project*.[31] Each city can be seen as at a *standstill*, a discrete and transitory image, an "arrêt sur image."[32] The Kublai/Marco couple then ends up grafting Benjamin's unfinished text onto Calvino's *Six Memos for the Next Millennium*, producing a strange and discrete flâneur for the next millennium. If the hypothesis of the graft holds, then

Calvino's work is a singular retake of the Benjaminian thematics[33] quite different from that of Manfredo Tafuri, influential historian and architectural critic of the Venice School. Writing in the same period, Tafuri observes, "Despite the acuteness of Benjamin's observations, neither in his essays on Baudelaire nor in 'Das Kunstwerk im Zeitalter seiner technischen Reproduzierbarkeit' does he relate this invasion of the ways of production in the urban morphology to the response of the avant-garde movements to the subject of the city."[34]

Tafuri implies in this passage, and later in the same chapter, that Benjamin did not understand how the avant-gardes were operating, how they based their practices in a new way of experiencing in modernity (an experiencing related to speed, simultaneity, and eclecticism, to mention only a few aspects that Tafuri considers). Tafuri does not bring to its extreme consequences the temporality intrinsic in Benjamin's reading, the rhythm of which attempts to indicate the unexpected explosion that resulted from new technologies and new means of production. One could say that Tafuri does not want to engage with an allegorical dimension that for Benjamin emerges as the past in the form of a divided present.[35] Calvino clearly seems to know something of Benjamin's writings and to have worked them out in a way quite different from Tafuri. The search for prefiguration in *Invisible Cities* does not halt with what exists but insists on the construction, and the construction of construction, of cities that refer to the invisible. Calvino does not create architecture but, instead, wants to facilitate a mental space for architecture, as a complex and ludic thought, as architecturability. He draws near to the Futurist notion of the invisible, but he does not make war, and he leaves open spaces for possibility, for change, and for a transformation in the singular negotiations between invention and reality.[36] The architectures of paper and of passage in *Invisible Cities* are in a provisional relationship with the *mass-mediauras* that Samuel Weber finds in certain of Benjamin's texts:[37] the architectures of the invisible cities are mass-mediauric architectures, and like lightning and shadows they themselves become media. A possible selective rereading by Calvino of the *Arcades Project* implied in *Invisible Cities* can be related to what the architectural critic Renato De Fusco opened up as a field of research, starting with his 1967 essay *Architettura come Mass Medium*.[38] De Fusco was one of the first Italian architectural critics of the 1970s to be attentive to phenomena other than functional architecture, and he thus opened up the interdisciplinary debate between architecture, semiology, and esthetics from Pop Art to utopian architecture. Significantly, in his writings De Fusco takes into consideration the most effervescent examples, from the American firm Venturi and Rauch to the pop culture cross-pollination with architecture, up to alternative counterdesign projects that stirred international debate at that time, what has been called the Radicals, and he also considers experimental Italian groups like Superstudio and Archizoom. Through highly evocative allegorical short films, collages, drawings, and writings, these groups reawakened and estranged the architectural practice; the possibility of the architectural practice was questioned in relation to mass production, economy, and technology.

No-Stop City, in which the relationship between the habitable and the uninhabitable, between consumer society and urbanism, between new technologies and lived spaces is graphically and architectonically interrogated, is one of the experimentations of the group Archizoom, and perhaps it is not by chance that only a few months later we find "le città continue" in *Invisible Cities*.

A description of Esmeralda, one of the series of "trading cities," follows the dialogue of Kublai and Marco about Venice. Esmeralda is created in an intricate and rhythmic cadence: "The network of routes is not arranged on one level, but follows instead an up-and-down course of steps, landings, cambered bridges, hanging streets. Combining segments of the various routes, elevated or on ground level, each inhabitant can enjoy every day the pleasure of a new itinerary to reach the same places. The most fixed and calm lives in Esmeralda are spent without any repetition" (88). But there are other trajectories, secret and adventurous roads, for example that of the cats and thieves who "move along higher, discontinuous ways" and "the routes of the swallows, who cut the air over the roofs, dropping long invisible parabolas with their still wings, darting to gulp a mosquito, spiraling upward, grazing a pinnacle, dominating from every point of their airy paths all the points of the city" (88). A map of all this would certainly require attention, for the complicated and multifarious Esmeralda is an allegory of stylization of the excess of directions and also of the theme of network and cartography. In considering this city, it is interesting to recall a very brief essay in which Calvino speaks of Supervenices, "Venice: Archetype and Utopia of the Aquatic City" (Venezia: archetipo e upopia della città acquatica).[39] Here Venice is captured in a vortex of skillful writing and inventive description, which seems a possible "*modello immaginario*" for escaping the crisis brought on by reflections on the metropolis and for inciting experimentation in the avant-garde and neo-avant-garde.

> One thing Venice shall not lose: the fact of being unique in its genre. The world will fill up with Venices, or rather Supervenices, in which multiple grids of various heights will overlap and enlace: navigable canals, paths and canals for hovercraft, underground or underwater or elevated railways, paths for bicycles, lanes for camels and horses, hanging gardens and pedestrian bridges, aerial cableways. Naturally vertical traffic will have similar extension and variety through elevators, helicopters, cranes, emergency ladders attached to the roofs of taxis or on watercraft of various types. (2692)[40]

Like all of the invisible cities, Supervenices is a stylized hybridization (or grafting), referring a bit to a city of exchanges, a bit to a city of the memory, a bit to a continuous city. The name Supervenices evokes a silent reference, both sententious and playful, to a group of experimental Italian architects of that period: Superstudio. Superstudio is one of the groups presented in the New York Museum of Modern Art (MoMA) exhibition *Italy: The New Domestic Landscape*, which I discuss in some detail in later chapters.[41] For now it suffices to note that in the videos, the collages, and the paper architecture of Superstudio, as in *Invisible Cities*, we find at work an estranging and reversible alternation between miniaturization and large dimensions, between high and low, in which the reflected architecture becomes a motif of invention; the necessity of thinking of the new relationship between large and small, between micro and macro, was also expressed by Andrea Branzi, one of the key figures of Radical Architecture, and was later taken up and rearticulated by Rem Koolhaas in *S,M,L,XL*.[42]

To conclude this interdisciplinary reading, I want to return through Lalage, a city that grows in lightness, and Octavia, spiderweb city. In the third dialogue Kublai tells Marco that he has had a dream.

> *"I shall tell you what I dreamed last night," he says to Marco. "In the midst of a flat and yellow land, dotted with meteorites and erratic boulders, I saw from a distance the spires of a city rise, slender pinnacles, made in such a way that the moon in her journey can rest now on one, now on another, or sway from the cables of the cranes."*
>
> *And Polo says: "The city of your dream is Lalage. Its inhabitants arranged these invitations to rest in the night sky so that the moon would grant everything in the city the power to grow and grow endlessly."*
>
> *"There is something you do not know," the Khan adds. "The grateful moon has granted the city of Lalage a rarer privilege: to grow in lightness."* (74)

Lalage is a dreamt city, and its inhabitants did not destroy the "chiaro di Luna." For the respect received, the moon has given the city a "rarest privilege [*privilegio più raro*]": to grow in lightness. Here there is a clear opposition to the Futurist manifesto "Let's Murder the Moonshine!," because of the possibility of bringing together melancholy and lightness in the same stroke. Or perhaps, considering that the lunar landing took place at that time, should we add that Calvino is indicating another new take on the moon? After Lalage follows the fifth thin city, Octavia:

> If you choose to believe me, good. Now I will tell how Octavia, the spider-web city, is made. There is a precipice between two steep mountains: the city is over the void, bound to the two crests with ropes and chains and catwalks. You walk on the little wooden ties, careful not to set your foot in the open spaces, or you cling to the hempen strands. Below there is nothing for hundreds and hundreds

> of feet: a few clouds glide past; farther down you can glimpse the chasm's bed.
>
> This is the foundation of the city: a net that serves as passage and as support. All the rest, instead of rising up, is hung below: rope ladders, hammocks, houses made like sacks, clothes hangers, terraces like gondolas, skins of water, gas jets, spits, baskets on strings, dumbwaiters, showers, trapezes and rings for children's games, cable cars, chandeliers, pots with trailing plants.
>
> Suspended over the abyss, the life of Octavia's inhabitants is less uncertain than in other cities. They know the net will last only so long. (75)

Octavia, which is preceded by a dream of a city that grows in lightness, is an ironical *soft city*.[43] *Invisible Cities* is also declined in the plural, as compared to the Invisible City of which Lewis Mumford speaks in the last paragraph of his *City in History*.[44] Mumford writes of the reorganization of the metropolitan complex "that derives from the de-materialization, or etherialization, of existing institutions," which he says "has already partly created the Invisible City" (563). Octavia has a singular logic, like the other cities, which are invisible cities in the plural, and not, in fact, the "Invisible City." According to this logic, the small and the large, the local and the global, the visible and the invisible, the flux and the network (or grid) lead to a necessary reconsideration of the relationships and the communications between the parts that make up the city. Mumford writes, "The electric grid, not the stone age container, provides the new image of the invisible city and the many processes it serves and furthers. It is not merely the pattern of the city itself, but every institution, organization, and association composing the city, that will be transformed by this development" (567). Calvino speaks to us in plural terms in relation to the invisible, and he is certainly not taken by the rage of the Dea Cibernetica (of which Mumford speaks), just as he is not taken by network fever. In his article "Network Fever," architectural critic Mark Wigley studies certain trends of these same years, which saw architectural planning ground itself on the strategy of network construction, a more recent version of the grid.[45] *Invisible Cities* dislocate and disarticulate any fixed relation; they ask us through the brevity of their descriptions to think of the reversibility implicit in the modernity that Baudelaire captured in his poetics and that Calvino remakes in an estranged and e-motive update.

The invisible cities are *multi-pli-cities*, multiplicities, "places" of experimentation and confrontation with other disciplines and with contemporaneity, in which many motifs of modernity and thus of our time are interrogated and invoked and implicated and set into the skillful and virtuoso Calvinian narrative. Here resides the contested and often criticized "lightness" of Calvino.

Thus the relationship between geography and city, between architecture and the media, must be rethought, and in this role we find Calvino, multiple and sometimes sybilline but constantly listening to his time and to modernity *at large*. My reading thus dramatically departs from that of Robert Dombroski in "Italo Calvino's *Invisible Cities* and Architecture."[46] My brief reading of the disoriented and interdisciplinary "horizons" in *Invisible Cities* should evoke a Calvino entirely different from Dombroski's: in Dombroski's words, Calvino "chooses architecture or city building as his postmodern paradigm. He understands that building implies a sense of optimism about the ideas of closure and unity that normally tend to be undercut by reason" (183). For Dombroski, Marco and Kublai are two separate individuals, while in my reading, they are superimposed and can be considered one in two, or two in one. As for the rest of *Invisible Cities*, all the inhabitants whose secrets and life are unknown, we are left with the task of thinking, imagining them, and perhaps thereby meeting them and listening to their storytelling; this should leave us with something to reflect on, perhaps in an allegorical way, even as it relates to the commonplaces of architecture, which is still understood by some as a closed, static, and reassuring discipline for which there is no principle of unity. Perhaps there is still the time and space for assimilating what Calvino writes, and, despite the sometimes blinding sparkle of the metropolis that still asks so much of anyone, everyone still must live, build, and discover a future there.[47]

Georges Perec's *Species of Spaces*: An Adventure of the 1970s

> "I was born . . . Rue de l'Atlas" (Georges Perec, *W, or, The Memory of Childhood*, 19)

> Instead, I think that the mass-media act as a challenge, that is to say it comes down to a chance: that the problems of writing have a chance to shed light (or to shatter) in light of the mass-media.
>
> Here the situation is different from other esthetic domains. We need not even mention architecture—which has nearly disappeared, leaving its place to urbanism—but, for example, performing arts: theater, painting. It seems to me that one can establish a fairly clear relation among techniques coming from mass-media and phenomena such as happenings or certain forms of pop art.
>
> (Text read at the colloquium "Mass-media e creazione immaginaria," *Fondazione Cini*, Venezia; G. Perec, "Ecriture et mass-media," *Preuves*, no. 202, December 1967)

In the 1960s, Georges Perec's newly published novel *Things: A Story of the Sixties* was immediately welcomed with much critical attention, not merely on the literary front but also by critics and theorists of contemporary society. Jean Baudrillard's reference to *Things* at the end of *The System of Objects*[48] stands out; for Baudrillard, the novel exemplifies the way things no longer have any symbolic value but are merely abstract signs that refer only to consumption and other empty signs. More recently, Kristin Ross gave considerable attention in *Fast Cars, Clean Bodies*[49] to Perec's novel, inserting it in a reading of postwar French society. Ross reads Georges Perec's story from a specific viewpoint that investigates and unsettles certain aspects of the modernization of French society; sociologist H. Lefebvre's elaboration of the term "everyday life," which becomes a specific key for interpreting the experience of the time, is a catalyst for many of Ross's analyses. In reference to this concept of "everyday life" Ross writes:

> Theoretical categories are not free-floating analytic devices, innocent in historical moment. If they instead find their origins in forms of experience, then the transitory importance of critical categories like "alienation" and "everyday life," or the move to the forefront of the concept of "reification" during these years, must then be another sign of the upheaval in social relations occasioned by the sudden, full-scale entry of capital into "style of life," into lived, daily, almost imperceptible rhythms. (6)

In opening another reading of selected texts of Perec, in particular *Species of Spaces* and *Life A User's Manual*, I want to shift attention from a history and adventure of the 1960s to a possible adventure of the 1970s.[50] *Species of Spaces*[51] shifts slightly (without going into completely different places) from the society of consumption and of things to what Paul Virilio and Perec called the "infra-ordinaire." As Perec wrote, "We wanted to do a sort of sociology of everyday life and one of the themes was the background noise, that is to say, what happens when nothing happens, which we called the 'infra-ordinary.' "[52] My reading moves from things to spaces (as in *Species of Spaces*, the page, the room, the neighborhood, or the city). *Species of Spaces*[53] is a hybrid book, a short book, that Perec wrote at the request of Virilio. This text should also be considered in the context of the meetings and debates that took place around *La Cause Commune*,[54] a journal in which Perec actively participated and which existed from 1972 until 1974, dedicating itself to societal problems and open to an interdisciplinary discussion among new media, sociology, philosophy, and literature. As one of the founders writes, in a rather post-1960s tone, "it was a matter of relocating 'this strange spirit of what one calls a subversive questioning' by adopting 'the eyes of man on man at ground level.' "[55] In a spoken and recorded discussion that took place in one meeting of the membership of *La Cause Commune* and is in fact called "Le grabuge," various participants in a vague way discussed what today we call globalization, as well as tensions between East, Middle East, and West. In a rather bizarre discussion, in which Virilio attempted to define completely the relationship between the image of society and the spectrum of the possible filters provided by art,[56] Perec replied that whatever these may be, even as far as the filter of globalized information, we are still dealing with the greatest of disparities: "There is not *one* society, there are millions of them" (129).

It was during the years of *La Cause Commune* that Perec wrote *Species of Spaces*. It deals, in fact, with kinds of spaces, types of simple everyday spaces that playfully insist on an interrogation of all that is nearest and most everyday. *Species of Spaces* is, on a certain level, divided chapter by chapter according to an expansive and linear logic. Or, as Perec said, it expands like the concentric circles that ripple in a pond into which one has tossed a pebble. In fact, the text begins with the space "closest" to the writer, the space of the white page, and, in a way that is fragmented yet linear as it relates to the expansive logic, goes on to speak of distant cosmic spaces in the final chapters. Space becomes written and at the same time becomes almost *infra-ordinaire* ether; one can move about in it, and one feels the differentiation of space in one's movement. In this text, space becomes a *passpartout* as Perec moves from the white sheet of the page, then delicately moves toward the space of the bed, then passes to the space of the room of *lightly* Proustian memory,[57] and circles through the various rooms of the apartment, to the space of the neighborhood, and then passes to the *infra-ordinaire* of the city and in the end even reaches uninhabitable space and the galaxies. Thus if in this text Perec follows a trajectory that departs from the small and near and arrives at the large and distant, he does so with a continuous eye for surprise and the unusual, provoking a slight unease, yet constantly invoking a playful interrogation of ordinary spaces. As Claude Burgelin wrote, this *système des espaces* "offers a 'journal' just as kaleidoscopic, unexpected and mobile as the very mobility that these spaces impose." It turns out that "the spaces find their strangeness when one obstinately questions obvious facts that let themselves dissolve before our eyes, be penetrated by words. In instants of vacillation, the familiar reveals itself as unknown and confides its part of the secret."[58]

In the premise, Perec underlines the fact that he deals with the act of writing and moving oneself within spaces both diversified and diversifying, both fragmented and fragmenting. "There isn't one space, a beautiful space, a beautiful space round about, a beautiful space all around us, there's a whole lot of small bits of spaces" (6). Perec then continues ironically with a small note on geographical and political space:

> Another—and here we suddenly enter into much more particularized spaces—originally quite modest in size, has attained fairly colossal dimensions and has become Paris. . . . Still another space, much larger and vaguely hexagonal, has been surrounded by a broad dotted line (innumerable events, some of them particularly weighty, had as their sole purpose the tracing out of this dotted line), and it has been decided that everything found *inside* this dotted line should be coloured purple and be called France, while everything found *outside*

> this dotted line should be in a different colour (although, outside the aforesaid hexagon, they weren't in the least anxious to be of a uniform colour: one bit of space wanted its colour and another bit wanted another one, whence the famous problem in topology of the four colours, unresolved to this day) and have a different name (in point of fact and for quite a few years, there was a strong insistence on colouring violet—and thereby calling France—bits of space that didn't belong to the aforesaid hexagon, but were often far distant from it, but, generally speaking, that didn't last half so well). (6)

Perec gives us this dotted minimal sketch of a map of France, in which he briefly and ironically makes a clear diachronic reference to France and its colonies, and thus to the French space (and in this sketch the limits are defined by suspension points, which for this reason leave room for the passage of, or at least an interrogation on, the borders); he then concludes the premise by pointing toward a multiple and diversified space, writing: "In short, spaces have multiplied, been broken up, and have diversified. There are spaces today of every kind and every size, for every use and every function. To live is to pass from one space to another, while doing your very best not to bump yourself" (6). Clearly, Perec is not simply offering advice not to bump oneself but is presenting a primer on space as storyteller.

The description of the various spaces pushes on in search of the possibility of being able to experience space and to say so in prose. Perec experiments with various genres, from description to degree zero, including prose, poetry, the relationship between the graphic and the written, the ordinary list of things to do or to catalogue in different spaces; each time a spatial aspect is written on the surface of the page it is interrupted by another with a different way to say it. Perec spaces things in such a way as to unsettle the ordinary in each chapter and each kind of space, insisting on a *chez-soi* made up also of doors, of places of passage, and indicating beyond the desire for a primal, nonvacillating place to start from, to refer to, to shelter in, a place that in the end, he tells us, does not exist. *Species of Spaces* concludes with these words:

> I would like there to exist places that are stable, unmoving, intangible, untouched and almost untouchable, unchanging, deep-rooted; places that might be points of reference, of departure, of origin: . . .
>
> Such places don't exist, and it's because they don't exist that space becomes a question, ceases to be self-evident, ceases to be incorporated, ceases to be appropriated. Space is a doubt: I have constantly to mark it, to designate it. It is never mine, never given to me, I have to conquer it. (91)

Among the various ways of marking (*marquer*) space, there are also several geographical maps. In fact, in addition to the map of France, other maps fill *Species of Spaces*, beginning with the strange and multiple introduction:[59] the first page of the introduction reproduces the empty *Map of the Ocean*, extracted from "The Hunting of the Snark" by Lewis Carroll. Or rather, the space of the text is marked by a beginning that reproduces a blank white map, taken from the short rhyming story by Lewis Carroll. Thus everything remains to be discovered; one must go in search of a chimera, the snark, through an ocean without horizons or points of reference. On the subject of maps and reinvented spaces, in the chapter "La page" we find an inserted didactic map on which a variety of geographical elements are represented. Of this physical map, reproduced in the *Petit Larousse Illustré*, Perec writes:

> Space as inventory, space as invention. Space begins with that model map in the old editions of the *Petit Larousse Illustré*, which used to represent something like 65 geographical terms in 60 sq. cm., miraculously brought together, deliberately abstract. Here is the desert, with its oasis, its wadi and its salt lake, here are the spring and the stream, the mountain torrent, the canal, the confluence. (13)

Thus Perec sniffs the air of his time and also gives a friendly wink to the experimentation of the Situationists, who at the end of the 1950s had already made reference to this map. The Situationists had been fascinated by this physical map, which they compared to a metropolis assembled of different buildings that presents itself in an estranging and layered way. And yet there are many differences between Perec and the Situationists, in particular in their way of thinking about psychogeographical space, which is understood and invested by the Situationists as a lived and psychic space. Perec, on the other hand, in *Species of Spaces* as in all his other writings, never allows the imagination of space to become overly invested and lived psychically or physically. Rather, he always prefers a certain distance from this emphatic tone, yet without denying the imaginary potential that space can permit: Perec is certainly aware of the potential that such a map brings with it. Like Guy Debord, who once compared it with a seascape by the Baroque painter Claude Lorrain,[60] Perec cites the didactic map and notes:

> Simulacrum of space, a simple pretext for a nomenclature. But you don't even need to close your eyes for the space evoked by these words, a dictionary space only, a paper space, to become alive, to be populated, to be filled: a long goods train drawn by a steam locomotive passes over a viaduct; barges laden with gravel ply the canals; small sailing boats manoeuvre on the lake; a big liner escorted by tugs enters the anchorage. (13–14; translation modified)

We find wedged into the text, now as explicit citations that give meaning to the page, now as memories of reading or as rewriting, citations of other authors (Jorge Luis Borges, Lewis Carroll, Michel Leiris, Jacques Roubaud, Raymond Roussel, to mention just a few); this level of the text provides us with other spatial-literary coordinates, which place the space of the book between the orienting and the disorienting, given the singularity with which each text inscribes space. Furthermore, one must indicate yet another level, that of the loose change and project ideas Perec had in stock, including *Places* and *Life A User's Manual*, which I will address shortly. Among the innumerable pleasing citations that flow from Perec's pen, perhaps the longest is that taken from one of Calvino's cosmicomics, "A sign in space." In this cosmicomic, Calvino, in a tour de force, uses the narration to shatter space understood as whole and stable, and he launches the potential and palindromic character Qfwfq, and the reader as well, into the adventure of a cosmic space, playing between possibility and the impossibility of living such an experience.[61] In this way Calvino reinvents the relationship between fiction, science, and semiotics. *Cosmicomics* is a place of experimentation with writing made fluid in cosmic space, where Calvino displaces the orientation between the comic and the cosmic. Calvino playfully places "in relationship" the infinite spaces and vast time periods of the universe with an imaginary character who in many ways is completely ordinary; Perec, on the other hand, in *Species of Spaces*, seems to take the opposite direction, attempting through a marked realism to draw near to realities, never too emphatic or emotively felt, or rather to "psychogeographies" through which he gives voice to nearby spaces and not to what he would define as the silence of the infinite spaces or of abstraction.

Perec gives a response of his own to the frequent discussion in those years on the "crisis of space." In *Species of Spaces*, space comes to be written and presented through the *infra-ordinaire* as much as through brief citations of authors in whose texts spaces played an active role.

Virilio, who had commissioned the text from Perec, published "La ville surexposée" (The overexposed city)[62] in *La Cause Commune* in 1974. His extreme thesis is well known. According to this idea, the space of the city enters into crisis starting with the massive use of new technologies, after which it passes from a physical threshold (the door and the window) to the immaterial one of the screen and the information door and control doors. This is the position on the reflection of contemporary space that in Virilio the critic will be continually intensified in texts such as *L'insécurité du territoire*, *L'écran du desert*, *L'horizon négatif*, *L'inertie polaire*; it is in relation to this perspective that Virilio speaks of writer and friend Perec:

> Moment of inertia, everything is already there in the *faux-jour* of a speed of liberation that effectively liberates us from voyages that give us the advantage of the attentive impatience of a missed meeting. Dead time, the paradoxical proximity of antipodes, of the stranger now and forever near us, the world keeps on arriving and we keep on

> waiting for it. . . . Georges Perec, the one who stands by, who plays with the measure of the space and time of words, in the absent center of a writer's study, the man scrupulous about a countdown of the history of objects and things, of the overtaken coma of places. [63]

Virilio touches on something essential in the writing of Perec—that sense of impatience felt by any reader faced with Perec's texts; we become impatient with the too-frequent delays and spatial and verbal detours, in which inertia sometimes surprises and sometimes immobilizes the reader. Leaving in the background of the reading some of these moments in the infra-ordinary adventure of the 1970s, I will now attempt to approach some of the loose change in *Life A User's Manual*, an immense building-book, in whose narration centripetal and centrifugal forces interchange. These forces exchange themselves, opening up, with brief glimpses, the immobility of an edifice to the outside; it is not by chance that this novel was defined as a Beaubourg novel, referring to the complexity of the Centre Georges Pompidou in Paris.

Life A User's Manual—Invisible Scaffolding, Rooms, and *Casse-tête*

> Paul Virilio: Let us come back to the current event that served as our starting point. A few minutes ago we talked about the problems of population displacement, of the exodus of populations. Doesn't this character, this Michel Siffre, make you think, when he suddenly says: "So there, I don't want to go anywhere else in space, I want to go somewhere else in time. I want to dissipate myself, not in surface dissipation but in a dissipation of duration. . . . We can no longer flee in space; we are going to flee in time. We are going to try to live differently, and we are going to try to disorient ourselves temporally."
>
> Georges Perec: In (his) experience, it is not so much that he deprived himself of time but that he deprived himself of others.
>
> ("Le grabuge," in Georges Perec, *Entretiens et Conférences*, vol. 1, 131)

One of the little construction sites of paper Perec refers to in *Species of Spaces* is, in fact, *Life A User's Manual*. In this building-novel the spatial relations are determined, but it is not a matter of describing something that may already be there, as in *Species of Spaces*. The space in which the text is framed is entirely mental, and in fact deals with construction articulated in relation to various *contraintes*: it does not represent a real space of Paris, even if it strongly resembles one (much as the invisible cities described by Marco are related to Venice).[64] The ordinariness of life in a Parisian building is unsettled through the constructive acrobatics that make up the novel.

In *Species of Spaces*, Perec writes: "I imagine a Parisian apartment building whose façade has been removed . . . so that all the rooms in the front, from the ground floor up to the attics, are instantly and simultaneously visible" (40). And in the same chapter he writes that one of the ideas from which the project originated came from a drawing by Saul Steinberg. "This project has multiple sources. One is a drawing by Saul Steinberg that appeared in *The Art of Living* (1952) and shows a rooming-house. . . . Part of the façade has been removed, allowing you to see the interior of some twenty-three rooms" (40–41). Afterward, Perec makes an inventory of this drawing, enumerating in great detail all of the objects present so as to emphasize the dizzying aspect created by the relationships represented in it (the absent objects—notices Perec—are the television and the radio) as in *Life A User's Manual*, which bursts with objects and relationships or nonrelationships between spaces and people. In relation to this graphic reference, it is important to remember that Calvino had written about Steinberg's drawings and had selected drawings in which he not merely underlined the intrinsic multidimensionality but also insisted on the relationship between movement and apparent movement, beginning with the graphic traces of the waves of a ship in one of Steinberg's drawings. Perec, on the other hand, selects a drawing that removes the front façade of a building, and the play of contrasts moves between the flat frontal effect of the façade (like wallpaper) and all the movement and agitation that dwell within each room.

In *Life A User's Manual*,[65] we find the story of the marvelously rich Bartlebooth,[66] who decides to give meaning to his life by studying the art of watercolor for ten years, traveling for twenty years, and making five hundred watercolors of harbors he visits. These watercolors are successively sent to Winckler, who makes them into puzzles; Bartlebooth spends another twenty years reassembling these puzzles, which are then sent to the place where they were made and dissolved in a solution that eliminates any trace of the painted watercolor. And yet the project is not completely brought to its end, because Winckler sets traps in the puzzles or because Bartlebooth becomes blind in 1972.

> If we can speak of a global failure, it is because Bartlebooth, in real terms, in concrete facts, did not manage to carry his challenge through to the end within the rules he had laid down: he wanted the whole project to come full circle without leaving a mark, like an oily sea closing over a drowning man; his aim was for nothing, nothing at all, to subsist, for nothing but the void to emerge from it, for only the immaculate whiteness of a blank to remain, only the gratuitous perfection of a project entirely devoid of utility; but though he did paint five hundred seascapes into puzzles each of seven hundred and fifty pieces, not all the puzzles were reassembled; and not all the reassembled puzzles were destroyed on the very site where the

> watercolours had been painted, roughly twenty years before. (391; translation modified)

Faced with the complexity and uselessness of life, Bartlebooth reacts by planning just such a use of it. Like the above passage, the book has many details, which compete to sketch out singular eccentric personalities, strange but also estranged, who end up, if not empty, at least far from a deep self. We know very little about Bartlebooth's travel adventures. Many geographical places, visited by Bartlebooth and by many other people, are named in the book (from postcard names such as Tunisia, regions of Africa and North and South America, and the Middle East to lesser known or smaller places, which indeed are disseminated in the novel in such a way that any stable and worldly representation is put into question), though details are always scarce.[67] But despite these worldly places everything incessantly returns to immobility and to the building on Rue Simon Crubellier; everything is framed within this building of ninety-nine rooms, as if a centripetal force brought everything back inside again and again. In chapter 72, "Basement, 3," which begins with a description of Bartlebooth's cellar, we read that he never speaks of his travels; the chapter instead narrates his mania for collecting objects once useful to him on a voyage: "Bartlebooth never talked very much about his travels, and for some years now he hasn't spoken of them at all. Smautf, for his part, quite enjoys recounting them, but his memory lets him down with increasing frequency" (346).

Not only does Bartlebooth not speak of his travels, but in fact he never talks at all, nor do most of the characters "living" in the book. While the book may speak of space, we never get the impression of spaciousness or openness (implicit in the spatial concept). Instead, when the narrated space makes reference to the extended one, it does so in a negative way; otherwise the narration takes place in the spaces of rooms, if not in the even smaller spaces of the puzzles. It is quite possible that Bartlebooth had strange and curious adventures to tell about, yet few details are given. One of the scarce times when space becomes a mysterious protagonist in adventure occurs in the description of how Winckler sets his traps with the puzzles. This space is empty enough to be invested emotionally by Bartlebooth.

> Each of Winckler's puzzles was a new, unique, and irreplaceable adventure for Bartlebooth. . . . The main problem was to stay neutral, objective, and above all flexible, that is to say free of preconceptions. But that was exactly where Gaspard Winckler laid his traps. As Bartlebooth grew more familiar with these little slivers of wood, he began to see them in specific ways, giving prominence to a particular angle, as if the pieces were being polarized, or vectorised, or were solidifying into a perceptual model which, with irresistible seductiveness, assimilated them to familiar images, familiar shapes, familiar contours: a

> hat, a fish, an amazingly accurate bird with a long tail, a long curved beak with a swelling at the base, just like one he remembered seeing in Australia; or again, it would be the exact outline of Australia, or of Africa, or of England, or of the Iberian peninsula, the heel of Italy, etc. . . . Of course the empty space no more looked like India than the piece which fitted it exactly looked like Britain: what mattered, in this instance, was that for as long as he carried on seeing a bird, a bloke, a badge, . . . he was quite unable to discover how the piece would slot into the others without being, very precisely, reversed, revolved, decentred, desymbolised: in a word, de-*formed*.
>
> Gaspard Winckler's illusions were essentially based on this principle: to oblige Bartlebooth to furnish the gaps with apparently anodine, obvious, easily named shapes . . . whilst at the same time pushing his perception of the pieces which would fit into the blanks in a completely different direction. (332–34)

Bartlebooth's obsessive relationship with the puzzle pieces points to a deforming desymbolization between the pieces of the puzzle, the shape of which can resemble a bird, a hat (perhaps seen on a particular trip), or the shape of a geographical representation; the shape of each individual piece and its referent contrast for each puzzle with the harbor depicted, which Bartlebooth must now reassemble. Winckler's sadistic illusionist game lies precisely in the collision of universes of formalization (of objects, of watercolors, of puzzles, and of geographies), so Bartlebooth emotionally invests a space with a logic according to which geography, landscapes, objects, and people enter into improbable relations of meaning. With incessant meticulousness, Perec combines the descriptions of the small spaces, those of the puzzles and of the rooms, articulating the novel and triggering the interweaving of many stories. Often from the description of a room at the beginning of a chapter, we move on into innumerable spaces visited by the protagonists of whom we have only the briefest flashes, which dissolve instantly into other places and other stories. On the other hand, when large common spaces are narrated, they are spoken of negatively, as in the glimpse of the space of the Paris of once upon a time, supplanted by the great projects of the 1970s.

When the narration opens up to global spaces, there are flashes of stories in rich oil countries, stories of unfortunate adventurers and passionate scholars, yet the experience of distant space is always interrupted and limited to a brief few pages.[68] The culmination of the negation of spaciousness is reached when the story of Bartlebooth (chapter 87) inserts itself, *malgré-lui*, into that of the great centers of nascent international tourism. One of the stories framed within the novel tells of Bartlebooth's torment by an art agent, who, having heard of his crazy project, wishes to buy the harbor paintings and put them throughout the world in luxury vacation hotels belonging to the chain Marvel Houses International, the agenda of which is defined as "the negation of space." This is a new chain of hotels created to compete with other groups of international hotels. These superluxurious hotels are conceived so as to permit the client to engage in a vast number of activities both in the hotel and outside it: "A good hotel, they believed, was one where a client can go out if he wants, and *not go out if going out is a burden for him*. Consequently, the primary characteristic of the hotels Marvel Houses International planned to build was that they would include *intra muros* everything that a demanding, wealthy, and lazy clientele could wish to see or to do without having to go outside" (423–24). Because the company's sole object is profit, it considers only geographical areas that meet three criteria:

> The first [criterion] was to find isolated sites, or sites that could easily be made isolated, offering abundant tourist facilities that were not yet fully exploited. . . . The second stratagem was to offer local, regional, and national authorities, in the places where Marvel Houses International wished to build, the full cost of constructing "culture parks," against an eighty-year concession. . . . Marvel Houses International's third stratagem was to plan to make their attractions profitable by developing—at least for the European sites, which comprised half of the total project—the possibilities for rotating features from one site to another; but this idea, initially designed only for staff (Balinese dancers, ragamuffins for the street parties, Tyrolean waitresses . . .), soon came to be applied to the equipment itself and resulted in what no doubt constituted the true originality of the entire project: the pure and simple negation of space. (424–26)

One percent of the budget has been set aside to purchase masterpieces of art, and Swiss critic Charles-Albert Beyssandre is chosen to make the acquisitions. After considering various possible artists (Klee, Morandi, Picasso, de Staël, Stella, Klein, and many others), Beyssandre comes to know of Bartlebooth's obsessive project. He attempts to purchase Bartlebooth's first works of art, which are to be destroyed, but he tries in vain.

This is a book in which the reader should *install* him- or herself, but this is difficult to do because of the continual shifts and interruptions placed in front of the stories, which are tangled together, starting with the rooms of the building. One could say that Perec makes a *détournement du détournement* of the Situationists and of the utopian idea of constructions of situations. In 1957, twenty years previously, Debord wrote on this subject in his "Report on the Construction of Situations":[69]

> Unitary urbanism is dynamic, that is, in close relation to styles of behavior. The most elementary unit of unitary urbanism is not the house, but the architectural complex, which combines all the factors conditioning an ambiance, or a series of clashing ambiances, on

> the scale of the constructed situation. The spatial development must take into account the emotional effects that the experimental city will determine. One of our comrades has advanced a theory of state-of-mind quarters according to which each quarter of a city would be designed to provoke a specific basic sentiment to which the subject would knowingly expose himself. (23)

While it's true that Perec constructs stories and situations, they imply the impossibility of fully relating with one another, always indicating an impossibility of connecting with one another in a community that would go beyond that of the big building that contains them. But perhaps the exterior space unites these stories? It would certainly seem not to, since there is really very little notion in the text of creating atmospheres and moods. We could almost say that *Life A User's Manual* presents the opposite of what Debord writes:

> The life of a person is a succession of fortuitous situations, and even if none of them is exactly the same as another the immense majority of them are so undifferentiated and so dull that they give a perfect impression of similitude. The corollary of this state of things is that the rare intensely engaging situations found in life strictly confine and limit this life. We must try to construct situations, that is to say, collective ambiances, ensembles of impressions determining the quality of a moment. (24)

The life of each character of *Life A User's Manual*, on the other hand, is made up of fortuitous meetings, and can scarcely be said to have coherence. An entire series of *détournements* is at work; internal and external spaces are constantly reconfigured and reinvented, and they always lead us to try to put together pieces of a puzzle of many stories. There is a continual *détournement* that repeatedly installs readers in a room only to displace them into another, and yet another, thus giving us a web of stories that frame one another but are at the same time separate. "The story" is a tapestry of countless stories (the secondary title is *Romans*); it is a novel Calvino cites in his *Six Memos for the Next Millennium* as a singular example of multiplicity. These stories and these lives, despite being crammed into a building, cannot be contained by it, nor are there any user's manuals for them.

These are stories that pursue, reconnect with, and interrupt one another each time a chapter concludes. Each room has the name of one of the inhabitants, which does not exclude but rather inscribes in its interior, in his or her own *chez-soi*, innumerable other characters who do not live there. One of the *contraintes* that Perec employs in moving from one room to another is the "knight's polygraph." Perec, in "Quatre figures pour *La Vie mode d'emploi*," writes: "It would have been tedious to describe the building floor by floor and apartment by apartment. But, even so, the succession of chapters could not be simply left to chance. Thus, I decided to apply a principle derived from an old problem well known to chess enthusiasts: the knight's polygraph (cf. F. Le Lionnais, *Dictionnaire des Echecs* [Paris: Presses universitaires de France, 1974], 304–305), which is a matter of moving the knight through the 64 squares of a chess board without stopping more than once on the same square."[70] As Paul A. Harris notes, the movement of the knight not only connects the spaces and allows the possibility "to touch each space, but in its irregular move, it actively alters the texture of the space it is traversing."[71] The things and their particular arrangements, like that of the rooms, become decisive for the way in which the narration moves, becoming pretexts for the narration, and though in each chapter we go beyond the space of the room, and we certainly go beyond the things in it, often the narration draws attention to particular objects, art, books, or photographs. Each object is charged with the potential to give words to the story; in this way Perec enlarges the life of each room, transporting the reader into the spaces of life, always beyond the thing and the setting, from the initial visual scene with which each chapter begins. Very often the chapters begin with a verb in the present tense to give an effect of presence, which, as soon as the story picks up, is contradicted, *detournée*, by the loose change of literary citations, memories, and stories of the past. And certainly very little is said about the future.

We read, for example, the beginning of the description of Winckler's first room (chapter 8), in which the objects and their arrangement in the room lead us to adventure stories and literary remakings that each character in the book brings there:

> Now we are in the room of Gaspard Winckler called the lounge. Of the three rooms in his flat, it is the one nearest the stairs, the furthest to the left from where we are standing. . . . It's a room in which Winckler didn't live very much. . . . It was only when he had guests whom he didn't know very well that he entertained them in his lounge. He had a round table with extension flaps that he couldn't have used very often, six straw-seated chairs, and a chest that he had carved himself with designs illustrating the principal scenes of *The Mysterious Island*: the landing of the balloon that had got away from Richmond, the miraculous finding of Cyrus Smith. (25)

Thus each chapter begins in a room that is for a moment before our eyes but then enlarges, not merely in the memory or references in the life of the inhabitant but also in brief citations or hidden or explicit references to other literary texts; the colportage of space becomes thicker and increasingly intricate in every room here. The reference to things, to objects, is so present and at the same time so exasperating that it explodes any facile interpretation of the "system of objects" as understood by Baudrillard. The way Perec inserts an impossible number of things and situations into six hundred pages, which is truly destabilizing, and as amusing as it is exasperating, pushes to the extreme each possibility of fixing a theory of the system of the objects. We find the most diverse things and situations placed in an inimitable allegorical mural, yet always with precision: book projects, many pictorial references and references to contemporary multimedia art, including the jukebox, electric billiards, stories of transvestites, advertising signs, mortuary signs, goldfish—even plastic life jackets.

The series of *contraintes* followed by Perec, several of the rules of which he has revealed, is the structure that holds together and articulates this building-novel. *L'échafaudage*, the system of scaffolding, is the logic that articulates the plot-twists and the characters' lives and rooms; now this complex scaffolding system has been rendered more explicit by the posthumous publication of the *Cahier des charges*,[72] made up of ninety-nine pages relating to the ninety-nine chapters, in which "appears the list of elements from which the chapter will be written." It is also according to the lists, the programs, the precise rules, analyzed by Hartje, Magné, and Neefs, that the narration advances in a novel in which, as Perec says, "there is no need to look for the scaffolding: the point of view of the construction is built into the narrative."[73] As the curators of the *Cahier des charges* note in their introduction, the structural logic of the novel, which has "programs," is quite different from that of the nineteenth-century novel;[74] the constructability at play with the constraints in *Life A User's Manual* voids the natural and internal laws of the novel. With all the structural rules Perec imposed, he pulverized the logic of the stories. And, as the curators of the *Cahier de charges* write: "A universe of narratives, of characters, of times, of dramas, is gathered there, but floating, fragmented, as if arranged in a constellation whose laws do not pertain to it" (12).

The characters are numerous, some say as many as fifteen hundred, and we know very little about them; they're not at all well-defined psychological representations of characters, and we have only tiny slices of stories for each of them. Yet despite the profusion of characters who all remain enigmas, they have at least a fictional potential that could find another life in a novel dedicated to each of them, with more elaborate descriptions. What does it mean that all are equivalent? Or, instead, what does it mean that the secret of each life is to think of the bond between singularity and multiplicity? Is it a matter of *choosing*, as a reader, one's own favorite characters? Calvino does, with a subtlety and lightness that leaves much to be interpreted, when he tells us of his preference for Cinoc, the killer of words, in whose name is an unhidden reference to *cinoche*, the French slang term for cinema.[75] The ensemble and the singularity of these characters, who all struggle to be recognized with the few traits they have been given, puzzle the reader. Jean Duvignaud writes of the subject of *Life A User's Manual*: "This powerful undertaking, that reconstructs in miniature, and as if microscopically, the diversity of possible existences in a contemporary Parisian apartment building's interior space, is not simply an exercise in style, nor is it simply an investigation of everyday life."[76]

They are discrete characters, discrete as the cities that constellate *Invisible Cities*. *Life A User's Manual* and *Invisible Cities* are in a strange relationship with each other, the first with an enormous number of characters, each with some trait making him or her specific, the second in which the protagonists are cities, each one sketched out in brief details and yet in clearly defined relationships. One of the *contraintes* imposed by Perec is that of the citations embedded in the story; for some of these, Perec explicitly cites the name in the "Post-scriptum." Many of these are hidden citations of Calvino. I would like to take notice of two that are particularly evident and derive from *Invisible Cities*. The first relates to Valdrada. In *Invisible Cities*, Valdrada is a city, or rather two cities, built on a lake: "one erect above the lake, and the other reflected, upside down. . . . The twin cities are not equal, because nothing that exists or happens in Valdrada is symmetrical: every face and gesture inverted, point by point. The two Valdradas live for each other, their eyes interlocked; but there is no love between them" (53–54). In chapter 50 of *Life A User's Manual*, we enter into a room that is not yet inhabited, in which, among the few objects present, we see a picture leaning against the wall, which is partially reflected in the dark mirror of the parquet floor. This picture represents a room, of which many particulars are given, followed by a description of the source of the painter Foulerot's inspiration:

> His painting was inspired by a detective story—*The Murder of the Goldfish*—the reading of which gave him such pleasure as to make him think of using it as the subject of a picture which would bring almost all the elements of the mystery together into a single scene.
>
> The action is set in an area quite reminiscent of the Italian lakes, not far from an imaginary city which the author named Valdrada. The narrator is a painter. (221–22)

Thus Perec takes several essential elements from the imaginary Calvinian city (the name, the mirrors, the lake), and then inscribes them in another narration (a double landscape reflected in the wood of the indoor parquet), in this case in a detective novel, the events of which take place between a splendid Renaissance villa in Italy and Bamako, in which inhuman cruelty is perpetrated by the rich inhabitants of the city. This technique of sampling and interruption of *Invisible Cities* is also used later in the book. At the beginning of chapter 78, "On the Stairs, 10," a child reads in *Le Journal de Tintin* a fictionalized biography of Carel von Loorens entitled "The Emperor's Messenger." The chapter gives us many details regarding this *touche-à-tout* character, who is interested in many disciplines without ever pursuing one of them in any definitive way. At one point in his life, he manages to become Napoleon's messenger to the Berber corsair Hokab el-Ouakt, metamorphosing himself into a merchant of the Persian Gulf and going by the name Haj Abdulaziz Abu Bakr. The meeting between Loorens and Hokab is one of the few moments in *Life A User's Manual* in which we find a dialogue—a brief one, certainly, in which the messenger speaks of the commercial offer he wishes to make Hokab, but it reminds us of the meeting between Marco and the Khan.

> At last, after nightfall, preceded by some of his bodyguards, Hokab appeared:
>
> "I've had your chests opened," he said, "and they were empty."
>
> "I have come to offer you four times as much gold as those chests could ever hold."
>
> "What need do I have of your gold? The smallest Spanish galleon gives me seven times as much."
>
> "When did you take your last galleon? The English sink them, and you daren't attack the English. Next to their three-masters, your galliots are bathtubs!"
>
> "Who sent you?"
>
> "You are an Eagle, and only another Eagle may address you! I come to you with a message from Napoleon I, Emperor of the French!" (374)

Almost immediately after this brief dialogue, we read:

> He [Hokab] invited him to stay in his palace, an immense fortress overhanging the sea, with terraces of enchanted gardens resplendent with jujube and carob trees, oleanders and tame gazelles, and he gave sumptuous feasts in his honour where he made him sample rare dishes from America and Asia. In return for this, Loorens spent whole afternoons telling the Arab of his adventures and describing to him the fabulous cities where he had sojourned: Diomira the city of sixty silver domes, Isaura the town of a thousand wells, Smeraldine the city of water, and Moriane with its alabaster gates transparent in the sunlight, its coral columns supporting pediments encrusted with serpentine, its villas all of glass, like aquariums where the shadows of dancing girls with silvery scales swim beneath medusa-shaped chandeliers. (374–75)

The crystalline beauty of the invisible city is destroyed, violated, and reduced to an adventure story, slightly historicized, and the presence and magic of Calvino's text are pulverized. It is a story taken from a comic book read by a child, immediately forgotten as soon as he begins the next chapter.[77]

Often, critics have compared *Life A User's Manual* with Butor's novel *Le passage de Milan*, a novel built around a building in which we follow the happenings of life throughout the course of a single night.[78] I would like to take an interpretive leap and, keeping in mind modernity as read in the *Arcades Project* by Walter Benjamin, give another opening into this book before reconnecting with *Invisible Cities*.

The motifs of the collector and of the interior, which Walter Benjamin focused on in his work and which one could easily connect with the collections incessantly mentioned by Perec, are well known. Perhaps one should add, as Calvino says, that "the demon of 'collectionism' is always beating its wings over Perec's pages. . . . I would say, [it] is a passion for the *unique*, that is, the collection of objects of which only one specimen exists. Yet a collector he was not, in life, except of words, of the data of knowledge, of things remembered."[79] In a fragment of the *Arcades Project* located in the *Konvolut* "Construction" (itself eccentric when compared with the rest of the *Konvolut*), Benjamin compares the puzzle, or *casse-tête*, and its fame in the nineteenth century, to the nascent concept of construction, which he immediately connects with the Cubist montage.

> The "Chinese puzzle," which comes into fashion during the Empire, reveals the century's awakening sense for construction. The problems that appear, in the puzzle of the period, as hatched portions of a landscape, a building, or a figure are a first presentiment of the cubist principle in the plastic arts. (To verify: whether, in an allegorical representation in the Cabinet des Etampes, the brainteaser undoes the kaleidoscope or vice versa.) (F6,2)[80]

Perec insists on this game of construction, in which one truly loses a sense of dimension: landscapes, apartments, or characters are recomposed within the building. He takes up the idea of the wooden map divided into a mobile puzzle, but he places in check the representative coherence that these puzzles had.[81]

There are many maps, *atlases*, in *Life A User's Manual*, but they are never a true instrument of orientation or a way of unequivocally locating the reading or a means to discover some new place. An example is the map with the contested title "COL B I A," which, after an entire story relating to its discovery and the hypotheses made by various scholars, we now find in Bartlebooth's office. One thing in particular makes this map unique in Bartlebooth's eyes and endows it with its sense of mystery and wonder, which is due less to its presentation of geographical spaces newly discovered at the time or to its historical value than to its particular deformation and reversed representation, fascinating to Bartlebooth for its cognitive similarity to the puzzles:

> It was not because it was unique that Bartlebooth, as a child, grew attached to this map, which he could look at in the great hall of the manor house where he grew up, but because it possessed another

> feature also: the map's north was not at the top, but at the bottom. This difference of orientation, much commoner in the period than is often realized, fascinated Bartlebooth to the highest degree: representations rotated not always by one hundred and eighty degrees, but sometimes by ninety or forty-five, completely subvert habitual perceptions of space; the outline of Europe, for instance, a shape familiar to anyone who has been only to junior school, when swung round ninety degrees to the right, with the west at the top, begins to look like Denmark. And in this minimal switch lay hidden the very image of his jigsaw-puzzle mind. (388–89)

The maps in *Life A User's Manual* are more interesting when they are disorienting, or at any rate when they call into question both orientation and representation. In the last section of dialogue in *Invisible Cities*, Kublai Khan and Marco speak of the Khan's atlas, in which many cities and maps are yet to be discovered and narrated: "The atlas has this quality: it reveals the form of cities that do not yet have a form or a name" (138).

Perec and Calvino are a two-of-a-kind couple, and while stylistically they differ in many ways, they can both be associated with the enterprise of pushing certain limits of modernity to their extremes: Calvino and the flâneur for the next millennium and, on the other hand, Perec and the *intérieur* for the next millennium. Both play with the abstractness of the concept of construction, making it unique and impossible to fix as a stable concept, and from there elaborate it in ways that are extremely different but perhaps not opposing in terms of the relationship, including the tension, between inside and outside. The tension and desire hidden in *Life A User's Manual* lie also in the desire to render complex and uncontainable the space of a room, while in *Invisible Cities* we find them in the desire to render visible, readable, and desirable the often chaotic space of the city. One thing that unites them is certainly the desire to hear still more stories in which space is an inventive narrator, a storyteller, full of surprises. It is not a matter of personal stories, and perhaps it is also for this reason that, in a first reading, the visceral-empathetic effect of the relationship between space and life may seem lacking. The subtraction of the lived experience from the storytelling could be interpreted as a strategy of offering to each one the possibility of reinventing and imagining spaces and their multiple relationships, to speak and listen to stories not merely with fear and anxiety but also with enchantment and desire.

At the end of the sixth of the *Six Memos for the Next Millennium*, "Multiplicity," Calvino writes:

> Someone might object that the more the work tends toward the multiplication of possibilities, the further it departs from that unicum which is the *self* of the writer, his inner sincerity and the discovery of his own truth. But I would answer: Who are we, who is each one

> of us, if not a combinatoria of experiences, information, books we have read, things imagined? Each life is an encyclopedia, a library, an inventory of objects, a series of styles, and everything can be constantly shuffled and reordered in every way conceivable. (124)

The enormous space, puzzle, and labyrinth in which the characters of *Life A User's Manual* live are described, as we read at the end in the final chapter, as being at a *standstill* or as a picture made in the moment of the death of Bartlebooth. Yet another wedge of the construction of *Life A User's Manual* reverses the narration, a narration that circulates in an enormous space and yet always points toward the interior, a space that allows many lives to be narrated in a single moment, the moment of death of a single person.

There is therefore both tenderness and tension between the texts of Calvino and Perec, where the imaginary geographies that fill the narration diverge in extreme ways and make us rethink the relationship between inside and outside, small and large, familiar and foreign. *Species of Spaces* and *Life A User's Manual* play with an apparent shutting of oneself into the private realm, and yet at the same time in each moment the narration ushers in the distant and the other. *Invisible Cities* appears to shift the attention toward the outside, toward the public, a public that then turns out to be eccentric, strange, estranged, and hidden. *Species of Spaces*, *Life A User's Manual*, and *Invisible Cities* bring together geographic zones of meaning, reinventing them each time, without imposing any single meaning. The books move toward a multiplicity of emotions, between the constructed and the yet-to-be-constructed, between the mapped and the not-yet-mapped. The sense of change, difference, and interruption continually raised in the words of *Life A User's Manual* and embedded in the text, as in a puzzle and *casse-tête*, also points to the sense of movement and emotion (and their contraries, inertia and dullness). In chapter 51, we find embedded the word "soul," as critic Claude Burgelin notes:

> At the heart of the book, in what Perec called "the" chapter LI, we see "the painter who will be in the painting," Valène-Perec followed by a crowd of seventy-nine of his characters in a sort of surprising parade-poem that obeys a strict principle of organization: the letter *a* moves in a perfect diagonal along the first sixty lines, the letter *m* the sixty following lines, the letter *e* the sixty (minus one) last lines. Thus was encrypted, both invisibly and visibly, a very un-perecian word, the word "âme" [soul]. Even so, there was the heart of the matter: *Life A User's Manual* is the autoportrait of a soul, of a psyche.

In the embedded words and stories resides emotion, the sense of movement that attempts at once to implode the immobility of the building on Rue Simon-Crubellier and that of the person who reads the stories.

Arrived without incident. We're at the Versailles Motel.
Food excellent. Interesting acquaintances. Love and kisses.

We're at the Hôtel Nadir. Sunning ourselves
on the beach with all the group. Kind thoughts.

We're at the Hôtel des Pins. We sunbathe on the beach
and play Scrabble. Many fond regards.

We're at the Pension Mimosa. Lots of lazing about,
sleeping and snacking. I've got sunburnt. Many fond regards.

(G. Perec, "Two Hundred and Forty-Three Postcards in Real Colour: For Italo Calvino," in *Species of Spaces and Other Pieces*, 222–39)

Chapter 4

✦

From Fictionalizing Function to Redefining the Now of the Urban

Part 1. Fictionalizing the Extremes of Functionality

A Few Glimpses of Superstudio: "Cautionary Tales," Education *Film Script, and "Multimediainfocenters"*

Among the multitude of experimental design groups that animated the international architectural scene in the 1960s and 1970s, Superstudio, an Italian experimental architectural group, combined its counterdesign projects with criticality and invention, achieving an astonishing conciseness. Criticality was directed toward monolithic uses (or abuses) of the legacy of the modern project, toward advances in technological constructions, and toward any contemporary utopian design. Invention was released not as real constructions, but via an intermediality that shook the boundaries of architecture, playing among many media: drawings, photography, montage, film, and language. In each of Superstudio's counterprojects, these media produced specific effects, always dwelling at the limit between the critical and the fictional realm. The first part of this chapter is devoted to studying a few of Superstudio's critical experimentations—mentioned only in passing in the previous chapter—to highlight how a specific intermediality at work in sophisticated literary and critical writings (and montages) clashes into proposing an almost–dead end for storytelling while also tackling the issue of what architecture should pay attention to. The second part of the chapter, departing from radical ground, traces marking moments along the singular trajectory of architect Bernard Tschumi. This second part follows, in passing, multiple experimentations, or "episodes," along a long span of time. The aim is to highlight how Tschumi works out a new way of imagining spaces that indeed leaves room for storytelling and for active participation, how Tschumi acts out an unprecedented architecturability among different media and their specific ways of operating.

Superstudio challenged or even mocked utopian flights of fancy like the mobile architectures exemplified by Yona Friedman and the psychedelic techno-utopianism launched by the British group Archigram, employing

Figure 4.1. Superstudio, *Misura nel Chianti*, furniture series, 1970. © Superstudio.

different Shklovskyian knight's moves (to which Superstudio often referred) to do so. *Continuous Monument* (1968–70), Superstudio's experimental project imagining an empty and endless megastructural architecture, countered Friedman's proposal that "the new urban society must not be shaped by the urbanist"—that, instead, "the new city must be an intensification of existing cities." Friedman's proposal was to activate a "three-dimensional technique" of *spatial urbanism* so as to juxtapose and superimpose parts of the city, whose structures "must be skeletons, to be *filled in* as desired."[1]

The *Histograms* series of furniture (*mobili*) that could be used and moved in any space was one of the few Superstudio projects that was actually produced and marketed. The *Histograms* were presented as a catalogue "of three-dimensional, non-continuous diagrams, a catalogue of histograms with reference to a grid interchangeable into different areas or scales."[2] The *Histograms* posed an alternative to a more pop style, as proposed, for example, by the *Superarchitetture* Italian radical interior design exhibition of 1966. With their catalogue-like minimalism, these objects were a way, Superstudio wrote, to "'*tricoter avec l'espace*,' . . . a form of madness or imbecility," whose grammar was based only on interchangeable scales: indeed, the grid is the same as that of *Continuous Monument*. The effect obtained by the use of the same plastic laminate print diagrams applied on three-dimensional small structures resulted in an abstract Cartesian "identical treatment of all the surfaces": the

Figure 4.2. Superstudio, *Landscape Office*, 1970. © Superstudio.

pieces lost their status as three-dimensional objects giving space to neutral surfaces. Such objects vary from easily identifiable furniture—often installed in outside spaces as the only built structures—to totally abstract experiments whose structure of support is merely horizontal, lying on the floor, exposed in gallery spaces as conceptual pieces (figure 4.1). Eventually, histogram tables were placed out of doors on a Florentine hill, used by Superstudio's members almost as advertisements for out-of-the-box landscape architecture practices (figure 4.2).

Architectures in Superstudio's counterdesigns are always imagined as having already gobbled up the entire space for functional and massive economical ends. In counterdesign projects like *12 Ideal Cities* (1971), Superstudio imagines possible cities whose architectural and infrastructural designs are mostly determined by a technology that dismisses fanciful ways of imagining cities, such as those of Archigram and other contemporary avant-garde or utopian projects. Indeed, with *12 Ideal Cities*, Superstudio injects dark scenarios of cities into the international alternative experimentations on architecture. These cities are constructed in prose accompanied by a few drawings, and the style of the prose resembles a Baroque abstract *concettismo* of dystopian architectures and cities. A strong contrast exists between the almost catalogue-like short descriptions and the heavy atmosphere created by the machinic power of the often oppressive technologies that constitute the cities (mechanical technologies as well as electronic ones). Each city emphasizes a technologically inflected aspect that is brought to the extreme of its functionality; the narrative strategy is similar to Calvino's *Invisible Cities*, but it differs in that *Invisible Cities* does not place the emphasis on functions and functionality and their biopower effects.

With *12 Ideal Cities*, Superstudio warns against a kind of Foucauldian biotechnological society of control as well as an impossible quest for a renewed way to do architecture, liberated from merely economical and functional ends. The *12 Ideal Cities*, identified as "Twelve Cautionary Tales for Christmas,"[3] with their mix of imagined functionalism, technologies, and special effects, have taken over the entire process of urbanization and architecture. In the first ideal city, the "2000-Ton City," functionalism is at the service of the control of the inhabitants' brains. The charm with which the description of the landscape begins is quickly annihilated by a vertical building whose interior is designed to simulate vistas in 3D, smells, sounds, and any kind of "sensations of living things" and is made to control the desires of individuals.

> Even and perfect, the city lies amid green lawns, sunny hills and wooded mountains; slim, tall sheets of continuous buildings intersect in a rigorous, square mesh, one league apart. The buildings, or rather the single, uninterrupted building consists of cubic cells 5 cubits each way; these cells are placed on the top of another in a single vertical stack, reaching a height of a third league above sea-level, so that the relative height of the building varies in relation to the level of the ground on which it rises. (*SLO*, 150)

The ceiling of the building/city is a brain-impulse receiver, and "in each cell is an individual whose brain impulses are continually transmitted to an electronic analyzer set at the top of the building; the analyzer selects, compares and interprets the desires of each individual, programming the life of the entire city moment by moment" (*SLO*, 150). If the analyzer detects a persistence of absurd thoughts, "the ceiling panel descends with a force of two thousand tons until it reaches the floor" (*SLO*, 150). These biotechno-Piranesian incarceration cities have constructions that function like an infernal screw ("Second City: Temporal Cochlea-City") or as a spaceship ("Fourth City: Spaceship City") in which the inhabitants only sleep with the help of a "dream generator": day and night, sleeping and waking are uniformly controlled. But the catalogue also includes a fabulous city, the "Sixth City: Barnum Jr.'s Magnificent and Fabulous City," which a generic "you" can visit for fifty cents a minute; there, with computer-generated role-playing, "you" can employ an avatar or "character" who "has a small quantity of practical knowledge that can be of use to you during your 'journey'":

> He knows which is his car, his house, his wife or girl, he can find his way in the city streets. . . . Watch out: during your journey, naturally, you can be attacked, run over. . . . (In any case, you won't feel any

> pain, this is the only type of sensation we don't provide for our normal characters. There are, however, 50,000 special characters with sensitivity to pain for those who like "special effects.") (*SLO*, 156)

Another ideal city, "Seventh City: Continuous Production Conveyor Belt City," presents itself as a machinic serpent / roller coaster devoted to polluting so as to negligently destroy the Earth. At its head this city has a "Grand Factory, 4 miles wide and 100 yards high, like the city it continuously produces. The Grand Factory exploits the land and the underground materials of the territory it crosses, and from these marvelously extracts all that it requires for the construction of the city" (*SLO*, 158). The spectacular and entertaining function of a roller coaster becomes a never-ending ride toward the destruction of the earth. The main public authority, the major, directs the "Tenth City: The City of Order"; the major has been in office for forty-five years. Why? "The reason for his long stay in office is simple: he has an exceptionally good idea. Instead of trying to suit the city to its inhabitants, like everyone else, he thought of suiting the inhabitants to their city" (*SLO*, 159).

A self-test similar to those found in weekly magazines concludes *12 Ideal Cities*. The scoring of this test shows that the more the reader desires the cities described, the more he is suited to be a head of state; the less he wants those cities, the more he is an unsaved idiot. In these "Cautionary Tales for Christmas," the apocalyptic tone of the writing prevails over the rarefied atmosphere of the images connected to the cities; in these images, mournful and desolated wastelands play a totally silent counter-role in relation to the writing, which always pretends to define clear functions and uses. Cristiano Toraldo di Francia, one of Superstudio's members, has recently written concerning the sense of Superstudio experimental practices that the avant-garde architect and designer becomes a creator of images. "The interest moves from the instrumental and technical significance of the visual image of a concrete object . . . to the significance of the image in relation to a specific concept or to a sequence of theoretical assertions."[4] In the contrasting relationship between short narratives and desolated and mournful images, readers and viewers are pushed to conceptually confront out-of-the-picture, inconvenient, and ultimately unnecessary possible scenarios and perhaps are asked to move toward inventive literary, visual, and architectural escapes. With writing drawn from sci-fi dystopian style, *12 Ideal Cities* seems to leave, or better to point toward, constructed scenarios in which there is no more eventful story to narrate or space for narrating.[5]

"Reflected Architecture" (1970–71)[6] is a series of photomontages, and the one depicting the vista of Niagara Falls dwells in a specific moment, whose time is kept secret, when a spectacular event will happen at the juncture of a marvelous natural landscape and a highly sophisticated engineering project that tickles the sublime. The montage presents a mirror-like effect—produced by a basin that reflects the sky and is built in front of the falls. The juncture

Figure 4.3. Superstudio, *Reflected Architecture: New Niagara*, 1970. © Superstudio.

between nature and engineering, between the power of reflection given by the glass-like contemporary skyscrapers and the geological and natural beauty of Niagara Falls, asks us to reflect, at least for a moment, on the practices of the osmosis between natural and constructed landscapes (figure 4.3). The eventful moment will occur when the basin collapses. In the short text that accompanies the photomontage we read:

> A basin of mirrors for vertical waters.
>
> The American side of Niagara Falls can be cut off, leaving only the Canadian (Horseshoe) Falls active. A rectangular basin can be built and covered in mirror-polished steel sheeting.
>
> When the water is turned on again, the basin will fill up in 33 minutes no seconds and 94 hundredths.
>
> Only in this fraction of time (extremely short in comparison with the 20,000 years of Niagara's existence) is the water situated next to the geometrically reflected clouds.
>
> Then the mirror surface of the basin vanishes. The structure has been calculated in such a way to resist underwater for some years. The collapse of the artificial structure causes a visible receding of the front of the American Falls, similar to the natural one of the Canadian Falls. The calculated time of collapse will be kept secret. Lots of people will go there, hoping to be there right in time for this terrific spectacle. (*SLO*, 84)

It may not be well known that the American side of Niagara Falls was dewatered in 1969 to evaluate erosion. The solution chosen was to keep everything as it was, even though some changes in the falling waters were expected. In this Superstudio vista the engineering function and use have no other apparent effect than to expose visitors to that moment in which they will eventually be present at an ephemeral spectacle in a location whose natural existence dates back centuries. It may be inferred, therefore, that Superstudio is gaming with this real colossal engineering enterprise, adding to Niagara its fictional constructions, constructions that indeed for their surface effect reflect also the disappearance of architecture.

Superstudio's Shklovskyian knight's move continues with the five screenplays of the *Fundamental Acts (Life, Education, Ceremony, Love*, and *Death*) (1971–73);[7] *Life* presents an "alternative model of Life on Earth." Earth is covered by supersurfaces whose network of energy can cover different percentages of the planet and is developed as a grid of horizontal structure. People will live in a continuous nomadism, without cities, houses, or objects. Indeed "almost everybody will take only himself from A to B, a single visible object, like a complete catalogue as an enormous Postal Market Catalogue" (*SLO*, 183). It is only with the arrival of a *parousia* of the earth without constructions that humans will get back to experiencing their bodies. "We'll keep silence to listen to our bodies, we'll hear the sound of blood in our ears. . . . We will watch ourselves living." In this way of living at the limit of navel-gazing and an immersed meditation state, the script announces a renewed possibility to perform and experience space, even if only mentally: "We'll do very complicated mental acrobatics. . . . We'll carry out astonishing mental operations" (*SLO*, 183). The journey in this mindscape ends in an eco-environment empty of three-dimensional structures, where life will acquire all its power:

> We'll look at the sun, the clouds, the stars.
> We will go to faraway places, just to look at them and hear them.
> Some people will become story-tellers: many will move to go and listen to them.
> Some will sing and play.
> Stories, songs, music, dancing will be the words we speak and tell ourselves. Life will be the only environmental art. (*SLO*, 183)

In this alternative, imagined future, enchanting for its perfectly achieved balance between environment and *Land Art*, it will again be possible to fully experience body perception and storytelling.

The coming of the new technology is at the core of another of the film scripts, *Education*. The script announces a time when researches will be brought on to achieve, for example, an "interplanetary information network; life as a permanent global form of education. . . . The twentieth century has seen the computer as an extension of our brain. On the one hand, we have seen a process of rationalization and on the other a de-conditioning in favor of new syntheses. Hardware is now sufficient and available while software is insufficient and limited. We need to plan many futures" (*SLO*, 189). The script is accompanied by vaguely scientific images, collages of secret connections between humans and technologies that in an outer space—if not an emptied-out space—represent moments of learning and thinking processes (figure 4.4). This search for new futures and new syntheses is, at the end, in question: "What can one say about the quality of teaching/learning? And what's going on in all these multimedia infocenters? Teach what? Learn what?" (*SLO*, 189).

Bernard Tschumi and Rem Koolhaas will be attentive to, if not inspired by, these alternative ways in which the space of comparison of architecture is confronted with its others, as a quest for renewal of ways of learning, teaching, researching, and constructing; yet they will do so by articulating multiple media differently, in order to activate unexpected spaces for invention.

Part 2. Bernard Tschumi: How to Trigger Architecture Radically

A Brief Note on Situated Technologies, before Their Time

Italian Radical experimentations circulated in galleries and museums as well as in some schools of architecture. At the Architectural Association School of Architecture (AA) in London, the production of Italian Radicals had been "a context of formation" to Bernard Tschumi, already a teacher, and Rem Koolhaas, a student and then a teacher.[8]

One of the very first publications by Tschumi, in collaboration with the architect Fernando Montes, *Do-It-Yourself-City* (1970), shares traits with Superstudio's intermedial experimentations and engagement with the networked cities to come.[9] *Do-It-Yourself-City* imagines possible interventions and interactions in the city to be activated by public and private access via hardware and software; the potential objective was to facilitate and improve the relational and multidimensional quality of life in the city; the question was, as Tschumi much later stated: "Can you merge the place of tectonics with the space of electronic flows? Or does the electronic space of flows become the invisible prosthesis for traditional urban space or vice versa?"[10] Similarities to Superstudio include the interest in thinking of the city as cabled and interactive, as well as the collages and drawings showing possible links and connections to be activated by citizens, and certainly the fictional tone, at a time when mobile and global communication and networked technologies had not yet, as today, become widely accessible or, if you like, predatory. The Italian Radicals' practices, particularly those of Archizoom and Superstudio, were a crucial confrontation but became reinscribed in Tschumi's theoretical investigation into space and eventually resurfaced in his later projects.[11]

Figure 4.4. Superstudio, *Fundamental Acts: Education*, 1971. © Superstudio.

Archizoom's counterdesign architectural projects of the late 1960s and early 1970s, from the "Homogeneous Housing Diagram: Hypothesis of Architectonic Language" to the *No-Stop City*, were a series of drawings and diagrams that imagined different but homogeneous ways of organizing interior and exterior spaces by modular typology and continuous plan (figure 4.5), with buildings stacked on different levels and fulfilling multiple and variable uses (emphasis was given to horizontal circulation with cars and vertical circulation with elevators).[12]

Andrea Branzi, one of the members of the group, affirmed:

> In 1968, the *No-Stop City*—a non-figurative architecture, for a non-figurative society that no longer had an external form, but had infinite interior forms—prefigured the central role of industrial products, merchandise, furniture, and service in the construction of fluid settings of the contemporary metropolis. This was the city seen as a conglomerate of habitable parking lots, as a system of topographical storages and free residential forests; this indicated a global system already lacking external space, where the city corresponds to the dimension of the global market and the system of networks spread across the land. The citizen is not he who lives in the city, but he who uses the industrial products and information supplied by telecommunications.[13]

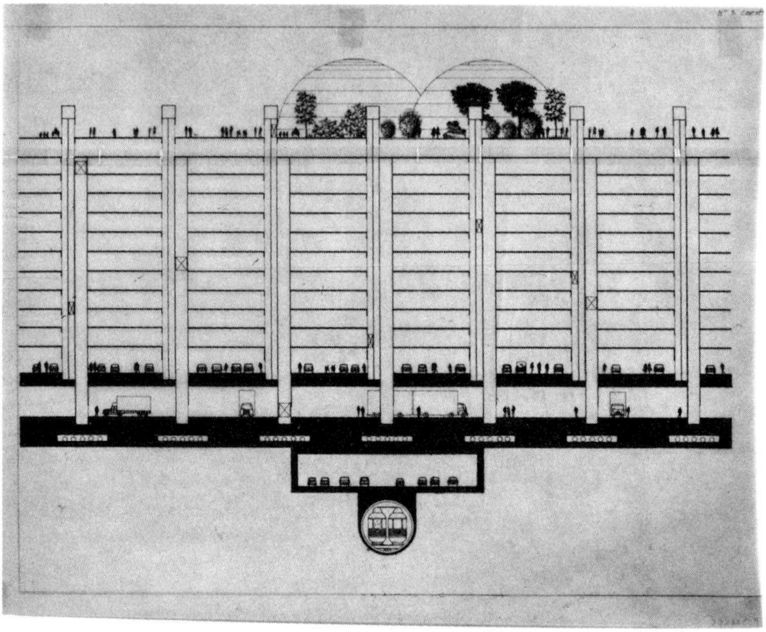

Figure 4.5. Archizoom, *No-Stop City*, 1971. © Archizoom/CSAC, Parma University.

Space within the *No-Stop City* was a neutral and repeatable surface, and architecture, similar in its typologies to parking lots or supermarkets, was part of one bigger system. Tschumi praises the *No-Stop City* project for its ability to convey criticality not with a written text but by "means of a project"; nevertheless, he remarks that this represents a way to "verify it [the system] and show where it is going. It also means that, paradoxically, one may someday find oneself in the situation of actually building one's verification" (*AD*, 19).[14] The experimentation among electronics and architecture was, after *Do-It-Yourself-City*, temporarily postponed.

Opening Up the Architectural Field through the Notion of Space

To approach Tschumi's singular trajectory requires spending some time passing through the works-in-progress laboratory of invention and investigation he undertook in the late 1970s and 1980s, which later coalesced in his built projects. Considering how in the recent years colorful images have saturated the architectural field, one could attempt to convey Tschumi's trajectory by overlooking these early investigations and paying attention mainly to a series of astonishing posters he did, but this would obscure Tschumi's long elaboration of his open-ended trajectory, his quest for a renewed sense of the intermingling of praxis and theory. Indeed, between 1976 and 1980, Tschumi

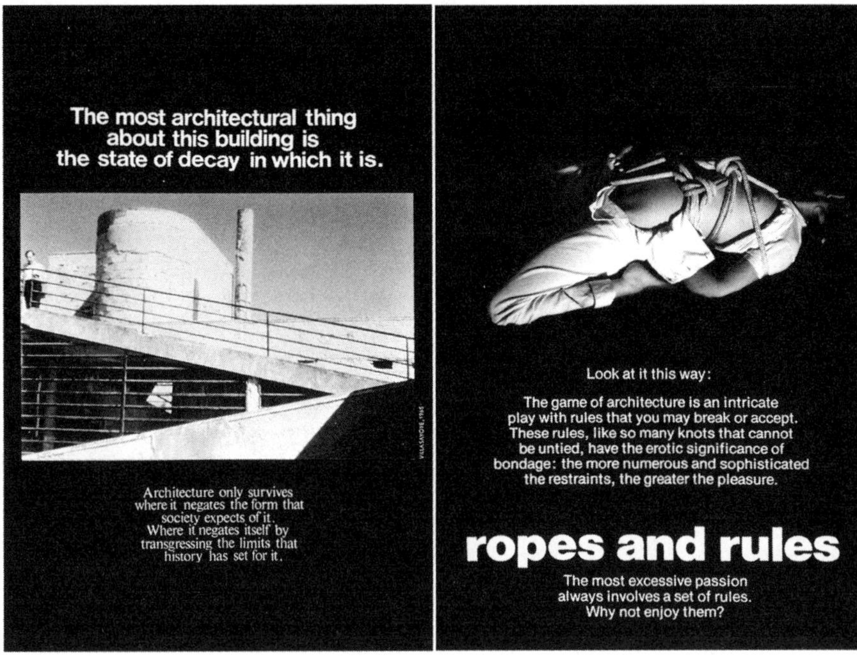

Figures 4.6 and 4.7. Bernard Tschumi, *Advertisements for Architecture*, 1976–80. © Bernard Tschumi.

produced a series of posters, *Advertisements for Architecture*, with which he captured attention for architecture by hijacking the advertisement medium. In one poster, a photo of the not useless but no longer in use Villa Savoye of Le Corbusier flashes out, questioning the heroic history of modern architecture with a short text that seems to echo Walter Benjamin's *Arcades Project*: "The most architectural thing about this building is the state of decay in which it is." In another poster, the photo of a man in ropes is accompanied by a text addressing the potential viewer/reader: "Look at it in this way: the game of architecture is an intricate play with rules that you may break or accept. These rules, like so many knots that cannot be untied, have the erotic significance of bondages: the more numerous and sophisticated the restraints, the greater the pleasure." Keeping these two images (figures 4.6 and 4.7) in mind, and before getting to Tschumi's built projects, I want to spotlight his publicly available laboratory of ideas, albeit only in short flashes, which in this instance is the best way.

In the 1970s Tschumi investigated a wide and open-ended notion of "space," importing in his experimentations and essays different rhetorical and critical frames and devices from a multiplicity of fields (literature, critical and literary theory, cinema and performing arts) so as to find alternative hinges from which to consider the "interplay between space and activities . . . as a possible route to bypass some of the obstacles that accompanied many anxieties about the social and the political role of architecture."[15] In a series of essays written between the late 1970s and the 1980s, later collected in *Questions of Space* (1990),[16] Tschumi articulates a part of his own inventive and conceptual laboratory of ideas, and in the introduction Tschumi notes that "taken together, these texts construct a discontinuous reality, whose fragments are less important than the spaces between them" (*QS*, 9). In the section that follows, I move among these essays, flashing out the ways they move, through intermedial lenses and interdisciplinary moving frames, beyond self-enclosed objects; this quick incursion into *Questions of Space* is also interwoven with other connected experimentations and with Tschumi's new modality of teaching, in order to show the way Tschumi operated: exploring in the first moment the extreme tension between the experience of space and the concept of space and later that among space, event, and movement.

"Questions of Space" (1975)[17] exposes the reader to a series of numbered questions. The incessant, Wittgensteinian style of this questioning about space fragments any unitary comprehension of space as a *res extensa*, and at the same time it constructs only generic and abstract questions from which answers, or essays, might emerge. The effect of this catalogue-like series of questions is to leave the reader in an ambiguous and anxious position, standing between the desire to answer with more nuance and to simply discard any ulterior investigation and move beyond.[18] This text seems to complement a performance Tschumi mounted in the same year: he distributed small cards to several persons, asking the participants to engage in the questioning of space; on the cards he wrote the "word *space* and a question mark. . . . A lot of people filled in the questions." Therefore, in a participatory mood, Tschumi performed a gesture that juxtaposed singular, impromptu notes with an abstract or general term: space; the term "space" could—he believed—"extend a bridge to other disciplines" (*Tschumi/Walker*, 21). An exhibit Tschumi organized in 1975 at the Royal College of Art in London (called, with an echo of Superstudio's style, *A Space: A Thousand Words*) was a parallel installment that launched an experimental quest: the call for participation, extended to artists and architects, asked for an image and a maximum of one thousand words and described the aims as being to resurface "opacity" from "transparency," to play with words and images so that indeed "words of architecture become the work of architecture."[19]

Tschumi introduces the exhibit by discussing in a mocking tone many recent and interpenetrating metatheories of space that eventually overlooked "the fact that space *was*." "Space seemed then to exist only as the interpenetration of quite different kinds of layers. Their names were the Mode of Production, the Collective Unconscious, the Linguistic Pattern, the Alternative Technology, even the Historical Precedent. They all intersected, infiltrated and superimposed upon the idea of space. . . . Space seemed to be rammed by so many discourses that it ceased to offer any resistance" ("A Space Is Worth a Thousand Words"). The exhibit aspired to access the wide motif of space in a transversal and inventive way, as Tschumi wrote: "Space *is*, and all it *does* is to suggest the refusal of any separation between politics and the pebbled beach, between critical analysis and secret desires, between words and figurations" ("A Space Is Worth a Thousand Words").[20] RoseLee Goldberg, performance artist and theorist of performance arts, joined the project; in the preface to the catalogue, she highlights the novelty of the exhibition, in which each piece is singular for the way "the relationship between text and image differs considerably from one work to another"; yet reflecting on the catalogue format, Goldberg, as an expert in performance and lived art, emphasizes the ambiguity of the discussion of space brought about with this kind of exhibit, in which space must be represented in two dimensions: "The viewer, rather than being subjected to real space, is given glimpses into different spatial possibilities—landscapes or mindscape."

Tschumi explicitly formulates Goldberg's concern in "The Architectural Paradox: The Pyramid and the Labyrinth" (1975), where we read that a paradox arises from, according to Tschumi, the "impossibility of questioning the nature of space and at the same time experiencing a spatial praxis" (*QS*, 12). While developing his argument, Tschumi notices a "surprising echo" between the Hegelian definition of architecture and some of the contemporary practices: both see architecture as something different from, a supplement to, use and utility. In Hegel's aesthetic theory, architecture was "whatever in a building did not point to utility. Architecture was a sort of 'artistic supplement' added to the simple building" (*QS*, 15–16), something therefore that escaped the utility of space. Similarly, the radical counterdesign searched for an autonomy that implies architecture dematerialized in the realm of concepts. The experiencing of space in a "purely sensory approach" stands opposed to the dematerialized architecture; for this direction Tschumi points to research spanning from the German *Raumempfindung* theory to the 1960s experimentations in dance and performance in search of new ways to articulate theory and experience. In the labyrinth, all "sensations, all feelings are enhanced, but no overview is present to provide a clue about where to get out" (*QS*, 23), because in an extreme space "the first moment of perception carries the experience itself" (*QS*, 23). In his search for ways to bridge sensorial/experiential aspects and reason, Tschumi delves further, via the concept of "pleasure"; disguising himself, if you will, as a Barthesian and Bataillean follower, he announces that "like eroticism, architecture needs both system and excess" (*QS*, 29). For Tschumi the pleasure of architecture "simultaneously contains (and dissolves) both mental constructs and sensuality. Neither space nor concepts alone are erotic, but the junction between the two is" ("The Pleasure of Architecture," *QS*, 54). The architecture that Tschumi looks for is similar to the Adornian fireworks: it is useless. "For if architecture is useless, and radically so, this very uselessness will signify strength in a world where cost/benefit justifications are required by social activists and corporate bankers alike. Once again, if there has lately been some reason to doubt the necessity of architecture, then the *necessity of architecture may well be its non-necessity*. As opposed to building, making architecture is not unlike burning matches without a purpose" (*QS*, 52). Fireworks would later be choreographed in his yet-to-be-finished Parc de la Villette.

While teaching at the AA School of Architecture, Tschumi experimented with new strategies among a mix of genres and media (writing, photography, performance, video, and conceptual art); he introduced inventive new angles of vision—of knowability—derived or colported from literature as well as from choreography and musical notation. Quite revolutionary in terms of intermediality, he selected texts by Borges, Calvino, and Joyce as architectural briefs for the studio he was teaching. These texts "provided programs or events on which students were to develop architectural works. The role of the text was fundamental in that it underlined some aspects of the complementing (or, occasionally, lack of complementing) of events and spaces" (*QS*, "Spaces and Events," 92). Encouraging almost incommensurable leaps between the literary "handling of the story"[21] and architectural imagination was the gesture with which Tschumi triggered the studio dynamic: in producing programs, students had to come to terms with another way of understanding the context, one that is never completed: that of literary events. To open up the static representations of plans, sections, and axonometrics and to inscribe in the project bodily movements, the students were asked to work with models of notation: "Movement notation derived from choreography and simultaneous scores derived from music notation were elaborated for architectural purpose. . . . A form of notation that was there to *recall* that architecture was also about the movement of bodies in space, that their language and the language of walls were ultimately complementary" (*QS*, 94). One of the projects published during these years was *Joyce's Garden*: "Tschumi made use of the potential of the point grid superimposed onto an existing urban context. Joyce's Garden employs the grid as a kind of vanishing mediator, linking the random everyday events of London's Covent Garden with the textual performance of James Joyce's *Finnegans Wake*, weaving the two incommensurable systems together even as the grid itself fades into nothing and leaves only its traces and effects."[22] The fascination with the intersection of literature and garden/city is as old as literature itself, but for Tschumi it began via Joyce, and eventually it formed one of the layers of his Parc de la Villette project. Before abandoning *Questions of Space*, it is necessary to consider one last thread that ties up with previous chapters, by taking note of two essays in *Questions of Space* partly devoted to Italian Futurism. In the essay "The Architecture of Dissidence" (1979) Tschumi announces the idea for a book that, he says, "traces a journey through the most original spaces of the twentieth century. . . . It will document the most dynamic episodes in the history of the twentieth-century spaces, emphasizing those moments when architects, artists and writers attempted to achieve radical breaks with the constricting rules of their time by devising impossible, shocking and often fabulous projects."[23] In this essay Tschumi sketches the different chapters of his proposed book as "episodes," therefore implying a writing more similar to screenplays than to historical or literary narrative. For the first one he plans to consider the "events staged by the Futurists in terms of architectural spaces" (*QS*, 81). The gesture of announcing a book unprecedented for its contents—many performative and radical episodes—without publishing it has itself the tone of a performance.

Futurist spaces are also the subject of the essay "Episodes of Geometry and Lust" (1981), which is divided into sections; the section "Spaces of Sensations" considers Futurist stage design and, in particular, Enrico Prampolini's manifesto "Futurist Atmosphere-Structure: Base for Architecture." What Tschumi highlights is Prampolini's remark that "no artistic activity has shown such a disdainfully anachronistic character as architecture" (*QS*, 42), as well as his attack on space "as a pictorial and separate fact."[24] In all the episodes, Tschumi points to the tension between life and death, ephemerality and permanence, geometry and sensuality; Tschumi emphasizes these tensions for their force of rupture from tradition and from their contexts, as well as for the fact that they were never resolved into a synthesis by the Futurists. Finally, Tschumi also produced a series of manifestos in which each project he had done "was reformatted and turned into a manifesto-like statement or theorem that had to be demonstrated" (*Tschumi/Walker*, 33). But then Tschumi moved his experimentations to another medium: film.

Inventing Cinematically Mutant Architectures

Leaving aside avant-garde performances, Tschumi starts to draw in a cinematic way: the relations among space, event, and movement are crucial in the *Manhattan Transcripts* (1976–81). The *Manhattan Transcripts* record four episodes articulated among three independent elements and transcribed with three different modes of notation (figure 4.8): space (architectural drawings), movement (outlined with lines and arrows), and event (with photos); these three elements are independent, "yet they stand in a new relation to one another, so that the conventional components of architecture are broken down and rebuilt along different axes."[25] These episodes unfold through a set of diagrams, plans, and drawings marking the movements "of the different protagonists—those people intruding into the architecture 'stage set'" (*MT*, 7). It is crucial to underline that in this way the protagonists participate in constructing with their acts and movements the unfolding of this paper architecture that is always in progress, mutant. In the different episodes (whose sequences have different modality: linear, repetitive, disjunctive, distorted, fading-in, and insertive), architecture and events unfold as a flux in time and

Figure 4.8. Bernard Tschumi, *The Manhattan Transcripts*, "The Block," 1980. © Bernard Tschumi.

space. In the *Manhattan Transcripts* architecture and cinema share a "frame-by-frame technique, the isolation of frozen bits of action. In both, spaces are not only composed, but also developed from shot to shot so that the final meaning of each shot depends on its context" (*MT*, 10). Because they are organized frame by frame, they create a cinematic narrativity; these are not self-contained images but instead "establish a memory of the preceding frame, of the course of events" (*MT*, 11). Each episode is introduced by a short and captivating beginning for the narrative, an incipit,[26] and by an aerial photo; these are quickly superseded by the simultaneous unfolding of the three axes; the viewer is exposed to a dynamic between conflict and reciprocity and constructs them in looking at the episodes. The filmic narrativity, one obtained by montage, is intended to expand the conventional architectural representation in order to imagine interrelations of spaces and their uses, by protagonists or just passersby, to imagine them not as self-contained objects but as objects that are incessantly transformed along with the events.

In this "work-in-progress," the flux of architectures and events unfold without any one being merely the backdrop and the other the action itself. Michael Hays has emphasized this complexity: "The actors (and we the readers) do not move in space so much as space moves with them (and us) as a constantly permutating *Umwelt* delineated as distorted architectural fragments, unfolding perspective, transforming across time. . . . It is as if part of the attempt is to render visible sensations beneath the surface of appearance—tremors and rhythms otherwise inaccessible."[27] Tschumi defines the "programmatic account" as the way in which the plot of each episode unfolds and intrinsically participates or conflicts with the architectural spaces. For example, in the first episode, "The Park" (*MT* 1), the mode of notation "underlines the deadly game of hide and seek between the suspect and the ever-changing architectural events. There, attitudes, plans, notations, movements are indissolubly linked. Only together do they define the architectural space of 'The Park' " (*MT*, 8). In contrast, in "The Block" (*MT* 4), "five inner courtyards of a simple city block witness contradictory events and programmatic impossibilities: acrobats, ice-skaters, dancers, soldiers, and football players all congregate and perform high-wire acts, games, or even the reenactment of famous battles, in a context usually alien to their activity" (*MT*, 8). In "The Block" disjunctions between spaces, movements, and programs are at play; each of them has a "distinct logic, while their confrontations produce the most unlikely combinations" (*MT*, 8).

In the words of Jeffrey Kipnis, who did not fail to see in the complex palimpsest the connection with Michelangelo Antonioni's film *Blow Up* (a murder mystery centered on a park), the *Manhattan Transcripts* are "perfect acts of architecture" that for more than a decade stood "as the study nonpareil of transformative architectural graphics."[28] The *Manhattan Transcript*'s drawings and diagrams set in motion something quite different from the nonfigurative architecture of Archizoom's *No-Stop City*—something more singular. They also produced acts, but not fundamental ones as in Superstudio's films *Fundamental Acts* (*Life*, *Education*, *Ceremony*, *Love*, and *Death*); instead, the *Manhattan Transcripts* activate mutual permutations among space, event, and movement, demonstrating a combinatory interplay, not just simple reversibility. If reversibility is in play at all, it is intended as something more complex than a simple transposition; somehow this is what is "advertised" in one of Tschumi's posters, in which a photomontage captures the moment when a lady seems to throw a man out of a window. We read: "Architecture is defined by the actions it witnesses as much as by the enclosure of its walls. Murder in the Street differs from Murder in the Cathedral in the same way as love in the street differs from the Street of Love. Radically." Tschumi does not apply or translate any devices or theory, but instead temporarily borrows, or as he says imports, debates and experiments from other disciplines, so to facilitate circulation, interaction, and conflict.[29]

The search for an architecture to be activated by space, event, and movement, and within transformative architectural drawings, took Tschumi's experimental journey in architecture beyond its disciplinary boundaries, but it was still missing a confrontation with a specific medium. As Tschumi affirms, "Each of those media has its own logic, and there was one more medium that I knew was coming—real materials."[30] Tschumi's entry in the competition for the Parc de la Villette (1982–98) in Paris, France, marked a turning point for him. Tschumi, acted out, not committing a murder or a suicide, but working for more than ten years on a built project.

Acting Out the Intermingle: Architectural Gestures at the Parc de la Villette

In the same year that the archives of *Arcades Project* was posthumously published in German (1982), Bernard Tschumi participated in the competition for the Parc de la Villette (a vast piece of land, emptied out and no longer in use, at the city border in the 19th arrondissement) and he won it the following year.[31] Imagined as an "Urban Park for the 21st Century," the park had a complex program of cultural and entertainment facilities (open-air theaters, restaurants, art galleries, music and painting workshops, playgrounds, video and computer displays, and gardens).[32] For the master plan Tschumi selected the grid because its spatial organization—defined by repetitive markings—negates hierarchy and allows for "a potentially infinite field of points of intensity: an incomplete, infinite extension."[33] Similar to Archizoom's project for the University of Florence (1970–71),[34] Tschumi's plan superimposed three different but autonomous systems: points, lines, and surfaces (figure 4.9). The first is the system of points, small-scale constructions (the twenty-six *folies*) at 120-meter intervals, each with a specific program. The second is the system of lines (arranged according to a coordinate structure and one curvilinear path, the Cinematic Promenade).[35] The third system, the system of surfaces, is divided into open spaces programmed for specific activities (for example, markets and outdoor entertainment) that contrast with "the leftover surfaces" with no specific program and "composed of compacted earth and gravel, a park material familiar to Parisians" (*EC2*, 57).

The superimposition of different systems plays with and disrupts the very concept of a system, and the grid "resisted the humanist claim of authorship, so it opposed the closure of ideal compositions and geometric dispositions" (*AD*, 194). The points of intensities in the park, the *folies* (a wordplay between a critical/clinical concept, madness, and an architectural term for a small building in a park), relate among themselves and with the other systems, disrupting any simple sameness: madness is grafted onto the French Cartesian rationality. Constructively, the starting point for the *folies* is a cube thirty-six feet on a side "divided in three in each direction, forming a cage with twelve feet between bars,"[36] which is then decomposed according to combinatory principles and supplemented with additional elements (one- or two-story cylindrical or triangular volumes, stairs, and ramps). A red enameled steel envelope covers the structural frame of each *folie*. The combinatory principle can accommodate the specific programmatic requirements related to each point of activity and can cross over into the other two systems. The *folies* are, in Jacques Derrida's words, performative marks, as he writes in his rhapsodic text on Bernard Tschumi, "Point de folie—maintenant

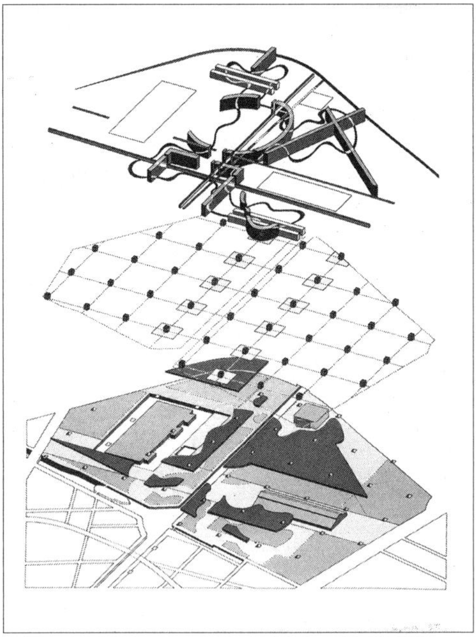

Figure 4.9. Bernard Tschumi, Parc de la Villette, Superposition: Points, Lines, Planes, 1982. Paris, France. © Bernard Tschumi.

l'architecture" (No [point of] madness—maintaining architecture). Derrida is careful in pointing at the spatiotemporal relationality at play in the park: "The performative mark *spaces*, is the event of spacing. The red points space, maintaining architecture in the dissociation of spacing. But this *maintenant* does not only maintain a past and tradition. It does not ensure a synthesis. It maintains the interruption."[37]

Considering the experimentations passing among different media in the *Manhattan Transcripts* and the Parc de la Villette, Derrida indeed speaks of transarchitecture, of invention, of event, of a scenography of passage:

> The invention, in this case, consists in crossing the architectural motif with what is most singular and most parallel in other writings which are themselves drawn into the said madness, in its plural, meaning photographic, cinematographic, choreographic. . . . An architectural writing interprets (in the Nietzschean sense of active productive, violent, transforming interpretation) events which are *marked* by photography or cinematography. Marked: provoked, determined *or* transcribed, captured, in any case always mobilized in a scenography of passage (transference, translation, transgression from one place to another, from a place of writing to another graft, hybridization). (575)

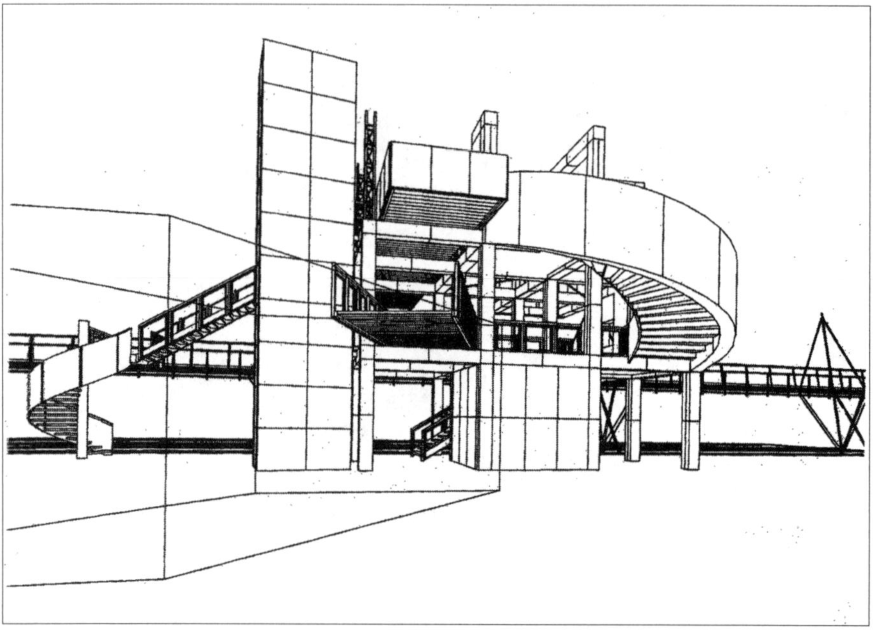

Figure 4.10. Bernard Tschumi, Parc de la Villette, Folie R5, 1982–98. Paris, France. © Bernard Tschumi.

The passersby take their turns in this scenography of passage and perform and move along the many experimental paths and programs. Just a few examples can give some glimpses of the interweaving at play in the park. The program for Folie R7 is a jazz club: the upper level has offices for the club, the intermediate level combines the garden and the waiting area, and the lower level is the space for the jazz club itself (and its related facilities). Folie R5 (figure 4.10) is another example of how these small buildings intersect with the system of lines. The program of this construction is a triple intersection on three levels: on the third upper story it intersects twice, once with a bridge that runs over the canal (a preexisting part of the site), and a second time with one path of the system of lines; the middle story intersects with the gallery on an elevated walkway along the canal; and finally, the ground level intersects with spaces of movement (elevators, stairs, and bridge).

Among the system of lines are the two galleries (two straight open-air paths, one running north–south and one running east–west), which interpenetrate the other systems. The North-South Gallery is "a brilliantly lit public street, open 24 hours a day and connecting the urban functions of the park: the Museum of Science and Industry, Cinema-*Folies*, Restaurant-*Folies*, Video-*Folies*, the 19th-century Grand Halle, a theater, and the City of Music" (*EC2*, 209). This gallery also collides with the "*Folies* it meets on its

Figure 4.11. Bernard Tschumi, Parc de la Villette, Cinematic Promenade, Garden of Mirrors, 1982–98. Paris, France. © Sophie Chivet.

trajectory . . . thus determining their respective architecture" (*EC2*, 209). The combinatory principle of the *folies* as a cross-programming and intermingling is *durchdringen*, to refer back to Benjamin.[38] At each level, the project spans a cross-programmed and intermingled constructed reality that the passersby can view and experience from a multiplicity of frames.

The curvilinear Cinematic Promenade, almost two miles long and part of the system of lines, derives from the montage-like architect's intervention (figure 4.11): the path is divided in parts (sequences) differentiated with different construction materials (on the ground, never at the same height, a mixture of mineral, vegetal, and plastic), different plants (*Acer sylvestris*, *Acer negundo*, bamboo . . .), different attractions (a sand box, a roller-skating space, a garden of mirrors, a garden of childhood frights, the Dragon Garden . . .), and spaces differently constructed for activities in the open air (jogging paths, meadows, sport fields, a skating rink . . .). Tschumi adopts the model of a strip of film to materialize the Cinematic Promenade. The walkway corresponds to the film's soundtrack, and the frames of individual and discrete gardens correspond to the image-track, each conceived as a different "episode." "Each part, each frame of a sequence qualifies, reinforces, or alters the parts that precede and follow it. . . . The cut between two garden sequences is established by means of an intersecting line of trees" (*EC2*, 70).

It is clear that this project is innervated with shocking and fabulous projects Tschumi had previously considered. This architect's intervention, which can be invisible or, if you prefer, perceived in a state of distraction, activates an atmosphere that potentially facilitates the unexpected. The way the cinematic device is immanent to the project differentiates it from the filmic experimentations in Superstudio's *Fundamental Acts*. Eventually it fosters space for storytelling.

> If the general structure of the sequence of gardens requires the indetermination of its content (hence the role of the chief architect as film director, overseeing the montage of sequences), its specific content implies determinacy (through the particular designs of individual designers). The park is also inhabited: sequences of events, use, activities, incidents are inevitably superimposed on those fixed spatial sequences. It suggests secret maps and impossible fictions, rambling collections of events all strung along a collection of spaces, frame after frame, garden after garden, episode after episode. (*EC2*, 70)

There are many other details and secret maps to discover in the project that would show how the conditions of design facilitate stimulating spatial interactions. At the Parc de la Villette the play among different systems, programs, and frames makes it difficult to have one image, to get a picture of it; instead, such play facilitates a moving experience in this "Urban Park for the 21st Century" that is permeated by many media Tschumi had previously investigated, always among manifold frameworks and angles of visions (just as a city is): the experience is similar to the experience of the city that Benjamin defines in his *Arcades Project* as a "vascular network of imagination."

Conceptualizing the Conditions for the Event-Cities

In "Six Concepts," a programmatic essay from 1991, Tschumi affirmatively adopts a stance other than those of the vernacular, historicist, contextualist, or high-tech and functionalist approaches, because according to him such stances repeat and apply superficial images of ready-made formulas without answering the question "How can architecture remain a means by which society explores new territories, develops new knowledge?" (*AD*, 237). Referring back to Benjamin's "Work of Art in the Age of Technological Reproducibility," which he calls a "classic," Tschumi argues that for architecture the "device of 'shock' may be an indispensable tool" (*AD*, 247). For Benjamin "the esthetic experience consisted of keeping defamiliarization alive" (*AD*, 246), and the defamiliarization originating from the shock of images was also "what allowed an image to stand out" (246); in a similar way, remarks Tschumi, it is better for architecture in the contemporary situation to find unfamiliar solutions than to repeat quieting and comforting ones.

> As opposed to nostalgic attempts to restore an impossible continuity of streets and plazas, this research implies making an event out of urban shock, intensifying and accelerating urban experience through clash and disjunction. . . . Over fifty years after the publication of Benjamin's text [*Work of Art*] we may have to say that shock is still all we have left to communicate in a time of generalized information. (247–48)

To intentionally activate shock seems to imply that the architect constructs not simply to disrupt but also to foster surprising spaces. Tschumi conceptualizes what Benjamin was considering or, if you wish, announcing in his *Arcades Project*, in which, in my interpretation, he understands architecture as a medium, not in a superficial way, but as a specific medium that changes and produces changes not only because of new mass-produced technologies but also because of its ability to communicate with other media in a mediatized society. Tschumi proposes not to "design a new definition of cities and their architecture" but to search for ways of "constructing conditions that will create a new city and new relationships between spaces and events" (*AD*, 259) and thereby of facilitating nonhierarchical and nontraditional society. Tschumi imports into architecture two crucial terms, one from Benjamin and one from Derrida. Benjamin's concept of shock is an effective device when combined with function or action; action means an "architecture of the event." If we accept what Derrida pointed out, that "the word 'event' shared roots with 'invention' " (*AD*, 257), then to eventualize, to invent, implies constructing architecture beyond any fixed or cause-and-effect relation between function and form, between programs and spaces.

Indeed, Tschumi's *Event-Cities 1* (1994), the first in a four-volume series, documents projects that invent and mobilize technologies of construction beyond tradition, projects that facilitate the circulation and communication of the different media as much as of people in everyday spaces, projects in which programs and uses converge in unexpected ways. In the introduction to *Event-Cities 1*, he affirms that his projects "disrupt and disfigure but, simultaneously, reconfigure, providing a rich texture of experiences that redefine urban actuality: city-events, event-cities" (*EC1*, 13).

Event-Cities 1, *2*, *3*, and *4*, with more than a dozen projects in each volume, share several common traits. They are all presented minutely, with sketches, details of drawings, and renderings in which "the construction detail, with its joints, screws and bolts, appears nearly obscene" (*EC1*, 12); a few grainy photos in black and white, suggestive more of newspapers than of glossy and colorful architectural publications, blend the projects with snapshots of everyday life. The projects are grouped according to main concepts that interlace, such as, in *EC1*, "Architectural Urbanism" and "Urban Architecture," or *EC3*, where the three nouns of the subtitle, "Concept vs. Context vs. Content," are connected and sometimes rendered in their gerundive forms: "Contextualizing Concept," "Conceptualizing Context," "Context Becoming Concept," "Large Scale: Concepts Becoming Contexts." Within this new mode of publication are presented a multiplicity of projects, and each amplifies and specifies the spectrum of experimentations that lie *in nuce*, unforeseen, in Tschumi's theoretical works. That is why I quickly flashed out some of them in the first part of this chapter, not so much in order to impose a rigid continuity as to indicate a trajectory. The mixing, combining, and crossing of these terms or concepts remain always bound to each occurrence (the project's constraints and demands), and this is certainly not done according to a hierarchical relationship between them. Then how? Only a close look at a few projects can make Tschumi's trajectory evident.

Event-Cities 1 opens with a specific part of the project for Parc de la Villette, presenting the most ephemeral component of it, the fireworks display, "in order to emphasize the 'event' dimension, the dimension of action, in what makes up a city" (*EC1*, 12). The fireworks, which took place in 1992, when the Parc had not yet been completed, are a three-dimensional version of the superimposition of the points, lines, and surfaces and are diagrammatically designed as a musical system of notation.

One project presented in *EC1*, included in the "Transient Events" section, is the *Groningen Video Glass Gallery* (1991), a pavilion built in a park for the display of pop music videos (figure 4.12). The pavilion is constructed completely in glass (glass beams, glass walls, glass partitions, glass stiffeners, glass roof) except for the tilted concrete base. Everything at first glance seems visible, apparent to the eye. But if we look more closely, there are several elements that delay an immediate reading of the pavilion: inside the pavilion several glass walls activate the movement and the space, and so do the video monitors that are arranged at different angles on metal racks. Tschumi creates a correspondence between the pavilion as a temporary construction (with a short-term use) and the videos' short duration, producing therefore at the same time a correspondence and a collision among different media. The strategy is to push to the extreme the concept of short duration and to render it in the (im)materiality of the building, and yet to maintain a sense of different spatiotemporal rhythms, a negation of a simple presence. A joke between words and materiality is obtained with the use of clips and their visibility: clips are the visible metal elements that keep together the glass sheets, but clips also refer to pop music videos. *Glass Video Gallery* shares, although pushed to the extreme, the normal principles of a pavilion, always a construction where inside and outside are blurred, where "inside and outside pass smartly one into another"; but it deviates from a typical pavilion because even if its "walls stand free like screens in spaces . . . and glass reflects a little of everything," it cannot be said that "slender columns carry an almost floating roof."[39] There are no columns, because the glass is structural and what remains of "columns" are only the metal racks that support the monitors.

Figure 4.12. Bernard Tschumi, Groningen Glass Video Gallery, 1990. Groningen, Netherlands. © Bernard Tschumi.

The pavilion destabilizes the visitor's optic and haptic dimensions, and glass not only delimits the inside and outside but is also present inside the pavilion so that it renders everything experienceable among multiple layers;[40] the monitors and the vision of the videos are in a situation that is inverted from a normal setting: they are not in the dark (at home or in a screening room) but are exposed to the outside (and most visible at night). Because the pavilion is inclined, bodily movement must be engaged with this inclination, and, as Greg Lynn has noticed, the pavilion conveys a floating experience in which the body "occupies multiple positions of stability." The floating sensation created in the Video Glass Gallery is "*aviary*, and involves the dematerialization of an object to the point at which it begins to float in the air. . . . [The pavilion] is perhaps the most radical in this regard. The transparency of the envelope, along with the structuring of the mass itself with the glass-bearing elements, dematerializes the mass of the pavilion. This dematerialization is linked to the elevation and sloping of the ground plane from the horizontal datum of the site."[41] One would be tempted to add that uncannily it seems to see and to materialize Depero's much earlier intuitions. Tschumi's calculated crossover—almost a mise-en-abyme—of different windows (the door, the window, the wall, and the screen) experiments with, and confronts architecture with, the apparent dematerialization brought forth by electronic technologies. As he wrote:

> Dematerialization in architecture cannot be separated from the development of technology. The more recent stages of dematerialization are not only structural but they introduce electricity and electronics as integral parts of architecture. Between the tectonic and the electronic, between the building and the billboard, between the city of places and the spaces of flows is a residual space that ultimately changes its own definition. This residual, non-designed, in-between space can be designated as one of the spaces of the events.[42]

In Tourcoing, France, at Le Fresnoy National Studio for Contemporary Arts (1991–97), these residual in-between spaces are activated via a multiplicity of constructive interventions and interpenetrations at many levels; Tschumi Architects has rehabilitated and transformed (while also adding to) an old leisure complex from the 1920s to create a center for crossovers of contemporary arts (a school, a film studio, a *mediathèque*, spectacle and exhibition halls, two cinemas, housing, laboratories for research and production, and other offices and facilities). They envisioned a center where "artists could deal with crossovers among disciplines—film, video, computer animation, performance art, installation art, and so forth" (*Tschumi/Walker*, 115). One of the main features of the project is the superimposition of a new roof, the *artifi-ciel* (*artificial-sky*), above the existing roofs of the complex. The *artifi-ciel* has transparent parts (clouds), and the relationship between clouds (transparent sheets of polycarbonate) and sky (steel roof) here is inverted because it is the cloud-shaped parts of the roof through which light can pass (during the day from the outside in, during the night from the inside out), so that the roof presents a negative image of a cloud-filled sky. We could ask, we could wonder, or even space could wonder, "Have the Futurist's clouds of the "Reconstruction of the Universe" finally landed in an architectural project?" And space could reply, "Apparently so." But one should notice the defamiliarizing invention—as shock—with the negative inversion at play here: between artificial and natural, between immaterial and material. In Superstudio's screenplay *Life*, looking at the clouds would have been again possible, as the voice-over indicated; here at Le Fresnoy anyone can have a look at them, now with an architecture innervated among media. The roof structure folds on one end to become the north façade of a box-shaped new structure. The trusses that support the roof are cinematic, because their frame-like structure activates spaces as potential movie stills or photos of performance. The potential of this architecture exceeds and explodes the notion of the container; in between the new roof structure and the old buildings are many spaces for gathering and for circulation: a cinema *en plein air*, a restaurant, and many catwalks allowing for free movement (figure 4.13); the heating, ventilation,

Figure 4.13. Bernard Tschumi, Le Fresnoy National Studio for Contemporary Arts, 1991–97. Tourcoing, France. © Bernard Tschumi.

air-conditioning ducts are also visible in the in-between spaces, creating additional architectural movement. Embracing affirmatively the constraints set by the old buildings, the project avoids any synthesis between form and function, and indeed "in this suspended space of pure circulations,"[43] as Silvia Lavin defined it, the connections between the different parts are often provided by suspended ramps and staircases that interpenetrate vertically, horizontally, and obliquely. Certainly, the surprising snapshots that could be taken from a multiplicity of viewpoints while moving inside Le Fresnoy would demonstrate Lavin's point that "by giving up a 'legible image' Le Fresnoy constructs the vertiginous effects of movement" (35); that is exactly what Le Fresnoy performs. The spatial crossovers that are in play here are certainly in tune with the multiple crossovers of artistic disciplines that this new electronic Bauhaus wants to foster.

The notion of performance has surfaced and infiltrated architecture with a new swerve since the beginning of the twenty-first century.[44] Performativity in architecture when "it's not just technology *per se*" but "architecture pushed to its limits"[45] is at play in the project by Tschumi Architects at Columbia University, Alfred Lerner Hall (1994–99). Asked to re-create a new student center on a campus that preserves its strong nineteenth-century identity (determined by single buildings devoted to different departments and by a fixed system of structure and cladding), Tschumi Architects (with Hugh Dutton, Gruzen Samton, and Ove Arup and Partners) deviated from

Figure 4.14. Bernard Tschumi, Lerner Hall Student Center, Columbia University, 1994–99. New York, USA. © Bernard Tschumi.

this norm, constructing an extraordinary performative but unprogrammed space of circulations. Tschumi Architects rehabilitated two buildings, one on Broadway and one inside the campus (with programmatic heterogeneity: i.e., bookstore, administrative spaces, auditorium, cinema, experimental theater) and placed in between a hub for multiple circulations and unexpected exchanges. The façade of the hub is not only an inclined curtain-wall, all in glass without structural columns (the glass being structural) and supported only by two trusses, but it is structurally joined with the ramps (with floor glazing): the ramps (intersecting triangulated plates with a diamond layout) and the curtain-wall support one another, sharing and performing forces and resistances. The project is performative because "the foregrounding of the structural logics stems from the fact that they provide the most direct and literal index of forces of matter, and thus are sensitive enough to register the complex interplay of program, structure, and flows."[46] In the same stroke, it also provides a space for everyday performance, offering to whoever looks at it or moves in it an open sense of airy circulations, exchange, and interaction: an "extra-ordinary" space (figure 4.14) that tackles the everyday life of campus. "At night, as light glows from the inside, figures in movement along this route [of the ramps] appear as if in a silent shadow theater."[47] The internal circulations and the crossing of programs are amplified by the use of more normative wall windows (as for the lounges or the dining room); the cinema on the third floor (inside one of the existing buildings) has a screen that can be lifted up so that it "becomes the balcony of the multipurpose auditorium below" (*EC2*, 331), and when the two are connected from the balcony, a big bay window cut into the wall gives a multilayered view that, passing through the layers of glasses, reaches out onto the outside campus. The project brings layers of permeability between interior and exterior spaces.

"Space is temporal because we move through it; time is spatial because, as architects, space is what we construct. It is through space that we are capable of addressing time. But time exists to activate our spaces, occasionally transforming them by challenging perceptions of their boundaries."[48] It is with this affirmation in mind that I close this chapter, an affirmation certainly pertinent for Tschumi Architects' project for a museum in Athens, Greece. To the challenge of constructing the New Acropolis Museum in Athens, Tschumi Architects responds in a specific way, swapping a palindrome of two terms between their gerundive and noun forms: "conceptualizing context and contextualizing concept." The museum, three hundred meters from the Parthenon, houses artifacts from early archeological finds, the Parthenon Marbles, and Roman Empire artifacts: these artifacts are displayed along a circulation loop that offers visitors a spatial experience inflected by time. The programmatic concept has been kept simple, we read in *EC3*, to avoid competing with the content and the context. This concept organizes three superimposed, autonomous parts made of three different materials (concrete, marble, glass); the base, the support for the museum, stands on several columns situated in such a way that archeological excavations of the ancient city are left untouched and made visible by glass-paneled floors (and a void) at the entrance. From the atrium, the visitors walk on ramps (built in part with glass-paneled floors showing other parts of the ancient city) and move among many artifacts; in the middle part of the building, in the Archaic Gallery, statues are situated on simple bases, and "twenty-nine concrete columns articulate an eight-meter-high space. As a result, the marble statues appear to populate this open space in casual arrangements of figures—the first and 'original' inhabitants of the Museum."[49] From the photos of this space, the haptic aspects of a possible strolling among "the inhabitants" (the statues) and new concrete columns make one wonder (if a jump-cut is allowed): how would a filmic sequence from Roberto Rossellini's *Journey to Italy* (1953–54), when the protagonist visits the National Archeological Museum in Naples, be remade here?[50] How would camera movements be choreographed in these spaces today and in this city? And what would they suggest?

The top floor, made almost only of glass, lets the frieze of the Parthenon Marbles (mounted on a rectangular concrete core) communicate from a distance with the Acropolis. The spatial experience of the top has an ulterior swerve because its orientation is the same as that of the visible Acropolis (figure 4.15). The different spatial and temporal layers, resulting from the circulation through the loop among the ancient artifacts, produce an interspersion of spaces and times, of proximities and distances, visible, perceptible, and also polemical. This polemical, out-of-joint, spatiotemporal dimension

Figure 4.15. Bernard Tschumi, New Acropolis Museum, 2001–9. Athens, Greece. © Bernard Tschumi.

suggests the past reclaiming the parts of the frieze that are missing, held at the British Museum; besides the orientation of the top floor, a clear difference in color tone between the original parts of the frieze and the cast copies (of the missing parts) reinforces the correspondence and the potential polemic at play in this context(s) and among these contents.

The frieze is in parts not only because of the missing pieces but also because it narrates a story (the Panathenaic Procession) that is only apprehensible if one moves or passes along it; Tschumi, with his previous experimentations in film narrativity, could not have failed to work through this analogy after Sergei Eisenstein. The narration can be apprehended in motion, Tschumi affirms, like the drawings from *The Street*, the first episode of the *Manhattan Transcripts*:

> An informing source for this and other early work was the Russian cinematographer Sergei M. Eisenstein, whose great essay from the 1930's "Montage and Architecture," was inspired by Greek architecture and in particular by the buildings of the Acropolis. The famous cavalcade scene in Eisenstein's film *Alexander Nevsky* shows a striking resemblance to the equestrian segments in the Parthenon Frieze. In the essay, rediscovered only in 1980, Eisenstein thinks analogically,

> referring to the Acropolis as "the perfect example of one of the most ancient films," uniquely capable of "fixing the total representation of a phenomenon in its full visual multidimensionality." Once again, the Acropolis appears in all its complexity, as an original "context" for thought.[51]

The New Acropolis Museum, more than "fixing the total representation," shows that architecture can invent the constructing, even among ruins, of multidimensional interpenetrations of different times, spaces, and media; in short, it can eventually conceptualize a context.

The aim of this chapter was to traverse in an extensive way moments, episodes, of Tschumi's trajectory that intersect with previous material examined in this book; Tschumi's trajectory, with its different incursions in the space of modernity triggering unexpected connections among times and spaces and among disciplines, demonstrates the consistency of its architecturability; "consistency" is indeed a term that Anthony Vidler only recently utilized, instead of unity, to praise Tschumi's work.[52]

Tschumi's ability to activate new and unexpected architectural innervations and interspersions in the city results in consistencies: it cannot be reduced to a series of flat images. Tschumi's architectures and texts need to be traversed to understand why and how architecture for him is a form of knowledge or, if you will, of knowability. At the risk of incurring the charge of cliché, one might say that, instead of images, Tschumi's works are closer to "script-images" and that Tschumi's architectures can be seen as parting from what Benjamin indicates is the relation of the what-has-been to the now—can be seen as suddenly emergent, *sprunghaft*, architectures that, cracking the continuity, are invented, imagining and activating conditions for constructing a relation between spaces and events in new ways.

Chapter 5

✦

Adventuring (in) the Architectural Field

Rem Koolhaas and the Office for Metropolitan Architecture

Part 1: *S,M,L,XL* and Its "Architecture-Characters"

The Novel(s) of Architecture

This final chapter moves between two publications of OMA (Office for Metropolitan Architecture), *S,M,L,XL* and *Content*, and it is divided into two parts in which I access my limited selective reading of the massive, multifarious, and fabulous works that OMA has produced since the 1970s. I do not intend for this reading to be exhaustive. Although this chapter and the previous one may seem to be parallel, my principal intention is not really to confront Bernard Tschumi and Rem Koolhaas but instead to see how OMA's architecturability relates—with several twists and turns—not just to Bernard Tschumi's experimentations but also to my other chapters. So while there is much that might be studied about the two architects' interactions from the time that Tschumi taught at the Architectural Association in London while Koolhaas was a student up to the many calls for projects in which the two architectural firms have participated or, needless to say, about their divergent styles of writing and of presenting their ideas, these are not the main focus of this chapter. The focus of my reading of OMA will be to look at the singularity of some moments of their trajectory and to see how, in this trajectory, a particular architecturability is at play. By the end of this chapter, we will turn back but also forward—in a double movement—to colportage, the term examined in the first chapter in relation to the *Arcades Project*: I now posit that OMA activates a colporting of architectures in contemporary space. There is no question of applying to this chapter a theory defined in the preceding chapters, or of finding here a final, definitive gathering together of the many threads identified earlier. Instead, my interdisciplinary reading dwells on considering how general questions of architecture and the urban are specifically thought and staged by OMA as they are interspersed within a certain theatricality and fictionality, always critical and yet inventive.

This said, the chapter jumps directly into *S,M,L,XL*,[1] leaving outside the frame all the projects and texts OMA did before; hopefully it will not seem illicit both to make such a jump and to posit that *S,M,L,XL*, among other things, is an "anti-procrustean" attempt to differentially free up architecture and the urban from historicism and postmodernism alike.[2] *S,M,L,XL*, a megabook, is all about an open-ended anti-procrustean dimensionality that simultaneously entails and fosters an architecture at play with technology, scale, numbers, needs—that aims at imagining new ways of performing in architecture, as mass medium, at the crossroads of a multiplicity of media that recast architecture's fabrics and urbanism's freedoms. The title *S,M,L,XL* is in part inspired by one of Branzi's "Radical Notes" titled "Small, Medium, Large,"[3] in which the Italian architect wrote that "the dimension is the only parameter we have to evaluate the differences which exist between the metropolis, the city, and the village."[4] Branzi himself affirms that Koolhaas makes an analogous use of his argument for which "there are no differences between the micro and macro scale, and as in clothing, the differences between people (I would say) are only a question of cut: small, medium, large, extra-large" (51). The analogy is present, and references to Archizoom and Superstudio surface throughout the book project, but they are complemented by a multiplicity of other layers that construct and give volume to it.

First of all there is the dependence of architecture on the world at large; the introduction of *S,M,L,XL* states that architects are "ostensibly involved in 'shaping' the world, for their thoughts to be mobilized architects depend on provocations of others—clients, individual or institutional" (xix). For architects, being confronted "with an arbitrary sequence of demands, with parameters they did not establish, in countries they hardly know," implies that "architecture is a *chaotic adventure*" (xix). The material presented follows such an adventure and offers the reader/viewer multiple ways of accessing it. There is no single project, and no single aspect of a project, that is presented in the same way; instead each project is presented within continuously shifting grounds and unstable staging modes, so as to resist any simple unpacking of OMA's adventures. On the back cover, the book is said to be "a novel about architecture. Conceived as . . . a free-fall in the space of the typographic imagination, the book's title, *Small, Medium, Large, Extra-Large*, is also its framework: projects and essays are arranged according to scale." Although this book has been compared for its force of innovation to Le Corbusier's *Toward a New Architecture*, certainly its typographical imagination also reminds one of the Futurist artist Fortunato Depero's autopromotional work *The Bolted Book* (1927). *S,M,L,XL*, published almost seventy years after *The Bolted Book*, can make use of a wider range of different media and supports, yet the two works share a highly complex and playful mode of display; the latter runs not as a CD-ROM but as a "CD-REM [that] side-steps the computer hardware altogether when first loaded, operating through the medium of a full-length print-out of the data itself."[5]

To state it in a more classical way, the book, as "a novel about architecture," uses multiple narrative strategies that relate to what is defined in literary terms as "in medias res": it starts the story not from the beginning but in medias res, in the middle of OMA's professional trajectory (the table of contents is structured to move from small projects to medium, large, and extralarge projects, but the complexity dwells for each cut); it is also *au pied de la lettre* in medias res because this is exactly the way OMA/Koolhaas address the projects and the built environments; it presents an architecture (alternative to one that "defines, excludes, limits, separates from the 'rest' ")[6] and an inventive and generous "new" urbanism ("obsessed . . . with the manipulation of infrastructure for endless intensifications and diversifications, shortcuts and redistributions—the reinvention of psychological space" [969]); both architecture and urbanism appear from the start, meshing and interpenetrating among many other media, and their appearance in the book is articulated among different genres (diaries, essays, fairy tales, manifestos). All these factors show architectures at *n* dimensions, and this megabook or hyperbook about OMA's galaxy, which doesn't present the projects in a typical architectural monograph (where indeed many details would have been more clearly defined), seems to spring off and to incessantly point toward a wide array of demands, programs, and inventions. *S,M,L,XL* narrates a multiplicity of enlaced stories for which architecture is embedded in the world, and with its "accumulation of words and images [the book] illuminates the condition of architecture today—its splendors and miseries—exploring and revealing the corrosive impact of politics, context, the economy, globalization—the world" (back cover). A mesh of sketches for constructive ideas, technical drawings, a massive amount of photos more or less in focus (of realized projects or of Styrofoam models), text-projects authored by Koolhaas: all these constellate this extraordinary book.

The projects are designated by enigmatic titles more suitable for short stories or chapters of a novel (never by the name of the architecture under consideration), which incorporate a fictional effect into the built (or buildable) architectures. Just two examples from the "Small" section give a glimpse into this last aspect: a project for the renovation of a hotel in the Swiss Alps is titled "Worth a Detour"; a project for a video bus stop in the Netherlands is titled "Only 90°, Please." It is up to the reader/viewer to engage with the fictional challenges implied in the title. Finally, if there is no critical external text analyzing OMA's projects, we find instead a curious ad hoc dictionary; indeed, the format of this book clearly resembles one. The dictionary's status and relevance in this palimpsest are ambiguous: the words (and the related texts) that comprise the dictionary are derived from multiple sources (critical theory, architectural theory, and literature, in large part) and are placed on the two external edges of many of the pages. This dictionary is composed of series of endless objets trouvés or perhaps just clichés, in any case, of splinters derived from broad architectural debates of the late twentieth century.

The list of the sources for the quotes, almost hidden, is found only in the last pages of the book, just before the images' copyright information.

But something more could be said in relation to this ad hoc dictionary and the rest of the book. Umberto Eco's challenge to a clear-cut difference between dictionary and encyclopedia can be useful in addressing this jungly megabook. Eco's argument, in a nutshell, might be stated in this way: while it is accepted that a dictionary is concerned with words and that an encyclopedia is instead concerned with things, even if a dictionary should contain what is universal and what constitutes linguistic competence, at the same time any linguistic competence is also encyclopedic, implying all the uses and practices, and therefore for Eco it is difficult to distinguish what is considered "necessary" and what is not.[7] In the expanded yet congested (to use one of Koolhaas's idioms) field produced by *S,M,L,XL*, while the dictionary stands out for marking the borders of a critical and interdisciplinary discourse about architecture and urbanism, the encyclopedic tone of stuff and things, present or implied (necessary or contingent), in the rest of the book points toward an encyclopedic-yet-experimental posture, in between the state of architecture at the end of the twentieth century and an autopromotional spectacular or enchanting presentation of OMA's enterprise and architectural journey.

Sarah Whiting, architect and critic, has written eloquently about the book that "rather than falling prey to the genre's anesthetizing logic of consumption, Koolhaas and Bruce Mau generated a monograph of incongruously ethereal density that defies facile appropriation (although notable efforts have been made.)"[8] I have no intention to appropriate the book so as to find the one main key of access to the book project or, if you prefer, a long-lost encyclopedic knowledge of architecture and urbanism (nor a comprehensive and exhaustive interpretation of the way architecture and urbanism have been imagined by OMA), but I would like to approach some aspects of a few projects, not only in order to shed light on the ways architecture, in its medium specificity, is imagined among other media as a contemporary in-progress research but also in order to meet some of the multitude of architecture-characters that spring from OMA's adventure and inhabit *S,M,L,XL*.

Perhaps, only perhaps, the tension between dictionary and encyclopedia may in part resolve the problematic swerve of the defense of the whole as proposed in "Bigness" (one of the four key texts in *S,M,L,XL*);[9] such a defense seems problematic on a general level as well, as it seems apparently distant from what in fact OMA performs in the many projects that repeatedly explode, expand, and break the limits of architecture and of any totality.

Three Glances at S *and* M*, or How to Effectively Render Projects in Intermedial Formats*

What follows in this section are just glances at aspects of OMA's adventures, considering how *S,M,L,XL* places the emphasis in relation to specific situations in which OMA operated, as well as which media are selected and mobilized for the presentation: a project in Japan that demonstrates a passion to learn more about this faraway land and its contemporary culture; a project in the city of Rotterdam that puts the spotlight on the tension occurring in the negotiation among public authority, developers, and architects; and finally a project in Morocco never achieved because of an international crisis.

Designing from a Distance

"+13,000 Points" is the title of one of the projects in S that presents OMA's built project for Nexus World Housing in Fukuoka, Japan (1991). The Japanese architect Arata Isozaki, in charge of a master plan "for a superblock with freestanding perimeter buildings for a client that wanted to introduce 'a new urban lifestyle' in Japan" (84), invited a chorus of architects to participate in the project (one from Japan and five "Westerners," as the book defines them). The pages presenting this project unfold in a specific way, adjusting the focus of the site and the project; in the first two leaves an aerial view embedded in a dark blue sky shows a blurred landscape below; the second two leaves depict an aerial photographic view of the area surrounding the site; and a third spread displays a map of the context in which the photos of the architects are signposts marking the map. OMA was assigned twenty-four individual houses, "each three stories high, packed together to form two blocks" (113). The photo on the next two leaves illustrates the already built project: undulate and floating roofs contrast with the block walls as well as with the series of anonymous conventional apartment buildings in the background; for each apartment, contrasts between enclosed and open spaces are at play; the first floors provide the entrance and a private stone garden; the second floors, dedicated to the bedrooms, have introverted spaces; and the top floors (a mix of dining and living areas and an additional room) are extroverted spaces with balconies open to the outside. The following twenty-four leaves have changing layouts and different contents, but they also share a repetitive pattern: on the outer borders of the left-hand pages appear fragments of images from Japan (maps, manga comics, photos of disturbing pornographic gestures, interiors, exteriors, infrastructures, and cityscapes, and some depicting OMA during the stay in Japan), and on the inner or right side of the same pages appear short written texts (travelogues, impressions of the city and of the encounter with the locale and the locals, reflections on and comparisons about the architecture); this diary in pieces enacts the Japanese adventure, sometimes with a freestyle prose. On the majority of the right-hand pages are photos showing details of OMA's built architecture. A contrasting effect is obtained between the volatile, accumulated traces of the Japanese adventure and the completed project, which breaks apart the very idea of the block.

This sequence of pages could be compared to raw materials the German film director Wim Wenders used when shooting his documentary *Tokio Ga*

(1985). *Tokio Ga* and the presentation of the project share a poetics that dwells within and beyond Roland Barthes's fascination with Japan; it is a poetics that pertains to a generation who grew up in the aftermath of World War II, in these two cases to Europeans who, immersed in the worlds of images, have experimented with a traveling cinematic gaze; among the stock of images, only glimpsed or steadily stared at by such an enchanted gaze, there are also those that have seen the fall of Berlin Wall and the coming of globalization.

This assemblage of images and texts is followed by several technical drawings and layouts of the floor plans, and the last two pages conclude the presentation with a black-and-white photo that shows two Japanese men in traditional costume apparently celebrating a ritual in a *terrain vague* not far from a freeway; such an image yet again seems to show the tension between tradition and modernization. This incursion into the presentation of the project shows how the authors of *S,M,L,XL*, rather than simply presenting photos of achieved projects, intersperse the projects themselves with experiential aspects that possibly, but not necessarily, converged into the executed projects.

Cartoonizing Developers' Taste: OMA's Junk

"Byzantium" offers another alternative way to present a project: this time the difficulties of negotiation between developers and architects is rendered as a comic illustrated by Thomas Koolhaas and Louis Price (figure 5.1). Byzantium, a mixed-use project, is a complex of housing, offices, and shops completed by OMA in 1991 in Amsterdam to replace a power plant in the downtown area. The cartoon narrates epic moments of tension between an innovative architect who believes in "integration and complication" and backward and greedy developers who declare OMA's first proposal "old junk" and "incompetence not integration" and yell, "Make it simple! All this costs money!!!" (357). Thinking through the project, a cartoon version of Koolhaas reflects, "I want it urban; you want it suburban. I want a round window; you make it square. Why the hell did you hire me?" (359). Despite the developers' opposition, the OMA proposal wins the competition, because "public opinion mobilizes behind OMA. . . . Critics and public unanimously endorse OMA's position. . . . Somehow, to the developers' horror, OMA WINS!!! A victory for complication" (361). The story ends with speech balloons that pop up from the new buildings: anonymous inhabitants comment, "Fantastic! Sensational! How they must envy us!" or "It is a miracle of integration!"; from the old buildings other voices comment, "They say the architect went out of his mind" and "I heard he already was crazy" (361). Despite its quite gloomy black-and-white tones, the graphic rendering of the negotiations among developers, authority, and architects—as well as between old and new ways of assembling architectures—gives hope that architects can defend their positions and not become totally surrounded.

Figure 5.1. OMA, *Byzantium*. Illustrations by Tomas Koolhaas and Louis Price. *S,M,L,XL*, p. 357. © OMA.

Turning Spaces Inside Out: A Mirage Project

OMA's project for the 1990 competition for the Palm Bay Seafront Hotel and Convention Center in the city of Agadir (Morocco) is introduced by a reproduction of the *Time* magazine article about the catastrophic earthquake that killed thousands of people and destroyed the city in 1960; this document is followed by and contrasted with a flashy montage of the king of Morocco's arrival aboard an Air France Concorde at the city's airport. The site for the project was located between the typically 1960s New Town (built after the earthquake) and the area that hosts one of the Moroccan king's five palaces: in *S,M,L,XL* we read that a group of "friends of the king" is planning to develop a "new Agadir" (376). OMA's project aims at respecting the beauty of the location between a beach and a forest of eucalyptus by designing a block sliced horizontally in two but with a curvilinear plane; in the lower part, the socle, "the heterogeneous elements of the convention center—auditoriums, conference rooms, foyers—form artificial dunes, a seamless continuation of the surroundings" (382). On the upper part stands a hotel, not with single rooms but with "individual apartments, each with its own exterior space" (382); private and public, artificial and natural, exterior and interior all intersperse. The lower and upper parts are thus divided by a void, and this configuration is poetically described as follows: "The floating upper half seems a mirage of the socle . . . the irregular forests of columns . . . the blue light that filters through the glass floor of the pool . . . the polished concrete, mosaic tiles, gold leaf: Islamic space turned inside out, Islam after Einstein" (382). The undulate shapes of the two parts have concrete "shells" cast upon the dunes to imitate the surrounding, and the upper shell is engineered to be sustained by columns that are different in height, thickness, and spacing.

Because of the tension in the international relations between Morocco and France (and the United States), this competition was abruptly and silently interrupted: the project became a mirage for OMA. A few words chronicle the situation: "The king was going to choose. No one answers the phone at the Palm Bay Company anymore" (382). While an unexpressive design was later selected, aspects of this enchanting design reappear in other, later OMA projects; indeed, a kind of repetition of structural architectural elements aimed at subverting and updating the canon of architecture and being responsive to the differentiation of each project's singularity within modernity and modernization is what reverberates in the firm's constant inventions. OMA approaches its goals with a calculated but inventive play operated by the synergy of engineering and architecture research: a kind of architecturability. The forest of columns will return as an element of another singular project, the Kunsthal Museum in Rotterdam.

A Theatrical Piece versus a Guided Tour, or the Space That Entertains

OMA participated twice in competitions related to a sustained effort that began in the mid-1980s to rehabilitate a *terrain vague* in Rotterdam with a Museum Park to host many different programs. OMA won the second competition, which involved only the building of a museum for temporary exhibitions. The site was quite urban and heterogeneous: the southern side was delimited by a highway (on the top of a dike), and the northern side, "a level lower, faces the Museum Park—conventional contemplation."[10] I approach this project with cross-referenced attention to the intricate way the architectural spaces are organized but also exposed and displayed among different layers both in *S,M,L,XL* and in Cecil Balmond's *Informal*.

In "Life in a Box?" OMA tells us that they chose the square as "a general envelope," and a few words introduce the working hypothesis foregrounding the project:

> The square would be crossed by two routes: one, the existing road running east–west; the other, a public ramp running north–south . . .
>
> These crossings would divide the square into four parts.
>
> The question then became:
>
> *How to imagine a spiral in four separate squares?* (431)

The Art Center is only apparently a box: the envelope is immediately contradicted from the outside, whose façades are all different: "The Kunsthal does appears hastily, even arbitrarily put together with an assortment of materials. Corrugated plastic and metal mesh mix with steel and travertine, exposed concrete meets wood."[11] In *S,M,L,XL* a series of photos of the already built project occupy entire pages, and around the photos are fragments from Samuel Beckett's high-modernist theatrical piece *Waiting for Godot*, printed in a huge font, while short sentences in a much smaller font form a narrative that suggests how to visit, as if the reader is there, to experience the spatial configuration of the building. The narrative aims at proximity, addressing the visitor or participant with a friendly "you." What could be the relevance of the fragments from Beckett's play? Perhaps Thomas Cousineau's study "*Waiting for Godot*": *Form in Movement* can give us some hinges. In this work, which appeared around the time of the Kunsthal projects in the early 1990s, the literary critic Cousineau reconsidered the choreographic aspects of gesture and physical movement in Beckett's play. Cousineau details the indications in the play and the rhythmical movements of Vladimir and Estragon; on a stage almost totally devoid of objects other than the stone and the tree, at times the characters are asked to move within a certain rectangularity that Cousineau reads as the characters' rigidity, "suggesting the idea of their entrapment with an enclosed space."[12] Through the formal patterns of motion described by the actors' trajectories, in which the tree and the stone are crucial, "the boredom into which our expectation of traditional action has led us is replaced by a fascination with the aesthetic effect that this 'form in movement' creates" (93). In this way, Cousineau argues, Beckett points toward a physical language that "communicates to a preverbal region of the psyche in which, long before we acquire words, we perceived the world in terms of shapes without bothering to ask their meanings" (93). For Cousineau there is a dissonance, a nondirect communication, between the lines and geometries described by gestures and movements and the human situation; in this resides one of the crucial aspects of the play.

In *S,M,L,XL*, the first photo of the Kunsthal is one taken in motion from the highway while driving by, the quote from Beckett's play is "I am not an historian," and the instruction for the visit is "Approach the building from the boulevard" (432–33). The second photo is taken in front of the Kunsthal, at night, echoing the play; it is accompanied by the indication "Enter the ramp toward the dike," and one of the quotes from the play is "The Tree?" Indeed, the picture, in blue ghostly or lunar tones, shows little groups of visitors and not the tree, but notice the juxtaposition of three different kinds of columns, a point to which I will return. The fragments of the theatrical piece and the short guide are arranged according to a dissonance or, better, an out-of-sync-ness that breaks apart continuity; and as Davidson has magisterially observed,[13] the firm's goal here is the breaking apart—through a specific way of connecting ramps and spaces—of an illustrious precedent of continuous circulation: Le Corbusier's congress hall for Strasbourg (1964), which aimed at a unified whole. This out-of-sync-ness starts from the initial ramp that cuts through the building before even giving access or entrance to it. Then, in Davidson's words, "inside, the 'spiral' that attempts to move through the fragmented square continuously breaks apart, sending the visitor into volumes of space before sucking him or her up into another progression" (40). These parts are well orchestrated and designed, but far from norms and linearity; the inside spiral permits and invites a circulation, yet the "spiraling affect," as Davidson writes, "produces no recognizable form. Here, movement and form are discontinuous" (40). An additional feature of the guiding fragments in the Kunsthal section of *S,M,L,XL* is that often the photos and the words don't perfectly match; there is a delay, a short wait before one can match words and images, provided either by a smaller photo embedded in the page or by a photo on the following page. For example, in the photo that looks down toward the ramp, on the left lower corner we read "It slopes down the park," and on the right corner we read "Halfway down, enter the auditorium," but only on the following page are we guided toward the flight of steps leading to the auditorium that slopes in the opposite direction; the tension and delay or alternate rhythms are played out in the architectural configuration and reverberate in the *S,M,L,XL* presentation, which points toward a decentered constructed space, a singular theatrical spacing that engages the ephemeral and the stable, movement and stasis (or pause).

From the bottom to the top, the building is as follows: in the basement are Exhibition Hall 1 and technical rooms on one side, and a restaurant on the other; then on a higher level the auditorium and Hall 2, and on the top Hall 3 and offices. The ramp moves along these intersecting parts up to the roof.

This is one of the first projects that welded OMA with the engineer Cecil Balmond, who writes: "Trapped by a Cartesian cage I wanted to break out. The *informal* beckoned . . . that opportunity came with Rem Koolhaas and the Kunsthal in Rotterdam."[14] In his book, *Informal*, Balmond tells a story of the making of this constructed space, of the way the project was made possible by activating *informally* the structures that, rebelling against monotony, produced the interruption of sameness.

In opposition to the Cartesian cage—to the formal structure "that marches to strict rhythms"—Balmond proposes the *informal*, which offers a Futurist poetics of engineered and staged architecture, "a syncopation—a rat-ta-ta-tat—instead of the dull metronomic one-two repeat of post and beam" (62). Throughout his text, Balmond records the design process and how it strives toward making an actor of the space: "Why not skip a beat? Incline the vertical, slope the horizontal. Or allow two adjacent lines of columns to slip past each other. Let space entertain us. Let's see other possibilities, other configurations of how buildings may be framed and stabilized" (62). With an avant-garde tone, Balmond narrates and details the inventory of ad hoc strategies that freed this architecture from "structural correctness and compulsive

Figure 5.2. OMA, Kunsthal II (1992). *S,M,L,XL*, p. 447. © OMA.

repetition" (75): "Structure *talks*" (75), it is in dialogue with architecture, "producing a range of events that go to make the Kunsthal an experiment in progress" (105).[15] For example, instead of braces dictated by a universal language (as in the roofs of factories and warehouses), "let the diagonals scatter across the vertical cross-section" (74). "A different solution of curving element can run right through a plan area—it works just as well, probably even with more efficiency" (75). In contrast to the "dumb skeleton," these new structures speak in the text: "'I am the thread propelling a story' and have structure as a generating path, rather than lay an unthinking grid map of columns and beams over the subdivision of space" (72).

These talking structures, delivering surprise and adventure, mimic the need of temporary exhibition spaces to permit continuously changing arrangements: this is how Balmond presents Hall 1. Columns are almost living characters, choreographed pantomimes; in Balmond's text they "'slip' past each other. Not squared up or standing to order in a formal subdivision of space, here, a local condition—a single out-of-phase movement—influences and informs the whole space" (76). From columns that activate the structure in this manner results a space not contained within an inside but instead in communication with the outside; the columns, metamorphosed into trees (figure 5.2), communicate in a canny way with the outside and eventually, one could argue, with the stone and tree of *Waiting for Godot*. The way

Balmond narrates this seems almost to bring us into the "primeval forest of OMA," to paraphrase Benjamin: "Hunks of timber were brought in to flesh the vertical shafts. Hall 1 of the Kunsthal was no longer a room or an enclosure, through an end glass wall its internal space travelled to join up with the park outside. Somewhere between artifice and nature the room for changing exhibitions became a twilight zone of the *informal*" (79).

Moving up in the building, the raking columns (leaning over at a sharp angle) of the Lecture Theatre, which are also on the slope that connects the different parts, create a self-sustaining system of forces. The alternative, informal engineering structure combines "raking columns and inclined slabs in a self sustaining network of bending and direct forces which in technical terms provided a moment frame" (81). An intentional "shift away from the norm" produces events in which the visitor is invited to participate; one example is outside the Kunsthal along the highway, where the juxtaposition of three different kinds of columns (one is concrete; two are steel, one an I-beam and the other castellated) "gives an energy to the idea of entry, and the three distinct natures mix and interface to offer '*threshold*' as an improvisation" (88).[16] Theatrical aspects participate in the making of this project; their effect is to interrupt a linear narrative as a way to experiment with the space of the project in a different and multilayered way.

Re-enabling the Manifesto Style for the Field of After-Architecture

OMA has staged many projects in collaboration with Balmond / Ove Arup Office, producing hybridities between architecture and engineering from which have emerged architecture-characters that inhabit *S,M,L,XL*, among interconnected stories—and among spatial jumps. Already for the first of the Kunsthal projects (1988), OMA/Arup invented a specific ad hoc structural system that would contrast with the concept of the box: the vierendeel beams formed an open-ended catalogue—one that shares similarities with Superstudio's *Histograms*—but with an effective engineering swerve that challenges the idea of a homogeneous catalogue.[17] The original hand-drawn and handwritten studies by Balmond for the vierendeels are found exactly at the core of *S,M,L,XL*—in the middle of it. Although these studies are found, or placed, in such a core position, they fluctuate in the book among the whirlpool of incredible projects; as we read in "Last Apples" (1993): "A mutual invasion of territory and the corresponding blurring of specific professional identities" (667) gave the possibility to "explore new potentials for the formation of space" (668).

To explore these new potentials implies accepting that there exists in buildings a dark zone, which "is not only strictly 'useless' . . . it also becomes conceptually inaccessible to the architect, who has become an intruder in his own project, boxed in, his domain a mere residue of the others' demands" (665). Accepting such a claim also means giving up "the aura of objectivity" to work with "a mutated architecture no longer obsessively committed to form making but to the creation of *conditions*, the fabrication of *content*—scriptwriting by tectonic means" (665). To bring in a brisk comparison, we see here the coalescing of at least two aspects that Tschumi worked through: here the "useless" is mostly considered for not being an external "given" for the architect to observe, and the quest for conditions to reimagine architecture is envisioned as specific type of scriptwriting. In contrast to Tschumi, who touched on the manifesto format only to then move on to drawing as filmic scriptwriting, "Last Apples" is paired with a well-known manifesto, "Bigness, or the Problem of Large" (1993), which becomes, in contrast to Branzi's notes, a "problem": not simply something to posit but also a resource. Certainly "Bigness" shares many common traits with the "classic" Futurist manifestos: from the will to reconsider the urban and the importance given to the materiality of any complex assemblage, to the production of an internal/external genealogy (in this case that of the OMA/Koolhaas trajectory and architecture at large) and the schematic division into concise parts; after an introduction, the text presents "theorems" and reduces, in a synthetic way, four principal points already considered by Koolhaas in his *Delirious New York*,[18] then adds a fifth one pointing at something radically distant from any stable context: "Bigness is no longer part of any urban tissue. It exists; at most, it coexists. Its subtext is *fuck* context" (502). Then, in a following part, a brisk reconsideration of "modernization," the manifesto spins toward the second half of the century and reaches out to many global locations (in between the late 1950s and the 1980s, and expanding into the New World as well as the Old) and splits into two coupled cusps. The first cusp was when Europe apparently surpassed "the threat of Bigness by theorizing it beyond the point of application" (504) with the megastructures; Yona Friedman's *urbanisme spatiale* "was emblematic: Bigness floats over Paris like a metallic blanket of clouds, promising unlimited but unfocused potential renewal of 'everything,' but never lands, never confronts, never claims its rightful place—criticism as decoration" (504). The other extreme of the first cusp is exemplified by the complex building Beaubourg in Paris (Centre Georges Pompidou) and defined as a "Platonic Loft"—because it had, from one side, "spaces where 'anything' was possible" (505) and on the other side implied a blindness toward the "neutrality realized without effort in the American skyscraper" (505). The second cusp, generated from the aftermath of the intellectual fabric of 1968, resolves in the manifesto into two "defensive lines: dismantlement and disappearance" (505). The first is defined as a weak opposition to form-follows-function, produced by fireworks and other intellectual sophistications; the other, drawing from "a patchwork of arguments scavenged since the sixties from American sociologists, ideologues, philosophers, French intellectuals, cybermystics, etc., suggests that architecture will be the first 'solid that melts into air' " (507–8). It goes without saying that certainly "Bigness" acquires the tone of a Futurist manifesto from its way of defying and quickly dismissing an incredible stock of experimentations and researches (and their genealogies).

The selection of quite dull or unsophisticated adjectives—"large" or "big"—is certainly meant to point at some state of things that is difficult to name, recognize, and theorize about, yet Bigness "can sustain a promiscuous proliferation of events in a single container" (511), and this may happen because it develops without operating within oppositions (independence and interdependence), through contamination (not purity), in quantity (not quality); in fact, the activities at the core of Bigness for their complexity "*demand* to interact, but Bigness also keeps them apart. . . . It is simply impossible to animate its entire mass with intention. Its vastness exhausts architecture's compulsive need to decide and determine. Zones will be left out, free from architecture" (512–13). In conclusion, the tension between interaction and apartness is a promising resource to look at. Tschumi's fireworks are implicitly dismissed as "intellectual sophistications," and the imaginary of ropes is reconsidered: whereas Tschumi in the 1970s conceptualized through a photomontage of a man in ropes (as we have seen previously) the potentiality in place within rules ("many knots that cannot be untied" and yet can be accepted or broken), here the rope metaphor is at work in "a web of umbilical cords to other disciplines whose performance is as critical as the architect's: like mountain climbers tied together by lifesaving ropes, the makers of Bigness are a *team* . . . . Beyond signature, Bigness means surrender to technologies; to engineers, contracts, manufactures; to politics; to others" (513–14). Ropes, rules, constraints, ordinary and extraordinary—if you like, also "signature, event, context," to quote an indelible text in the humanities[19]—received an alternative consideration that while always performative, at least in its presentation, presses toward motion from the more conceptual into the more material realm.

Finally, to consider the tension between architecture and the urban, between the classical city and what no longer belongs to the "urban tissue," it is worth noticing how questions of theater or of representing Bigness on the stage are turned upside-down (if such a comparison and jump is accepted) in relation to Depero's "Magic Theater": using various font sizes, just as "Bigness" does, Depero declares that the new set design should be achieved with disproportions, difference in sizes and dimensions, but he also proposes a new way to construct set design in order to bring the life of the cityscapes onto the theatrical stage. What is announced instead in the final section of "Bigness" is an architecture transformed in such a way that apparently there is no longer even an avant-garde stage where the city happens: "The exterior of the city is no longer a collective theater where 'it' happens; there's no collective 'it' left. The street has become residue, organizational device. . . . Not only is Bigness incapable of establishing relationships with the classic city—*at most, it coexists*—but in the quantity and complexity of the facilities it offers, it is itself urban" (514–15). The same attraction and apartness defined within architecture is now at work in the tension between architecture and urbanism: "If urbanism generates potential and architecture exploits it, Bigness enlists the generosity of urbanism against the meanness of architecture. . . . [Bigness] gravitates opportunistically to locations of maximum infrastructural promise. . . . Bigness surrenders the field to after-architecture" (515–16). One of OMA's projects of the 1990s that exemplifies these aspects of Bigness is Euralille, a project enlaced in *S,M,L,XL* as an "infernal" enterprise of many actors.

Metropolitan Moments and Montages: Euralille

> We were surrounded by a group of people who said, "Please solve this!" There is an *ur*-scene at the beginning of every architectural enterprise: the architect, knowing almost nothing about the situation into which he is dropped, has to convince those who know everything, who have wrestled sometimes for years with the same issues—the most ignorant must persuade the most skeptical. It requires suspension of disbelief from which, sometimes, neither side recovers. (1162)

The passage above is part of the narrative Koolhaas wrote in "Quantum Leap" in commenting on the first completed phase of Euralille in 1994, a project that involved many entities and phases, before and after OMA's selection as the design team; in many of its moments, such a narrative clearly shows not a knowledge already established but a kind of knowability in progress accompanied by a positive attitude that will risk surprising with quite unorthodox proposals, for "a Freudian flight forward" (1164).

"Bigness" is one of the best-known project-texts by Koolhaas that spring from the intense practice OMA conducted in the 1990s while simultaneously participating in many competitions at enormous scales, located in exceptional sites, with complex programs devoted to collective activities. OMA's scriptwriting of architecture attentive to the "infrastructural potential" is evident in the huge project done in Lille, France. Through Euralille, the city was meant to become a "European city Hub" to be "competitive with the major metropoles of Europe":[20] OMA had to meet the needs of the several planned activities and the specificity of the site. Many negotiations and decisions were to be taken at the national and European level, between public and private actors and contactors, to come up with a project whose programs were supposed to connect with existing buildings; new ones included the TGV station and railroad, a European business center, shops, offices, parking structures, hotels, housing, a concert hall, and a congress Expo center. For Euralille, OMA's hinging point was to intensify the existing or potential network of infrastructures, so OMA played the game to exacerbate complication at many levels. The project has received incredible attention and is the subject of many publications. A Euralille-focused work that is fascinating

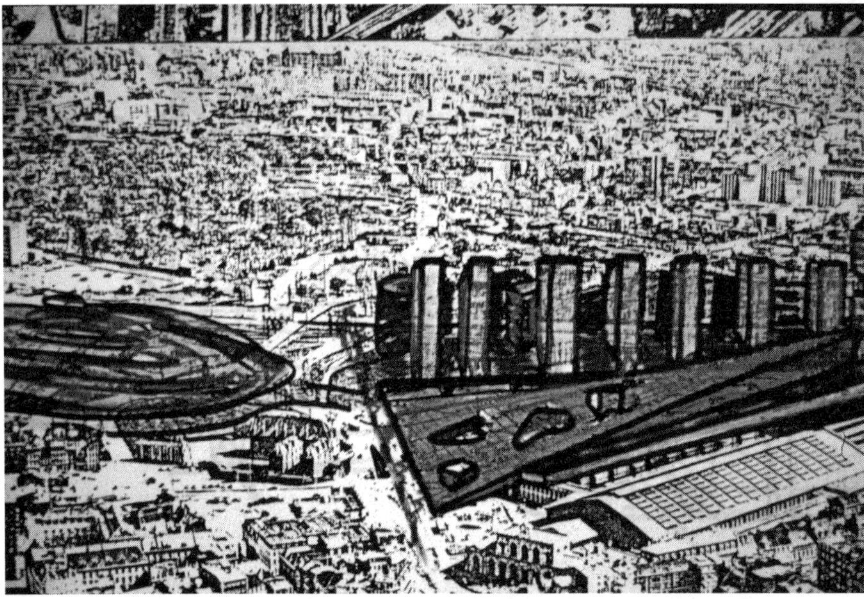

Figure 5.3. OMA, Euralille, early sketch, 1994. © OMA.

for its simplicity is the video by Richard Copans,[21] in which Koolhaas candidly explains, drawing on a white paper lines that connect European states (England, Belgium, Germany, the Netherlands) to France and to Lille, how the project was approached in a city with a historical configuration and a preexisting infrastructure (from traces of old city walls to the existing system of transportation).

What emerges from the beginning of the film is that Lille, with the reduction of distances brought by the TGV high-speed rail line, was to become a center of gravity or intensity for a community of 50 million Europeans; far was going to be near, and the challenge was to disentangle a Gordian knot: the TGV railway would run underground, but this line was still in conflict with another vector, that of the highway. OMA proposed to reroute the freeway and have it run underground parallel to the TGV. Between the old train station and the new TGV station there was a triangle: instead of a simple square or, worse, a residual space, to highlight the TGV station as a marker of the site, OMA imagined that triangular space "as a plane that could rotate along its axis, one part would emerge from the ground to become building while the other would descend far enough to expose the flank of the TGV tunnel [figure 5.3]: the train could be revealed through a 300-meter-long 'window'" (1166). The strategy of superimposition (for example, the construction of other buildings on top of the TGV station) was used so that this complex of buildings was less a place and more an interconnection of programs and distances; Lille, we read in *S,M,L,XL*, "would redefine the idea of 'address.' . . . What is important about this place is not where it *is* but where it *leads*, and how quickly. We imagined a series of skyscrapers straddling the station, towers that would suggest not a *place*, but a distance in *time* from the various cities. The address would be defined as '70 minutes from London,' '50 minutes from Paris,' '18 minutes from Brussels' " (1170). Is it by accident that the many entries from the ad hoc dictionary that gravitate around this project include those for "slow," "slowly," "so far," "space-time," "speed" (four entries), "stories," "styles," "synthetic," "technology," "through," "time"? Probably not.

In order to avoid any "boring" uniformity, OMA invited several architects to design the different buildings, with very different styles. OMA worked as a supervisor or, to put it in a more poetic way, to produce a mise-en-scène, or act as a filmmaker, and Euralille appears as a montage of programs.[22] OMA defined sections, levels, relationships, interfaces, and many interviewing strategies, and designed only the highest point of infrastructural density. OMA created a void, a hole to exalt the play of lines of circulation, as one of the metropolitan moments at Euralille,[23] what OMA called the Espace Piranesien.

The numerous publications that this project awakened detail critical points and motifs within the project as well as operative decisions taken, and here my intent is to be brief, just to capture the explicitly expressed will of producing a synthesis within the complex network—what one could define as the invention of metropolitan moments and montages. The hypothesis introducing the project in *S,M,L,XL* read: "Until recently, Lille (pop. 1,000,000), a formerly significant city, was leading a slightly melancholy existence. Once a mining and textile town, it had fallen on hard times. But two new givens—the tunnel between England and the continent and the TGV network (the French superfast train that will run through it)—will transform Lille as if by magic and make it important in a completely synthetic way" (1156). Certainly this project has also attracted harsh criticisms: one of the most interesting is the one by the architectural historian Jean-Louis Cohen, who has detailed the project's many faults and errors with the aim of showing how "Koolhaas's culture, intellectual capacity, talent and energy"[24] failed to pass the test of construction. In this review of the project, Cohen's final flight in synthesizing his views reads this way: "Although the slogan of 'Bigness' may remain, associated as in this case with a type of architecture which verges on cheap modern junk, it could well turn out to be a barren concept" (181). We will return shortly to the idea of junk, which soon became a question for Koolhaas, but let us for a moment dwell on the question of faults.

An Intermission: About Networks and Traveling

Koolhaas, presenting the Euralille project in the early 1990s, points toward a paradox inherent to the end of the twentieth century and concisely states that "the expression of the ambitions of Prometheus—the desire to change the destiny of an entire city—continues to be taboo."[25] And then, announcing a radical future, he opines: "In Lille, the TGV line is projected for the site of old fortifications, now engulfed by a proliferating periphery. A gigantic futurist project will be built two paces from the old quarter, resulting in an uncommon, hybrid condition that will permit the insertion of activities considered to be peripheral into the heart of the city" (93).

Now if you will allow me a jump cut (indeed, in this section that I expressly call an "intermission" I make several jump cuts), I would like to mention what the contemporary French philosopher Bernard Stiegler was saying in the 1990s considering the relation of networks and territories: "The territory is woven, there is only a becoming-network of the territory of the earth,"[26] and when its framing conditions change, due to the acceleration of technology (which evolves faster than culture), we experience radical deterritorialization. In the short essay "Developing Deterritorialization," Stiegler synthesizes his thought about technology's primary duplicity (and shortly afterward he published his first volume, *Technics and Time 1: The Fault of Epimetheus*). Reconsidering this question from Plato up to Leroi-Gourhan, he strives for an original prostheticity. Stiegler argues that the conflict between logos (truth) and technics (artifact, arbitrary) is already at work in Plato: "It is necessary to distinguish between logos and techne, insofar as the latter—as the domain of the artifacts—is also that of the arbitrary and of the worst kind of *ubris*, the violence of humans, who see themselves as gods, against *phusis*. Contrarily, logos is the site where *aletheia* appeared, the truth that is also *metron*—measure or reserve" (21). But Stiegler does not want to think in terms of an opposition, which indeed he questions in Greek thought when he performs a reading of the myth of Prometheus and Epimetheus in Plato's *Protagoras*. The two were ordered by the gods to equip mortal creatures and "distribute to them their proper qualities" (21). Because Epimetheus in his distribution forgot humans, Prometheus "stole the mechanical arts of Hephaestus and Athena, and fire" (21) to give to humans; in so doing, Prometheus placed "man outside of himself" (21). Humans invent prostheses, and exteriorization is thus "originary"; logos and technics, technics and indetermination, technics and social, are all bound together; a similar tension could then be retraced in the way OMA approached the becoming-network of Lille. Koolhaas forgets Epimetheus and puts forward Prometheus, but OMA seems to care for something similar to that with which Stiegler concludes his essay: "The power of radical deterritorialization of territories that sets to work the global fulfillment of technology today is thus only a final consequence of an original—but originally forgotten—process. (Epimetheus is the forgetful one)" (23). Euralille, whose actors are many besides Koolhaas and the OMA team, seems to look for a politics similar to the one Stiegler refers to at the end of his essay, a politics that "would be that of a development [*aménagement*] of deterritorialization, according to which one's definition of oneself is received from elsewhere, from a nonlocal and larger network, according to which one only finds one's definition in one's manner of receiving, of being destined" (23).

While Koolhaas speaks, as we have just seen concerning Euralille (and here I come to my second jump cut in this intermission), of a "gigantic futurist project," Futurism, the historical avant-garde, is never mentioned: in *S,M,L,XL* there is no reference to the heroic architectural Futurist moments. Instead, the meanings of the words "Futurist" and "Futuristic" fluctuate at times in many projects. "Futurist," as a generic adjective, gets a negative spin when Koolhaas, acute observer that he is, puts on paper with virtuosic bravura his take on Atlanta. In "Atlanta" (1987–94), after supplying some data about the city and introducing many points (the presence there of CNN, one of the biggest airports in the world, etc.), the author writes that Atlanta "has changed at an unbelievable speed, like in a nature film when a tree grows in five seconds" (836), and its growth has annihilated any reason to even consider the opposition between center and periphery. Koolhaas writes that his first visit to Atlanta was in 1973 at the time of the crisis of downtowns in the United States; in Atlanta he discovered instead a peculiar rebirth of downtown, a renaissance. Much was due to John Portman, architect and developer, who created "*a city of clones*" so abstract as to be capable of invading the entire globe.

What is an architectural firm in this condition? Located in idyllic places, "dense forests, hills, and lakes" and within "corporate villas," the partners could generate in an afternoon an entire project; such a situation is compared to "a new branch of physics, the outcome of the dynamics of force field in perpetual motion," but, without tension between architect and investor, there was no new unknown, no spark of inspiration, no "breaking of rules" (847). The reference to the force field and to the question of knowability has now returned, with a different spin from the consideration of Benjamin in chapter 1. In a provocative written montage, Koolhaas tells us that this is postmodernism: "Post-inspirational, past erudition, intimately connected with speed, a futurism, postmodernism is a mutation that will be from now on part of architectural practice—an architecture of the flight forward" (848).

S,M,L,XL nonetheless includes in the dictionary a few excerpts from *The Futurist Cookbook* (1932), edited by F. T. Marinetti, including a short story, several manifestos, and many Futurist recipes. To put this Futurist publication in context, it came out at the time in the 1930s when Futurism, far beyond its founding and heroic moments, was expanding its experimentations into many aspects of everyday life (advertising, cooking, design, and fashion, to mention just a few), injecting into these fields the sense of the ephemeral of Futurist poetics. None has defined the cultural production of the competing avant-gardes in the 1930s in Italy better than Claudio Fogu, who stated that "fascist culture was a signifier with no fixed referent, [and] it was structurally (not just opportunistically) open to the competitive interplay of many artistic groups and intellectuals. . . . Futurism, placed in this context, was neither leftist nor Fascist; it was, instead, a unique avant-garde within the broader phenomenon of modernism, unique because it sought to take a leading role within the development of mass culture in advanced capitalism, doing so via the aestheticization of both politics and economics."[27] The entry "edible" in *S,M,L,XL* quotes a curious and theatrical short story by Marinetti wherein several Futurists, including Prampolini, in one night are able to create twenty-two edible sculptures and a catalogue to accompany them. I have considered how Tschumi highlighted the importance of Futurist set design and the force of dissidence that he recognized in it. Instead, more than ten years later, Koolhaas inserts just a few excerpts of one of the most ephemeral of the Futurist productions, one that certainly also implies the coupling of performing and sharing.[28] At the "sculpture" entry in *S,M,L,XL*, there is another quote from the *Futurist Cookbook*, this time one about recipes (called *formulas*), "Network in the Sky" by the sculptor Mimmo Rosso; it is a pastry imagined in architectural shapes and with many colors. If the gesture of just sprinkling—to retain the culinary trope—these few quotes from Futurism into *S,M,L,XL* seems to imply less a resistance than a mostly avant-gardist take on this historical avant-garde ("I am not an historian" is, as we have seen, one of the first quotes from *Waiting from Godot*), then what one may dwell on is the attention toward the aerial view and the trope of flight, which Futurist aeropoetry of the 1930s invented and experimented on, contending with other modernist movements.

OMA's office is an endless, traveling experimental journey, as is expressed graphically on the first pages of *S,M,L,XL* in "OMA Travel Behavior" (xiii). Traveling in search of motivating commissions is natural for this architectural studio, always curious to confront the unknown (as well as the overly known), and eventually to give answers, albeit temporary ones, that aim toward interdisciplinarity. To come back to Calvino's *Invisible Cities*, OMA's incredible and unprecedented way of experiencing the practice of architecture has become the forerunner, with Bernard Tschumi's studio, of a new way of leading forward and toward new Marco Polo architects.[29]

Sedating the Classical City: The Generic City

> The Generic City is the apotheosis of the multiple-choice concept: all boxes crossed, an anthology of *all* the options. (1253)

To return to OMA's metropolitan moments, Jean-Paul Baietto, the director of the Euralille enterprise, defined OMA's project as "a *dynamique d'enfer*, a dynamic from hell. . . . So complex become all the interconnections, the mutual dependencies, the proliferation of interfaces, the superimposition of users and owners that together they form a group of prisoners" (1208). Here Baietto also wanted to highlight the intrication of actors and the inventiveness that the enterprise was able to put forward at the end of the twentieth century. We may place this in parallel with one of the few quotations in *S,M,L,XL* drawn from *Invisible Cities*, a quotation omnipresent in any study on Calvino and beyond, found at the entry "inferno":

> And Polo said "The inferno of the living is not something that will be; if there is one, it is what is already here, the inferno where we live every day, that we form by being together. There are two ways to escape suffering it. The first is easy for many: accept the inferno and become such a part of it that you can no longer see it. The second is risky and demands constant vigilance and apprehension: seek and learn to recognize who and what, in the midst of the inferno, are not inferno, then make them endure, give them space." (796–800)

Beyond a Koolhaas able to participate in the production of an extraordinary "dynamique d'enfer" exists another productive Koolhaas—which by no means relates to the first on the basis of simple opposition—the implacable observer of contemporary architecture, such as the one writing "The Generic City: Guide" (1994). This piece performs an involved observation of the extreme and massive trend of contemporary constructions as opposed to invention, innovation, and craft at the crossroads of urbanism and architecture. The text immediately gave a new and timely perspective on the state of contemporary cities: for the simultaneity and concentration of the classical city, the Generic City substitutes "individual 'moments' spaced apart to create a trance of almost unnoticeable aesthetic experience" (1250); it shares some traits with Calvino's *Invisible Cities* as well as with Superstudio's *Ideal Cities*, but it departs markedly from these two texts because here the subject is one city; although Calvino's poetics maintained an intriguing relationship with the generic[30] and Superstudio's fictional cities exacerbated in each ideal city one aspect of the contemporary city, neither achieved the homogeneity addressed in the singular Generic City. A few words on the way the contents are aggregated: in *S,M,L,XL*, while the text is divided into sections with specific titles, the effect on the reader is one of a continuous and uninterrupted accumulation of observations and comments; such an effect is created not only by the way the contents and the arguments are packed together but also by the layout, which does not differentiate the parts of the text.

"Generic" came into widespread use as a term to refer to any kind of unbranded product and became particularly associated with drugs during the 1990s; in the Generic City the metropolitan innervation and interspersion among the architectural cityscape are sedated. In the very first of Koolhaas's statements, the generic is bluntly countered by another key word that was circulating in the humanities at that time, "identity." The generic in many of its facets circulates without rest in the text, mining every possible singularity; indeed, the singularity of an old city like Barcelona, "oversimplifying its identity . . . becomes transparent, like a logo" (1250). The identity of a city weakens and loses its centrality: "As the sphere of influence expands, the area characterized by the center becomes larger and larger, hopelessly diluting both the strength and the authority of the core" (1248). As a consequence, the periphery—without a center—loses its importance. Such a contemporary phenomenon can be observed generically and also statistically at a global scale in Asia, Europe, Australia, Africa, and America, and it relates to the enormous increase of inhabitants of the Generic City.[31] The Generic City is far away from the clamor of the metropolis; instead, the Generic City is *sedated*, and its serenity "is achieved by the *evacuation* of the public realm, as in an emergency fire drill" (1251). In the Generic City, the public is held together by nothing, or, better, only by the *residual*.[32] The only aggregation left is what discourages association and alterity; "golf courses are all that is left of otherness" (1251). With a highly performative gesture, Koolhaas, mimicking genericity, brings together different aspects that should demarcate a city only to demonstrate the lack of urgency; the *residual* is the "refuge of the illegal, the uncontrolled," but because of its continuous manipulation it appears as a strange aggregate: "It represents a simultaneous triumph of the manicured and the primeval" (1253), a primeval that is anything but a contested field of inquiries. There is no interaction in the Generic City, whose density exists only in isolation, a pattern that housing follows: "Housing is not a problem. It has either been completely solved or totally left to chance; in the first case it is legal, in the second 'illegal'; in the first case, towers or, usually, slabs (at most, 15 meters deep), in the second (in perfect complementarity) a crust of improvised hovels. One solution consumes the sky, the other the ground" (1253). The force and the potential of urbanism in the Generic City deploys only as "*decks, bridges, tunnels, motorways*—a huge proliferation of the paraphernalia of connection": there is no space for walking. "The roads are only for cars. People (pedestrians) are led on rides (as in an amusement park), on 'promenades' that lift them off the ground, then subject them to a catalog of exaggerated conditions—wind, heat, steepness, cold, interior, exterior, smells, fumes—in a sequence that is a grotesque caricature of life in the historic city" (1254). There is nothing positive about the situation into which urbanism is thrown, and certainly not about the so-called New Towns, which flourish and perish in an unproductive pendulum; the text signals to the reader that their quick aging process seems like a kind of progeria.

It is clear that Koolhaas's Generic City—where bits of the reality of its architectural and urban contemporaneity are fictionally packaged so as to form a whole—is far from storytelling about singular interspersion of people and inhabited locations, as much as it is distant from any authentic relation with memory or history, about which nevertheless a comment is granted: in any Generic City there is a quarter, often called Lipservice (with some ironic variants: Afterthought, Waterfront, Too Late, 42nd Street, the Village . . .), that shows off its insincere hypocrisy. "Instead of specific memories, the associations the Generic City mobilizes are general memories, memories of memories: if not all memories at the same time, then at least an abstract, token memory, a déjà vu that never ends, generic memory" (1257); moreover, because no new aura is produced, "the value of established aura skyrockets" (1257). When, in the text, architecture directly falls under scrutiny, it appears to be a claustrophobic inside that never ends, which doesn't give any access to the outside in a time when hotels are "now containers . . . imprisonment, voluntary house arrest; there is no competing place left to go; you come and stay. Cumulatively, it describes a city of ten million all locked in their rooms, a kind of reverse animation—density imploded" (1260). In the Generic City architecture is air-conditioned, and everything of the outside is simulated in an endless inside: within the building one finds "the climatic conditions that once 'happened' outside—sudden storms, mini-tornadoes, freezing spells in the cafeteria, heat waves, even mist" (1261). Such a scenario is reminiscent of Marvelous Houses International, the fictional chain of hotels from Perec's novel *Life A User's Manual*, and of Fredric Jameson's comments on the Bonaventure Hotel in Los Angeles (designed by John Portman).

The tone that flows in the entire text stands in between a hallucinating monologue and a one-man show, and indeed it finishes by imagining two improbable spectacles. Walter Benjamin, in his "Paris, the Capital of the Nineteenth Century" (1935), compares the world exhibitions and the propagation of the universe of commodities to Grandville's drawings. "Saturn's ring becomes a cast-iron balcony on which the inhabitants of Saturn take the evening air."[33] Grandville's drawings of the Ring of Saturn are an exemplary image of the camouflage of commodification of the universe in a utopian form. Now, Koolhaas winks at such an image in the second-to-last paragraph, titled "Culture," pointing at the phantasmagorical aspect of the Generic City: "In each time zone, there are at least three performances of *Cats*. The world is surrounded by a Saturn's ring of meowing" (1264). The last paragraph, "End," imagines "a Hollywood movie about the Bible" (1264). This end abruptly brings the readers in front of a stage. Several sequences of the script are just sketched within a baroque cacophonic scenario; we read about a mix of humanity and animality first in compulsive gesturing and shouting at an open market and then retroceding, leaving emptiness and silence on the stage: "That is the story of the city. The city is no longer. We can leave the theater now . . ." (1264). The theatrical aspects of the writing do not need to be analyzed further. A series of fuzzy photos in a seemingly tropical but metropolitan area preceded the text, and now a series of photos of a Generic City with a terse blue sky shot one after the other from a point of view in movement close the text.

S,M,L,XL—which here I have touched upon only in sprinkles—is almost over except for an added postscript.

Exiting the Book: A Flâneur for the Twenty-First Century and Awaiting China's Adventures

The megabook concludes with a postscript—positioned after the copyright credits—that presents one last project titled, in the gerundive form, "Unraveling": the project "Deux Bibliothèques" (1992) is shown through different representational methods: photos of the existing site; stills from a video in which the architect's hands demonstrate, by cutting a sheet of paper with scissors, "the design process [whereby] the paper is raised, folded and cut"[34] to obtain a pliable surface; a quite minimalist model shown in close-up photos to inspect the project; an abstract drawing of the continuous circulation; and endless sections passing among the levels, underlining how "sections of each level are manipulated to touch those above and below; all the planes are connected by a single trajectory, a warped interior boulevard that exposes and relates all programmatic elements" (1318–23). The project, which won the competition for ideas in 1993, was an architectural intervention in the Parisian Jussieu campus—the Faculty of Sciences—started in 1964 by Éduard Albert, the architect appointed by André Malraux, but left incomplete because of the turmoil of 1968. OMA is fascinated by Albert's project, by its "three-dimensional network" as opposed to a building, by its "endless connections [that] absorb all circulation" but that also unfortunately "psychologically exhaust in advance any attempt to inhabit it" (1309). Because the area of the project intervention is the *parvis*—the roof of the auditorium—OMA considers the necessity to emphasize it as "the stage for social appearance," not to be experienced "as residue, a mere slice of void sandwiched between socle and building" (1309); OMA's gestures of unraveling are meant to give social and imaginary potential. The *parvis* stands between the double library—science is embedded in the ground, the humanities rise upward—and the multiplication of ways of representing the project underlines that the complex is not a container but an interior space that makes connections and facilitates motion, an urbanized complex intended as much for linking other parts of the campus and the cityscape as for facilitating access to the books and other collections. The general structure is conceived in a way that "generates a system of supra-programmatic 'urban' elements in the interior: plazas, parks, monumental staircases, cafés, shops" (1326) with a calculated design of paths, escalators, and elevators, but, in addition, its "program can change continuously, without affecting architectural character" (1329). The *parvis*, the central stage, is an expanded point of energy; it becomes an *acceuil* that facilitates the connections on the south with the metro station and on the north with the Seine. Such a "magic carpet," as OMA calls it, is intended also to bring a certain density, as opposed to dispersal, that communicates with the cityscape but with "minimal enclosure."

The project insists on the assemblage of a certain duplication, with its twinned libraries, and this perhaps also points toward a graft between science

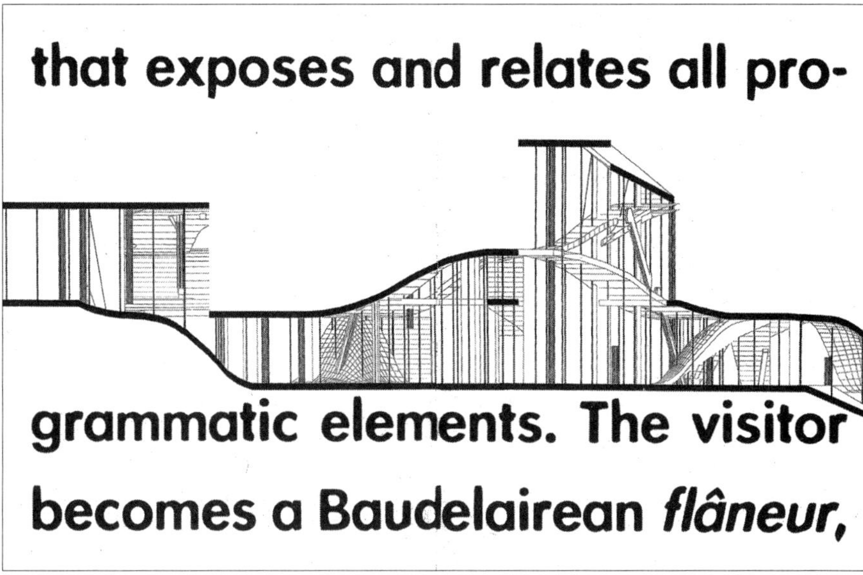

Figure 5.4. OMA, 2 Bibliothèques Jussieu (1993), Paris France Competition. *S,M,L,XL*, pp. 1322–23. © OMA.

and humanities, between engineering and architecture. Such a duality is also reinforced graphically in the presentation, from the first imposing page where the existing building is presented as a negative, or as an X-ray (perhaps to signal also the fact that one of the reasons for this project was to remove the asbestos present in the existing complex), to the rest of the pages, where on the upper half we see images and on the lower half we read text; then, at a certain point, black and white are reversed both in the text and in the background of the images. The text is quite succinct, hence this shift of format happens within the sections showing the potential of the complex's continuous internal circulation, when the text moves along in bigger fonts that poetically invite the visitor to be a flâneur "inspecting and being seduced by a world of books and information—by the urban scenario" (1324; figure 5.4). The inside of the library certainly exceeds the interior and exchanges, or mirrors, the outside spaces. The Baudelairean figure is invoked, with a light nostalgia, to foster a desire for the public realm, a flâneur for the new millennium, and perhaps also to gain the attention of the Parisian jury for the competition.

Hence with a geographical jump, which eventually will announce a futurity much beyond architecture and urbanism yet one where these two generic terms/disciplines are deeply concerned, the last two pages of the book are occupied by excerpts from the *Hong Kong Standard* newspaper from September 1994; the few readable passages are about the possible upcoming Olympic Games in China. In the center of the page stands a photo depicting people in the Working People's Palace of Culture looking at a billboard-sized, montage-like propaganda painting; the caption reads, "Beijing residents admire a painting depicting Deng Xiaoping's tour of southern China in 1992." The effect obtained with this montage-like painting is *naïf* yet spectacular for the astonished viewers: modernist constructions appear in the background, and the work captures the persona of Deng Xiaoping, speaking with firm and reassuring gestures.

S,M,L,XL's continuous mixing of genres and of presentation formats, pointing incessantly to what is outside its borders, often showing but not telling or vice versa, keeps its projects investigating beyond the aftermath of the modern movement and its different avatars. OMA's travels are as much in space as among different media.

China will be one of the frontiers, we have learned from the very recent past history, where star architects will further develop projects spanning a spectrum that touches at extremes of spectacularity and criticality. OMA too will launch its operative energy toward this part of the world with built projects, and will also split its practice with the introduction of an alternative and palindromic enterprise; AMO ("I love" in Latin or Italian, Koolhaas likes to say about this acronym, and possibly "Architecture Media Organization") investigates, thinks through massive changes, but doesn't produce architecture in a "proper" sense.

Part 2: Cartoonish "Architecture-Characters" Popping Up from Junkspace

From AMO's Atlases to the Builtscape as an Endless, Consuming Inside ("Junkspace")

AMO has produced graphically and conceptually astonishing atlases, such as "Atlas, Worldwide" (2002). Mimicking the simplifying method of the logosphere with these atlases, AMO visualizes information available at a global scale to "show the political, economical and social trends which affect the metropolis" and to help orientation to their possible futures; the information conveyed with these new atlases is, for AMO, "fluid and the way in which the world presents itself is not bound to geographical shape. New constellations or alliances appear. The global movements which determine our current life, are surrounding us as nebulous mass, sticking out as newspaper headings to then disappear again."[35] The atlases are many: the best-known is the ¥€$ map of the world, but others include one that considers the proliferation of city agglomerations (the "urban core"), another on world air travels ("Transatlantic Waning, Eurasian Gaining"), and a third titled "Enter and Exit 'Fortress Europe'" (figure 5.5).

With these atlases, conceived at the beginning of the new millennium, AMO proposed new potential constellations in which to consider architecture and

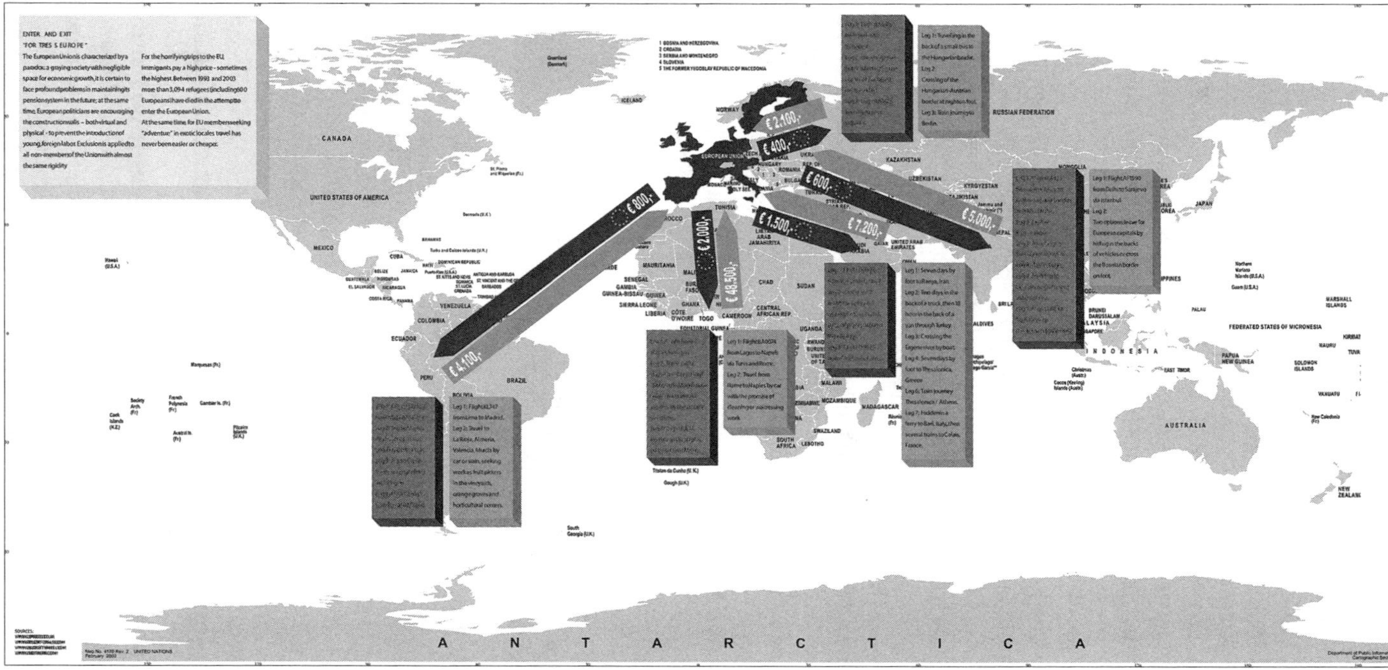

Figure 5.5. OMA/AMO, *Enter and Exit "Fortress Europe,"* AMO Projects, 2002. © OMA/AMO.

the urban. In the same years, Koolhaas wrote extensively about space and about architecture's junk side.

"Junkspace" (2000) is a major text by Koolhaas, published in many OMA/AMO venues and so well known beyond the field of architecture that it became a sort of pop hit of the first decade of the twenty-first century. In their cartoonish incarnations in *S,M,L,XL*, developers called OMA's projects junk, and the architectural critic Jean-Luis Cohen referred to the Euralille project as trending toward junk; now it is Koolhaas who attacks the entire global way of constructing as junk. In "Junkspace," whose compound neologism reminds one immediately of food consumption and bad nutrition, space and architecture are now questioned and observed, not as useless or no longer in use but as massively in use; indeed, space, not architecture, becomes the junk with which Koolhaas entertains his readers.

"Junkspace" is a follow-up to "The Generic City." The change from "The Generic City" to "Junkspace" has a convoluted twist. If in "The Generic City" we saw the builtscape from the outside transform into an inside without exteriority, now in this second text everything is embedded inextricably in the inside. Similar to the shift we have seen in chapter 1, which Benjamin underlines, from the Baroque allegory that sees the corpse from the outside to the Baudelairean one that sees it from within, here Koolhaas talks about the cacophony of a worldly builtscape that in many instances doesn't let space breathe or have any effects, except junky ones, on participants. The farcical effect such a text produces shows the resistance of what is out there and what any architect who operatively intends to imagine and produce alternative architecture must cope with. The result is that outside and inside become too complex to be clearly opposed.

Whereas melting the words of the title "The Generic City" produces "genericity," a noun only recently in use in English (the *OED* gives 1964 as the first instance of its use and 2002 as its most recent) and therefore pointing at an almost oxymoronic consistency, "Junkspace" is a newly coined compound indicating an odd singularity. Junkspace, "the residue mankind leaves on the planet,"[36] is a continuous interior and an endless series of containers expanded throughout a world where consumption and construction collide and proliferate; it is an allegory of the state of the art of construction, a "web without a spider" (179) of stuffs and uses. The text is preceded by the words on a billboard—*Logan Airport: A World-Class Upgrade for the Twenty-First Century*—and the first place mentioned is LAX. The distance and the difference between Boston and Los Angeles are performatively void with the airplane transportation system. Los Angeles, instead of being a tilting point for arrival in a new world and the discovery of invention, as it was in the early 1970s for architectural historian Reyner Banham, breathless and prancing as he explored the city in his BBC documentary,[37] becomes a metonymic place to tell something about the entire planet: "The built (more about that later) product of modernization is not modern architecture but Junkspace."[38]

The experience of reading the entire text, even silently, resounds as if one is listening to another one-man show that doesn't stop, spelling out Junkspace in its endless continuity, always "interior, so extensive that you rarely perceive limits" (175); it is "a non-stop 'performance' of the built space, not just of the contemporary city, but of a whole universe on the point of fusing into a kind of all-purpose indeterminate magma."[39]

Junkspace has a never-ending series of definitions whose vocabulary is often derived from realms of everyday life and from middle-class products either affordable or desirable, not derived from the realm of architecture;[40] when space is in question, it is only to demonstrate the belatedness and inoperativity of any recent conceptualization.

> Because it costs money, is no longer free, conditioned space inevitably becomes conditional space; sooner or later all conditional space turns into Junkspace. . . . When we think about space, we have only looked at its containers. As if space itself is invisible, all theory for the production of space is based on an obsessive preoccupation with its opposite: substance and objects, i.e., architecture. Architects could never explain space; Junkspace is our punishment for their mystifications. O.K., let's talk about space then. The beauty of airports, especially after each upgrade. The luster of renovations. The subtlety of the shopping center. Let's explore public space, discover casinos, spend time in theme parks. . . . Junkspace is the body double of space, a territory of impaired vision, limited expectation, reduced earnestness. Junkspace is a Bermuda Triangle of concepts. (176)

What remains of modern architecture is only its most indifferent side: "Structures emerge like springs from a mattress" (177), and "transparency only reveals everything in which you cannot partake" (177); instead of going against the grain of the modernist motto "Form follows function," here architecture's trouble is that "forms search for function like hermit crabs looking for a vacant shell" (178). The craft and intelligence of architecture have totally turned away from any flight of critical montage, as in a fallout defined by gestures: "clamp, stick, fold, dump, glue, shoot, double, fuse—have become indispensable" (178). The movements in Junkspace are all in sync (escalators, near exits, automated tellers) or are flows leading toward disaster like "the stampedes triggered by warring compartments of soccer fans" (180); otherwise, movements and their traffic (airspace, subways, or highway) are "clogged by its users" (180). To airports in need of more space, as if their use was meant to be (bad) choreography, are added pieces, and a patchwork of materials so that "only a perverse modernist choreography can explain the twists and turns, the ascents and descents, the sudden reversals that comprise the typical path from the check-in" (181). For public life, we read, is substituted Public Space™ or "what remains of the city once the unpredictable has been removed. . . . Space for 'honoring,' 'sharing,' 'caring,' 'grieving,' and 'healing' . . . civility imposed by an overdose of serif" (184); in language, the new frontier of Junkspace produces unheard oxymorons like "reality/TV," "museum/store," and "food/court," and the political side of Junkspace "depends on the central removal of the critical faculty in the name of comfort and pleasure" (183); the dynamic between public and economy is defined in a ghastly way: "for culture 'engraved donor bricks'; for everything else: cash, rentals, leases, franchises, the underpinning of brands. Junkspace expands with the economy but its footprint cannot contract—when it is no longer needed, it thins" (184). Ecology is also considered in light of the blanket of Junkspace: "Landscape has become Junkspace, foliage as spoilage: Trees are tortured, lawns cover human manipulations like thick pelts, or even toupees. . . . Seemingly at the opposite end of Junkspace, the golf course is, in fact, its conceptual double: empty, serene, free of commercial debris" (186–87).

The end immerses the reader in a junksphere, where cyberspace has become the outside and the inside of the body is colonized and invaded by vibes of cell phones, Botox, and gene therapy; it terminates with a series of questions, such as "What if space started looking at mankind?" and "Is each of us a mini-construction site?" (189–90); as has been noted, this ending seems to make reference to the movie *Fantastic Voyage*.[41]

This piece relates to a series of shorter ones on space written for a special issue that the magazine *Wired* commissioned AMO to produce; such a carpet/inventory of novel spaces aims at redefining the language of space in front of the mutated conditions of contemporaneity.[42] What certainly should be noticed is that such a contribution seems like a remake (or, better still, an *état des lieux* of worldly spaces depicted in aggravated tones) of Perec's *Species of Spaces*.

Is "Junkspace" only a grotesque armor and caricature of the ordinary as an allied and artifactual background from which OMA defines its projects? Perhaps this is partly correct, if we understand it as an autopromotional strategy with which to mobilize the attention of the avant-gardist force that sustains the projects,[43] and so we will now examine a few of the most recent ones.

Yet Another Ambiguous Publication: Colporting *Architectures in Space*

Projects OMA undertook after *S,M,L,XL* and during the dawn of the new millennium received a new presentation with another hybrid and junk-like publication, something between a magazine and a book: *Content: Triumph of Realization*.[44] This work presents the "architect's ambiguous relations with the forces of globalization"; the architect is a "vagabond rowing, searching for an opportunity to realize the visions that make remaining at home tortuous."[45] The title and what the book collects seem to allude to satisfaction with the achievement and recognition obtained at the time when the question of context and content has been extremely reformulated in the OMA/AMO spheres of actions. Contents and projects presented here are to be related (or countered) not to "container" (clearly derided in "Junkspace") nor to "form," but—as the architectural critic R. E. Somol posits in "12 Reasons to Get Back into Shape"[46]—in relation to "illicit shapes": "Shape is EMPTY. If a relatively neglected territory within architecture, shape has had a more energetic discussion in art . . . The OMA shape projects don't only operate with the graphic immediacy of logos, generating new identity, but they are also holes in the skyline that reframe the city. One doesn't look *at* them so much as through them or from them. To radically paraphrase Carl Andre, a shape is a hole in a thing it is not" (86–87).

Koolhaas's writing figures in *Content: Triumph of Realization* as a short introduction underlining how slow architecture is in relation to the "contemporary maelstrom"; he indicates the gap between an "ancient knowledge" and a "contemporary practice." The one-page introduction adopts a quite humble tone despite the graphic font format already at play in "Bigness," which starts with a huge font that decreases along the page, stating:

> Architecture is
> a fuzzy amalgamation
> of ancient knowledge and contemporary practice. (20)

Architecture, we read, is therefore an "awkward way to look at the world and an inadequate medium to operate on it" (20). Yet from outside the profession "architecture" is often still called in question because it "embodies the lingering hope . . . that shape, form, coherence could be imposed on the violent surf of information that washes over us daily" (20).

The OMA/AMO field of action is also introduced with a "maybe": "Maybe architecture doesn't have to be stupid after all. Liberated from the obligation to construct, it can become a way of thinking about anything—a discipline that represents relationships, proportions, connections, effects, the diagrams of everything" (20). Koolhaas introduces AMO/OMA's split relationship using a dance terminology: "a 'split'—a *grand écart*, the fiendishly difficult moment, immobile, on the ground of classical ballet—the maximum stretch between two opposite forces, realization and speculation" (20).

Many hybrid-like entities populate the publication. Instead of a cartoonish depiction of the architects' struggles in defending a project, here OMA's architectures are transformed into cartoonish shapes who wonder, Is it a book? A magazine?

The publication has been opened widely, in comparison with *S,M,L,XL*, beyond Koolhaas's writings, to many contributors who have at least temporarily shared fields of investigation with OMA/AMO. The table of contents

Figure 5.6. OMA/AMO, Contents, *Content*, 2004. © OMA/AMO.

is embedded in pages whose background is a cityscape generated by a city-building-like video game with anonymous constructions and OMA's cartoon-like shapes with wicked looks; the view is from above, and indeed some FOCKA F-2 aircraft, perhaps drones, spot the context in an almost aeropoetry Futurist's style; an angry gorilla, a wink to both the film *King Kong* and one of Italian Radical Design's icons,[47] circulates in this cityscape (figure 5.6).

The pieces in *Content* present the many OMA/AMO projects that extend throughout the world; there are also singular interventions on contemporary themes and events from affirmed cultural critics (Michael Hardt and Scott Lash) and from less well-known ones; in addition, there are refreshing interviews, ranging from one conducted innocently, but with hidden malice, by Beatriz Colomina and Koolhaas with Martha Stewart ("No More Surprises") to one done by Koolhaas and the ur-curator Hans Ulrich Obrist with Robert Venturi and Denise Scott Brown. The magazine format urges brevity on all these contributions, which in general are also presented in small characters and bombarded by many different fonts and images: to get the picture while browsing or reading among them may require close attention. Overall, *Content*, as if despising monumentality, aims to be an almanac of AMO/OMA's recent production.

But what is an almanac? In its more concise sense it is a yearly calendar giving statistical information about temporal data such as the phases of the moon, the tides, and so forth; the *OED* indicates that the word is derived from Middle French *almanac*, *almanach*, *almenach*, which in turn connects with Arabic and Spanish. Going back to French, *Le Petit Larousse Illustré* provides this entry:

> **ALMANACH:** [almana] n.m. (ar. *al-manākh*). Calendrier, souvent illustré, comportant des indications astronomiques, météorologiques, ainsi que des renseignements d'ordre varié (médecine, cuisine, astrologie, etc.).[48]

Certainly *Content* is an almanac that with its "GO EST" motto indicates a spatial move, and eventually a carrying around, in this case of researches, and the propagation and dissemination of them. And what if we look back at terms such as *colporter* and *colportage*? The *Petit Larousse Illustré* tells us:

> **COLPORTER:** v.t. (lat. comportare, transporter). **1.** Vieilli. Transporter de petites marchandises de place en place pour les vendre. **2.** Fig. Répandre, propager des bruits, des nouvelles.
>
> **COLPORTAGE:** n.m. **1.** Action, fait de colporter. **2.** Métier de colporteur. ◊ *Littérature de colportage*: ouvrages populaires de petit format, très divers (almanachs, ouvrages pieux, contes de fées, romans sentimentaux, guides pratiques d'agriculture, etc.), qui étaient vendus par des marchands ambulants entre le XVIeme et le XIXeme s.

This hybrid publication performs with all its contents a colportage of ideas, of inventions, of studies and analysis, of spaces also, mimicking too the unpleasant noises and the blinding visuality of the market, which aims to divert even as it produces Junkspace.

The final part of the book, "Property 1993–2003 Architectural Adventures?," is the list of all OMA/AMO projects organized according to the country in which they were undertaken. There is one final kind of invention introduced in the publication: the fifteen "Universal Modernization Patents."[49] They are identified not with the name of a specific building but with a concept design, and they are briefly detailed with a diagram and an abstract. The almost Baudelairean tone of the brief text with which they are introduced downplays the fleeting attention to architectural inventions: "The half-life of architects' collective memory is now around six months. Ideas emerge, inspire, and are conveniently forgotten. Here, OMA stakes its claims of eternity" (73). The patent for "Loop-Trick" (1987) is defined as "a system of intersecting ramps that destroys the status of individual floor" (76); an initial application was with the Kunsthal in Rotterdam, and the abstract gives additional design concepts on how it eliminates the notion of above and below.

Dewey Decimal System / MLA's Style

> The client defined a public library as a place where everyone feels welcome and at home, where *anyone*—from old people to small children, from homeless to schizophrenics—can go for shelter, learning and inspiration. The written word is the path to liberation, emancipation and growth, but people also spend important moments of their lives in a library. My Seattle dinner companions—all women—reflected on the fact that they all, without exception, encounter their first love, their first book or their first kiss in a library! Also, libraries in America often house sport facilities, showers and coffee shops, so just imagine: you can read, kiss, write, wash, eat, love, study, scribble, sport, discover and sleep in a library . . . you don't have to go anywhere else: this is a world in itself. (Petra Blaisse, "Undoing Boundaries—Seattle Central Library, Seattle, USA," in *Inside Outside*)

One exceptional OMA project of the new millennium is the Seattle Public Library (SPL), which captured—at least in a distracted way—the attention of humanities professionals: it was featured on the cover of the *PMLA* issue for the 2012 convention. In *Content*, bits of SPL appear more than once; the first time, in "Material Fetish," we see photos of fragments of the work-in-progress with basic descriptions of the materials and the way to process them: each material is highlighted—to give a captivating, generic sense of it— such as "I ♥ CONCRETE"—"I ♥ STEEL."

OMA's aim was to work through the essence of the public as free, not to produce "sophisticated and entertaining forms of the Private," as we read in "Seattle Public (seattle: 37°47'N 122° 26'W)" (139); the building was to be public and open to the outside. To this end, OMA has activated many interconnected lines. SPL, in glass and steel, relates to different levels of the site and connects to the outside with spectacular views toward Mt. Rainer and Elliott Bay.[50] But the connection to the outside reaches out beyond the site, mixing, or even "combing," the very idea of access and of outside/inside, close/distant, at the time of data flows; OMA rethinks this institution for the twenty-first century as a place that can host not just books but both old and new media. "As new media emerge and gain currency, the library seems threatened, a fortress ready to be taken by a marauding hoard [*sic*] of technologies. In this fairytale, the electronic becomes barbaric" (139). OMA therefore wanted the library to have a social role (no cost, service programs, young adult services, readers' advisory, art exhibits, bibliotherapy, discussion groups, video, voter registrations, adult education, increased community prominence, training the disadvantaged) and access to "new equalities" (e-book, World Wide Web, database, magazines, newspapers, CD-ROM . . .).

OMA decided to design a flexible connection of "programmatic clusters—five of stability and four of instability." The former are called platforms (the

Figure 5.7. OMA, Seattle Public Library, Living Room, 2004. © Laura Chiesa.

parking, the staff spaces, the meeting spaces, the spiral, and the headquarters) and the latter, called in-betweens, are spaces where circulation and flow is continuous (spaces for kids, the living room and the entrances, the mixing chamber, and the reading room). Because the platforms and the in-betweens have different purposes, they differ in size, density, and opacity.

Entering from Fourth Street, one can access on the left the Children's Center, constructed of a combination of different materials—"soft, shiny, smooth and spongy"—colored in red, pink, and yellow; from the ceiling are "hanging many bulbs . . . clouds of lights" (205, *Inside Outside*); in the center there is an expandable auditorium that at maximum size reaches to the floor of the opposite entrance on Fifth Avenue, to the Living Room. The Living Room (figure 5.7), "the biggest civic space of the surrounding areas," offers singular haptic and visual experiences, and it hosts many uses: there are rest areas, check-in and check-out, the Teens' Library, and bookshelves with spokes heading in different directions that give dynamism to the space. The firm Inside Outside has orchestrated a pleasant atmosphere, with a stunning mix of plants and carpets on which are printed plants in many tones of green, "carpets—not wall-to-wall but loose carpets—give the floor plane colour and direction, which helps orientation and gives the room a narrative" (*Inside Outside*, 203); one could add that Inside Outside participates in creating room for storytelling. From

Figure 5.8. OMA, Seattle Public Library, Mixing Chamber, 2004. © Laura Chiesa.

Figure 5.9. OMA, Seattle Public Library, The Spiral, 2004. © Laura Chiesa.

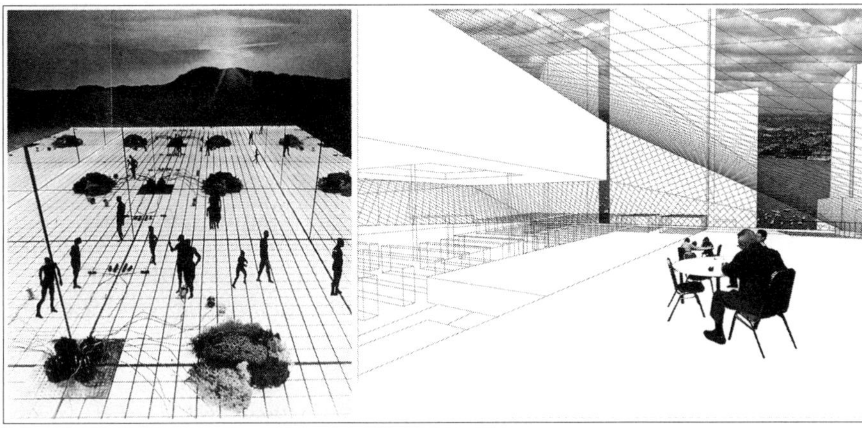

Figures 5.10 and 5.11. Superstudio, *Environments*, 1972, and OMA, Seattle Public Library, View from Elliott Bay. © OMA.

the entrance on Fifth Street, on the left side of the Living Room, a ramp of stairs—in concrete but painted red (signaling the heart of SPL)[51]—brings the staff areas and the meeting platforms up to the in-between space of the Mixing Chamber. The Mixing Chamber is a "trading floor for information," where humans and technology merge: the visitors find the librarians' expertise and help, free-access computers, and billboard-size screens that indicate the flows of books (checked out, read, new titles), as well as other events (lectures, films) and local and international news (figure 5.8). As an interface between different platforms, this in-between facilitates interaction and play.

A thin, superlong escalator, which seems to lead toward outer space, is divided in two sections (uncannily similar to the one in the building located on the block just below Fourth Street) and leads directly to the top floor; its yellow-green artificial color, achieved by neon lighting, gives almost a vertigo or a sense of reaching an outer space. From the first section of the escalator, one arrives at the stable platform: the Book Spiral. The Book Spiral rethinks the spaces in view of the Dewey Decimal System, as a continuous ribbon "running from '000' to '999,' " not as a stack of floors, with a pleasant internal promenade offering access to the entire collection (figure 5.9).[52]

The virtual spaces and the real spaces of the library converge toward a new and open synthesis, and it is no wonder that in presenting the project OMA effectively borrowed its collage-like visualization from the Italian experimental architectural group Superstudio, which already in the early 1970s was questioning the tension between the virtual and the real (figures 5.10 and 5.11). Finally, the uneven horizontal spatial compartments are cut vertically by a huge void—similar to the one in Euralille—"and a colossal pylon in reinforced concrete containing the elevators."[53] Such a void is visible and experienceable from different points of view—the Living Room, the Mixing

Room, and up to the last floor; the huge pylon is the screen for projections of video materials. Old and new media, visual and verbal inventions, are given space just as much as the visitors are.

The external metal framework of irregular surfaces of tilted diamond shapes, articulated with different inclinations, define the internal spaces in relation to the specificity of the site,[54] but they also have an astonishing public effect to the outside: day and night, passersby and several modes of transportation and their movements are reflected and momentarily captured in the multiplicity of the tilted diamond shapes: such fleeting effects all reverberating in the outside concur in signaling the exceptionality of this public space in relation to a more orthodox and perhaps more private downtown.

A Gigantic Built Palindrome: Performing an Allegory of Data Flows

> Who says that structure should not be re-invented? Who says that the regime of gravity that we have suffered from under capitalism and communism, the one regime that unites us all, who says that that regime is sacrosanct, who says that reinventing structure cannot be creative, I simply ask you to clarify the terms by which you name this structure unworkable. It is workable. . . . It is simply a way of supporting and enabling other forms of architecture to emerge. ("Discussion at Tsinghua University, 5 August 2003," in *Content*, 499)

As an apt conclusion to this chapter I would like now to turn briefly to a gigantic project that interrogates the question of public in the mediascape from very different angles of vision. The play between the norm and inventiveness, between the real and the virtual, between data and experiential spaces, and the meshing of inside and outside and the calculated insistence on transparency as a way to open up the public in a building: all these are also at the conceptual core of OMA's huge project begun in 2003 and only recently completed, the headquarters of the Chinese television network CCTV (575,000 square meters of program space) in the new Central Business District in Beijing. The objective was to integrate all the TV production facilities (previously isolated in scattered zones outside the city center) and to create a magnificent complex to house the tension between the media data flow and architecture. CCTV is an acronym for a proper name—Chinese Central Television—but also for a set of control devices, closed-circuit television: indeed this project brings to its extremes questions related to the "society of control" and to contemporary network broadcasting. This allegorical tension operates on many levels of the project (figure 5.12).[55]

The program has been divided among four buildings, all designed by OMA: the CCTV (which hosts the administrative spaces, the broadcasting center, the news production facilities, the media production, the staff facilities);[56] TVCC, the near-palindrome of CCTV, which stands for Television

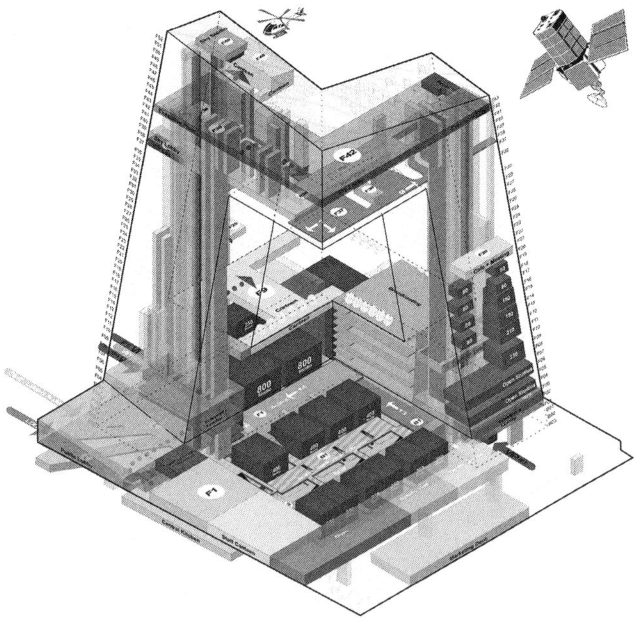

Figure 5.12. OMA, CCTV, Loop. © OMA.

Cultural Center (housing multiple cultural facilities and a hotel); the Service Building (with the central energy center, parking for broadcasting vehicles, and the guard dormitory); the Media Park that connects the complex to the city and, by hosting a range of public events, "establishes a programmatic gradient from nature to media from real to virtual" ("CCTV by OMA," 164). Instead of adding yet another skyscraper to the cityscape, OMA/AMO thought about alternative configurations.[57] A "Universal Modernization Patent" has been registered out of the CCTV project—"Skyscraper Loop" 2003—wherein the isolation of a high-rise is broken down by "turning four segments into a loop" (*Content*, 511). CCTV can host ten thousand staff members (whose number is increased by visitors), therefore the "spaces have been conceived as infrastructural systems, able to guide, disperse and direct all different groups to their various destinations" ("CCTV by OMA," 77). Structurally, CCTV is a rectangular tube communicating in a loop and constructed of two vertical high-rises and two horizontal L-shaped sections that sustain the structure; because the upper part is oblique, on one side (Tower 1) it rises fifty floors and on the other side (Tower 2) only forty-two. The CCTV building, designed by OMA in collaboration with the engineers Rory McGowan, Ove Arup & Partners, because of the singularity of the concept for the structure (not covered by the applicable Chinese and International Codes), passed through serious performance-based design tests.[58]

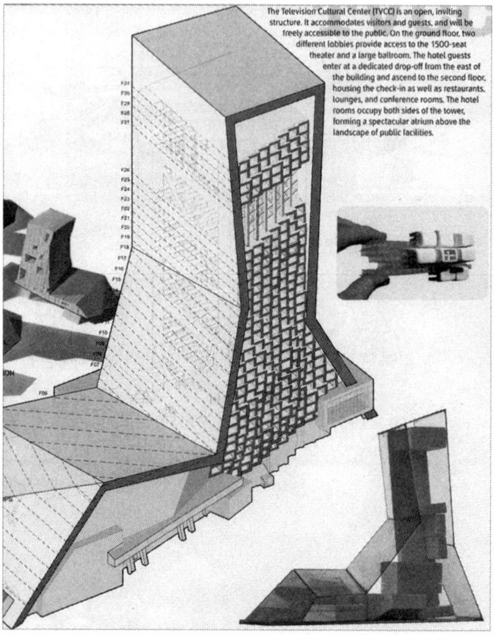

Figure 5.13. OMA, TVCC. *Content*, p. 493 © OMA.

The loop promotes interdependence rather than isolation among the many activities that take place at the CCTV, and it is also accessible to the public, who can inspect—through glass partitions—what is going on inside and at the same time gain multiple views and perspectives on the city. Such an apparently transparent possibility to inspect, for many reasons related to the artifactuality of television broadcasting, seems to signal an allegory of the contemporary mediascape more strongly than anything else.

Finally, the other project coupled in the palindrome is the TVCC (figure 5.13), which caught fire at an advanced stage of construction, during the celebration of the New Year in 2009, probably ignited by fireworks. The project articulates many requests from the brief, assembling them "in a loose and seemingly random manner—volumes joined, stacked and piled form a loose and penetrable accumulation of public programs" ("CCTV by OMA," 120). Such an apparently random assemblage is defined as a "freeze-frame"—a term that relates either to a film shooting device or to a live performance gesture (both refer to an instability within stillness)—and has an envelope whose name derives from cooking tools; indeed, there is a Universal Modernization Patent for "Cake-Tin Architecture" (2002): such a formula collects "all the contradictory demands of a complex program without attempting to resolve them" but instead casts "them in a totally arbitrary, pleasing form, charm can be generated on a big scale from heterogeneous elements" (*Content*, 512).

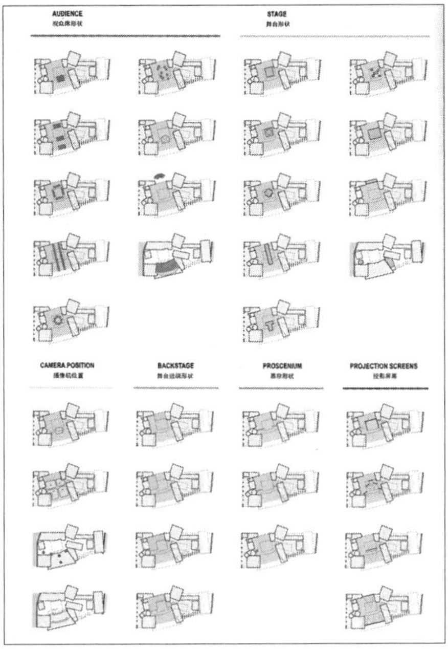

Figure 5.14. OMA, TVCC, Theater. © OMA.

On the ground is obtained the same random continuous aggregation of programs (a theater, audio studios, digital cinemas, a ballroom, an AV room, the new release hall, and the exhibition spaces) that mesh the exterior and the interior and therefore the public flows. Details of the continuous interstitial spaces created by calculated plays with randomness are many. If performativity and performance are at stake on an architectural/engineering level, all the spaces also are stages that invite performance and participation. Among those, certainly the theater, for which the minimum equipment of a fixed stage is included and the audience seating is constructed to be mobile, is designed to allow "maximum contact between the performers and the audience" ("CCTV by OMA," 137). The positions of audience, stage, camera, backstage, proscenium, and projection screens are movable. Mobility is obtained by disconnecting the fixed relation between audience and stage; "the ground plane is entirely liberated; entrance lobby and stage connect horizontally and allow for a multitude of stage arrangements and performance types" ("CCTV by OMA," 137). The spaces of performances have not been lost but have instead been multiplied in a radicalized experimental field (figure 5.14). Two minimal questions at least can be posited: first, will TVCC be rebuilt? Second, what kinds of performances will take place, and how will the audience participate?

CODA

OMA's adventures are still on the move with an almost countless series of projects. I will mention just two of these works with a particular connection to this book. The Dee and Charles Wyly Theater in Dallas, Texas (2009), has a simple but highly sophisticated design that allows for a radically new, if not Futurist, way of performing. Its stagecraft in fact reminds one, to define it at a moving conceptual-visual level, of a freeze-frame of the vision F. T. Marinetti announced in the postscript of the manifesto "The Futurist Synthetic Theater (*A-technical-Dynamic-Simultaneous-Autonomous*)." The other project, started in 2012, announces itself as groundbreaking because of the encounters of extraordinary actors in the expanding field of performance and performativity: it is the Marina Abramović Institute for the Preservation of Performance Art, to be built in Hudson, New York.

The few glances at *S,M,L,XL* in chapter 5 make clear both how, for OMA, architectures are always thought of as intermedial and in relation with other fields and also how OMA's operativity expands and explores, considering modernity and modernization both attentively and creatively. *S,M,L,XL* has one main theme—architecture and urbanism—that is regarded as embedded and enlaced in a network of realities, and this creates a connection to the other books considered in this study, Perec's *Life A User's Manual*, Calvino's *Invisible Cities*, and Benjamin's *Arcades Project*. Concepts, sentences and syntax, genres, and imaginability and projectuality are at work in concurrent ways with reference to the medium-specificity of architecture: we can say, borrowing Marjorie Perloff's words, that OMA/AMO in their productions show an "unoriginal genius" in their ability to mix different levels of understanding and of representation. *Content* activates a "colportage of architectures" among contemporary spaces and the mediascape; from perspectives that survey the scattered and disarrayed junkspace, OMA/Koolhaas allow to emerge new inventions, architecturability. OMA/AMO has launched a series of fieldwork studies (in conjunction with Koolhaas's appointment at Harvard) that consider massive urban mutations at a global scale. The spaces and places under scrutiny are seen at quite a distance from a traditional sense of place or of "genius loci." *Projects on the City* are among AMO/OMA's recent publications. A study that considered the impact of shopping on the city and culminated in a publication titled *The Harvard Design School Guide to Shopping* traces a genealogy of the marketplace, from the old market to the arcades and on up to the shopping mall. This study is coupled to the design specificity and the physical and psychological effects that the recent "predatory and voracious" market phenomenon and its *residual space* may produce. Certainly *The Guide to Shopping* is another instance in which OMA/AMO loops us back, through twists and turns, to the *Arcades Project*: indeed, a reading of the *Guide* induces both awareness of the case studied and a kind of boredom, to quote one of the *Konvolute* titles from Benjamin's *Arcades Project*.

Redundancy of/in attention is what OMA/AMO productions incessantly require. A forty-thousand-page book collecting thirty-five years of writing by OMA/AMO was exhibited at the Architectural Association in London in spring 2010; titled *OMA Book Machine*, it is a compressed, archived version on paper of just such a production. Although it is contained within the enclosed space of a gallery, once one begins to look at or read it, one is transported far beyond any disciplinary boundaries or physical walls.

As I show a little earlier in this book, Bernard Tschumi's radical exploration and invention of spaces for comparison offer the public new spaces for storytelling, at first with precise and brisk incursions, searching for momentary new allies in other fields and practices (historical avant-gardes and neo-avant-gardes, theater, literature, cinema, video). Then later, like atomic fission, Tschumi reintroduces them in built or buildable projects, with an architecturabilty that never simply repeats itself. Indeed, one might be tempted to ask how Tschumi's design for De Passage in The Hague (2014) differentiated it from a shopping mall. One could dream of knowing more about the reasons that Tschumi dedicated to Calvino his astonishing design for the renovation of MoMA (1997). These are additional potential relations and connections that this book looks for, but in order to find them it needs to activate several jumps.

Placed in the middle of this book, selected works by Calvino and Perec—with their estranging effects that cross over into the infraordinary—demonstrate the force of the literary imagination, scintillating with new and unexpected potential literary geographies, atlases of invention. The literary experimentations of Calvino and Perec do indeed impel readers toward the quest for space as storyteller, a space that is always interspersed, multiple, and multidimensional. These experimentations mark the distance of Calvino and Perec from the historical avant-gardes; yet, in updated but parallel ways, they play with interspersions of fields, just as the historical avant-gardes did.

To step back, to retrocede, or (even better) to jump back further into the book, the study of a selection of scattered materials from the "first" of the historical avant-gardes undertakes to show how, in Futurist experimentations, interspersion and compenetration took place on mobile stages, along a trajectory that moved from a more experiential mood—yet always abstract and fleeting—to a more allegorical one, quasi-Futurist, not standardized. The space of theater became the one privileged to imagine new spaces of modernity.

Finally, to step all the way back to the book's beginning, a selection of parts from the unfinished *Arcades Project*—aimed at studying the primeval moments of modernity—provides the opportunity to articulate a relationality among three notions that circulate among all the chapters: space as storyteller, architecturability, and colportage of space. Therefore the *Arcades Project* can be considered the origin of this book, though only in the Benjaminian sense of the word "origin": origin in the Benjaminian idiom is anything but a unified concept or term. The Benjaminian origin, instead, allows thinking and writing to leap or to jump—always in motion—in different and even opposite directions, to adopt divergent and opposing perspectives.

NOTES

Introduction

1. Walter Benjamin, "The Storyteller," in *Selected Writings, Vol. 3: 1935–1938*, ed. Marcus Bullock, Howard Eiland, and Michael W. Jennings, trans. Harry Zohn (Cambridge, MA: Harvard University Press, 2002), 142.

2. Giuliana Bruno, *Atlas of Emotion: Journeys in Art, Architecture and Film* (New York: Verso, 2002), 4.

3. Anthony Vidler, *Warped Space: Art, Architecture and Anxiety in Modern Culture* (Cambridge, MA: MIT Press, 2000), viii.

4. Samuel Weber, *Theatricality as Medium* (New York: Fordham University Press, 2004), x.

5. Jacques Derrida, "Point de folie: Maintenant l'architecture," in *Architecture Theory since 1968*, ed. K. Michael Hays, trans. Kate Linker (Cambridge, MA: MIT Press, 1998), 579.

6. Brigid Doherty has opened a path toward the study of the notion of the "colportage phenomenon of space" in Benjamin's texts. Brigid Doherty, "The 'Colportage Phenomenon of Space' and the Place of Montage in *The Arcades Project*," *Germanic Review* 81, no. 1 (2006): 37–64. Doherty posits that "Benjamin's efforts to conceptualize the colportage phenomenon of space and montage involved an attempt to rethink nineteenth-century painting as a form of perception [*Anschauungsform*], a source of knowledge, and an archive of things to be imitated and thereby transported—phantasmatically, in hash trances, and actually, in technological reproductions—into the space, or the rooms, of the present" (51). In studying the relation between painting and montage and their role in the writing of *The Arcades Project* Doherty concludes:

> Fundamental, then, to Benjamin's conception of montage is that montage had the potential to emerge as a medium for composing history in new, and newly perceptible—newly vivid, newly graphic, perhaps newly palpable—forms. A medium first dreamed, and dreamed in, by the generations of the nineteenth century, montage corresponds to an *Anschauungsform* framed in its utopian guise by a history painter such as Wiertz. To Benjamin's invocation of Wiertz, I suggest we add Delaroche and his pictorial inventions of historical spaces habitable by plaster effigies of princes posed as if within an especially well-decorated theatrical set. In the hash experiment, Benjamin imagines his own plastic inventions outstripping the accomplishments of the avant-garde scenographer Erwin Piscator. He fantasizes taking hold of the levers that control stage lighting, and finds in his own imagined theatrical experiments an explanation for why he "collect[s] colportage images." In the *Arcades Project*, montage corresponds to the

> ordinary, oneiric stagings of the nineteenth century's bourgeois interiors, and to the restagings of those interiors in painting, and in writing about painting, of that epoch. With regard to his own age, Benjamin promulgated montage as a technique of awakening that, in contemporary art, especially Dada and Surrealism, attempted to actualize, often in imitation of the effects of present-day cinema and nineteenth-century colportage alike, the *gesteigerte Anschaulichkeit* to which he himself aspired in reconceptualizing the writing of history. (60)

7. Luca Somigli, *Legitimizing the Artist: Manifesto Writing and European Modernism, 1885–1915* (Toronto: University of Toronto Press, 2003), 21.
8. Günter Berghaus, ed., *Futurism and the Technological Imagination* (Amsterdam: Rodopi, 2009).
9. Claudia Salaris, *Artecrazia: L'avanguardia futurista negli anni del fascismo* (Florence: La Nuova Italia, 1992), 3.
10. For Marinetti's relation to Venice, see Paolo Valesio, "Il Portasigarette Ritrovato," introduction to F. T. Marinetti, *Venzianella e Studentaccio*, ed. Patrizio Ceccagnoli and Paolo Valesio (Milan: Oscar Mondadori, 2013).
11. Fredric Jameson, *The Geopolitical Aesthetic* (Bloomington: Indiana University Press, 1995), 154.
12. Alex Woloch, *The One vs. the Many: Minor Characters and the Space of the Protagonist in the Novel* (Princeton, NJ: Princeton University Press, 2004), 18.
13. Franco Moretti, *Graphs, Maps, Trees: Abstract Models for Literary History* (London: Verso, 2005), 64.
14. Haun Saussy, "The Dimensionality of Literature," *Neohelicon* 38 (2011): 293.
15. Albena Yaneva, *Made by the Office for Metropolitan Architecture: An Ethnography of Design* (Rotterdam: 010 Publishers, 2009), 14.
16. David Joselit, *After Art* (Princeton, NJ: Princeton University Press, 2012), 56.
17. Charles Jencks, *The Story of Post-Modernism* (Chichester, UK: John Wiley & Sons, 2011); see in particular p. 231 for the many possible references and metaphors implied in the shape of this building.
18. OMA, CCTV Headquarters, http://oma.eu/projects/2002/cctv-%E2%80%93-headquarters (accessed November 1, 2015).

Chapter 1

1. Anthony Vidler, "The Architecture of Estrangement: Simmel, Kracauer, Benjamin," in *Warped Space: Art, Architecture and Anxiety in Modern Culture* (Cambridge, MA: MIT Press, 2000), 66–67.
2. Walter Benjamin, *Arcades Project*, ed. Roy Tiedemann, trans. Howard Eiland and Kevin McLaughlin (Cambridge, MA: Harvard University Press, 1999). References to individual sections follow the annotations in this edition (N2a,3, in this case).
3. Walter Benjamin, "Paris Diary," in *Selected Writings, Vol. 2: 1927–1934*, ed. Howard Eiland, Michael W. Jennings, and Gary Smith, trans. Rodney Livingstone (Cambridge, MA: Harvard University Press, 1999), 337, 351.

4. Michael Jennings, "Walter Benjamin and the European Avant-Garde," in *The Cambridge Companion to Walter Benjamin*, ed. David S. Ferris (Cambridge: Cambridge University Press, 2004), 31.

5. Samuel Weber, *Benjamin's -abilities* (Cambridge, MA: Harvard University Press, 2008), 309.

6. For this question of the fields of knowledge—as *Gebieten*—it is important to expand on Benjamin's reading of Kant, in particular of "On the Program of the Coming Philosophy." Geoffrey Bennington's "RIP," in *Futures: Of Jacques Derrida*, ed. Richard Rand (Stanford, CA: Stanford University Press, 2001), which moves quickly between Kant and Derrida on the question of future, would be an interesting starting point. Bennington focuses on the beginning of the *Critique of Judgment* and the relationship between the transcendental and the contingent; the hinge of his argument is found in the term *Gebiet* (and in the shifting topology of this term among *domain*, *terrain*, *territory*, *region*, and *field*).

7. Kevin McLaughlin has elegantly unfolded how the notion in physics of the force field was translated by Benjamin into the realm of aesthetics in order to define aesthetic conservation principles that did not rely on substance-based ones. The notion was employed by Benjamin with the aim to replace a theory of aesthetic content and was defined by two other key terms: divisibility and virtuality. See Kevin McLaughlin, "The Coming of Paper: Aesthetic Value from Ruskin to Benjamin," *MLN* 114, no. 5 (1999): 975–76.

8. Theodor W. Adorno, "A Portrait of Walter Benjamin," in *Prisms*, trans. Samuel Weber and Shierry Weber (Cambridge, MA: MIT Press, 1981), 230.

9. I am incorporating these few words from Kwinter's argument on field theory and Futurism. "The Einsteinian field, and its corresponding notion of space-time, dispensed entirely with the need to posit a material substratum as a carrier for forces and events by identifying the electromagnetic field with the new metrical one. . . . The field describes a space of propagation, of effects. It contains no matter or material points, but rather functions, vectors, and speeds." Sanford Kwinter, *Architectures of Time: Toward a Theory of the Event in Modernist Culture* (Cambridge, MA: MIT Press, 2001), 59–60. In chapter 2, I analyze Kwinter's interpretation of field theory in relation to Futurism.

10. For Benjamin's writing in relation to the German suffix *-barkeit*, see Weber, *Benjamin's abilities-*.

11. Samuel Weber, "Storming the Work: Allegory and Theatricality in Benjamin's *Origin of the German Mourning Play*," in *Theatricality as Medium* (New York: Fordham University Press, 2004), 174.

12. While writing this part, I read a recent text by Jean-Luc Nancy, "L''éthique originaire' de Heidegger," in *La pensée dérobée* (Paris: Galilée, 2001). In a footnote, Nancy writes:

> In reality, Heidegger's formulation is more difficult to interpret unequivocally: the word translated [into French] as "structure" is *Gerüst*, which means either a supporting structure such as a scaffolding or, as the architects say, a "load-bearing" structure. We might therefore hesitate between the idea of the structure of the opening itself (= as any opening is structured) and the idea of a load-bearing structure of the opening: the general form of referring-to, which is the form of meaning [*sens*], as bearer of the

> opening. This latter is the opening "that belongs to the understanding," and the "understanding" is that by means of which there is meaning. But meaning in this sense would be equally both what can be understood and what bears the possibility of understanding, and in the understanding itself, of being-open. This being-open (to being, or from being) would itself be not meaning but rather what meaning as existential disposition makes possible, and in relation to which it remains secondary, like scaffolding. (96)

Nancy's argument on the ambiguity of the term *Gerüst* in Heidegger could be expanded in the confrontation with Benjamin's thought. What I want to underline is that in Benjamin it is a question of structure that goes beyond a stable meaning to become the structure "supporting the opening," for which the dissemination of meaning is as important as the specificity of the architecture that springs from that time. This hesitation between these two interpretations should be allowed to remain, for in it resides the strength of Benjamin's articulation of thought.

13. Walter Benjamin, "Paris, the Capital of the Nineteenth Century" (1935), in *Arcades Project*, 3–13.

14. Letter 39 of 2–4 and 5.8.1935, in Theodor W. Adorno and Walter Benjamin, *The Complete Correspondence 1928–1940*, trans. Nicholas Walker (Cambridge, MA: Harvard University Press, 1999), 109.

15. There are many passages in the *Arcades Project* that demonstrate that Benjamin was attentive to the split and the friction between engineering and beaux arts in specific moments. For example, passage F1a,2:

> "Every tradesman imitates the materials and methods of others, and thinks he has accomplished a miracle of taste when he brings out porcelain cups resembling the work of a cooper, glasses resembling porcelains, gold jewelry like leather thongs, iron tables with the look of rattan, and so on. Into this arena rushes the confectioner as well—quite forgetting his proper domain, and the touchstone of his taste—aspiring to be a sculptor and architect." Jacob Falke, *Geschichte des modernen Geschmacks*, p. 380. This perplexity derived in part from the superabundance of technical processes and new materials that had suddenly become available. The effort to assimilate them more thoroughly led to mistakes and failures. On the other hand, these vain attempts are the most authentic proof that technological production, at the beginning, was in the grip of dreams. (Not architecture alone but all technology is, at certain stages, evidence of a collective dream.) (151–52)

16. Sigfried Giedion, *Building in France, Building in Iron, Building in Ferroconcrete*, trans. J. Duncan Berry (Santa Monica, CA: Getty Center for the History of Art and the Humanities, 1995).

17. Ibid., 53.

18. Samuel Weber, *Mass Mediauras: Form, Technics, Media* (Stanford, CA: Stanford University Press, 1996), 97.

19. Sokratis Georgiadis, introduction to Giedion, *Building in France, Building in Iron, Building in Ferroconcrete*, 9.

> Semper's negative attitude toward the extensive architectural use of iron was also based on another important factor. He had discussed the material as early as 1849 in an article reviewing the Jardin d'hiver in Paris, and there altogether rejected the open display of it, at least in monumental buildings. As a constructional material iron should "by its nature be used as slender rods and sometimes as cables." Due to the small surface displayed in these forms, the more perfect the construction, the more the iron visually disappears. It is in this sense that Semper spoke of it as an "invisible material." Barely fifteen years later he repeated this assessment in his principal work *Der Stil in den technischen und tektonischen Künsten; oder, Praktische Ästhetik* (Style in the technical and tectonic arts; or, Practical esthetics). We have in metal-rod construction, he noted, "a poor soil for art! There can be no question of a monumental style with cast-iron rods; its very ideal is *invisible architecture*! For the thinner metal is spun, the more perfect is its manner." Clearly Semper could not tolerate a dematerialized architecture. (8)

20. Letter 39 of 2–4 and 5.8.1935, in Adorno and Benjamin, *The Complete Correspondence 1928–1940*, 109.

21. Letter 40 from Benjamin to Adorno, 16.8.1935, in Adorno and Benjamin, *The Complete Correspondence 1928–1940*, 117–18.

Benjamin writes as follows:

> I would certainly not wish these lines to appear as too meagre a response, let me be bold enough to offer just a few quite provisional remarks—although this runs certain risks as well . . .
>
> One thing I would like to say immediately: if your letter makes such emphatic reference to the "first" sketch of the Arcades, I can confirm that absolutely nothing has been abandoned, and not a single word relinquished, from this "first" version. And the piece you had in front of you is not, if I could put it this way, the "second" sketch but rather a different one. The two sketches have a polar relationship to one another. They represent the thesis and the antithesis of the work. Consequently, as far as I am concerned, this second one is far from being a conclusion. The necessity for it lies in the fact that the insights contained in the first sketch cannot be articulated immediately—except perhaps in an impermissibly "poetical" fashion. Hence the subtitle, long since abandoned, of the first sketch: "A Poetic Fairy-Tale."
>
> Now I have the two ends of the bow in hand—but still lack the strength to bend and string it properly. Only a long period of "training" can prepare me for this, and directly working in the material itself is one element, amongst others, of the process. My unfortunate circumstances also mean that those other elements have had to recede in favor of the first one during the second period of my work on the project. I am aware of this. And the somewhat dilatory character of my method reflects this awareness. I do not wish to let any mistake disturb the calculated plan of the whole.

22. Letter 40 from Benjamin to Adorno, 16.8.1935, in Adorno and Benjamin, *The Complete Correspondence 1928–1940*, 118.

23. Letter 10 from Benjamin to Adorno, 1.12.1932, in Adorno and Benjamin, *The Complete Correspondence 1928–1940*, 20.

24. "In the interior, he [the private individual] brings together the far away and the long ago. His living room is a box in the theater of the world." "Paris, the Capital of the Nineteenth Century," 9.

25. I use *ontopology* in the way Derrida writes about it in *Specters of Marx*, trans. Peggy Kamuf (London: Routledge, 1994):

> (By *ontopology* we mean an axiomatics linking indissociably the ontological value of present-being [*on*] to its *situation*, to the stable and presentable determination of a locality, the *topos* of territory, native soil, city, body in general). For having spread in an unheard-of fashion, which is more and more differentiated and more and more accelerated (it is acceleration itself, beyond the norms of speed that have until now informed human culture), the process of dislocation is no less arch-originary, that is, just as "archaic" as the archaism that it has always dislodged. This process is, moreover, the positive condition of the stabilization that it constantly relaunches. All stability in a place being but a stabilization or a sedentarization, it will have been necessary that the local differance, the spacing of a displacement gives the movement its start. And gives places and gives rise [*donne lieu*]. All national rootedness, for example, is rooted first of all in the memory or the anxiety of a displaced—or displaceable—population. It is not only time that is "out of joint," but space in time, spacing. (102–3)

26. For the philosophical question related to the interplay of place and space in the philosophical history of the concepts, see the rich study by Edward W. Casey, *The Fate of Place: A Philosophical History* (Berkeley: University of California Press, 1997). The fact that Benjamin's writing is not included in this crucial selection and display of the history of philosophy is quite intriguing.

27. I am indebted to Samuel Weber for this alternative translation.

28. Samuel Weber, "Ability and Style," in *Benjamin's -abilities*, 117.

29. Vidler, *Warped Space*.

30. In a note in the *Arcades Project* we find a quite suggestive dialectical diagram of Benjamin's process (910).

31. Aragon opens and prefaces his *Paris Peasant* (Louis Aragon, *Paris Peasant*, trans. Simon W. Taylor [Boston: Exact Change, 1994]) with an introduction to a modern mythology. In the first chapter dedicated to the "passage de l'Opéra," we read: "How oddly this light suffuses the covered arcades which abound in Paris in the vicinity of the main boulevards and which are rather disturbingly named passages, as though no one had the right to linger for more than an instant in those sunless corridors" (13–14). As Aragon considers these elements of a phantasmatic cityscape, he inscribes them as one part of the modern myth:

> The great American passion for city planning, imported into Paris by a prefect of police during the Second Empire and now being applied to the task of redrawing the map of our capital in straight lines, will soon spell the doom of these human aquariums. Although the life that originally quickened them has drained away, they deserve, nevertheless, to be

> regarded as the secret repositories of several modern myths: it is only today, when the pickaxe menaces them, that they have at last become the true sanctuaries of a cult of the ephemeral, the ghostly landscape of damnable pleasures and professions. Places that were incomprehensible yesterday, and that tomorrow will never know. (14)

32. "The classic passage on awakening at night in a dark room and the ensuing orientation: 'When I awoke like this, and my mind struggled in an unsuccessful attempt to discover where I was, everything would be moving round me through the darkness: things, places, years. My body, still too heavy with sleep to move, would make an effort to construe the form which its tiredness took as an orientation of its various members, so as to induce from that where the wall lay and the furniture stood, to piece together and to give a name to the house in which it must be living. Its memory, the composite memory of its ribs, knees, and shoulder-blades, offered it a whole series of rooms in which it had at one time or another slept, while the unseen walls kept changing, adapting themselves to the shape of each successive room that it remembered, whirling madly through the darkness. And even before my brain . . . had collected sufficient impressions . . . to identify the room, it, my body, would recall from each room in succession what the bed was like, where the doors were, how daylight came in at the windows, whether there was a passage outside, what I had in my mind when I went to sleep, and had found there when I awoke.' Marcel Proust, *Du côté de chez Swann*, vol. 1, p. 15" (K8a,2).

33. Samuel Weber, "Benjamin's Writing Style," in *Encyclopedia of Aesthetics*, vol. 1 (New York: Oxford University Press, 1998), 262.

34. "'Le Corbusier's houses depend on neither spatial nor plastic articulation: the air passes through them! Air becomes a constitutive factor! What matters, therefore, is neither spatiality per se nor plasticity per se but only relation and interfusion. There is but one indivisible space. The integuments separating inside from outside fall away.' Sigfried Giedion, *Bauen in Frankreich*, Berlin 1928, p. 85" (M3a,3).

35. The tangential dimension to which I am referring resembles the way that Benjamin, in his text on language and translatability, "The Task of the Translator," in *Selected Writings, Vol. 1: 1913–1926* (Cambridge, MA: Harvard University Press, 1996), addresses the relationship between the original and the copy. Among the images that he exposes to the reader we find the following:

> It is the task of the translator to release in his own language that pure language which is exiled among alien tongues, to liberate the language imprisoned in a work in his re-creation of that work. For the sake of language, he breaks through decayed barriers of his own language. Luther, Voss, Hölderlin, and George, have extended the boundaries of the German language.—What remains for sense, in its importance for the relationship between translation and the original, may be expressed in the following simile. Just as a tangent touches a circle lightly and at but one point—establishing, with this touch rather than with the point, the law according to which it is to continue on its straight path to infinity—a translation touches the original lightly and only at the infinitely small point of the

sense, thereupon pursuing its own course according to the laws of fidelity in the freedom of linguistic flux. (261)

36. The following quote from Meyer in the *Arcades Project* helps to explain this relation:

> "The arcade as iron construction stands on the verge of horizontal extension. That is a decisive condition for its 'old-fashioned' appearance. It displays, in this regard, a hybrid character, analogous in certain respect to that of the Baroque church—'the vaulted hall' that comprehends the chapels only as an extension of its own proper space, which is wider than ever before. Nevertheless, an attraction 'from on high' is also at work in the Baroque hall—an upward-tending ecstasy, such as jubilates from the frescoes on the ceiling . . ." A. G. Meyer, *Eisenbauten*, p. 74. On the other hand, it may be said that something sacral, a vestige of the nave, still attaches to this row of commodities that is the arcade. From a functional point of view, the arcade already occupies the field of horizontal amplitude; architecturally, however, it still stands within the conceptual field of the old "hall." (F4,5)

37. See, for example, Benjamin's annotation in J54a,1: "Concerning the 'strange sectioning of time,' the final stanza of 'L'Avertisseur':

> Despite what he may hope or plan,
> There is no moment left when man
> Is not subject to the constant
> Warnings of this odious Serpent.

To be compared with 'L'Horloge' and 'Rêve parisien.' "

38. "With regard to the 'sectioning of time': the hidden construction of 'Le vin des amants' is grounded in the fact that only rather far along does the now surprising light fall on the situation at hand: the ecstatic drunkenness which the lovers owe to the wine is a morning drunkenness. 'Into the blue crystal of the morning'—this is the seventh line of this fourteen-line poem" (J68a,6).

39. Weber, "Storming the Work."

40. And the passage continues: "This *gestus* is found again in the 'ebbings' of his prosodic construction [*Versbaus*]—something that, for several commentators, is the most precious element of his *ars poetica*" (J52,2).

41. Walter Benjamin, "The Paris of the Second Empire in Baudelaire," in *Selected Writings, Vol. 4: 1938–1940*, ed. Marcus Bullock, Howard Eiland, and Gary Smith, trans. Edmund Jephcott (Cambridge, MA: Harvard University Press, 2003), 59.

42. In the *Petit Robert* we find:

> COLPORTAGE: Action de colporter.
>
> COLPORTER: (1539; a. fr. *comporter*; lat. *comportare* "transporter," modifié par *col*; Cf. Coltiner). 1. Transporter avec soi des marchandises pour le vendre. *Colporter des marchandises, des livres*. 2. Transmettre (une information) à des nombreuses personnes (souvent pey.). V. Divulguer, propager, rapporter, répandre. *Colporter une nouvelle, une histoire scandaleuse*: la raconter à l'un et à l'autre.

43. Walter Benjamin, "The Work of Art in the Age of Its Technological Reproducibility," in *Selected Writings, Vol. 3: 1935–1938*, ed. Marcus Bullock, Howard Eiland, and Michael W. Jennings, trans. Harry Zohn (Cambridge, MA: Harvard University Press, 2002).

44. Walter Benjamin, *Gesammelte Schriften*, Bd.7 T.1 (Frankfurt am Main: Suhrkamp Verlag, 1972), 380.

45. John Macarthur, "Movement and Tactility: Benjamin and Wölfflin on Imitation in Architecture," *Journal of Architecture* 12, no. 5 (2007): 482; Walter Benjamin, "The Rigorous Study of Art," in *Selected Writings, Vol. 2: 1927–1934*, 670.

46. Macarthur, "Movement and Tactility," 482.

47. Mark Hansen, *Embodying Technesis: Technology beyond Writing* (Ann Arbor: University of Michigan Press, 2000), 254.

48. For a brief but fascinating history of glass, which considers it in its uses and its technology from the most ancient to contemporary optical fibers, see Pascal Richet, *L'âge du verre* (Paris: Découvertes Gallimard Techniques, 2000).

49. I do not intend to here delve into the play between mirrors, *psyché*, and space in Benjamin's writing, which would lead us further to Freud, Derrida, and Nancy. For the moment, I will address the subject only by citing some aphorisms: Benjamin's "Mallarmé: genius of mirrors" (R1a,1) and "What is *une psyché*?" (F°,1); Freud's "*Psyche ist ausgedehnt: weiss nichts davon*" and Nancy's fascination with this phrase of Freud's in *Corpus* (Paris: Ed. Metaillé, 1992), 22. Two long texts by Derrida, "La double séance" in *La dissémination* (Paris: Éditions du Seuil, 1972), 215–347, and *Le toucher* (Paris: Éditions Galilée, 2000), would be helpful in order to elaborate these aphorisms.

50. Weber, *Mass Mediauras*, 100.

Chapter 2

1. Walter Benjamin, "Experience and Poverty," in *Selected Writings, Vol. 2: 1927–1934*, ed. Howard Eiland, Michael W. Jennings, and Gary Smith, trans. Rodney Livingstone (Cambridge, MA: Harvard University Press, 1999), 731–36.

2. For a study of Paul Scheerbart, see John Stuart's introduction to *The Gray Cloth: Paul Scheerbart's Novel on Glass Architecture*, trans. John A. Stuart (Cambridge, MA: MIT Press, 2001).

3. Sanford Kwinter, *Architectures of Time: Toward a Theory of the Event in Modernist Culture* (Cambridge, MA: MIT, 2001), 35.

4. For this reason, adds Kwinter, it is necessary to think of fragment and multiplicity together. The fragment should not be considered a piece that refers to a whole; instead it should be considered "in the element of its positivity, as a specific characterization of matter within a continuous, fluctuating, and time-imbued multiplicity" (38). Space and time are no longer distinct categories; Kwinter underlines that this is not a question of a "modernist antitemporal stillness," which would return again within a closed time. Rather, the phenomena are comprehensible only *in time*, in the process of their *becoming*.

5. Among the endless and labyrinthine Futurist archives, I have done a very minimal selection, and I will not refer here to Futurist architects such as Sant'Elia, Mario Chiattone, Guido Fiorini, Virgilio Marchi, and Tullio Crali, just to mention a few.

6. Manfredo Tafuri, "The Stage as 'Virtual City': From Fuchs to Totaltheater," in *The Sphere and the Labyrinth: Avant-Gardes and Architecture from Piranesi to the 1970s* (Cambridge, MA: MIT Press, 1987), 99.

7. Enrico Crispolti, ed., *Ricostruzione futurista dell'universo* (Turin: Assessorato per la cultura, Musei Civici, 1980), 25.

8. In a study dedicated entirely to Prampolini, the specificity of this moment is given: "Rome becomes the center of the new Futurist creative activity, driven toward a simultaneous emotional merging of perceived events, but operating through analogical plastic forms, and therefore imaginatively quite liberating." Enrico Crispolti and Rosella Siligato, eds., *Prampolini dal futurismo all'informale* (Rome: Edizioni Carte segrete, 1992), 103.

9. Fortunato Depero, "Complessità Plastica—Libero Gioco Futurista—L'Essere Vivente Artificiale" [Plastic Complexity—Free Futurist Game—The Artificial Living Being], in *Casa Balla e il futurismo a Roma*, ed. Enrico Crispolti (Rome: Istituto Poligrafico e Zecca dello Stato, 1989), 225.

10. S.v. "complexity," *OED Online*, September 2015, http://www.oed.com.gate.lib.buffalo.edu/view/Entry/37689?redirectedFrom=complexity& (accessed October 31, 2015).

11. F. T. Marinetti, "Technical Manifesto of Futurist Literature," in *Futurism: An Anthology*, ed. Lawrence Rainey, Christine Poggi, and Laura Wittman (New Haven, CT: Yale University Press, 2009), 122; emphasis in original.

12. Luigi Ballerini has drawn attention to the interaction and reconfiguration that takes place in the Futurist poetics between written language and the object-language:

> The idea of a privileged verbal language is not only in question, but literally outdated, and one proceeds, perhaps for the first time, to a linguistic investiture of nonverbal material signs, which is to say to the acknowledgement of their grammatological potential. The distinction between the act of writing inside the verbal language and the act of creating—while writing—an object-language of which the verbal one is a part not so much (not exclusively) for its condition of semantic vocation but more for what this vocation produces at the plastic-formal level, it is an essential step to understand one of the most important conquests of Futurism: the substantial reciprocity of the principles of interaction (verbal-plastic and verbal-material etc.) and of the simultaneity of linguistic perception. (Luigi Ballerini, *La piramide capovolta* [Venice: Marsilio, 1975], 72)

13. Giacomo Balla and Fortunato Depero, "Futurist Reconstruction of the Universe," in Rainey, Poggi, and Wittman, *Futurism: An Anthology*, 209.

14. Günter Berghaus, *Italian Futurist Theatre 1909–1944* (Oxford: Calderon, 1998), 296. As Berghaus emphasizes, this Futurist complex had been already presented by Depero's previous manifesto, which announced the "ARTIFICIAL LIVING BEING"—an assemblage of playful mechanisms.

15. John Rajchman, *Constructions* (Cambridge, MA: MIT Press, 1998), 76.

16. F. T. Marinetti, Emilio Settimelli, and Bruno Corrà, "The Futurist Synthetic Theater," in Rainey, Poggi, and Wittman, *Futurism: An Anthology*.

17. The Futurists used the term "passéist" to refer to anything that was excessively concerned with traditional or older forms that the Futurists considered outmoded.

18. In a recent edition of Marinetti's texts, the editors felt compelled to avoid a literal translation of the Italian adjective *sintetico* because such an equivalence in English is misleading.

> The term *sintesi* does not have a direct equivalent in English and is usually translated as "synthetic." We have called the dramatic genre "Theater of Essential Brevity" and the plays "minidramas"; the adjective *sintetico* has been rendered as "compressed," "condensed," or "compact." (F. T. Marinetti, *Critical Writings*, ed. Günter Berghaus, trans. Doug Thompson [New York: Farrar, Straus and Giroux, 2006], 464)

While one could investigate Futurist theater in its relation to the philosophical implications of the adjective *sintetico*, I will for the sake of brevity not consider these implications. The literal translation, even if it brings foreignness to English, gets close to the use that Futurists wanted to make of the term. Moreover, beside the fact that everyday Italian is embedded also with the conceptuality of the philosophical tradition, the Futurists were no doubt aware of the force that they were imposing in using "synthetic," and therefore wanted, with theatrical gestures, to point toward the question of synthesis in relation to time and temporality.

19. See Paolo Valesio, "'The Most Enduring and Most Honored Name': Marinetti as a Poet," in *F. T. Marinetti: Selected Poems and Related Prose*, sel. Luce Marinetti, trans. Elizabeth R. Napier and Barbara R. Studholme (New Haven, CT: Yale University Press, 2002), 152.

20. Samuel Weber, "Theatricality as Medium: Introduction," in *Theatricality as Medium* (New York: Fordham University Press, 2004), 11.

21. Giovanni Lista, *La scène futuriste* (Paris: Éditions du Centre national de la recherche scientifique, 1989), 140.

22. However, this rapport with physical sensations is not what is later proposed by Artaud. In his proposal to reconstruct the set and remove the supremacy of the word, Artaud resembles the Futurists, but Futurist theater is not, as Derrida emphasizes with respect to Artaud, "representation, then, as the autopresentation of pure visibility and pure sensibility." Neither is it the opposite of distancing, as in Derrida, "The Theater of Cruelty and the Closure of Representation," in *Writing and Difference* (Chicago: University of Chicago Press, 1978), 238.

23. Acceptance into the Futurist movement eluded him, despite his efforts over many years. On this aspect, see Lista, *La scène futuriste*, and Berghaus, *Italian Futurist Theatre 1909–1944*.

24. Enrico Prampolini, "The Atmosphere-Structure—Bases for a Futurist Architecture," in *Attraverso l'architettura futurista*, ed. Enrico Crispolti (Modena: Galleria Fonte d'Abisso Edizioni, 1984), 88–89.

25. Enrico Prampolini, "A New Art? Absolute Construction of Movement-Noise," in *Attraverso l'architettura futurista*, 24–25.

26. Enrico Prampolini, "Futurist Stage Design," in Rainey, Poggi, and Wittman, *Futurism: An Anthology*, 212–15.

27. Enrico Prampolini, "Pittura pura" [Pure Painting], *L'artista moderno* 14, fasc. I, January 1915, reprinted in *Casa Balla e il futurismo a Roma*, ed. Enrico Crispolti (Rome: Istituto Poligrafico e Zecca dello Stato, 1989), 227–28. Of particular interest in this regard are Mark A. Cheetham's analyses of Kandinsky in his *The Rhetoric of Purity: Essentialist Theory and the Advent of Abstract*

Painting (New York: Cambridge University Press, 1991). For Kandinsky's work in theater at the beginning of the century and its relation to Symbolism, as well as successive moments in theater, see the chapter titled "Kandinskij e la sintesi scenica astratta" in Silvana Sinisi, *Cambi di scena: Teatro e arti visive nelle poetiche del Novecento* (Rome: Bulzoni, 1995).

28. In many of the theatrical explorations undertaken in Futurism, the marionette occupied a central position. The recurrence of the marionette can be viewed as a product of the desire to create a stronger relationship between the stage and the public, at the expense of the actor. Thus the manifesto, besides stressing the importance of the set design, directly opposes the actor's privileged position as diva or star that was dominant at the time.

29. "Quivering and luminous forms (produced by electrical currents + colored gases) will be unleashed in dynamic writhings, genuine *gas-actors* will replace real actors in a theater of the unknown. *Gas-actors* rustling, hissing sharply, producing bizarre noises, will easily endow works with unprecedented interpretative meanings, express variegated emotive tonalities far more efficiently than some celebrated actor" (215). Lista draws particular attention to distinguishing Prampolini from the important precedents set by Loïe Fuller and Edward Gordon Craig: "Prampolini was aiming at shattering the spectator by means of dissonance 'of unexpected dynamic effects' whereas Craig wanted to obtain a kinetics made of 'gentle and gracious, serious and somber, haughty and splendid movements' " (Lista, *La scène futuriste*, 302).

30. Berghaus, *Italian Futurist Theatre 1909–1944*, 282. Lista describes it as follows: "Prampolini, for the stage, constituted of chromatic and rotating panels, designed what he called 'luminous architectures,' totally abstract. In the first act the scenery was articulated with an ensemble of asymmetrical diagonals, with a strong dynamic overtone. In the second act on the contrary the scenery was composed of two convergent planes" (Lista, *La scène futuriste*, 347).

31. Rainey, Poggi, and Wittman, *Futurism: An Anthology*, 272–73 (translation modified).

32. Maria Elena Versari, "Futurist Machine Age, Constructivism and the Modernity of Mechanization," in *Futurism and the Technological Imagination*, ed. Günter Berghaus (Amsterdam: Rodopi, 2009).

> The schism produced at the Congress is seen nowadays as the affirmation of the progressive principles of Constructivism against the models of individual stylistic production embodied by Expressionism. . . . In the many statements that accompanied the relocation of Russian Constructivism to Western Europe, explicit political references became fewer and fewer; the *progressivism* characterizing the new search for a *constructive* style ended up spinning upon itself in a formalistic Utopian ideology of *efficacy* . . . . The ideological contradiction of "International" Constructivism thus derived from the Utopian status of the artist within it. It was his task to embody, with his work, the "fundamental feature of the present age, [that] is the triumph of the constructive method." In this way, the Constructivist artist was responsible for finding an effective way of realizing the modernization of today's society, working from within (and against) the current social structure. The artist's work would therefore mirror not so much the

> content of modernity (the machine), but its internal constitutive structure (the method). (163–64)

The first critic who developed this theme was Enrico Crispolti in his *Il mito della macchina e altri temi del Futurismo* (Trapani: Celebes Editore, 1969).

33. Crispolti, *Casa Balla e il futurismo a Roma*, 174–75.

34. Prampolini, in the catalogue of the New York exhibition *Machine Age Exposition*, restates this point. He writes: "The plastic exaltation of the Machine and the mechanical elements must now be conceived in their interior reality, this is not in the formal representation of the elements which makes up the machine itself, but rather in the plastic mechanical analogy that the Machine suggests to us in connection with various spiritual realities." "The Aesthetic of the Machine and Mechanical Instrospection in Art," in "*Machine Age Exposition*, May 16–28 NYC, 1927," special issue, *Little Review* 12 (1927): 10.

35. Lisa Phillips and Dieter Bogner, *Frederick Kiesler* (New York: Whitney Museum of American Art, 1989), 39.

36. *Futurist Performance*, ed. Michael Kirby, trans. Victoria Nes Kirby (New York: Paj, 1971), 225–31.

37. Phillips and Bogner, *Frederick Kiesler*, 49. Prampolini's and Kiesler's ideas on stage design were moving in parallel directions, as is documented in the catalogue of the *International Theatre Exposition* organized by Kiesler in New York in 1926. In his "Debacle of the Modern Theatre: Picture-Stage, Actors, Space-Stage" (*Little Review* 11, no. 2 [Winter 1926]: 67), where he calls for a "space-stage," as opposed to a "picture-stage," Kiesler writes: "The contemporary theatre calls for the vitality of life itself, a vitality which has the force and the tempo of the age. For such energy the proscenium with its angles, its here-and-there, is not enough. Its breath fills the entire stage; it demands depth, freedom of movement, space in the truest sense of the word. It cannot get this on the picture-stage, where the action and the scenery are designed for a decorative frontal effect. The new spirit bursts the stage, which is not merely *a priori* space, but also *appears* as space."

38. "For the sound action the noises of metallic structures alternating with human voice, whose suggestive power constituted for Prampolini an essential element of the space-actor, had been planned." Giovanni Lista, quoted in Crispolti and Siligato, *Prampolini dal Futurismo all'informale*, 234.

39. Prampolini produced several stage designs and costumes for *The Dance of the Propeller* (1923) and a ballet by Casavola, as well as many stage designs for Marinetti's theatrical syntheses: *Drum of Fire* (1922), *Prisoners* (1925), and *Vulcan* (1926), to mention only a few.

40. Enrico Prampolini, *Théâtre de la Pantomime Futuriste*, directed by Maria Ricciotti and Enrico Prampolini (Paris: M. et J. De Brunoff, 1927).

41. "Ultime teatrali: 'Pantomima futurista' al Lirico," *Corriere della sera*, March 22, 1928, reprinted in Berghaus, *Italian Futurist Theatre 1909–1944*, 259.

42. Berghaus, *Italian Futurist Theatre 1909–1944*, 451.

43. The *rumorarmonio*, or noise-harmonium, was an instrument designed by Russolo that connected several noise-generating machines to a keyboard. On Russolo, see Luciano Chessa, *Luigi Russolo: Noise, Visual Arts and the Occult* (Berkeley: University of California Press, 2012).

44. Fortunato Depero, *Depero Futurista*, Edizione Dinamo-Azari (Milan: Dinamo-Azari,1927; repr. 1978).

45. "Teatro Magico" [Magic Theater], in *Depero e la scena: Da "Colori" alla scena mobile, 1913–1930*, ed. Bruno Passamani (Turin: Martano Editore, 1970), 101.

46. From 1928 to 1930 Depero lived in New York. There he continued his activities involving graphics and publicity, interior architectures, and theatrical set designs, among which is the noteworthy *The New Babel*, which was never staged. See Laura Chiesa, "Transnational Multimedia: Fortunato Depero's Impressions of New York City (1928–1930)," *California Italian Studies* 1, no. 2 (2010), doi: ismrg_cisj_8891.

47. Kwinter, *Architectures of Time*, 90.

48. Lista, *La scène futuriste*, 271–82.

49. Giovanni Calendoli, preface to *Teatro: F. T. Marinetti* (Rome: Vito Bianco, 1960), lxvi. Characters are integrally abstract, as in the example of "Simultaneity of the multiple personality," a character "constructed by the overlapping of infinite characters that would not have been able to coexist in a 'psychological' reality" (lxix).

50. *Ricostruire l'Italia con architettura futurista Sant'Elia*, in *Teatro*, ed. Jeffrey T. Schnapp (Milan: Oscar Mondadori, 2004), 477. We do not know the exact date when the play was written, but most likely, as Schnapp suggests, it was the late 1920s or early 1930s.

51. Ezio Godoli has documented the debates and meetings of the period, beginning with the periodicals established in 1932, *La città nuova* and *Il Futurismo*, continuing up through the magazines *Sant'Elia*, *La Terra dei Vivi*, and *Artecrazia*, which did not last long beyond its first issues. The closing of this magazine followed some explicit criticism by many Futurists, including Marinetti and Prampolini, against the art exposition in Munich, *Entartete Kunst* (*Degenerate Art*), which opened in June 1937. Ezio Godoli, *Guide all'architettura moderna: Il Futurismo* (Bari: Laterza, 1983). See also Luciano Paletta, *L'architettura in Italia: 1919–1943: Le polemiche* (Milan: Clup, 1972); Riccardo Mariani, *Razionalismo e architettura moderna: Storia di una polemica* (Milan: Edizioni Comunità, 1989); Giorgio Ciucci, *Gli architetti e il fascismo* (Turin: Einaudi, 1989); Carlo Melograni, *Architettura italiana sotto il fascismo* (Turin: Bollati Boringhieri, 2008).

52. F. T. Marinetti, Angiolo Mazzoni, and Mino Somenzi, "Manifesto futurista dell'architettura aerea" [Futurist Manifesto of Aerial Architecture], in *La metropoli futurista: Progetti im-Possibili*, ed. Vincenzo Capalbo and Ezio Godoli (Florence: Officina del Novecento, 1999), 92.

53. For an accurate analysis, see David Rifkind, "Quadrante and the Politicization of Architectural Discourse in Fascist Italy," PhD diss., Columbia University, 2007, which has since appeared as David Rifkind, *The Battle for Modernism: Quadrante and the Politicization of Architectural Discourse in Fascist Italy* (Vicenza and Venice: CISA Andrea Palladio and Marsilio Editori, 2012).

54. "Corsivo n. 90," in *Quadrante*, no. 9, 1934: 22. Reprinted in Massimo Bontempelli, *L'avventura Novecentista* (Florence: Vallecchi Editore, 1974), 328.

55. For the effect of color in architecture, see Sylvia Lavin, "What Color Is It Now?," *Perspecta, the Yale Architectural Journal* 35 (2004): 98–111.

56. This seems to refer to proposals made by Claude Parent and Paul Virilio in their architectural drawings from the 1960s, which were presented in 1960 at the *Mostra dell'architettura* in Venice. See "La fonction de l'oblique," in *Architecture Principe, 1966–1996* (Paris: Les Éditions de l'Imprimeur, 1997). Our contemporary constructed avant-garde architectures grow out of this constructive spatial research.

57. Volt [Vincenzo Fani], "La casa futurista. Indipendente—mobile—smontabile—meccanica—esilarante. Manifesto," in *La metropoli futurista: Progetti im-Possibili*, ed. Vincenzo Capalbo and Ezio Godoli (Florence: Officina del Novecento, 1999), 88–90.

58. This is clearly a reference to the internal logic of the Futurist proposals, particularly that of Balla and Depero, and for the development of "polymaterism" elaborated by Prampolini in the 1930s.

59. Rainey, Poggi, and Wittman, *Futurism: An Anthology*, 99.

60. "The avant-garde, while it defines itself ideologically by its polemical (and at times scornful) attitude toward every form of historiographic meditation, cannot even begin to conceive of itself as a form of organization if it does not see itself as a radically historical creature, almost obsessively attentive to all the nuances of the 'before' and 'after' " (Valesio, *F. T. Marinetti: Selected Poems and Related Prose*, 153).

61. Rainey, Poggi, and Wittman, *Futurism: An Anthology*, 67.

62. Berghaus, *Italian Futurist Theatre 1909–1944*, 69. The author has produced the best documented and most detailed history of the different phases of Futurist theater. These performances, held by Marinetti and other Futurist artists, preceded the Futurist Variety Theater and Synthetic Theater.

63. L. Rainey, "Introduction: F. T. Marinetti and the Development of Futurism," in Rainey, Poggi, and Wittman, *Futurism: An Anthology*, 10.

64. Cinzia Sartini Blum, *The Other Modernism: F. T. Marinetti's Futurist Fiction of Power* (Berkeley: University of California Press, 1996).

65. Italo Calvino, *Six Memos for the Next Millennium*, trans. Patrick Creagh (New York: Vintage International Edition, 1993), 71. In chapter 3 I will also question whether the city is just a symbol in Calvino's *Invisible Cities*.

66. Anthony Vidler, ed., *Architecture between Spectacle and Use* (Williamstown, MA: Sterling and Francine Clark Art Institute, 2008), vi.

Chapter 3

1. Inaugural in this line of interpretation is Lucia Re's text, *Calvino and the Age of Neorealism: Fables of Estrangement* (Stanford, CA: Stanford University Press, 1990). For *Invisible Cities,* see also Lucia Re's "Testi letterari e testi architettonici: *Le città invisibili* di Italo Calvino," in *Cultura della conservazione e istanza del progetto*, ed. Francesco Alberti and Sandro Scarrocchia (Florence: Alinea, 1998), 31–40.

2. Consider, for example, Manet van Montfrans, *Georges Perec: La contrainte du réel* (Amsterdam: Rodopi, 1999), and Michael Sheringham, *Everyday Life: Theories and Practices from Surrealism to the Present* (Oxford: Oxford University Press, 2006).

3. Calvino was introduced to the Oulipo group by Raymond Queneau and first participated in the group as a "foreign correspondent" (while living in Paris) in

1973. He became an official member in 1980 (having already returned to Rome). Perec was accepted as a "new member" in 1967.

4. Oulipo, *Atlas de littérature potentielle* (Paris: Gallimard, 1981). Calvino's suggestion of the use of "atlas" in the title is confirmed by a letter from Paul Fournel to the writer. It welcomed with *félicitation* the idea of using "atlas": "You have triumphed," Fournel writes to Calvino. "The Oulipians have given me the task of congratulating you." In Italo Calvino, *Romanzi e Racconti*, ed. Claudio Milanini, vol. 3 (Milan: Mondadori, 1994), 1241.

5. Giuliana Bruno, *Atlas of Emotion: Journeys in Art, Architecture and Film* (New York: Verso, 2002).

6. Walter Benjamin, *Arcades Project*, ed. Roy Tiedemann, trans. Howard Eiland and Kevin McLaughlin (Cambridge, MA: Harvard University Press, 1999), M1,4.

7. Italo Calvino, *Saggi*, ed. Mario Berenghi, vol. 1 (Milan: Mondadori, 1995), 417–25.

8. Calvino, *Saggi*, vol. 1, 426–33. Here Calvino comments on a much visited and discussed exhibition, organized at the Centre Georges Pompidou, entitled *Cartes et Figures de la Terre* (Paris: Centre Georges Pompidou, Centre de création industrielle, 1980).

9. Or rather, on a conceptual plane, one could say that "l'espace ne préexiste pas à sa carte," as the cartographer Christian Jacob wrote; the philosopher Bernard Stiegler recently elaborated on this idea, calling into question the relationship between phenomenology and technology. However, this does not remove the possibility of adventure, or of the nonprogrammable, but rather plays between the spectral quality of the *grafia*, in this case of the cartography, and the indeterminate and unplannable. Christian Jacob, *The Sovereign Map: Theoretical Approaches in Cartography throughout History*, ed. Edward H. Dahl, trans. Tom Conley (Chicago: University of Chicago Press, 2006); Bernard Stiegler, "Etre-là-bas: Phénoménologie et orientation," in "Espace et imagination," special issue, *Alter: Revue de phénoménologie* 4 (1996): 263–80.

10. This tension between the deep and the vast can be compared with one of Freud's final brief notes, which the philosopher J.-L. Nancy has highlighted: "La psyché est étendue: n'en sait rien." Jean-Luc Nancy, *Corpus* (Paris: Métailié, 1992). I leave it to this aphoristic citation to expand silently throughout my chapter.

11. Calvino, *Saggi*, vol. 1, 242–51.

12. Calvino, *Romanzi e Racconti*, vol. 2, 357–498; Italo Calvino, *Invisible Cities*, trans. William Weaver (Orlando, FL: Harcourt, 1974).

13. Claudio Milanini, *L'utopia discontinua: Saggio su Italo Calvino* (Milan: Garzanti, 1990), 129.

14. Kevin Lynch, *The Image of the City* (Cambridge, MA: MIT Press, 1960). Sylvia Lavin has clearly defined how Lynch's concept of "imageability" implies a stabilized interaction between viewers and the environment.

> In the 1960 *The Image of the City*, Kevin Lynch defined the image as the result of the interaction between immediate sensation and memory of past experience. Through this interaction of raw perception and cognitive processing, according to Lynch, subjects construct images that function to provide orienting structures of meaning and relation. . . . For

> Lynch, forms are to be positively evaluated on the basis of what he called "imageability," the capacity to evoke in the observer a vivid apparency and legibility. Images in this scenario are comforting devices that enable not merely the interaction of observer and environment but that stabilize, monitor, and freeze the potentially fluid, illegible indeterminacy of viewing subjects of the world. Imageability thus functions as an instrument of striation transforming the perceptible field into a map as knowable ahead of time as a perspectival grid. (Sylvia Lavin, "Inter-Objective Criticism: Bernard Tschumi and Le Fresnoy," in "How the Critic Sees: Seven Critics on Seven Buildings," special issue, *ANY* 21 [1997]: 35)

For a rapid but very pertinent analysis of Lynch's research, see also Anthony Vidler, *Warped Space: Art, Architecture and Anxiety in Modern Culture* (Cambridge, MA: MIT Press, 2000), 174–75.

15. Marina Zancan clarifies the relationship between what she calls the italic subtext (eighteen unnumbered pieces) and the roman subtext (fifty-five cities). For Zancan, the italic sections make up the metanarrative location of the text, while the cities, the roman subtext, locate the fabula. Marina Zancan, "*Le città invisibili* di Italo Calvino," in *Letteratura Italiana: Le Opere*, ed. Alberto Asor Rosa, vol. 4, *Il Novecento* (Turin: Einaudi, 1996). In particular, see "Struttura," 890–98.

16. Marcello Carlino elaborates this question of discourse-silence in the dialogues between Marco and Kublai, demonstrating that silences are "just-as-much messages" rather than *blackouts*. And it is certain that their silences are messages as well, and that their communication does not suffer from desolating blackouts, if they revitalize it by turns when it is "less happy than it was": silences instead of words and words instead of silences. Marcello Carlino, "Il discorso-silenzio e i racconti 'possibili' di Calvino," *Nuova Corrente* 34, no. 99 (January–June 1987): 107–24.

17. Cristina Della Coletta identifies, in a Deleuzian reading, the relationship in *Invisible Cities* between Orient and Occident, between difference and repetition in the narrative form, in the formal structure, and in the thematic contents of the text. Cristina Della Coletta, "L'Oriente tra ripetizione e differenza nelle 'Città Invisibili' di Italo Calvino," *Studi Novecenteschi* 24, no. 54 (1997): 411–31.

18. Yuri Tynianov, *The Problem of Verse Language*, ed. and trans. Michael Sosa and Brent Harvey (Ann Arbor, MI: Ardis, 1981), 33. On the other hand, on the exchanges of *Il Milione* by Marco Polo and *Le città invisibili* with Shklovsky, see Roberto Ludovico, "Dietro le *Città Invisibili*, V. Sklovskij narratore," *Quaderni d'Italianistica* 20, nos. 1–2 (1999): 217–26.

19. In this skillful framework, it becomes difficult to follow the reading in order to be able to delimit the series of cities (cities of memory, of desire . . .). Symptomatic in this sense is French critic Frasson-Marin's attempt, which cannot succeed, to define a fixed linear schema for the book. On the other hand, the end of Frasson's chapter on *Invisible Cities* confirms my hypothesis that the interdisciplinary geographies that subtend Calvino's text are varied and hidden. A series of final questions concludes the chapter; I present only a few: "The reader can certainly do a 'pleasant' reading of Calvino's book, lingering on his unique, 'clever' construction. But would this reading take into account all of the aspects

of *Invisible Cities*? We do not believe so. It would neglect what makes the work profoundly original: its quality of a gracious 'mathesis' displaying an aggregate of knowledge, interests and culture from our time not only by means of writing, images and the sign but with humor as well." Regarding this knowledge of the culture of "our time," however, Frasson is silent. Aurore Frasson-Marin, *Italo Calvino et l'imaginaire* (Geneva and Paris: Slatkine, 1986), 282.

20. Bruno Zevi, *Architecture as Space: How to Look at Architecture*, ed. Joseph A. Barry, trans. Milton Gendel (New York: Da Capo Press, 1993).

21. Franco Ricci is the scholar who most coherently elaborates and reads Calvinian texts from this perspective, which moves between word and image. Franco Ricci, *Painting with Words, Writing with Pictures: Word and Image in the Work of Italo Calvino* (Toronto: University of Toronto Press, 2001).

22. Calvino, "The Pen in the First Person: For the Drawings of Saul Steinberg," in *The Uses of Literature*, trans. William Weaver (Orlando, FL: Harcourt Brace, 1982), 294–95.

23. Italo Calvino, "Marco Polo," in *Romanzi e Racconti*, vol. 3, 509–86.

24. "It was in the Forties that ethical tension had marked—then too between conservatism and innovation—his intellectual wavering between Turin (Pavese) and Milan (Vittorini); and which now, between Paris and Milan, allows him a long-distance dialogue—a distance accentuated by death—with the later Vittorini (*La ragione conoscitiva, Le due tensioni, Le città del mondo*), with which they associate him—beyond the continuity of their shared experiences—the questions that they both address to culture, to science, to literature, and of which the answers to some of the fundamental questions differentiate him: 'In short, Vittorini is a man who believes that the world exists, that discourse about the world matters because beyond discourse there is the world' " (Zancan, "*Le Città Invisibili* di Italo Calvino," 918).

25. Bruno Falcetto, "Le cose e le ombre. 'Marco Polo': Calvino scrittore per il cinema," *La visione dell'invisibile: Saggi e materiali su le* Città Invisibili *di Italo Calvino*, ed. Mario Berenghi, Gianni Canova, and Bruno Falcetto (Milan: Mondadori, 2002), 62–73.

26. In particular, see Italo Calvino, "Vittorini: Progettazione e letteratura," in *Saggi*, vol. 1, 160–87.

27. For the Venice School, I refer to a network of criticism and history of architecture research, carried on throughout the 1970s and 1980s by Manfredo Tafuri and Massimo Cacciari, among others, with critical ties to influential personalities such as A. Rosa, which had a pervasive and lasting international echo. The attention paid to architecture and the avant-garde as urban phenomena of modernity that emerged from this research was, for some time, too critical, or shall we say "not open" to experimentation. For critical readings of Tafuri in particular, see Fredric Jameson, "Architecture and the Critique of Ideology," in *Architecture, Criticism, Ideology*, ed. Joan Ockman (Princeton, NJ: Princeton Architectural Press, 1985), 51–88. See also the special issue dedicated to Manfredo Tafuri, "Being Manfredo Tafuri," ed. Ignasi De Sola-Morales, *ANY*, nos. 25–26 (2000).

28. It is important to remember that what Benjamin says about Paris seems to repeat what Henry James said about Venice.

29. There are many possible and important references to Benjamin subtended in Calvino's writing. For a more ample reading of the period, see Marco Belpoliti,

Settanta (Turin: Einaudi, 2001). This text is as dense as a Calvinian forest and teems with rich and determining details of recent history; it also brings to our attention many elements of passage and exchange between French and Italian intellectuals. Among these, we must not forget a magazine project in which Calvino took part, along with Gianni Celati and Giorgio Agamben, the title of which, "Ali Babà," leaves much to be discovered and investigated.

30. Terms used by Calvino in his presentation upon the Italian publication of the works of Charles Fourier. Italo Calvino, "Per Fourier. 2. L'ordinatore dei desideri," in *Saggi*, vol. 1, 279–306. For an overview of the relationship between writing/travel and *Invisible Cities*, see Sergio Zatti, "Viaggi sedentari," *Annali d'Italianistica* 21 (2003): 57–70.

31. I have elaborated in greater depth a selective reading of the *Arcades Project* in chapter 1. Howard Caygill is the only scholar who, writing on Benjamin, has referred, even in passing, to the fascinating possible relationships to consider between Benjamin's cities (Naples, Moscow, Berlin, and Paris), in the relationship between experience, imagination, and thought, and *Invisible Cities* by Italo Calvino. (An unfortunate typo renders the title as *Imagined Cities.*) Howard Caygill, *Walter Benjamin: The Colour of Experience* (London: Routledge, 1998), 119.

32. For the question of the digital image, see Bernard Stiegler, "The Discrete Image," in Jacques Derrida and Bernard Stiegler, *Echographies of Television: Filmed Interviews*, trans. Jennifer Bajorek (Cambridge, UK: Polity, 2002), 145–62. For a reading of the cinematographic experience and its relationship with *Invisible Cities*, see Gianni Canova, "All'ombra delle nostre palpebre abbassate: Il paradosso del non-visibile in Calvino e nel cinema contemporaneo," in Berenghi, Canova, and Falcetto, *La visione dell'invisibile*, 132–33. On the relationship between contemporary philosophy and the question of flux and real and virtual movement in the metropolis, see Henry Sussman, "The Writing of System: Borges's Library and Calvino's Traffic," in *Literary Philosophers: Borges, Calvino, Eco*, ed. Rodolphe Gasché (New York: Routledge, 2002).

33. On several occasions, Calvino makes reference to Benjamin's French texts. In a brief text written ten years after the publication of *Invisible Cities*, Calvino reviews *Le rovine di Parigi* by Giovanni Macchia; Calvino defines it as a "superbook" that springs from the *Arcades Project*'s ruins, so that Macchia's book becomes somehow the ghost of Benjamin's unfinished one. The tone of both is—for Calvino—not apocalyptic but one of getting acquainted with the vision of the end of the world so that the world will go on. In this essay on Macchia, he writes: "Already in books like *La Caduta della Luna* (1973) this aspect began to become apparent, and now seems even more evident, even making its way with another collected tradition. In fact *Le Rovine di Parigi*, both theme and title, take their starting point from the ruins of the book that Walter Benjamin wanted to write on the city 'of arcades,' of which only fragments and a mountain of citations remain. The authors of Benjamin's citations are the same that Macchia works on, reshaping the same figure in his own discourse." Italo Calvino, "Giovanni Macchia: Le rovine di Parigi," in *Saggi*, vol. 1, 1142–48.

34. Manfredo Tafuri, *Architecture and Utopia: Design and Capitalist Development*, trans. Barbara Luigia La Penta (Cambridge, MA: MIT Press, 1979), 83. For Tafuri, both the Russian Formalists (including the Futurists) and the Surrealists have tendencies that are perpetuated from their very beginnings to "today." On

one hand is the Russians' Formalism, in which the defense of autonomy was posed as "irreconcilable to reasons extraneous to its own construction" (62), and on the other is Surrealism, which made use "of the political terrain in order to safeguard a final border" (65); according to Tafuri, both have the common goal of attempting to leave off productive labor and defend intellectual labor.

35. On allegory and modernity in Benjamin, see Samuel Weber, "Genealogy of Modernity: History, Myth and Allegory in Benjamin's *Origin of the German Mourning Play*," *MLN* 106, no. 3 (1991): 465–500.

36. Derrida's brief text on the strategies of the contemporary architect Bernard Tschumi also sheds some light on *Invisible Cities* by Calvino: "One does not declare war. Another strategy weaves itself between hostilities and negotiations. . . . The meaning of 'grid' does not achieve assembled totality. It crosses through. . . . Furthermore, such crossing does not move through an already existing texture; it weaves this texture, it invents the histological structure of a text." Jacques Derrida, "Point de folie—maintenant l'architecture," in *Psyché* (Paris: Edition Galilée, 1987), 488; reprinted in K. Michael Hays, ed., *Architecture Theory since 1968*, trans. Kate Linker (Cambridge, MA: MIT Press, 1998), 578.

37. "To the extent to which it eludes or exceeds signification, such an event can only be fugitive, fleeting, like a falling star or a flash. What this meteoric event leaves behind in its wake is what I would be tempted to call—if a neologism can be allowed—the *mediauric*: auratic flashes and shadows that are not just produced and reproduced by the media but which *are* themselves the media, since they come to pass in places that are literally inter-mediary, in the interstices of a process of reproduction and of recording—*Aufnahme*—that is above all a mass movement of collection and dispersion, of banding and disbanding." Samuel Weber, *Mass Mediauras: Form, Technics and Media* (Stanford, CA: Stanford University Press, 1996), 106.

38. Renato De Fusco, *Architettura come Mass Medium: Note per una semiologia architettonica* (Bari: Dedalo Libri, 1967).

39. Italo Calvino, "Venezia: archetipo e utopia della città acquatica," in *Saggi*, vol. 2, 2688–92.

40. On cartography and the challenge posed by the shape of Venice to the cartographic paradigm, see Kristin Pilz, "Reconceptualizing Thought and Space: Labyrinths and Cities in Calvino's Fictions," *Italica* 80, no. 2 (2003): 229–42. In the article, Pilz writes: "Venice is of course also the Renaissance centre of cartography. And ironically it is this aquatic city that defies mapping as Calvino explains in a review of a Paris cartography exhibition: 'It is a city in which the dominant spatial theme is incertitude and variability, given that the limits between earth and water continually change: Venice, where the maps of the lagoon always must be rewritten' (*S.*, vol. 1, 431)" (234).

41. Dominique Rouillard's article "'Radical' architettura," in *Tschumi, une architecture en projet: Le Fresnoy* (Paris: Le Fresnoy, CGP, 1993), hints at a possible relationship between Calvino and Superstudio, who had sent to Calvino, as an editor, their text *Twelve Cautionary Tales for Christmas*.

42. The invisible cities, especially the continuous ones, but not merely these, bring to mind the experimentations of another Italian group, Archizoom, and their *No-Stop City* (1970–72). The continuous cities in *Invisible Cities* bear

traces of an essay by Rem Koolhaas, "The Generic City," in Rem Koolhaas and Bruce Mau, *S,M,L,XL* (Rotterdam: 010 Publishers, 1995).

43. Remo Ceserani, speaking of the "euphoric post-modernism of architects," writes:

> For J. Rabam [*Soft City*] the city escapes the controls and rational designs of urban planners and architects; it is, like the masses and movements of the Sixties, a vital entity, provided with communicative powers; it is "malleable, ascribable to a vertiginous and sensual variety of lives, dreams, interpretations," it is theater, emporium, encyclopedia, labyrinth, and inside of it single individual humans may take shape in creative ways:
>
> Cities, unlike villages and small towns, are plastic by nature. We mould them in our images: they, in their turn, shape us by the resistance they offer when we try to impose our own personal form on them. . . . The city as we imagine it, the soft city of illusion, myth, aspiration, nightmare, is as real, maybe more real, than the hard city one can locate on maps, in statistics, in monographs on urban sociology and demography and architecture.

Remo Ceserani, *Raccontare il postmoderno* (Turin: Bollati Boringhieri, 1997), 51.

44. Lewis Mumford, *The City in History: Its Origins, Its Transformations, and Its Prospects* (New York: Harcourt, Brace & World, 1961).

45. Mark Wigley, "Network Fever," *Grey Room* 4 (2001): 82–122. "Doxiadis launched the field of 'Ekistics' in the mid-fifties and founded the Athens Technological Institute in 1958 as a research center and architecture school based on the idea of global statistics. The idea was to think at the largest possible scale by domesticating vast amounts of global information. If the data could be controlled, cities could be controlled. Courses in statistical analysis become 'indispensable' for architectural training. Spatial patterns would follow from detecting patterns in the flow of information. Design would begin with precisely calibrated charts rather than artistic sketches" (87). "An image of the invisible extension of the physical was always the central goal of the Delos meetings. . . . Following Doxiadis's lead, the Delos events were all about making a certain kind of drawing, trying to visualize the invisible by conjuring up a coherent picture of an unseen order" (92). Certainly *dulcis in fundo* in this direction one must also remember the text of the Japanese architect Araka Isozaki entitled "Invisible City" (1967) in *Architecture Culture 1943–1968*, ed. Joan Ockman (New York: Rizzoli, 1993), 403–7.

46. Robert S. Dombroski, *Proprieties of Writing: Ideological Discourse in Modern Italian Fiction* (Baltimore: John Hopkins University Press, 1994). In comparison to the dichotomies proposed by Dombroski, and in contraposition to him, it is necessary to remember Teresa De Lauretis, "Semiotics Models, *Invisible Cities*," *Yale Italian Studies* 2 (1978): 13–37, which is mostly important for the reading of *Invisible Cities* elaborated with semiotics and critical theory; see p. 30, in particular.

47. The allegorical use of and emphasis on architecture point to the idea of ethical relation. This is the direction taken by Steven Shankman, who compares some moments of Emanuel Levinas and Calvino. Steven Shankman, "Ethics,

Transcendence, and the Other: Milione of Marco Polo and Calvino's *Le città invisibili*," *Annali d'Italianistica: Official Journal of the Canadian Society for Italian Studies* 19 (2001): 137–52. I would also mention the work of Simonetta Chessa Wright, who has the merit of studying the works of Italo Calvino as they relate to the Baroque as studied in German culture, from W. Worringer to A. Riegl up to a reprise proposed by Severo Sarduy and Gilles Deleuze. Simonetta Chessa Wright, *La poetica neobarocca in Italo Calvino* (Ravenna: Longo Editore, 1998). Certain reservations must however remain when applying such an interpretive tradition to the singularity of the works of an author. These reservations can be posed as J. Derrida did, when he differentiated between "form" and "force" in the essay "Force and Signification," in *Writing and Difference*, trans. Alan Bass (Chicago: University of Chicago Press, 1978), 3–30.

48. Jean Baudrillard, *Le système des objets* (Paris: Gallimard, 1968).

49. Kristin Ross, *Fast Cars, Clean Bodies: Decolonization and the Reordering of French Culture* (Cambridge, MA: MIT Press, 1995). For Perec's point of view on consumer society, see several of the interviews with Perec from 1966 to 1970, published in Georges Perec, *Entretiens et Conférences*, vol. 1, ed. Dominique Bertelli and Mireille Ribière (Paris: Joseph K., 2003). In a text given at a colloquium, now famous among Perec scholars, the writer says: "You see, I can define my writing as a sort of journey—Michaux wrote an incredibly beautiful sentence: 'I write to traverse myself'—as a sort of journey, a sort of itinerary that I try to describe starting with, let's say, a vague idea, an irritation. . . . From there, I try, you see, to say everything that can be said about the theme from which I started. It's what rhetoricians called rhetorical places. *Things* are the rhetorical places of fascination; it's everything that can be said about that fascination that objects exercise on us" ("Pouvoirs et limites du romancier français contemporain," in Perec, *Entretiens et Conférences*, vol. 1, 84).

50. "Une histoire des années soixante" is the subtitle of *Things*, and "Une aventure des années soixante" is the subtitle given to a posthumous collection of the writings of Georges Perec. This is a collection of essays written in the 1960s in which the writer defines his poetics and his theoretical position in dialogue with other intellectuals of the time. Here, he redefines his position in relation to the *nouveau roman*, existentialism, and realism; Perec also makes clear his attention to the method of editing as theorized by Eisenstein, theories that Perec reinterprets theoretically as possibilities of montage and narrative construction. See the preface by Claude Burgelin in Georges Perec, *L.G.: Une aventure des années soixante* (Paris: La Librerie du XXe Siècle, Éditions du Seuil, 1992).

51. On the reviews immediately following the period, see in particular Perec, *Entretiens et Conférences*, vol. 1, 140–41.

52. Georges Perec, "Ce qu'il se passe quand il ne se passe rien," *Entretiens et Conférences*, vol. 1, 214.

53. Georges Perec, in *Species of Spaces and Other Stories*, ed. and trans. John Sturrock (London: Penguin, 1997).

54. Besides Paul Virilio, Jacques Dauvinaud also took part in the magazine, and texts by Henri Lefevre, Marshall McLuhan, and Pierre Shaeffer were published in it.

55. Perec, *Entretiens et Conférences*, vol. 1, 121.

56. Virilio says: "Have we really touched upon societies with ethnology, with sociology? Everybody knows that the answer is 'no.' We have made an image of primitive society, an image of advanced society. But through this cultural image of society, do we not go from a classical period, let's say the period that prepares social perspective, that prepares a classical order, to expressionist societies, informal societies? Are there not perhaps sociological styles comparable to styles in plastic arts? Could our image of society be in fact a cultural image that can undergo the esthetic variations that our perception of reality has undergone through painting, through sculpture?" (Perec, *Entretiens et Conférences*, vol. 1, 128).

57. In the entire chapter "The Bedroom," the space of the bedroom is tightly related to bodily memories and a direct reference to Proust flashes out (and at the same time relates to another of Perec's projects, *Lieux où j'ai dormi*): "It's no doubt because the space of the bedroom works for me like a Proustian madeleine (the whole project is of course invoked by this; it is all nothing more than a rigorous extension of paragraphs 6 and 7 of the first chapter of the first part ["Combray"] of the first volume [*Du côté de chez Swann*] of *A la recherche du temps perdu*) that I undertook, several years ago now, to make an inventory, as exhaustive and as accurate as possible, of all the 'Places Where I Have Slept'" (Perec, *Species of Spaces*, 23).

58. Claude Burgelin, *Georges Perec* (Paris: Éditions du Seuil, 1990), 125–27.

59. The introduction is made up of five parts: a first part made up of a list of ways to say "space," and which is spaced vertically along the page, bringing into play the graphic relationship between vertical and horizontal (3–4):

SPACE

OPEN SPACE

ENCLOSED SPACE

OUTER SPACE

SPACE SUIT

SPACE AGE

. . .

LACK OF SPACE

. . .

SPACE ODYSSEY

. . .

BLANK SPACE

SPACE OUT

. . .

WASTED SPACE

This is followed by the premise, of which we have cited several excerpts; then comes a brief theatrical text uttered by a voice offstage telling us that space is without horizon, made of blackness and nothingness; and then finally a fifth citation of a poem, or implication, taken from Paul Eluard's children's song and divided into two inverse parts of which the first begins with a Parisian "rue" and goes on to eggs and birds, while the second speculatively begins with the bird and leads on to a small revolution in which "la rue renversa la ville de Paris [the street knocked the town of Paris over]" (Perec, *Species of Spaces*, 8).

60. Guy Debord, "Deux comptes rendus de dérive," *Les Lèvres nues*, no. 8 (1956): 10–12.

61. In *Cosmicomics*, Calvino crafts a spatial reflection on ordinary life; the space becomes thought and at the same time becomes comic, with several somehow estranging elements of daily life. Here I refer to the Calvino of *Cosmicomics,* but one could say that in all of his texts in all their diversity, space is heraldic. Space becomes the "origin" of narration in Calvinian writing, whether in relation to the plastic arts or as a poetically phenomenological approach. The singular way in which Calvino touches on the spatial theme, each time differently, makes space new, prismatic, different, and always entirely to be discovered. See also many of the written texts regarding the figurative arts, on De Chirico, Arakawa, Melotti, Paolini, now collected in Calvino, *Saggi*, vol. 2.

Gianni Celati has compared the prose of Calvino's world (in particular the late Calvino) to that of Perec, bringing them together for their manner of describing, which implies a certain abandonment, almost Heideggerian, to the world understood as a fullness. "Looking over an essay describing a meadow in Calvino's book, or a room in *La Vie mode d'emploi* by his friend Georges Perec, one may notice that here descriptions have become a habit of treating words like traces that appear on the paper. The observer dedicates himself to cataloguing or inventing them, as one does with everything that arises from a zone of the unknown. In the end what counts with a description are its borders and limits, beyond which opens the spatial emptiness into which we have put ourselves. And all the shapes or characteristics that we recognize in that space are traces of words that have furrowed it." Gianni Celati, "Palomar, nella prosa del mondo," *Nuova Corrente* 34 (1987): 227–42.

62. Later published in Paul Virilio, *L'espace critique: essai* (Paris: Christian Bourgois, 1984).

63. Paul Virilio, "L'inertie du moment," *L'Arc*, no. 76 (1979): 20–22.

64. In a speech at a colloquium on architectonic space, Perec says: "There is something that pertains to the domain, not at all of spatialization . . . how to express it? Of brick and stone spatialization . . . anyway, I mean: something that would be from the domain of the constructed but is a mental construction. The building in *Life A User's Manual* doesn't exist, but even I went to see if it existed, in the middle" ("À propos de la description," in Perec, *Entretiens et Conférences*, vol. 2, 240).

65. Georges Perec, *La Vie mode d'emploi. Romans* (Paris: Hachette, Le Livre de Poche, 1978); *Life A User's Manual. Fictions*, rev. ed., trans. David Bellos (London: Random House, 2008).

66. As Perec said on numerous occasions on the subject of this name: "His name is Bartlebooth, a mixture of Bartleby, Melville's scrivener, and Barnabooth,

Larbaud's traveler; the two most fascinating literary characters I know, one who is poverty, absolute bareness, the other who is richness and also a search for the absolute." Perec, "La maison des romans," in *Entretiens et Conférences*, vol. 1, 238.

67. Chapter 15 focuses on recounting a part of the travel notebook and the maps which Smauft, Bartlebooth's helper, kept. The multiplicity and the quantity of names of places is alphabetically catalogued in the fifty-eight-page index, along with places of gathering and spectacle, associations, institutions, ethnic groups, artists, scientists, politicians, and fictional characters from other sources and from *Life A User's Manual*.

68. Calvino, in "Perec, *La vita istruzioni per l'uso*," always alert to the motives of travel and adventure, emphasizes precisely this aspect:

> There is the story of an adventurer who, aware that among the peoples of Arabia and Africa they still use shells as units of exchange, tries to exploit the situation and ends up ruined by an inflation of the shell market.
>
> There is the story of an ethnologist who after having finally reached the unknown tribe in the hinterlands of Sumatra finds himself ignored by all the inhabitants of the village as if he did not exist; nobody deigns to grant him a word or a glance, though he passes years among them. Having returned home, he understood that just as those inhabitants he had observed did not admit of being observed by him, he had to abstain from communicating the results of his observation, and he withdrew into deep silence. (Calvino, *Saggi*, vol. 1, 1400)

69. Guy Debord, "Report on the Construction of Situations," in *Situationist International Anthology*, ed. and trans. Ken Knabb (Berkeley: Bureau of Public Secrets, 1981).

70. Georges Perec, "Quatre figures pour *La Vie mode d'emploi*," *L'arc*, no. 76 (1979): 50–53.

71. Paul A. Harris, "The Invention of Forms: Perec's *Life A User's Manual* and a Virtual Sense of the Real," *SubStance* 23, no. 2 (1994): 73.

72. George Perec, *Cahier des charges de La Vie mode d'emploi*, ed. Hans Hartje, Bernard Magné, and Jacques Neefs (Paris: Ed. Zulma/CNRS, 1993). For a recent in-depth analysis of the function of constraints in Perec, see Alison James, *Constraining Chance: Georges Perec and the Oulipo* (Evanston, IL: Northwestern University Press, 2009). In her study of Perec, James rearticulates the singular problematization at play between chance and intentionality, between infraordinary and extraordinary, between constraint and excess of language. Working on specific examples from Perec's texts and the *Cahier de charges*, James shows that "the combinatory distribution of elements [in the *Cahier de charges*] produces this diversity, while at the same time guaranteeing a level of coherence and continuity thanks to the repetition of the elements of the general table" (150). Also interesting is Gilles Deleuze and Félix Guattari's concept of diagram, "a site of potentiality that provides the conditions of possibility for the creation of forms" (153), through which James reads unforeseen configurations in Perec's writings.

73. Perec, "Entretien with Gérard Dupuy," in *Entretiens et Conférences*, vol. 1, 234.

74. The nineteenth-century novel also took its strength from the order and arrangement of its scenes:

> To lead into the just, effective form which will be that of the novel, to conceive the work, its rhythm, its internal diversions, its very volume, is to organize the internal equilibrium of fiction in relation to the mimetic presence and coherence for which the narrative aims, and in relation to the narrative developments that the envisioned story or stories can offer. On the other hand, the "programs" of *Life A User's Manual*, in the setting fully established from the start, allow and impose (or impose and allow, as you wish) the constitution of the material of fiction by following predetermined routes and the pulverization of the logic of stories in the structure that effectuates it. It is a matter of explicitly and radically dissociating the rules of the novel's production and construction from what could be considered as internal, "natural" laws of the narrated fiction. The narrative framework is then the resolution, for the reader, of a sort of immense puzzle composed of all the narratives thus produced from rules of passage and distribution. The logic of the structure is primary, perfectly indifferent to the imaginable determinations of fiction. (*Cahier des charges,* 12)

For the relationship between the characters and the space of the city and plot in the nineteenth-century novel, see Shannon Marcus, *Apartment Stories: City and Home in Nineteenth-Century Paris and London* (Berkeley: University of California Press, 1999), and Alex Woloch, *The One vs. the Many: Minor Characters and the Space of the Protagonist in the Novel* (Princeton, NJ: Princeton University Press, 2004).

75. Italo Calvino, "Perec, *La vita istruzioni per l'uso*," in *Saggi*, vol. 2, 1400.

76. Jean Duvignaud, "Effet d'éloignement par rapport aux choses," *L'Arc*, no. 76 (1979): 23–27.

77. And the following chapter opens on the stairs of the building, where the rich Mrs. Rorschash leaves for her fifty-sixth world tour. "The Rorschashs' double door is wide open. Two trunks have been dragged onto the landing. . . . Olivia Rorschash entrains at midnight tonight at the Saint-Lazare railway for her 56th world tour" (380). Very often critics underline textual references of names used by Perec. These too are puzzles, and it's strange that no one has ever written anything on this name, which grafts the name of the psychologist Hermann Rorschach and the rich family Rothschild who, as is well known, invested in the construction of buildings rented at low prices to the workers of Paris from the beginning of the twentieth century on.

78. Michel Butor, *Passage de Milan* (Paris: Éditions de Minuit, 1954). Butor, on the subject of this novel, says: "In *Passage de Milan*, I had a Parisian apartment building with seven floors, I think, and that was taken from seven at night until seven in the morning. I thus had a superposition of floors and this superposition of floors, I studied through a succession of hours. Each hour corresponded to a chapter and in each chapter, I studied some of the superposed elements in the building." Michel Butor, *Entretiens avec Georges Charbonnier* (Paris: Gallimard, 1967), 106.

79. Italo Calvino, *Six Memos for the Next Millennium*, trans. Patrick Creagh (New York: Vintage International Edition, 1993), 122.

80. Benjamin, *Arcades Project*, 164.

81. The historian of cartography Christian Jacob discusses this type of map/puzzle, underlining its recreational and didactic value. "Now a brief reflection on maps that are both mobile *and* apt to be sectioned: namely, wooden maps cut into puzzles. This type of map has an obvious pedagogical as well as amusement value by putting into play an array of strategies of search, as well as much trial and error, based on a double logic: that of the mechanical assembling of cut-out pieces, and that of reference to a previously given image and field of knowledge, namely, geography" (Jacob, *The Sovereign Map*, 85).

Chapter 4

1. Yona Friedman, "Manifesto: L'architecture mobile," in *Yona Friedman: Structures Serving the Unpredictable*, ed. Sabine Lebesque and Helene Fentener van Vlissingen (Amsterdam: NAi Press, 1999), 21–22.

2. Superstudio, "Histograms," reprinted in Peter Lang and William Menking, *Superstudio: Life without Objects* (Milan: Skira Editore, 2003), 114. On Superstudio, see Roberto Gargiani and Beatrice Lampariello, *Superstudio* (Milan: Laterza, 2010).

3. Superstudio, "Twelve Cautionary Tales for Christmas," in Lang and Menking, *Superstudio: Life without Objects*.

4. Cristiano Toraldo di Francia, "Superstudio & Radicaux," in *Architecture radicale* (Orléans: Institut d'art contemporain Villeurbanne with HYX, 2002), 205–6.

5. Felicity Scott underlines that experimentations such as those of the Italian Radicals, when "open to a critical engagement with contingent forces and hence to a broader social, technical, and political matrix" (3), belong to a group of marginal practices that "can reveal the very contours of a new type of historical space." Felicity D. Scott, *Architecture or Techno-Utopia: Politics after Modernism* (Cambridge, MA: MIT Press, 2007), 3.

6. Superstudio, "Reflected Architecture," in Lang and Menking, *Superstudio: Life without Objects*, 84–94.

7. Reprinted in Lang and Menking, *Superstudio: Life without Objects*.

8. Dominique Rouillard, *Superarchitecture: Le futur de l'architecture 1950–1970* (Paris: Éditions de la Villette, 2004), 511–26.

9. Fernando Montes and Bernard Tschumi, "Do-It-Yourself-City," *L'Architecture d'Aujourd'hui* 148, no. 148 (1970): 98–105. Although Tschumi's project is as yet unrealized, it is reminiscent, to use a very contemporary comparison, of the *Situated Technologies* experiments done in the last few years by the architects Omar Khan, Mark Shepard, and Trebor Scholz or those discussed in Kazys Varnelis, ed. *Networked Publics* (Cambridge, MA: MIT Press, 2008). For the ongoing project *Situated Technologies,* see http://www.situatedtechnologies.net.

10. Bernard Tschumi, "Ten Points, Ten Examples," *ANY*, November/December 1993, 42.

11. See Bernard Tschumi, introduction to *Architecture and Disjunction* (Cambridge, MA: MIT Press, 1996), subsequently abbreviated as *AD*; *Tschumi on Architecture: Conversations with Enrique Walker* (New York: Monacelli, 2006), subsequently abbreviated as *Tschumi/Walker*.

12. *No-Stop City* was not only presented in drawings but also in other media, as for example with optical devices created out of an urban trash container from

which one can view the incredibly Yayoi Kusama–like enclosed mise-en-abyme environments of the *No-Stop City*. All the detailed analysis of Archizoom projects of these years as well as its possible connections with the specific Italian political-critical climate can be found in Roberto Gargiani, *Dall'onda pop alla superficie neutra: Archizoom Associati 1966–1974* (Milan: Electra, 2007).

13. Andrea Branzi, *Weak and Diffuse Modernity: The World of Projects at the Beginning of the 21st Century* (Milan: Skira, 2006), 71.

14. In *Tschumi/Walker*, talking about Archizoom and Superstudio, Tschumi affirmed that the latter was "more predictable, populist, and metaphorical" (19). Tschumi discussed the Radicals' counterdesign strategies in one of his first essays: "The Environmental Trigger," in *A Continuing Experiment: Learning and Teaching at the Architectural Association*, ed. James Gowan (London: Architectural Press, 1975), 89–99; see also Bernard Tschumi, introduction to *AD*.

15. *AD*, 16. Tschumi was interested in Henri Lefebvre's work, but he quickly shifted his questioning on space toward a more performance-based experimentality. On this, see Bernard Tschumi, "Henri Lefebvre 'Le droit à la ville,'" *Architectural Design* 42, no. 9 (1972): 581–82, and *Tschumi/Walker*.

16. Bernard Tschumi, *Questions of Space* (London: Architectural Association, 1990); subsequently abbreviated as *QS*.

17. Tschumi, "Questions of Space," pp. 31–35 in *QS*.

18. The listed questions vary widely:

Is space a material thing in which all material things are to be located? . . .

1.71 If other geometries give a clearer understanding of space than the Euclidean geometry, has space itself changed with the construction of spaces with d-dimensions? . . .

2.52 Architecturally, if space is the medium for the materialization of theory, is a space the materialization of the architectural concept? . . .

2.72 Does the experience of space determine the space of experience?

2.73 If such a question is said to be absurd, does (architectural) space exist independently of the experiencing body? . . .

4.3 If space is neither a social product (an end result) nor a pure category (a starting point) is it an in-between (an intermediary)?

4.4 If space is an in-between, is it a political instrument in the hands of the state, a mould as well as a reflection of society? (*QS*, 32–35)

19. "The distinction between the talk about space and the creation of space vanishes, as well as any primacy of either the visual or the verbal. Dilemmas like buildings or non-buildings, concepts or percepts, mental space or physical space disappear. Ultimately, the words of architecture become the work of architecture." Bernard Tschumi, "A Space Is Worth a Thousand Words," in *A Space: A Thousand Words* (London and Milan: Royal College of Art with Dieci Libri, 1975), exhibition catalogue, unpaginated.

20. Among the participants (Daniel Buren, Dan Graham, Lapo Binazzi, Fernando Montes, and Zoe and Elia Zenghelis, to mention just a few), Tschumi proposed his useless fireworks concept: "Just as all the erotic forces contained in your movement have been consumed for nothing, good architecture must be conceived, erected and burned in vain. The greatest architecture of all is

the fireworkers': it perfectly shows the gratuitous consumption of pleasure" (Tschumi, "Fireworks," in *A Space: A Thousand Words*).

21. Bernard Tschumi, "Joyce's Garden," in *The Discourse of Events* (London: Architectural Association, 1983), 39.

22. Michael Hays, *Architecture's Desire: Reading the Late Avant-Garde* (Cambridge, MA: MIT Press, 2010), 160.

23. *QS*, 80.

24. "Prampolini, in his text, suggested that *space must live in actions* in their dynamic synthesis. Speaking of theater, he demanded the 'exclusion of the elements of stage architecture which are incapable of producing new sensations.' He dreamed of electro-chemical colours sensitive to electric currents and to the luminous colouration of tones, in accordance with combinations of neon with other gases" (*QS*, 42–43).

25. Bernard Tschumi, *The Manhattan Transcripts* (London: Academy Group, 1994), 7; subsequently abbreviated as *MT*.

26. For example, MT1, "The Park," has this incipit: "They found the Transcripts by accident. Just one little tap and the wall split open, revealing a life-time's worth of metropolitan pleasures—pleasures that they had no intention of giving up. So when she threatened to run and tell the authorities, they had no alternative but to stop her. And that's when the second accident occurred—the accident of the murder. . . . They had to get out of the Park—quick. But one man was tracked by enemies he didn't know—and didn't ever see—until it was too late. THE PARK." *MT*, 14.

27. Hays, *Architecture's Desire*, 153. For Hays, *The Manhattan Transcripts* conceptualize an architectural Real "as an unrealizable, a negativity which becomes present in effect and as event only through displacement and negation—in the gaps, holes, and cracks that are the marks of architectural desire" (153).

28. Jeffrey Kipnis, *Perfect Acts of Architecture* (New York: MOMA/Wexner Center for the Arts, 2001), 58.

29. "Those who say that architecture is impure if it must borrow its arguments from other disciplines not only forget the inevitable interferences of culture, economy, and politics but also underestimate the ability of architecture to accelerate the working of culture by contributing to its polemic. As practice and as theory, architecture must import and export. . . . In my case, theoretical writing had for its aim not only to expand architectural concepts but also to negotiate the relationship between cultural practice of architecture and the interrelated spheres of politics, literature, or the arts. In no way was I interested in translating or transposing literary or film motives into architecture. Quite the contrary. But also I needed these allies to support a key architectural argument. The research in other fields corroborated my view that the inherent disjunction of architecture was its strength and its subversive power. . . . Architecture, then, could not only import certain notions from other disciplines but could also export its findings into the production of culture. In this sense, architecture could be considered as a form of knowledge." *AD*, 17–18.

30. *Tschumi/Walker*, 44.

31. This competition, one of the competitions of the time of France's *Grands Projects*, was meant to "redevelop La Villette, an area in northeast Paris that was originally slated for a modern-day slaughterhouse. . . . La Villette involved a

135-acre site set amidst the intersection of two lines of water, the Ourcq Canal running from east to west and the Saint-Denis Canal running from north to south. . . . He made inquiries, dissected the project brief, and reviewed its creation in 1867 under Napoleon III up to the controversial closing in 1974 of the slaughterhouses and cattle market, located at its north and south portals respectively." Gilles de Bure, *Bernard Tschumi* (Basel: Birkhäuser, 2008), 47.

32. Bernard Tschumi, *Event-Cities 2* (Cambridge, MA: MIT Press, 2000), 53; subsequently abbreviated *EC2*.

33. *AD*, 194.

34. For this Archizoom project see Gargiani, *Archizoom*, 260. There is a similarity in the ways gridded and random lines superimpose in the two projects, which can be added to the much debated filiations and origins of the point grid matrix: Le Corbusier's Hospital in Venice (1965), Tschumi's *Joyce's Garden* (1977), and Peter Eisenman's Cannaregio project (1978); see Jacques Derrida and Peter Eisenman, *Chora L Works*, ed. Jeffrey Kipnis and Thomas Leeser (New York: Monacelli, 1997).

35. Among the coordinate paths are two main ones: one connects the park to the city along a north–south and east–west axis ("an elevated track, a sort of balcony overlooking the Museum of Science and Industry": *EC2*, 209); another path is an open, but covered, structure that facilitates links between the park, the *folies*, and the buildings designed by other architects, such as the City of Music.

36. *EC2*, 63.

37. Jacques Derrida, "Point de folie: Maintenant l'architecture," in K. Michael Hays, ed., *Architecture Theory since 1968* (Cambridge, MA: MIT Press, 1998), 580. "On the one hand, the point concentrates, folds back toward itself the greatest force of attraction, *contracting* lines toward the center. Wholly self-referential, within a grid which is also autonomous, it fascinates and magnetizes. . . . At the same time, through its force of magnetic attraction (Tschumi speaks here of a magnet which would 'reassemble' the 'fragments of an exploded system'), the point seems to bind, as Freud would say, the energy freely available within a given field. It exerts its attraction through its very punctuality, the *stigmè* of instantaneous *maintenant* toward which everything converges and where it seems to individuate itself; but also from the fact that, in stopping madness, it constitutes the point of transaction with the architecture which it in turn deconstructs or divides" (579).

38. "Form and function" is not the leading principle: "The cause-effect relationship sanctified by modernism, by which form follows function (or vice versa) needs to be abandoned in favor of promiscuous collisions of programs and spaces, in which the terms intermingle, combine and implicate one another in the production of a new architectural reality." *Event-Cities 1* (Cambridge, MA: MIT Press, 1999), 13; subsequently abbreviated as *EC1*.

39. Jan de Graaf, "Milestones," in *What a Wonderful World: Music Videos in Architecture* (Groningen: Groninger Museum, Dienst Ruintelijke Ordening Gemeente Groningen, 1990), 18.

40. Early in 1978 Tschumi pointed to Marcel Duchamp's antiretinal gesture: "His anti-retinal attitude became strongly apparent in the *Large Glass*, which interacted with its surrounding space in a way that no painting or sculpture had done before. It stood 'in-between,' acting as a very special—and spatial—filter. . . .

While the mainstream of the Modern Movement would, *ad nauseam*, exhaust the nineteenth-century possibilities of functionalism through the transparent—and retinal—mirror of Cubism, Duchamp was hinting at another type of spatial relationship made up of empathy, reference and wit" ("Architecture and Its Double," *QS*, 65).

41. Greg Lynn, "Differential Gravities," in "Lightness," special issue, *ANY 5* (March/April 1994): 22.

42. Bernard Tschumi, "Ten Points, Ten Examples," in "Electrotecture: Architecture and the Electronic Future," special issue, *ANY* 3 (November/December 1993): 41.

43. Sylvia Lavin, "Inter-Objective Criticism: Bernard Tschumi and Le Fresnoy," in "How the Critic Sees: Seven Critics on Seven Buildings," special issue, *ANY* 21 (1997): 34. "Urban in its zoning of functions, which separates sites of display from areas of production from districts of leisure, and thereby distinguishes public from private, and urban in its agglomerative form, Le Fresnoy is post-urban in its preference for surprise events over a stable city image" (35).

44. For this tension between performance and performativity see Hannah Dorita and Omar Khan, eds., "Performance Architecture," special issue, *Journal of Architectural Education* 61, no. 4 (2008). See also Chris Salter, *Entangled: Technology and the Transformation of Performance* (Cambridge, MA: MIT Press, 2010).

45. Bernard Tschumi and Hugh Dutton, *Glass Ramps / Glass Wall: Deviations from the Normative* (London: Architectural Association, 2001), 63.

46. Jesse Reiser, "Introduction," in Tschumi and Dutton, *Glass Ramps / Glass Wall*, 16.

47. Bernard Tschumi, "Deviation from the Normative," in Tschumi and Dutton, *Glass Ramps / Glass Wall*, 23.

48. *EC2*, 13.

49. Bernard Tschumi, "Conceptualizing Context," in *The New Acropolis Museum*, ed. B. Tschumi Architects (New York: Skira Rizzoli, 2009), 85.

50. For an analysis of this sequence and the entire film, see the extraordinary pages in Giuliana Bruno, *Atlas of Emotion*.

51. Bernard Tschumi, "Conceptualizing Context," in *The New Acropolis Museum*, ed. Bernard Tschumi Architects (New York: Skira Rizzoli, 2009), 86. For an enlightening reading at the crossroads of architecture, film, and psychoanalysis (Le Corbusier–Eisenstein-Freud), see Anthony Vidler, *Warped Space: Art, Architecture and Anxiety in Modern Culture* (Cambridge, MA: MIT Press, 2001).

52. Anthony Vidler, "After the Event," *Architectural Review* 236, no. 1411 (September 2014): 87–95. Vidler wrote this piece on the occasion of the exhibition devoted to Bernard Tschumi at the Centre Georges Pompidou in 2014: "The exhibition as a whole demonstrates a 'consistency' in Tschumi's work from the beginning to the present, as well as a conceptual 'development' that continually circles back to remember former exercises and projects. But this consistency does not rely on a forced unity of theory, nor on a self-conscious adoption of change and evolution. For while the analytical approach is ever-present in words, sketches, diagrams, programmatic research, that endow a strategic clarity to the resulting architectural construct, it is continually refreshed by encountering new programmes and environmental conditions. For in the end, what this exhibition reveals, and for the first time comprehensively, as we trace and retrace our

notated dance through concepts and forms, is that, for Tschumi at least, there is no theory without practice, nor practice without theory. In fact it would be invidious to try to separate the two, and even better to jettison the categories altogether" (95).

Chapter 5

1. Rem Koolhaas and Bruce Mau, *S,M,L,XL* (Rotterdam: 010 Publishers, 1995).

2. I derive this term from Koolhaas's text "The New Sobriety," written to accompany the installation OMA created for the Venice Biennale exhibition *La strada novissima* (1980). Reprinted in Jacques Lucan and Rem Koolhaas, *OMA–Rem Koolhaas: Architecture, 1970–1990* (New York: Princeton Architectural Press, 1991), 153. Many recent authoritative texts dwell on Koolhaas/OMA's works prior to *S,M,L,XL*.

3. Andrea Branzi, "Piccolo, medio, grande," in "Radical Notes," *Casabella* 379 (1973). "Radical Notes" is a series of editorial short texts that Andrea Branzi wrote during the 1970s in the architecture magazine *Casabella*.

4. François Burkhardt and Cristina Morozzi, eds., *Andrea Branzi* (Paris: Éditions Dis Voir, 1997), 50.

5. Anthony Vidler, "A REM-Based Program for Interactive Architecture," in "Urbanism vs. Architecture: The Bigness of Rem Koolhaas," special issue, *ANY* 9 (November/December 1994): 58.

6. Rem Koolhaas, "What Ever Happened to Urbanism?," in *S,M,L,XL*, 967.

7. Umberto Eco, *Semiotics and the Philosophy of Language* (Bloomington: Indiana University Press, 1986); and *Dall'albero al labirinto* (Milan: Bompiani, 2007).

8. Sara Whiting, "Spot Check: A Conversation between Rem Koolhaas and Sarah Whiting," *Assemblage* 40 (December 1, 1999): 38.

9. "Because there is no theory of Bigness, we don't know what to do with it, we don't know where to put it, we don't know where to use it, we don't know how to plan it. Big mistakes are our only connections to Bigness. But in spite of its dumb name, Bigness is a theoretical domain at this *fin de siècle*: in a landscape of disarray, disassembly, dissociation, disclamation, the attraction of Bigness is its potential to reconstruct the Whole, resurrect the Real, reinvent the collective, reclaim maximum possibility. Only through Bigness can architecture dissociate itself from the exhausted artistic/ideological movements of modernism and formalism to regain its instrumentality as vehicle of modernization." "Bigness," in *S,M,L,XL*, 509–10. Roberto Gargiani considers that there are four key texts in *S,M,L,XL* ("Typical Plan: Meditation" [1993], "Bigness, or the Problem of Large: Manifesto" [1994], "Last Apples: Speculations on Structure and Service" [1993], and "The Generic City: Guide" [1994]) with which Koolhaas "outlines the principles of a theory that involves the idea of the plan, the size of the project, the role of the structure, and the contemporary megalopolis." Roberto Gargiani, *Rem Koolhaas/OMA: The Construction of Merveilles,* trans. Stephen Piccolo (Lausanne and Oxford: EPFL, 2008), 223.

10. "Kunsthal [Temporary Arts Center]," *El Croquis—1987–1998 oma/rem koolhaas*, 53+79 (1998): 196.

11. Cynthia Davidson, "Koolhaas and the Kunsthal: History Lesions," in "How the Critic Sees: Seven Critics on Seven Buildings," special issue, *ANY* 21 (1997): 39.

12. Thomas Cousineau, *Waiting for Godot: Form in Movement* (Boston: Twayne, 1990), 90–91.

13. Davidson, "Koolhaas and the Kunsthal," 39.

14. Cecil Balmond, *Informal* (Munich: Prestel Verlag, 2002), 59.

15. In *Informal*, four new structural configurations are explained that deliver "surprise at the Kunsthal: brace, slip, frame and juxtaposition [an ad hoc new vocabulary of technology]" (Balmond, *Informal*, 72).

16. Even at the level of the ramp many mixes are at play, as for example: "The floor of a gallery loses its substance spectacularly in the form of a metal grille over the void, giving the visitor a scary passage; ramp columns impede or encourage the journey below, as one dodges or meets a changing perspective of the building in relation to the park" (Balmond, *Informal*, 105).

17. "The vierendeels form a catalog: each one is different, from the regular and closely spaced to a logarithmic sequence of ever-increasing intervals and structural dimensions . . . in Kunsthal I the apparently chaotic aspect of the compressed perspective of the beams—a random anti-grid—destabilizes the regular form; its logic becomes apparent only in passing through the different planes of the structure" (*S,M,L,XL*, 429).

18. "Fuelled initially by the thoughtless energy of the purely quantitative, Bigness has been, for nearly a century, a condition almost without thinkers, a revolution without program. *Delirious New York* implied a latent 'Theory of Bigness' based on five theorems" (*S,M,L,XL*, 499). The four points are: "A Big Building cannot be controlled by a single architectural gesture" (499), but it is not a question of simple fragmentation; 2. The elevator "render[s] null and void the classical repertoire of architecture" (500); 3. Core and envelope separate so much that the façade cannot reveal the inside, and to reveal Bigness transforms the city "into an accumulation of mysteries" (501); 4. "Buildings enter an amoral domain, beyond good or bad" (502).

19. "Signature, Event, Context," in Jacques Derrida, *Limited Inc.*, trans. Samuel Weber (Evanston, IL: Northwestern University Press, 1988).

20. Espace croisé, ed., *Euralille: The Making of a New City Center* (Basel: Birkhäuser, 1996), 15. The book documents throughout many aspects of the making of the project, from the way the different entities involved in the project converged to the seminars lead by OMA/Koolhaas, with comments deriving from a wide spectrum of fields of interest.

21. *Euralille by Rem Koolhaas* (Paris: Les films d'ici, 1997).

22. "Face à la rupture. Les mutations urbaines," in *Deux Conversations avec Rem Koolhaas et caetera*, ed. François Chaslin (Paris: sens@tonka, 2001). For the question of the mise-en-scène, see p. 101; for the relation to cinema, Koolhaas affirms, "What played the key role . . . were the systems and techniques internal to film, and especially those related to editing. In architecture, there is always a desire for continuity whereas film is based on a system of systematic and intelligent ruptures. For the most part, my involvement and relationship with film consists of my affinity for this system of rupture rather than that of the imaginary of continuity" (162–63).

23. "At the point of greatest infrastructural density, an *absence* of building reveals the highway, railway, three levels of parking, and the metro, which dives underneath the whole complex, in one overtly metropolitan moment—Espace Piranesien" (*S,M,L,XL*, 1200).

24. Jean-Louis Cohen, "Euralille: 'Bigness' Put to the Test of Construction," in Espace croisé, *Euralille: The Making of a New City Center*, 179.

25. Rem Koolhaas, "Urbanism after Innocence: Four Projects: The Reinvention of Geometry," *Assemblage* 18 (August 1992): 93.

26. Bernard Stiegler, "Developing Deterritorialization," *ANY* 1, no. 3 (November/December 1993): 20.

27. Claudio Fogu, "Futurism and Politics: Anarchist Rebellion and Fascist Reaction, 1909–1944" (book review), *Modernism and Modernity* 4, no. 1 (1997): 179–80.

28. Without any intention to homogenize different artistic experimentations in time, it is worth noting that one of the emerging artists in the 1990s, Rirkrit Tiravanija, became one of the most influential artists with his performances that included cooking and sharing.

29. Beatriz Colomina, "Toward a Global Architect," in *Architects' Journeys: Building, Traveling, Thinking/Los viajes de los arquitectos: Construir, viajar, pensar*, ed. Craig Buckley and Pollyanna Rhee (New York/Pamplona: GSAPP Books/T6 Ediciones, 2011), 20–49.

30. If it is permissible to grasp floating terms, in this case "genericity," this can be retraced in many of his texts, but I will give only two examples. In *The Watcher* (1963) he writes: "Generic terms like 'left-wing party' and 'religious institution' are not used here to avoid calling things by their real name but because even declaring, *d'emblée*, that Amerigo Ormega's party was the Communist party and the polls were located inside Turin's famous 'Cottolengo Hospital for Incurables' would represent a more apparent than real progress toward precision." *The Watcher and Other* Stories, trans. William Weaver (New York: Harcourt Brace Jovanovich, 1975), 5. Much later, he wrote in "Multiplicity" about Georges Perec as a collector and his passion for the *unique* that "a collector he was not, in life, except in words, of the data of knowledge, of things remembered. Terminological exactitude was his way of possessing things. Perec collected and gave a name to whatever comprises the uniqueness of every event, person or thing. No one was ever more immune than Perec to the worst blight in modern writing—which is vagueness [*genericità*]." Italo Calvino, *Six Memos for the Next Millennium*, trans. Patrick Creagh (New York: Vintage International Edition, 1993), 123.

31. Koolhaas writes this text at the time when he "spends a major portion of his life in airplanes, observing human settlements and continents from above. He passes through airports and crosses time zones and geographical boundaries, creating an accumulation of images in his imagination that emerges, in *Generic City*, as a synthetic, poetic interpretation of the phenomenon of human congestion on the earth's surface"(Gargiani, *Rem Koolhaas/OMA*, 230).

32. "The Generic City is held together, not by an over-demanding public realm—progressively debased in a surprisingly long sequence in which the Roman Forum is to the Greek agora what the shopping mall is to the high street—but by the *residual*. In the original model of the moderns, the residual was merely green, its controlled neatness a moralistic assertion of good intentions, discouraging

association, use. In the Generic City, because the crust of its civilization is so thin, and through its immanent tropicality, the vegetal is transformed into *Edenic* Residue, the main carrier of its identity: a hybrid of politics and landscape" (*S,M,L,XL*, 1252–53).

33. Walter Benjamin, *Arcades Project*, ed. Roy Tiedemann, trans. Howard Eiland and Kevin McLaughlin (Cambridge, MA: Harvard University Press, 1999). 8. See Margaret Cohen, "Benjamin's Phantasmagoria: The *Arcades Project*," in *The Cambridge Companion to Walter Benjamin*, ed. David S. Ferris (Cambridge: Cambridge University Press, 2004), 199–220.

34. Gargiani, *Koolhaas/OMA*, 193.

35. OMA, "Atlas," http://oma.eu/projects/2002/amo-atlas (accessed May 7, 2015).

36. Rem Koolhaas, "Junkspace," *October* 100 (Spring 2002): 175.

37. See Reyner Banham's documentary produced by the BBC in 1972, *Reyner Banham Loves Los Angeles*. The architectural historian's discovery of a new reality arriving at LAX and that of Koolhaas are almost two opposite gestures. Here a further study could expand on the facts that during these years Koolhaas was teaching at Harvard and that OMA participated after 1996 in a series of competitions with astonishing projects, the majority of them not built, such as one for the New Headquarters for Universal Studios in Universal City in 1996, the Los Angeles County Museum of Art extension in 2001, and the new headquarters for the California Department of Transportation in 2001.

38. Koolhaas, "Junkspace," 175.

39. Fredric Jameson, "Future City," *New Left Review* 21 (May/June 2003): 73.

40. Just to extract a few quotations: "a colossal security blanket that covers the earth in a stranglehold of seduction" (176), "a perpetual Jacuzzi with millions of your best friends" (176), "additive, layered, and lightweight, not articulated in different parts but subdivided" (176), "structure groans invisibly underneath decoration, or worse, has become ornamental" (176), "it is flamboyant yet unmemorable like a screen saver" (177), "Junkspace's modules are dimensioned to carry brands; myths can be shared, brands husband aura at the mercy of focus groups" (177), "'space' is scooped out of Junkspace as from a soggy block of ice cream that has languished too long in the freezer" (182), "Junkspace turns into biojunk; ecology into ecospace" (187).

41. Vidler, in a short but provocative text, at first take seems to criticize what he calls the Koolhaasworld, but at the end it is clear that he is instead endorsing it because of the radical force it contains. Anthony Vidler, "Still Wired after All These Years," *Log* 1, no. 1 (Fall 2003): 59–63.

42. As an introduction, Koolhaas writes "For this special issue of *Wired*, we at AMO have invited a cadre of writers, researchers, critics, and artists to report on the world as they see it. What follows are 30 spaces that fall into three rough clusters: waning spaces once celebrated, now hemorrhaging aura; contested spaces, continuously refined by the battles for their dominion; and new spaces, only recently understood as space at all. Together they form the beginning of an inventory, a fragment of an image, a pixelated map of an emerging world." "The New World: 30 Spaces for the 21st Century," *Wired* 11, no. 6 (June 2003): 117, http://archive.wired.com/wired/archive/11.06/newworld.html.

43. In *Deux conversations avec Rem Koolhaas et caetera*, the architect suggests, "Junkspace means that there is a contemporary experience of space universal and grounded on values totally un-architectural. . . . One observes a kind of dismantling of architecture, an intensification of its spectacular qualities (in a sense architectural) but with a totally different conceptual or sensible effect. . . . I find it astonishing that, if one identifies junkspace as the production of space probably the most important of the last twenty years, it becomes possible to read the architecture of Gehry or other our contemporaries, or even mine, as junkspace. An absolute arbitrary rules in the manipulation of signs." François Chaslin, *Deux conversations avec Rem Koolhaas et caetera* (Paris: Sens & Tonka, 2001), 143.

44. Rem Koolhaas and Brendan McGetrick, eds., *Content: Triumph of Realization* (Cologne: Taschen, 2004). *Content* came out on the occasion of the exhibit of Rem Koolhaas/OMA/AMO at the Neue Nationalgalerie in Berlin (November 2003–January 2004).

45. Rem Koolhaas, *Content*, 16. "*Content* is a follow-up to *S,M,L,XL*, an inventory of seven years of OMA's tireless labor. In many ways it is structured according to what its predecessor is not—dense, cheap, disposable. . . . The relentless internal logic that propelled *S,M,L,XL* is here counteracted by the incorporation of critical, external voices. Subjects are not arranged according to size, but by geographical proximity: the trajectory moves ever eastward, beginning in San Francisco, ending in Tokyo. *Content* is dominated by a single theme—'Go East' at once response to 9/11's mounting wreckage and acknowledgment of the eastward moment that has, through AMO's political involvement with the EU and an increasing density of Chinese projects, redirected the office's energy" (16). It is a smaller and more handy publication, but still thick, consisting of 544 pages.

46. Robert E. Somol, "12 Reasons to Get Back into Shape," in *Content*, 86–87.

47. For this image and its context in relation to the Radical Architecture see Beatriz Colomina and Craig Buckley, eds., *Clip, Stamp, Fold: The Radical Architecture of Little Magazines 196X–197X* (Barcelona: ACTAR, 2010), 130.

48. *Al-Manakh 1* (2007) and *Al-Manakh Gulf Cont'd* (2009) are two later massive publications in which OMA/AMO, in collaboration with many other external contributors and organizations, offers detailed analyses of Gulf cities like Abu Dhabi, Doha, Dubai, and Kuwait City.

49. "Patent Office," in *Content: Triumph of Realization*, ed. Rem Koolhaas and Brendan McGetrick (Cologne: Taschen, 2004), 73–83.

50. "The various slippages of the floors take the views and urban characteristics of the site into account. Along 5th Avenue only the last level of the library remains aligned with the street, because the group of floors in the middle part is pushed back, as if the library were pulling back from the United States Court House and its garden. On the opposite side, along 4th Avenue, the slippage of the same group stops at the borderline of the traditional buildings. On Spring Street, too, the façade of the cantilevered group of levels is pushed to the border of the continuous storefront, while on the opposite side, along Madison Street, this shift generates a cavity that amplifies that of the terraces created by the backdrop of skyscrapers. The shifts of floors also create other urban design solutions, from the gallery created by the sector framework without glazing, along 5th Avenue, where the main entrance is located, to the grand canopy created by the groups of

overhanging floors along Spring Street and 4th Avenue, where plots for plantings in the form of bands are inserted" (Gargiani, *Rem Koolhaas/OMA*, 286–87).

51. The mixing of colors and materials expands in the entire library so as "to keep the public alert and interested by leading them not only from one space to another but also from one experience to another" (Blaisse, *Inside Outside*, 200). Different colors are at play as one moves from the Living Room to the Assembly and to the Mixing Chamber: "To define the Teens' Library on the Living Room level, the floor bluntly changes from white-stained wood to red polyurethane. Moving up on the floor to the 'in-between space' called the Assembly, you enter a soft and warm organic space . . . , the inside of the heart: red, dark red, pink, orange and orange-brown cover rounded forms and narrow, winding corridors. From this boiling hot and pumping space, doors open into brightly lit, clinic-like workspaces (white, light grey and blue; with here and there a brown or black plane). Stairs climb up to the steel-cold floor above: the digital library—or the Mixing Chamber" (Blaisse, *Inside Outside*, 206–7).

52. "The Spiral's 6,223 bookcases are guaranteed to house 780,000 books upon opening, with the flexibility to add 1,450,000 books in the future (without adding bookcases)" (*Content*, 142).

53. Gargiani, *Rem Koolhaas/OMA*, 290.

54. Noriko Tsukui, ed., "OMA@work," special issue, *Architecture and Urbanism*, May 2000, 91. The framework of diamond shapes of the library appears transparent, "clad in two layers of glass, between which are steel tubes that join together to form a lattice of diamond shapes. The steel-tubes skin not only provides the main structural support for the building, but also modulates light and, with built-in coolers and filters, controls internal air temperature" (Tsukui, "OMA@work," 102). From the top floor one can see more than one triangular construction on top of other buildings: these are the elevators' pylon roofs, and one can wonder if the entire framework of SPL is not also a *clin-d'oeil* to them.

55. Having already finished the entire manuscript for this book, I stumbled onto Sven-Olov Wallenstein's essay that dwells on the question of allegory in relation to CCTV, "Looping Ideology: The CCTV Center in Beijing," in *Media Houses: Architecture, Media, and the Production of Centrality*, ed. Staffan Ericson and Kristina Riegert (New York: Peter Lang, 2010). While I share some of Wallenstein's points, what is most important is that one of my book's hinges is to work through the question of allegory.

56. The administrative spaces with "extra large floor plates of over 8,000 m^2 allow for ultimate flexibility of the office layout and future changes in their configuration" ("CCTV by OMA," special issue, *Architecture and Urbanism* [July 2005]: 50); the broadcasting "is the heart of the building—connecting and collecting all its signals and tightly monitoring the quality of transmission" (48); "with its 24-hour operation, the news section will be—together with the broadcasting center—the engine for continuous activity within the building" (46) and media production with fifteen production studios and seventeen news studios of different sizes accessible to the audience from the plaza; also included are staff facilities with canteens, cafes, lounges, meeting rooms as well as recreational facilities "from basketball court to a gym, a health club and a medical center" (52).

57. One of the AMO atlases shows the rush into building more and more high-rises and notes that "on the last day of August 2003 the number of Asian high rise buildings surpassed that of North America for the first time" (*Content*, 470).

58. "The surfaces of the building's continuous rectangular form provide the optimum zone for the building's primary structure. Together, all surfaces form a structural tube with no beginning or end, a loop, which provides a strong yet flexible, economical, robust and safe means of realizing the CCTV building in the highly seismic area of Beijing. The tube surface is a triangular structural mesh, which has been modified and optimized according to strict procedures" ("CCTV by OMA," 105). OMA details that "performance-based design involves going back to the first principles of engineering and demonstrating by calculation and modeling the detailed performance of the building against criteria which were determined by the design team in conjunction with the Client and Expert Panel. These criteria cover such issues as building movement, robustness (ability to find alternative load paths), performance under various levels of earthquake, and material proprieties" (108).

WORKS CITED

Adorno, Theodor W. "A Portrait of Walter Benjamin." In *Prisms*, translated by Samuel Weber and Shierry Weber, 227–41. Cambridge, MA: MIT Press, 1981.

Adorno, Theodor W., and Walter Benjamin. *The Complete Correspondence 1928–1940*. Edited by Henri Lonitz. Translated by Nicholas Walker. Cambridge, MA: Harvard University Press, 1999.

Aragon, Louis. *Paris Peasant*. Translated by Simon W. Taylor. Boston: Exact Change, 1994.

Balla, Giacomo, and Fortunato Depero. "Futurist Reconstruction of the Universe." In Rainey, Poggi, and Wittman, *Futurism: An Anthology*, 209–12.

Ballerini, Luigi. *La piramide capovolta*. Venice: Marsilio, 1975.

Balmond, Cecil. *Informal*. Munich: Prestel Verlag, 2002.

Barenghi, Mario. "Poesie e invenzioni oulipiennes." In Calvino, *Romanzi e Racconti*, vol. 3, 1241.

Baudrillard, Jean. *Le système des objets*. Paris: Gallimard, 1968.

Belpoliti, Marco. *Settanta*. Turin: Einaudi, 2001.

Benjamin, Walter. *Arcades Project*. Edited by Roy Tiedemann. Translated by Howard Eiland and Kevin McLaughlin. Cambridge, MA: Harvard University Press, 1999.

———. "Experience and Poverty." In *Selected Writings, Vol. 2: 1927–1934*, edited by Howard Eiland, Michael W. Jennings, and Gary Smith, translated by Rodney Livingstone, 731–36. Cambridge, MA: Harvard University Press, 1999.

———. "Das Kunstwerk im Zeitalter seiner technischen Reproduzierbarkeit." In *Gesammelte Schriften*, Bd.7 T.1, 350–84. Frankfurt am Main: Suhrkamp Verlag, 1972.

———. "Paris Diary." In *Selected Writings, Vol. 2: 1927–1934*, edited by Howard Eiland, Michael W. Jennings, and Gary Smith, translated by Rodney Livingstone, 337–54. Cambridge, MA: Harvard University Press, 1999.

———. "The Paris of the Second Empire in Baudelaire." In *Selected Writings, Vol. 4: 1938–1940*, edited by Marcus Bullock, Howard Eiland, and Gary Smith, translated by Edmund Jephcott, 3–94. Cambridge, MA: Harvard University Press, 2003.

———. "The Rigorous Study of Art." In *Selected Writings, Vol. 2: 1927–1934*, edited by Marcus Bullock, Howard Eiland, and Gary Smith, translated by Thomas Y. Levin, 666–72. Cambridge, MA: Harvard University Press, 1999.

———. "The Storyteller." In *Selected Writings, Vol. 3: 1935–1938*, edited by Marcus Bullock, Howard Eiland, and Michael W. Jennings, translated by Harry Zohn, 143–66. Cambridge, MA: Harvard University Press, 2002.

———. "The Task of the Translator." In *Selected Writings, Vol. 1: 1913–1926*, edited by Marcus Bullock and Michael W. Jennings, translated by Harry Zohn, 253–63. Cambridge, MA: Harvard University Press, 1996.

———. "The Work of Art in the Age of Its Technological Reproducibility." In *Selected Writings, Vol. 3: 1935–1938*, edited by Marcus Bullock, Howard Eiland, and Gary Smith, translated by Edmund Jephcott and Harry Zohn, 101–33. Cambridge, MA: Harvard University Press, 2002.

Bennington, Geoffrey. "RIP." In *Futures: Of Jacques Derrida*, edited by Richard Rand, 1–17. Stanford, CA: Stanford University Press, 2001.

Berghaus, Günter, ed. *Futurism and the Technological Imagination*. Amsterdam: Rodopi, 2009.

———. *Italian Futurist Theatre 1909–1944*. Oxford: Calderon, 1998.

Blaisse, Petra. *Inside Outside*. Edited by Ota Kayoko. New York: Monacelli, 2009.

Blum, Cinzia Sartini. *The Other Modernism: F. T. Marinetti's Futurist Fiction of Power*. Berkeley: University of California Press, 1996.

Bontempelli, Massimo. "Corsivo n. 90." In Massimo Bontempelli, *L'avventura Novecentista*, 328–29. Florence: Vallecchi Editore, 1974.

Branzi, Andrea. "Piccolo, medio, grande." In "Radical Notes," *Casabella* 379 (1973): 12.

———. *Weak and Diffuse Modernity: The World of Projects at the Beginning of the 21st Century*. Milan: Skira, 2006.

Bruno, Giuliana. *Atlas of Emotion: Journeys in Art, Architecture and Film*. New York: Verso, 2002.

Buckley, Craig, and Beatriz Colomina, eds., *Clip, Stamp, Fold: The Radical Architecture of Little Magazines 196X–197X*. Barcelona: ACTAR, 2010.

Bure, Gilles de. *Bernard Tschumi*. Basel: Birkhäuser, 2008.

Burgelin, Claude. *Georges Perec*. Paris: Éditions du Seuil, 1990.

Burkhardt, François, and Cristina Morozzi, eds. *Andrea Branzi*. Paris: Éditions Dis Voir, 1997.

Butor, Michel. *Entretiens avec Georges Charbonnier*. Paris: Gallimard, 1967.

———. *Passage de Milan*. Paris: Éditions de Minuit, 1954.

Calendoli, Giovanni. Preface to *Teatro: F. T. Marinetti*, iii–lxxxi. Rome: Vito Bianco, 1960.

Calvino, Italo. *Le città invisibili*. In *Romanzi e Racconti*, vol. 2, 357–498. Translated by William Weaver as *Invisible Cities* (Orlando, FL: Harcourt, 1974).

———. "Com'era nuovo il Nuovo Mondo." In *Saggi*, vol. 1, 417–25.

———. "Giovanni Macchia: Le rovine di Parigi." In *Saggi*, vol. 1, 1142–48.

———. "La letteratura come proiezione del desiderio." In *Saggi*, vol. 1, 242–51.

———. "Marco Polo." In *Romanzi e Racconti*, vol. 3, 509–86.

———. "The Pen in the First Person: For the Drawings of Saul Steinberg." In *The Uses of Literature*, translated by William Weaver, 291–99. Orlando, FL: Harcourt Brace, 1982.

———. "Per Fourier. 2. L'ordinatore dei desideri." In *Saggi*, vol. 1, 279–306.

———. "Perec, *La vita istruzioni per l'uso*." In *Saggi*, vol. 1, 1393–1400.

———. *Romanzi e Racconti*. Edited by Mario Barenghi, Bruno Falcetto, and Claudio Milanini. Vol. 2. Milan: Mondadori, 1992.

———. *Romanzi e Racconti*. Edited by Mario Barenghi, Bruno Falcetto, and Claudio Milanini. Vol. 3. Milan: Mondadori, 1994.

———. *Saggi*. Edited by Mario Barenghi. 2 vols. Milan: Mondadori, 1995.

———. *Six Memos for the Next Millennium*. Translated by Patrick Creagh. New York: Vintage International Edition, 1993.

———. "Venezia: archetipo e utopia della città acquatica." In *Saggi*, vol. 2, 2688–92.

———. "Il viandante nella mappa." In *Saggi*, vol. 1, 426–33.

———. "Vittorini: Progettazione e letteratura." In *Saggi*, vol. 1, 160–87.

———. *The Watcher and Other Stories*. Translated by William Weaver. New York: Harcourt Brace Jovanovich, 1975.

Canova, Gianni. "All'ombra delle nostre palpebre abbassate: Il paradosso del non-visibile in Calvino e nel cinema contemporaneo." In *La visione dell'invisibile: Saggi e materiali su Le* Città Invisibili *di Italo Calvino*, edited by Mario Berenghi, Gianni Canova, and Bruno Falcetto, 131–39. Milan: Mondadori, 2002.

Carlino, Marcello. "Il discorso-silenzio e i racconti 'possibili' di Calvino." *Nuova Corrente* 34, no. 99 (January–June 1987): 107–24.

Casey, Edward W. *The Fate of Place: A Philosophical History*. Berkeley: University of California Press, 1997.

Caygill, Howard. *Walter Benjamin: The Colour of Experience*. London: Routledge, 1998.

Celati, Gianni. "Palomar, nella prosa del mondo." *Nuova Corrente* 34 (1987): 227–42.

Ceserani, Remo. *Raccontare il postmoderno*. Turin: Bollati Boringhieri, 1997.

Chaslin, François. *Deux conversations avec Rem Koolhaas et caetera*. Paris: Sens & Tonka, 2001.

Cheetham, Mark A. *The Rhetoric of Purity: Essentialist Theory and the Advent of Abstract Painting*. New York: Cambridge University Press, 1991.

Chessa, Luciano. *Luigi Russolo: Noise, Visual Arts and the Occult*. Berkeley: University of California Press, 2012.

Chessa Wright, Simonetta. *La poetica neobarocca in Italo Calvino*. Ravenna: Longo Editore, 1998.

Chiesa, Laura. "Transnational Multimedia: Fortunato Depero's Impressions of New York City (1928–1930)." *California Italian Studies* 1, no. 2 (2010). doi: ismrg_cisj_8891.

Ciucci, Giorgio. *Gli architetti e il fascismo*. Turin: Einaudi, 1989.

Cohen, Jean-Louis. "Euralille: 'Bigness' Put to the Test of Construction." In Espace croisé, ed., *Euralille: The Making of New City Center: Koolhaas, Nouvel, Portzamparc, Vasconti, Duthilleul: Architects*. Basel: Birkhäuser, 1996.

Cohen, Margaret. "Benjamin's Phantasmagoria: The *Arcades Project*." In *The Cambridge Companion to Walter Benjamin*, edited by David S. Ferris, 199–220. Cambridge: Cambridge University Press, 2004.

Colomina, Beatriz. "Toward a Global Architect." In *Architects' Journeys: Building, Traveling, Thinking/Los viajes de los arquitectos: Construir, viajar, pensar*, edited by Craig Buckley and Pollyanna Rhee, 20–49. New York/Pamplona: GSAPP Books/T6 Ediciones, 2011.

Copans, Richard. *Euralille by Rem Koolhaas*. Paris: Les films d'ici, 1997. DVD.

Cousineau, Thomas. *Waiting for Godot: Form in Movement*. Boston: Twayne, 1990.

Crispolti, Enrico, ed. *Casa Balla e il futurismo a Roma*. Rome: Istituto Poligrafico e Zecca dello Stato, 1989.

———. *Il mito della macchina e altri temi del Futurismo*. Trapani: Celebes Editore, 1969.

———. ed. *Ricostruzione futurista dell'universo*. Turin: Assessorato per la cultura, Musei Civici, 1980.

Crispolti, Enrico, and Rosella Siligato, eds. *Prampolini dal futurismo all'informale*. Rome: Edizioni Carte segrete, 1992. Exhibition catalogue.

Davidson, Cynthia. "Koolhaas and the Kunsthal: History Lesions." In "How the Critic Sees: Seven Critics on Seven Buildings," special issue, *ANY* 21 (December 1997): 36–41.

Debord, Guy. "Deux comptes rendus de dérive." *Les Lèvres nues*, no. 8 (1956): 10–12.

———. "Report on the Construction of Situations." In *Situationist International Anthology*, edited and translated by Ken Knabb, 17–25. Berkeley: Bureau of Public Secrets, 1981.

De Fusco, Renato. *Architettura come Mass Medium: Note per una semiologia architettonica*. Bari: Dedalo Libri, 1967.

de Graaf, Jan. "Milestones." In *What a Wonderful World: Music Videos in Architecture*, 18. Groningen: Groninger Museum, Dienst Ruintelijke Ordening Geemente Groningen, 1990.

De Lauretis, Teresa. "Semiotics Models, *Invisible Cities*." *Yale Italian Studies* 2 (1978): 13–37.

De Sola-Morales, Ignasi, ed. "Being Manfredo Tafuri." Special issue, *ANY*, nos. 25–26 (February 2000).

Della Coletta, Cristina. "L'Oriente tra ripetizione e differenza nelle 'Città Invisibili' di Italo Calvino." *Studi Novecenteschi* 24, no. 54 (1997): 411–31.

Depero, Fortunato. "Complessità Plastica—Libero Gioco Futurista—L'Essere Vivente Artificiale" [Plastic Complexity—Free Futurist Game—The Artificial Living Being]. In *Casa Balla e il futurismo a Roma*, edited by Enrico Crispolti, 225–26. Rome: Istituto Poligrafico e Zecca dello Stato, 1989.

———. *Depero Futurista*. Edizione Dinamo-Azari. Milan: Dinamo-Azari, 1927—reprinted 1978.

———. "Teatro Magico" [Magic Theater]. In *Depero e la scena: Da "Colori" alla scena mobile, 1913–1930*, edited by Bruno Passamani, 101–3. Turin: Martano Editore, 1970.

Derrida, Jacques. "Force and Signification." In *Writing and Difference*, translated by Alan Bass, 3–30. Chicago: University of Chicago Press, 1978.

———. "Point de folie: Maintenant l'architecture." In *Architecture Theory since 1968*, edited by K. Michael Hays, translated by Kate Linker, 570–81. Cambridge, MA: MIT Press, 1998.

———. "Signature, Event, Context." In Jacques Derrida, *Limited Inc.*, translated by Samuel Weber. Evanston, IL: Northwestern University Press, 1988.

———. *Specters of Marx*. Translated by Peggy Kamuf. London: Routledge, 1994.

———. *Writing and Difference*. Translated by Alan Bass. Chicago: University of Chicago Press, 1978.

Derrida, Jacques, and Peter Eisenman. *Chora L Works*. Edited by Jeffrey Kipnis and Thomas Leeser. New York: Monacelli, 1997.

Dombroski, Robert S. *Proprieties of Writing: Ideological Discourse in Modern Italian Fiction*. Baltimore: John Hopkins University Press, 1994.

Dorita, Hannah, and Omar Khan, eds. "Performance Architecture." Special issue, *Journal of Architectural Education* 61, no. 4 (2008).

Duvignaud, Jean. "Effet d'éloignement par rapport aux choses." *L'Arc*, no. 76 (1979): 23–27.
Eco, Umberto. *Dall'albero al labirinto*. Milan: Bompiani, 2007.
———. *Semiotics and the Philosophy of Language*. Bloomington: Indiana University Press, 1986.
Espace croisé, ed. *Euralille: The Making of New City Center: Koolhaas, Nouvel, Portzamparc, Vasconti, Duthilleul: Architects*. Basel: Birkhäuser, 1996.
Falcetto, Bruno. "Le cose e le ombre. 'Marco Polo': Calvino scrittore per il cinema." In *La visione dell'invisibile: Saggi e materiali su le* Città Invisibili *di Italo Calvino*, edited by Mario Berenghi, Gianni Canova, and Bruno Falcetto, 62–73. Milan: Mondadori, 2002.
Fogu, Claudio. "Futurism and Politics: Anarchist Rebellion and Fascist Reaction, 1909–1944" (book review). *Modernism and Modernity* 4, no. 1 (1997): 178–81.
Frasson-Marin, Aurore. *Italo Calvino et l'imaginaire*. Geneva and Paris: Slatkine, 1986.
Friedman, Yona. "Manifesto: L'architecture mobile." In *Yona Friedman: Structures Serving the Unpredictable*, edited by Sabine Lebesque and Helene Fentener van Vlissingen, 21–22. Amsterdam: NAi Press, 1999.
Gargiani, Roberto. *Dall'onda pop alla superficie neutra: Archizoom Associati 1966–1974*. Milan: Electra, 2007.
———. *Rem Koolhaas/OMA: The Construction of Merveilles*. Translated by Stephen Piccolo. Lausanne: EPFL, 2008.
Gargiani, Roberto, and Beatrice Lampariello. *Superstudio*. Milan: Laterza, 2010.
Giedion, Sigfried. *Building in France, Building in Iron, Building in Ferroconcrete*. Introduction by Sokratis Georgiadis, translated by J. Duncan Berry. Santa Monica, CA: Getty Center for the History of Art and the Humanities, 1995.
Godoli, Ezio. *Guide all'architettura moderna: Il Futurismo*. Bari: Laterza, 1983.
Hansen, Mark. *Embodying Technesis: Technology beyond Writing*. Ann Arbor: University of Michigan Press, 2000.
Harris, Paul A. "The Invention of Forms: Perec's *Life A User's Manual* and a Virtual Sense of the Real." *SubStance* 23, no. 2 (1994): 56–85.
Hays, Michael. *Architecture's Desire: Reading the Late Avant-Garde*. Cambridge, MA: MIT Press, 2010.
Isozaki, Arata. "Invisible City." In *Architecture Culture 1943–1968*, edited by Joan Ockman, 403–7. New York: Rizzoli, 1993.
Jacob, Christian. *The Sovereign Map: Theoretical Approaches in Cartography throughout History*. Edited by Edward H. Dahl. Translated by Tom Conley. Chicago: University of Chicago Press, 2006.
James, Alison. *Constraining Chance: Georges Perec and the Oulipo*. Evanston, IL: Northwestern University Press, 2009.
Jameson, Fredric. "Architecture and the Critique of Ideology." In *Architecture, Criticism, Ideology*, edited by Joan Ockman, 51–88. Princeton, NJ: Princeton Architectural Press, 1985.
———. "Future City." *New Left Review* 21 (May/June 2003): 65–79.
———. *The Geopolitical Aesthetic*. Bloomington: Indiana University Press, 1995.
Jencks, Charles. *The Story of Post-Modernism*. Chichester, UK: John Wiley & Sons, 2011.

Jennings, Michael. "Walter Benjamin and the European Avant-Garde." In *The Cambridge Companion to Walter Benjamin*, edited by David S. Ferris, 18–34. Cambridge: Cambridge University Press, 2004.

Joselit, David. *After Art*. Princeton, NJ: Princeton University Press, 2012.

Kiesler, Frederick. "Debacle of the Modern Theatre: Picture-Stage, Actors, Space-Stage." *Little Review* 11, no. 2 (Winter 1926): 61–72.

Kipnis, Jeffrey. *Perfect Acts of Architecture*. New York: MoMA/Wexner Center for the Arts, 2001.

Kirby, Michael, ed. *Futurist Performance*. Translated by Victoria Nes Kirby. New York: Paj, 1971.

Koolhaas, Rem. "Junkspace." *October* 100 (Spring 2002): 175–90.

———. "The New Sobriety." In Jacques Lucan and Rem Koolhaas, *OMA-Rem Koolhaas: Architecture, 1970–1990*. New York: Princeton Architectural Press, 1991.

———. "The New World: 30 Spaces for the 21st Century." *Wired* 11, no. 6 (June 2003). http://archive.wired.com/wired/archive/11.06/newworld.html.

———. "Urbanism after Innocence: Four Projects: The Reinvention of Geometry." *Assemblage* 18 (August 1992): 83–113.

Koolhaas, Rem, and Bruce Mau. *S,M,L,XL*. Rotterdam: 010 Publishers, 1995.

Koolhaas, Rem, and Brendan McGetrick. *Content: Triumph of Realization*. Cologne: Taschen, 2004.

Kwinter, Sanford. *Architectures of Time: Toward a Theory of the Event in Modernist Culture*. Cambridge, MA: MIT Press, 2001.

Lang, Peter, and William Menking. *Superstudio: Life without Objects*. Milan: Skira Editore, 2003.

Lavin, Sylvia. "Inter-Objective Criticism: Bernard Tschumi and Le Fresnoy." In "How the Critic Sees: Seven Critics on Seven Buildings," special issue, *ANY* 21 (1997): 32–35.

———. "What Color Is It Now?" *Perspecta, the Yale Architectural Journal* 35 (2004): 98–111.

Lista, Giovanni. *La scène futuriste*. Paris: Éditions du Centre national de la recherche scientifique, 1989.

Ludovico, Roberto. "Dietro le *Città Invisibili*, V. Sklovskij narratore." *Quaderni d'Italianistica* 20, nos. 1–2 (1999): 217–26.

Lynch, Kevin. *The Image of the City*. Cambridge, MA: MIT Press, 1960.

Lynn, Greg. "Differential Gravities." In "Lightness," special issue, *ANY* 5 (March/April 1994): 20–23.

Macarthur, John. "Movement and Tactility: Benjamin and Wölfflin on Imitation in Architecture." *Journal of Architecture* 12, no. 5 (2007): 477–87.

Marcus, Shannon. *Apartment Stories: City and Home in Nineteenth-Century Paris and London*. Berkeley: University of California Press, 1999.

Mariani, Riccardo. *Razionalismo e architettura moderna: Storia di una polemica*. Milan: Edizioni Comunità, 1989.

Marinetti, F. T. *Critical Writings*. Edited by Günter Berghaus. Translated by Doug Thompson. New York: Farrar, Straus and Giroux, 2006.

———. "Electrical War." In Rainey, Poggi, and Wittman, *Futurism: An Anthology*, 98–104.

———. *Ricostruire l'Italia con architettura futurista San'Elia* [*Reconstruct Italy with Futurist Sant'Elia Architecture*]. In F. T. Marinetti, *Teatro*, edited by Jeffrey T. Schnapp, 477–533. Milan: Oscar Mondadori, 2004.
———. "Technical Manifesto of Futurist Literature." In Rainey, Poggi, and Wittman, *Futurism: An Anthology*, 119–25.
Marinetti, F. T., Umberto Boccioni, Carlo Carrà, and Luigi Russolo. "Against Passéist Venice." In Rainey, Poggi, and Wittman, *Futurism: An Anthology*, 67–70.
Marinetti, F. T., Angiolo Mazzoni, and Mino Somenzi. "Manifesto futurista dell'architettura aerea" [Futurist Manifesto of Aerial Architecture]. In *La metropoli futurista: progetti im-possibili*, edited by Vincenzo Capalbo and Ezio Godoli, 91–93. Florence: Officina del Novecento, 1999.
Marinetti, F. T., Emilio Settimelli, and Bruno Corrà. "The Futurist Synthetic Theater." In Rainey, Poggi, and Wittman, *Futurism: An Anthology*, 204–9.
McLaughlin, Kevin. "The Coming of Paper: Aesthetic Value from Ruskin to Benjamin." *MLN* 114, no. 5 (1999): 962–90.
Melograni, Carlo. *Architettura italiana sotto il fascismo*. Turin: Bollati Boringhieri, 2008.
Milanini, Claudio. *L'utopia discontinua: Saggio su Italo Calvino*. Milan: Garzanti, 1990.
Montes, Fernando, and Bernard Tschumi. "Do-It-Yourself-City." *L'Architecture d'Aujourd'hui* 148, no. 148 (1970): 98–105.
Montfrans, Manet van. *Georges Perec: La contrainte du réel*. Amsterdam: Rodopi, 1999.
Moretti, Franco. *Graphs, Maps, Trees: Abstract Models for Literary History*. London: Verso, 2005.
Mumford, Lewis. *The City in History: Its Origins, Its Transformations, and Its Prospects*. New York: Harcourt, Brace & World, 1961.
Nancy, Jean-Luc. *Corpus*. Paris: Métailié, 1992.
———. *La pensée dérobée*. Paris: Galilée, 2001.
OMA. "Atlas." http://oma.eu/projects/2002/amo-atlas. Accessed May 7, 2015.
———. "CCTV by OMA." Special issue, *Architecture and Urbanism*, July 2005.
———. "CCTV Headquarters." http://oma.eu/projects/2002/cctv-%E2%80%93-headquarters. Accessed May 7, 2015.
———. "Kunsthal [Temporary Arts Center]." *El Croquis—1987–1998 oma/rem koolhaas*, 53+79 (1998): 196–227.
———. "OMA@work," edited by Noriko Tsukui. Special issue, *Architecture and Urbanism*, May 2000.
Oulipo. *Atlas de littérature potentielle*. Paris: Gallimard, 1981.
Paletta, Luciano. *L'architettura in Italia: 1919–1943: Le polemiche*. Milan: Clup, 1972.
Pannaggi, Ivo, and Vinicio Paladini. "Manifesto of Futurist Mechanical Art." In Rainey, Poggi, and Wittman, *Futurism: An Anthology*, 272–73.
Parent, Claude, and Paul Virilio. "La fonction de l'oblique." In Claude Parent and Paul Virilio, *Architecture Principe, 1966–1996*. Paris: Les Éditions de l'Imprimeur, 1997.
Perec, Georges. "À propos de la description." In *Entretiens et Conférences*, vol. 2, 240.

———. *Cahier des charges de La Vie mode d'emploi*. Edited by Hans Hartje, Bernard Magné, and Jacques Neefs. Paris: Ed. Zulma/CNRS, 1993.

———. "Ce qu'il se passe quand il ne se passe rien." In *Entretiens et Conférences*, vol. 1, 214–16.

———. *Entretiens et Conférences*. Edited by Dominique Bertelli and Mireille Ribière. 2 vols. Paris: Joseph K., 2003.

———. "Entretien with Gérard Dupuy." In *Entretiens et Conférences*, vol. 1, 232–35.

———. *L.G.: Une aventure des années soixante*. Preface by Claude Burgelin. Paris: La Librerie du XXe Siècle, Éditions du Seuil, 1992.

———. "La maison des romans." In *Entretiens et Conférences*, vol. 1, 236–44.

———. "Pouvoirs et limites du romancier français contemporain." In *Entretiens et Conférences*, vol. 1, 76–88.

———. "Quatre figures pour *La Vie mode d'emploi*." *L'Arc*, no. 76 (1979): 50–53.

———. *Species of Spaces and Other Stories*. Edited and translated by John Sturrock. London: Penguin, 1997.

———. *La Vie mode d'emploi. Romans*. Paris: Hachette, Le Livre de Poche, 1978. Translated by David Bellos as *Life A User's Manual. Fictions* (rev. ed., London: Random House, 2008).

———. *W, or, The Memory of Childhood*. Translated by David Bellos. Boston: David R. Godine, 2003.

Perec, Georges, Jean Duvignaud, and Paul Virilio. "Le Grabuge." In *Entretiens et Conférences*, vol. 1, 121–34.

Phillips, Lisa, and Dieter Bogner. *Frederick Kiesler*. New York: Whitney Museum of American Art, 1989.

Pilz, Kristin. "Reconceptualizing Thought and Space: Labyrinths and Cities in Calvino's Fictions." *Italica* 80, no. 2 (2003): 229–42.

Prampolini, Enrico. "The Aesthetic of the Machine and Mechanical Introspection in Art." In "*Machine Age Exposition*, May 16–28 NYC, 1927," special issue, *Little Review* 12 (1927): 9–11.

———. "Arte meccanica—manifesto futurista" [Mechanical Art—Futurist Manifesto]. In Enrico Crispolti and Ivo Pannaggi, *Pannaggi e l'arte meccanica futurista*, 174–75. Milan: Mazzotta, 1995.

———. "Un'arte nuova? Costuzione Assoluta di Moto-Rumore" [A New Art? Absolute Construction of Movement-Noise]. In *Attraverso l'architettura futurista*, edited by Enrico Crispolti, 98–99. Modena: Galleria Fonte d'Abisso Edizioni, 1984. Exhibition catalogue.

———. "L'atmosfera-struttura—Basi per un'architettura futurista" [The Atmosphere-Structure—Bases for a Futurist Architecture]. In *Attraverso l'architettura futurista*, edited by Enrico Crispolti, 88–89. Modena: Galleria Fonte d'Abisso Edizioni, 1984. Exhibition catalogue.

———. "Futurist Scenic Atmosphere." In *Futurist Performance*, edited by Michael Kirby, translated by Victoria Nes Kirby, 225–31. New York: Paj, 1971.

———. "Futurist Stage Design." In Rainey, Poggi, and Wittman, *Futurism: An Anthology*, 212–15.

———. "Pittura pura" [Pure Painting]. In *Casa Balla e il futurismo a Roma*, edited by Enrico Crispolti, 227–28. Rome: Istituto Poligrafico e Zecca dello Stato, 1989.

———. *Prampolini dal futurismo all'informale*, edited by Enrico Crispolti and Rosella Siligato. Rome: Edizioni Carte segrete, 1992. Exhibition catalogue.

———. *Théâtre de la Pantomime Futuriste*. Paris: M. et J. De Brunoff, 1927.

Rainey, Lawrence. "Introduction: F. T. Marinetti and the Development of Futurism." In Rainey, Poggi, and Wittman, *Futurism: An Anthology*, 1–39.

Rainey, Lawrence, Christine Poggi, and Laura Wittman, eds. *Futurism: An Anthology*. New Haven, CT: Yale University Press, 2009.

Rajchman, John. *Constructions*. Cambridge, MA: MIT Press, 1998.

Re, Lucia. *Calvino and the Age of Neorealism: Fables of Estrangement*. Stanford, CA: Stanford University Press, 1990.

———. "Testi letterari e testi architettonici: *Le città invisibili* di Italo Calvino." In *Cultura della conservazione e istanza del progetto*, edited by Francesco Alberti and Sandro Scarrocchia, 31–40. Florence: Alinea, 1998.

Reiser, Jesse. "Introduction." In Bernard Tschumi and Hugh Dutton, *Glass Ramps / Glass Wall, Deviations from the Normative*, 11–17. London: Architectural Association, 2001.

Ricci, Franco. *Painting with Words, Writing with Pictures: Word and Image in the Work of Italo Calvino*. Toronto: University of Toronto Press, 2001.

Richet, Pascal. *L'âge du verre*. Paris: Découvertes Gallimard Techniques, 2000.

Rifkind, David. *The Battle for Modernism: Quadrante and the Politicization of Architectural Discourse in Fascist Italy*. Vicenza and Venice: CISA Andrea Palladio and Marsilio Editori, 2012.

Ross, Kristin. *Fast Cars, Clean Bodies: Decolonization and the Reordering of French Culture*. Cambridge, MA: MIT Press, 1995.

Rouillard, Dominique. "'Radical' architettura." In *Tschumi, une architecture en projet: Le Fresnoy*, 89–112. Paris: Le Fresnoy, CGP, 1993.

———. *Superarchitecture: Le futur de l'architecture 1950–1970*. Paris: Éditions de la Villette, 2004.

Salaris, Claudia. *Artecrazia: L'avanguardia futurista negli anni del fascismo*. Florence: La Nuova Italia, 1992.

Salter, Chris. *Entangled: Technology and the Transformation of Performance*. Cambridge, MA: MIT Press, 2010.

Saussy, Haun. "The Dimensionality of Literature." *Neohelicon* 38 (2011): 289–94.

Scott, Felicity D. *Architecture or Techno-Utopia: Politics after Modernism*. Cambridge, MA: MIT Press, 2007.

Shankman, Steven. "Ethics, Transcendence, and the Other: Milione of Marco Polo and Calvino's *Le città invisibili*." *Annali d'Italianistica: Official Journal of the Canadian Society for Italian Studies* 19 (2001): 137–52.

Sheringham, Michael. *Everyday Life: Theories and Practices from Surrealism to the Present*. Oxford: Oxford University Press, 2006.

Sinisi, Silvana. *Cambi di scena: Teatro e arti visive nelle poetiche del Novecento*. Rome: Bulzoni, 1995.

Somigli, Luca. *Legitimizing the Artist: Manifesto Writing and European Modernism, 1885–1915*. Toronto: University of Toronto Press, 2003.

Somol, Robert E. "12 Reasons to Get Back into Shape." In Rem Koolhaas and Brendan McGetrick, *Content: Triumph of Realization*, 86–87. Cologne: Taschen, 2004.

Stiegler, Bernard. "Developing Deterritorialization." In "Electrotecture: Architecture and the Electronic Future," special issue, *ANY* 3 (November/December 1993): 18–23.

———. "The Discrete Image." In Jacques Derrida and Bernard Stiegler, *Echographies of Television: Filmed Interviews*, translated by Jennifer Bajorek, 145–62. Cambridge, UK: Polity, 2002.

———. "Etre-là-bas: Phénoménologie et orientation." In "Espace et imagination," special issue, *Alter: Revue de phénoménologie* 4 (1996): 263–80.

Stuart, John. "Introduction." In *The Gray Cloth: Paul Scheerbart's Novel on Glass Architecture*, translated by John A. Stuart. Cambridge, MA: MIT Press, 2001.

Superstudio. "Fundamental Acts (Life, Education, Ceremony, Love, and Death, 1971–1973)." In Lang, *Superstudio: Life without Objects*, 175–205.

———. "Histograms." In Lang, *Superstudio: Life without Objects*, 114–15.

———. "Reflected Architecture." In Lang, *Superstudio: Life without Objects*, 84–94.

———. "Twelve Cautionary Tales for Christmas." In Lang, *Superstudio: Life without Objects*, 150–61.

Sussman, Henry. "The Writing of System: Borges's Library and Calvino's Traffic." In *Literary Philosophers: Borges, Calvino, Eco*, edited by Rodolphe Gasché. New York: Routledge, 2002.

Tafuri, Manfredo. *Architecture and Utopia: Design and Capitalist Development.* Translated by Barbara Luigia La Penta. Cambridge, MA: MIT Press, 1979.

———. *The Sphere and the Labyrinth: Avant-Gardes and Architecture from Piranesi to the 1970s.* Cambridge, MA: MIT Press, 1987.

Toraldo di Francia, Cristiano. "Superstudio & Radicaux." In *Architecture radicale*, 153–243. Orléans: Institut d'art contemporain Villeurbanne with HYX, 2002. Exhibition catalogue.

Tschumi, Bernard. *Architecture and Disjunction.* Cambridge, MA: MIT Press, 1996.

———. "Architecture and Its Double." In *Questions of Space*, 61–77.

———. "The Architecture of Dissidence." In *Questions of Space*, 79–86.

———. "Conceptualizing Context." In *The New Acropolis Museum*, edited by Bernard Tschumi Architects, 82–89. New York: Skira Rizzoli, 2009.

———. "Deviation from the Normative." In Bernard Tschumi and Hugh Dutton, *Glass Ramps / Glass Wall, Deviations from the Normative*, 19–24. London: Architectural Association, 2001.

———. "The Environmental Trigger." In *A Continuing Experiment: Learning and Teaching at the Architectural Association*, edited by James Gowan, 89–99. London: Architectural Press, 1975.

———. "Episodes of Geometry and Lust." In Tschumi, *Questions of Space*, 37–45.

———. *Event-Cities 1*. Cambridge, MA: MIT Press, 1999.

———. *Event-Cities 2*. Cambridge, MA: MIT Press, 2000.

———. *Event-Cities 3: Concept vs Context vs Content.* Cambridge, MA: MIT Press, 2000.

———. "Henri Lefebvre 'Le droit à la ville.'" *Architectural Design* 42, no. 9 (1972): 581–82.

———. "Joyce's Garden." In *The Discourse of Events*, 38–41. London: Architectural Association, 1983.
———. *The Manhattan Transcripts*. London: Academy Group, 1994.
———. *Questions of Space*. London: Architectural Association, 1990.
———. "Questions of Space." In Tschumi, *Questions of Space*, 31–35.
———. "A Space Is Worth a Thousand Words." In *A Space: A Thousand Words*, unpaginated. London and Milan: Royal College of Art with Dieci Libri, 1975. Exhibition catalogue.
———. "Ten Points, Ten Examples." In "Electrotecture: Architecture and the Electronic Future," special issue, *ANY* 3 (November/December 1993): 40–43.
Tschumi, Bernard, and Enrique Walker. *Tschumi on Architecture: Conversations with Enrique Walker*. New York: Monacelli, 2006.
Tsukui, Noriko, ed. "OMA@work." Special issue, *Architecture and Urbanism*, May 2000.
Tynianov, Yuri. "The Concept of 'Construction.' " In *The Problem of Verse Language*, edited and translated by Michael Sosa and Brent Harvey, 31–35. Ann Arbor, MI: Ardis, 1981.
Valesio, Paolo. " 'The Most Enduring and Most Honored Name': Marinetti as a Poet." In *F. T. Marinetti: Selected Poems and Related Prose*, selected by Luce Marinetti, translated by Elizabeth R. Napier and Barbara R. Studholme, 149–65. New Haven, CT: Yale University Press, 2002.
———. "Il Portasigarette Ritrovato." Introduction to F. T. Marinetti, *Venzianella e Studentaccio*, edited by Patrizio Ceccagnoli and Paolo Valesio. Milan: Oscar Mondadori, 2013.
Varnelis, Kazys, ed. *Networked Publics*. Cambridge, MA: MIT Press, 2008.
Versari, Maria Elena. "Futurist Machine Age, Constructivism and the Modernity of Mechanization." In *Futurism and the Technological Imagination*, edited by Günter Berghaus, 149–75. Amsterdam: Rodopi, 2009.
Vidler, Anthony. "After the Event." *Architectural Review* 236, no. 1411 (September 2014): 87–95.
———. ed. *Architecture between Spectacle and Use*. Williamstown, MA: Sterling and Francine Clark Art Institute, 2008.
———. "A REM-Based Program for Interactive Architecture." In "Urbanism vs. Architecture: The Bigness of Rem Koolhaas," special issue, *ANY* 9 (November/December 1994): 58–59.
———. "Still Wired after All These Years." *Log* 1, no. 1 (Fall 2003): 59–63.
———. *Warped Space: Art, Architecture and Anxiety in Modern Culture*. Cambridge, MA: MIT Press, 2000.
Virilio, Paul. "L'inertie du moment." *L'Arc*, no. 76 (1979): 20–22.
———. "La ville surexposée." In *L'espace critique: essai*. Paris: Christian Bourgois, 1984.
Volt [Fani, Vincenzo]. "La casa futurista. Indipendente—mobile—smontabile—meccanica—esilarante. Manifesto." In *La metropoli futurista: progetti im-possibili*, edited by Vincenzo Capalbo and Ezio Godoli, 88–90. Florence: Officina del Novecento, 1999.
Wallenstein, Sven-Olov. "Looping Ideology: The CCTV Center in Beijing." In *Media Houses: Architecture, Media, and the Production of Centrality*, edited by Staffan Ericson and Kristina Riegert, 163–82. New York: Peter Lang, 2010.

Weber, Samuel. *Benjamin's -abilities*. Cambridge, MA: Harvard University Press, 2008.

———. "Benjamin's Writing Style." In *Encyclopedia of Aesthetics*, vol. 1, 261–64. New York: Oxford University Press, 1998.

———. "Genealogy of Modernity: History, Myth and Allegory in Benjamin's *Origin of the German Mourning Play*." *MLN* 106, no. 3 (1991): 465–500.

———. *Mass Mediauras: Form, Technics, Media*. Stanford, CA: Stanford University Press, 1996.

———. *Theatricality as Medium*. New York: Fordham University Press, 2004.

Whiting, Sarah. "Spot Check: A Conversation between Rem Koolhaas and Sarah Whiting." *Assemblage* 40 (December 1, 1999): 36–55.

Wigley, Mark. "Network Fever." *Grey Room* 4 (2001): 82–122.

Woloch, Alex. *The One vs. the Many: Minor Characters and the Space of the Protagonist in the Novel*. Princeton, NJ: Princeton University Press, 2004.

Yaneva, Albena. *Made by the Office for Metropolitan Architecture: An Ethnography of Design*. Rotterdam: 010 Publishers, 2009.

Zancan, Marina. "*Le città invisibili* di Italo Calvino." In *Letteratura Italiana: Le Opere*, edited by Alberto Asor Rosa, vol. 4, *Il Novecento*, 875–929. Turin: Einaudi, 1996.

Zatti, Sergio. "Viaggi sedentari." *Annali d'Italianistica* 21 (2003): 57–70.

Zevi, Bruno. *Architecture as Space: How to Look at Architecture*. Edited by Joseph A. Barry. Translated by Milton Gendel. New York: Da Capo Press, 1999.

INDEX

Page numbers in **boldface** refer to illustrations.